Policy Evaluation with Computable General Equilibrium Models

Computable General Equilibrium (CGE) modelling is a relatively new field in economics. While the first papers appeared in the early seventies, it is now a well-established field of research, based at the intersection between theoretical and applied economics. A variety of institutions, including the IMF, the World Bank, and the OECD uses CGE-models to quantitatively evaluate policy reform proposals.

This book deals with some of the most urgent international economic policy problems. It is divided into five sections, each focusing on particular issues:

- Methodology: indicates future lines of research and discusses methodological issues in applying CGE-models of policy problems.
- Imperfect competition: discusses the recent advances in CGE modelling in incorporating imperfect competition.
- Environment: analyses the implications of the Kyoto Protocol and voluntary agreements on emission reductions.
- Pension reform: deals with the problems of an ageing population within the sphere of overlapping generations models.
- Miscellaneous: examines various issues from the economic efficiency of income taxation, to a discussion of the changes in the Polish economy arising from accession to the European Union.

Professionals and academics working in the field of policy analysis and economic modelling will find this work a valuable resource.

Amedeo Fossati is full professor of Public Finance at the University of Genova. His most recent publications examine local finance and tax reform. He is a member of the Italian Association of Public Finance, of the International Institute of Public Finance and of the European Economic Association.

Wolfgang Wiegard is full professor of Economics at the University of Regensburg. Since 1997 he has been the editor of the review *Finanzarchiv*. He is a member of the German Council of the Economic Advisors and Chairman of the Council of Economics Advisors to the German Institute for Economic Research (DIW, Berlin).

Routledge Applied Economics

1 Policy Evaluation with Computable General Equilibrium Models
Edited by Amedeo Fossati and Wolfgang Wiegard

Policy Evaluation with Computable General Equilibrium Models

Edited by
Amedeo Fossati
and
Wolfgang Wiegard

Routledge
Taylor & Francis Group

LONDON AND NEW YORK

First published 2002
by Routledge
2 Park Square, Milton Park, Abingdon, Oxfordshire OX14 4RN

Simultaneously published in the USA and Canada
by Routledge
711 Third Avenue, New York, NY 10017

First issued in paperback 2014

Routledge is an imprint of the Taylor and Francis Group, an informa business

Typeset in 10/12 pt Baskerville by Newgen Imaging Systems (P) Ltd., Chennai, India

British Library Cataloguing in Publication Data
A catalogue record for this book is available
from the British Library

Library of Congress Cataloging in Publication Data
Policy evaluation with computable general equilibrium models/edited
by Amedeo Fossati and Wolfgang Wiegard.
     p. cm.
   Includes bibliographical references and index.
   1. Equilibrium (Economics)—Econometric models—Evaluation.
   2. Economic policy—Econometric models—Evaluation.
   I. Fossati, Amedeo, 1937–   II. Wiegard, Wolfgang.
HB145.P647 2001
339.5'01'5195–dc21

ISBN 13: 978-1-138-86596-9 (pbk)
ISBN 13: 978-0-415-25671-1 (hbk)

Contents

List of figures and charts   viii
List of tables   xi
List of contributors   xiv
Acknowledgements   xvi
Introduction   xvii

PART I
Methodology   1

**1 Studying the past and future with
    infinite-horizon simulation models**   3
CHARLES BALLARD

2 Policy reform without tears   20
GLENN W. HARRISON, JESPER JENSEN, MORTEN I. LAU AND
THOMAS F. RUTHERFORD

**3 The marginal cost of public funds in
    developing countries**   39
SHANTAYANAN DEVARAJAN, KAREN E. THIERFELDER AND
SETHAPUT SUTHIWART-NARUEPUT

**4 CGE models for practical policy analysis:
    The Australian experience**   56
PETER B. DIXON, BRIAN R. PARMENTER AND MAUREEN T. RIMMER

PART II
Imperfect competition 83

5 An applied intertemporal general equilibrium
model of trade and production with scale economies,
product differentiation and imperfect competition 85
JEAN MERCENIER

6 A conjectural variation computable general
equilibrium model with free entry 105
ROBERTO A. DE SANTIS

7 Market power in a liberalized power market:
The case of Italy 122
GIANCARLO PIREDDU AND CHRISTIAN M. DUFOURNAUD

PART III
Environment 137

8 The Kyoto Protocol: Implications of international
capital mobility on trade and regional welfare 139
KATRIN SPRINGER

9 Carbon taxation and various pollutants in Europe:
Combining general equilibrium and integrated
system approaches 160
T. HUW EDWARDS AND JOHN P. HUTTON

10 The efficiency costs of voluntary agreements in
environmental policy 182
CHRISTOPH BÖHRINGER AND THOMAS F. RUTHERFORD

PART IV
Pension reform 201

11 The ageing of the population and justice
between generations: A CGE and generational
accounting approach for Belgium 203
PHILIPPE LIÉGEOIS

12 Ageing population and pension reform in Italy 216
BARBARA CAVALLETTI AND ECKHARD LÜBKE

13 **Pension funding reforms in a small open welfare state**   232
HANS FEHR AND ERLING STEIGUM

14 **Social security in an ageing society: An applied
general equilibrium analysis**   249
D. PETER BROER

**PART V
Miscellaneous**   269

15 **Can tax progression raise employment?
A study of four European economies**   271
JOHN P. HUTTON AND ANNA RUOCCO

16 **Introducing idiosyncratic uncertainty in a
life-cycle CGE-model**   300
TOKE WARD PETERSEN

17 **International spillover effects of a
demographic shock when fiscal policy is
politically responsive**   325
MEHMET SERKAN TOSUN

18 **An intertemporal evaluation of accession to the
European Union**   344
DANIEL PIAZOLO

Index   363

Figures and charts

Figures

3.1	Tariff elimination and welfare	43
3.2	Factor market distortions	49
3.3	Welfare effects of tax changes	53
4.1	Comparative-static percentage changes from ORANI	58
4.2	Forecast average annual growth rates and policy deviations in MONASH	60
4.3	Capital accumulation in MONASH	61
5.1	Sensitivity of computed paths of capital and consumption to alternative choices of time grid	98
6.1	The demand system	106
8.1	Production structure of industry sector	143
8.2	Production structure of the investment good sector	144
8.3	Household/government production structure	145
8.4	Structure of foreign trade	146
8.5	Household decision	148
8.6	Capital demand in each region	149
8.7	Benchmark capital in- and outflows in 1993	152
8.8	Welfare effects of the Kyoto protocol	153
8.9	Change in sectoral output in 2010	154
8.10	Leakage rate in per cent	156
10.1	Output distortions of VA programs	185
10.2	Welfare effects – competitive economy	191
10.3	Employment effects – competitive economy	192
10.4	Output effects – competitive economy	192
10.5	Welfare effects – imperfect competition	193
10.6	Output per firm – imperfect competition	194
11.1	The dependency rate	207
11.2	The 'International' interest rate and the public debt/GDP ratio	209
11.3	The rate of tax on wages	210

11.4	The generational accounts	210
11.5	Complementary individual public transfers relative to GDP per head	213
11.6	Debt/GDP ratio	214
12.1	Definitions of a PAYG pension scheme	221
12.2	Alternative reform proposal	223
12.3	Simulation results – contribution rate	228
12.4	Simulation results – social security reserves	228
13.1	The pension function	235
13.2	Marginal tax rate schedule for wage and pension income	236
14.1	Population growth in the Netherlands, 1995–2194	253
14.2	Income tax and marginal burden on labour	254
14.3	Participation rates	254
14.4	Growth of labour supply	255
14.5	Market wage growth	255
14.6	Total tax burden as a fraction of GDP	256
14.7	Social security contribution rates	256
14.8	Health insurance contribution rates	257
14.9	Consumption ratios	258
14.10	Current account surplus and savings as a fraction of GDP	258
14.11	Compensating variations per generation, relative to the 1976 generation	259
14.12	Compensating variations for a 10 per cent reduction in PAYG benefits	261
14.13	Compensating variations for a transition to premium smoothing for the PAYG fund	263
14.14	Growth rate of GDP per capita	264
15.1	Fixed labour supply, $b = 0.8$	278
15.2	Fixed labour supply, $b = 0$	279
15.3	Variable labour supply, $b = 0.8$	279
15.4	Variable labour supply, $b = 0$	280
16.1	Assets	315
16.2	Leisure	317
16.3	Labour earnings in the deterministic model	319
16.4	Labour earnings with idiosyncratic earnings uncertainty	320
16.5	Consumption	320
17.1	Projected old-age dependency ratio in developed countries	326
17.2	Tax rate transitions in A and B	333
17.3	Human capital transitions in A and B	334
17.4	Capital stock transitions in A and B	335
17.5	World net interest rate transition	335
17.6	Balance of payments transitions for the ageing country	336

17.7   Income transitions in A and B   336
17.8   Consumption transitions of old and young generations
        in A and B   337
17.9   Welfare transitions in A and B   338
18.1   Overall effects of EU membership on consumption,
        exports, imports and domestic good production   356
18.2   Overall effects of EU membership on investment,
        capital stock, borrowing and debt   357

Charts

4.1   Real GDP and factor inputs   71
4.2   Real investment and consumption   71
4.3   Aggregate export and import volumes   72
4.4   Real exchange rate   72
4.5   Real wage rates and aggregate employment   73
4.6   Terms of trade   73
4.7   Percentage point contributions to the growth in real GDP   74
4.8   Output of the main losers   74
4.9   Output of the main winners   75
4.10   Gross regional state product   78

Tables

2.1	Sectors in the Danish model	24
2.2	Excise tax rates and expenditures at the industry level	28
2.3	Welfare effects of excise tax reform on households	31
2.4	Effecting compensation to losers	33
3.1	Some previous MCF estimates	41
3.2	Marginal cost of public funds for selected sectors	44
3.3	Detailed MCF results for Bangladesh	45
3.4	Detailed MCF results for Cameroon	46
3.5	Detailed MCF results for Indonesia	47
3.6	Marginal welfare cost of public funds in Cameroon	49
3.7	Sample key distortions in Cameroon	50
3.8	Production effects of increase in cash crop tax	51
3.9	Production effects of increase in intermediate goods tax	52
3.10	Full CGE versus heuristic MCF estimates	53
4.1	Expenditure of foreign students in Australia, 1996–97	64
4.2	Assumptions about numbers of foreign students, 1997–98 to 2004–5	65
4.3	Assumptions about regional distribution of foreign students, 1997–98 to 2004–5	66
4.4	Base-case forecasts: macroeconomic variables	68
4.5	Base-case forecasts: output by selected industry	69
4.6	Selected regional data	79
5.1	Selected results for the British pharmaceutical industry	99
5.2	Welfare gains from European trade integration	101
6.1	The benchmark data set for Turkey	113
6.2	Calibrated conjectures and firms' price elasticities	114
6.3	The economic impact of tariff liberalization and competition policies	116
7.1	Domestic production, spot imports and market share in the benchmark	129
7.2	Scenario and simulation equilibria	130
7.3	Production, imports, equilibrium prices, market shares and operating surplus index variations	131

7.4	Cournot–Nash and competitive equilibria after Enel break-up and spot imports liberalization	132
8.1	Regions and commodities in the 11 by 10 GTAP aggregation	150
8.2	Key elasticities	151
8.3	Dynamic key parameters for the off-steady state scenario for the year 1993	151
8.4	Parameterization of imperfect capital mobility	151
8.5	Shares of capital in- and outflows relative to total capital use	152
9.1	Elasticity assumptions	164
9.2	Energy statistics from the database	166
9.3	European multi-country CGE model	168
9.4	Change on 1995 base (A) Sulphur emissions (B) NO_x emissions	170
9.5	RAINS model excess deposition change from a 30 ECU carbon (A) Sulphur (B) Nitrogen	172
10.1	Benchmark data and key elasticities	190
11.1	Calibration of the model	208
12.1	Normal retirement age in 1991	225
12.2	Retirement age in detail	226
12.3	Age of retirement and average working period in the simulation	226
12.4	Economic parameter values in the simulations	227
12.5	Demographic parameter values in the simulations	227
13.1	Population projections	238
13.2	Macroeconomic structure in the base year 1995 (per cent of output)	239
13.3	Baseline growth path (percentage deviation from base year)	240
13.4	Macroeconomic effects of pension reforms (in per cent)	242
13.5	Intergenerational welfare changes (in per cent)	243
13.6	Household welfare changes (in per cent)	245
14.1	Effects of a decrease of 10 per cent in PAYG benefits	260
14.2	Effects of a transition to contribution rate smoothing for the PAYG contribution rate	263
14.3	Percentage of current generations that benefit from a pension reform	265
15.1	Direct tax rates modelled in 1992 benchmark	288
15.2	Effects of increased progression on employment and unemployment: Germany (1992 benchmark)	288
15.3	Increase in tax progression by increasing the marginal tax rate keeping the average constant and letting allowances vary. Germany	289

15.4 Increase in tax progression, by increasing the marginal tax
     rate keeping the average constant and letting allowances
     vary. France   290
15.5 Increase in tax progression, by increasing the marginal
     tax rate keeping the average constant and letting
     allowances vary. Italy   291
15.6 Increase in tax progression, by increasing the marginal
     tax rate keeping the average constant and letting
     allowances vary. UK   292
16.1 Summary in the deterministic model with one
     productivity level   310
16.2 Summary in the deterministic model with two
     productivity levels   311
16.3 Decomposition of the labour supply effect on two
     productivity levels   311
16.4 Summary with idiosyncratic uncertainty   312
16.5 Decomposition of the labour supply effect
     with uncertainty   313
17.1 Benchmark values of the parameters used in the
     two-country OLG model   333
17.2 Closed versus open economy results   339
17.3 Sensitivity of simulation results to various values of ψ 340
18.1 Poland's trade with partner countries in 1996 and 1997:
     (a) Imports, (b) Exports   346
18.2 SAM for Poland 1996 in million Zloties   350
18.3 Simulations of full EU membership effects for
     Poland – relative to the reference run   355

Contributors

Ballard, Charles: Michigan State University, USA;
e-mail: ballard@pilot.msu.edu

Böhringer, Christoph: Centre for European Economic Research,
Mannheim, Germany; e-mail: boehringer@zew.de

Broer, D. Peter: Erasmus University Rotterdam and CPB Netherlands Bureau
of Economic Policy Analysis, The Netherlands; e-mail: broer@cpb.nl

Cavalletti, Barbara: University of Genova, Italy;
e-mail: cavallet@economia.unige.it

De Santis, Roberto A.: European Central Bank, Frankfurt am Main, Germany;
e-mail: roberto.de_santis@ecb.int

Devarajan, Shantayanan: World Bank, Washington, USA;
e-mail: sdevarajan@worldbank.org

Dixon, Peter B.: Centre of Policy Studies, Monash University, Australia;
e-mail: peter.dixon@buseco.monash.edu.au

Dufournaud, Christian M.: University of Waterloo, Canada;
e-mail: cdufourn@watser1.uwaterloo.ca

Edwards, T. Huw: Centre for the Study of Globalisation and Regionalisation,
Warwick, UK; e-mail: terence_huw_edwards@compuserve.com

Fehr, Hans: University of Würzburg, Germany;
e-mail: hans.fehr@mail. uni-wuerzburg.de

Harrison, Glenn W.: University of South Carolina, USA;
e-mail: harrison@darla.badm.sc.edu

Hutton, John P.: University of York, UK; e-mail: jph1@york.ac.uk

Jensen, Jesper: Copenhagen Economics, Denmark;
e-mail: jj@copenhageneconomics.com

Lau, Morten I.: Centre for Economic and Business Research, Danish Ministry of Trade and Industry, Denmark; e-mail: mol@efs.dk

Liégeois, Philippe: ECARE, Université Libre de Bruxelles and CORE, Université Catholique de Louvain, Belgium; e-mail: phliege@ulb.ac.be

Lübke, Eckhard: University of Münster, Germany; e-mail: luebke@dr-luebke.de

Mercenier, Jean: Thema and University of Cergy-Pontoise, France; e-mail: mercenie@u-cergy.fr

Parmenter, Brian R.: Centre of Policy Studies, Monash University, Australia; e-mail: parmenter@t_gm.com.au

Petersen, Toke Ward: University of Copenhagen and Statistics Denmark; e-mail: twp@dst.dk

Piazolo, Daniel: Institute of World Economics, Kiel, Germany; e-mail: dpiazolo@ifw.uni-kiel.de

Pireddu, Giancarlo: PricewaterhouseCoopers Corporate Finance and University of Milano Bicocca, Italy; e-mail: giancarlo.pireddu@it.pwcglobal.com

Rimmer, Maureen T.: Centre of Policy Studies, Monash University, Australia; e-mail: maureen.rimmer@buseco.monash.edu.au

Ruocco, Anna: University of Regensburg, Germany; e-mail: anna_ruocco.confindustria@confindustria.it

Rutherford, Thomas F.: University of Colorado, Boulder, USA; e-mail: rutherford@colorado.edu

Springer, Katrin: Institute of World Economics, Kiel, Germany; e-mail: kspringer@ifw.uni-kiel.de

Steigum, Erling: Norwegian School of Management, Oslo; e-mail: erling.steigum@bi.no

Suthiwart-Narueput, Sethaput: Ministry of Finance, Thailand and World Bank, USA; e-mail: sethaput@vayu.mof.go.th

Thierfelder, Karen E.: U.S Naval Academy, USA; e-mail: thier@usna.edu

Tosun, Mehmet Serkan: Syracuse University, USA; e-mail: mstosun@maxwell.syr.edu

Acknowledgements

We would like to express our appreciation to Bernadette Burke for revising the English language version, and to Orietta Bertonasco for her patient and skilful secretarial assistance.

Introduction

Applied General Equilibrium – perhaps more often named Computable General Equilibrium (CGE) modelling is a relatively new field in economics. The fact is that CGE modelling, by applying the Walrasian approach to real economies, is a very useful tool for policy makers in matters where market linkages are the dominant characteristic. CGE modelling has advanced considerably from the first seminal approach, with confidence in and the reliability of the results becoming ever more widespread, provided that the model is used correctly and the right questions posed. In fact, CGE models must be tailored to the particular policy issue under investigation, in order to quantify the effects of policy changes. A first peculiarity of the approach is that results are not just qualitative, but quantitative too, since computable models are complex systems of quantitative linkages among variables. A second, more important, characteristic is the complexity of the scenarios that can be specified within the model considered: such peculiarity permits analysis automatically excluded by other approaches. To put it briefly, CGE models allow specification of economies with the desired level of detail both as regards the behaviour of the economic agents and as regards sector and factor markets linkages.

The trivial drawback is, of course, that any result is strictly dependent on functional forms considered and the parameter values chosen. From that angle, however, CGE-models are no different from other economic tools, and in particular from econometric models.

On 29/30 October 1999 an international conference was held in Genova, Italy, entitled 'Policy Evaluation with Computable General Equilibrium Models'. The idea of the conference was to bring together well-known experts and younger professionals from the CGE-community throughout the world. While the international experts evaluated what had been achieved, the younger economists presented their work, all of which is at the very frontier of current research. This book gathers together a large collection of the papers which were presented at the conference, subdivided under the headings Methodology, Imperfect Competition, Environment, Pension Reform, Miscellaneous. The volume also deals with some of the most urgent policy problems such as pension reform, environmental policy and industrial policy. In addition, the book contains some informative and ambitious papers on methodological issues.

One major problem of most CGE papers is that they usually come as 'black boxes' to the general reader since the theoretical models, the computer codes and the data cannot be presented in length due to severe space constraints. It is common practice just to roughly outline the analytical framework of the simulation model in the main paper and to concentrate on the interpretation of the results obtained. This, however, is somewhat unsatisfactory. For most papers contained in our book, we therefore provide additional information about coding structures, data sets and other details at the web-address http://www. uni–regensburg.de/Fakultaeten/WiWi/Wiegard/CGE-book/index.htm.   This allows interested readers to gain additional insights into each author's work.

Part I: Methodology

This section of the book is devoted to present ideas about the state of the art, indicates future lines of research and discusses methodological issues in applying CGE-models to policy problems. In the first chapter *Studying the past and the future with infinite-horizon simulation models*, Charles Ballard's intention is to find new solutions to the old problem of testing the capability of models in respect of their cognitive value as regards the future. Over the last generation, economists have used a great variety of CGE-models to analyse the effects of policy changes, with the open or virtual goal of learning about what might occur in the future, were a particular change implemented. But the counterfactual equilibrium, even in dynamic CGE-models, is couched in a conventional time, if any, that does not correspond with the evolution of real time in real economies. The purpose of Ballard's chapter is to explore a new approach to validation and testing of the models. This new approach involves looking into the past, and using the model to analyse the effects of an actual policy change.

In Chapter 2, *Policy reform without tears*, Glenn W. Harrison, Jesper Jensen, Morten I. Lau and Thomas F. Rutherford consider an important methodological point in applied research, that is, the search for the character of Pareto improvement in reforms. The point is based on the fact that a policy reform must be accepted by the people, and the pursuit of consent is central to any sound reform. Hence, it follows that it is insufficient simply to ascertain the effects of possible reforms, and that the Pareto improvement character of reforms should be considered at the very beginning of any reform proposal, using CGE models tailored to such a purpose.

In Chapter 3, *The marginal cost of public funds in developing countries*, Shantayanan Devarajan, Karen E. Thierfelder and Sethaput Suthiwart-Narueput use CGE approach to evaluate the marginal cost of raising public funds. The interesting starting point is that despite its great economic potential – in particular for developing countries – the marginal cost of funds has produced only a modest corpus on its theoretical properties and empirical magnitude. The chapter attempts to partially remedy this situation by providing CGE estimates of the marginal cost of funds for Cameroon, Bangladesh and Indonesia. Since the marginal cost of taxation is quite different across sectors and instruments, the potential for tax reforms in developing countries is considerable.

In Chapter 4 *CGE-models for practical policy analysis: The Australian experience*, Peter B. Dixon, Brian Parmenter and Maureen T. Rimmer review the Australian experience of using CGE-models for practical policy analysis. The specific policy issue addressed is the effect on the Australian economy of a slowdown in foreign-student numbers such as was thought likely to ensue after the recent crisis in the Asian economies. However, the reader's interest is focused mainly on the methodological issues raised, which differentiate Australian experience in CGE modelling from other academic positions. What is important is that, while elsewhere much of the current work on dynamic CGE modelling is using steady-state base solutions, in the MONASH dynamic simulations realistic base cases are projected. Therefore, in assessing the effects of shocks in a future year, MONASH is first used to obtain a base-case forecast, that is, a plausible representation of the economy for that year with no shock. The differentials between such forecasts and the simulations values are then evaluated to reflect the policy shocks.

Part II: Imperfect competition

The incorporation of imperfect competition is one of the recent advances in CGE-modelling efforts. This is important for the analysis of industrial policy, for issues of economic integration and international trade. In Chapter 5 *An applied intertemporal general equilibrium model of trade and production with scale economies, product differentiation and imperfect competition*, Jean Mercenier presents a state-of-the-art, intertemporal, multicountry, multisector general equilibrium application, with trade and production, increasing returns to scale internal to a firm, imperfect competition and product differentiation at the individual producer level. The emphasis is on the description of the mathematical structure of the model, calibration techniques, temporal aggregation issues and computational considerations. The model is used to investigate European trade integration effects.

In Chapter 6 *A conjectural variation computable general equilibrium model with free entry*, Roberto A. De Santis considers CGE models with industrial organisation features, since he deals with markets when domestic and foreign firms compete in a quantity setting oligopoly with constant conjectures and free entry. His main contribution is methodological: he proposes a procedure to incorporate the conjectural variation approach in CGE analysis so that the strategic interaction among rival firms in international markets can be modelled. It should be noted that the conjectural approach is rarely used in CGE modelling because the strategic behaviour of the firms can occur at different stages of the multi-stage demand trees usually employed. In the chapter, Roberto De Santis derives a general formulation for the price markup, where the price elasticity of demand is a function of the conjectured reactions of both the rival domestic and foreign firms.

Chapter 7 *Market power in a liberalized power market: The case of Italy*, analyses the role of dominant firms in the liberalized power market and their ability to influence price formation through strategic behaviour. Giancarlo Pireddu and Christian Dufournaud, using standard conjectural variations, present a CGE-model of electricity generation activity for Italy in order to measure market power in terms of equilibrium price, market shares of firms and welfare. Each firm is endowed with a specific set of technologies available to meet its market demand both in peak and off-peak periods. Using Italian published data, a benchmark scenario reflecting the situation prior to liberalization is compared to gains and losses from competitive and strategic behaviours (Cournot–Nash).

Part III: Environment

Environmental policy has become one of the main fields of CGE-models application. In this section of the book the relative topics analysed are welfare and trade implications of the Kyoto Protocol and voluntary agreements on emission reductions. Katrin Springer in Chapter 8 *The Kyoto protocol: Implications of international capital mobility on trade and regional welfare*, analyses the implications of the Kyoto Protocol when carbon emission reduction targets are imposed in different world regions. The chapter adopts a recursive dynamic global, multi-regional, multi-sectoral CGE model where the regions are linked by bilateral trade and capital flows. Ten sectors are modelled, and two types of physical capital (domestic and foreign) are implemented considering, however, imperfect substitution between them. The model assumptions reflect imperfections in the world capital market, increased risks inherent to foreign investment, legal restrictions on ownership of foreign property, and asymmetric information between domestic and foreign investors. The issue examined is to what extent the common modelling practice of ignoring international capital mobility and foreign cross-ownership of capital in computable general equilibrium models for analysing the effects of certain climate policies may give rise to distorted predictions.

In Chapter 9, *Carbon taxation and various pollutants in Europe: Combining general equilibrium and integrated system approaches*, T. Huw Edwards and John Hutton outline the development of a static multi-country CGE model as a tool to analyse issues relating to the introduction of environmental taxation, such as interaction with other taxes, revenue recycling, international carbon 'leakage' and tax export effects. The model is linked to IIASA's RAINS model to expand the analysis to cover other cross-boundary pollution.

In Chapter 10, *The efficiency costs of voluntary agreements in environmental policy*, Christoph Böhringer and Thomas Rutherford dispute the notion that voluntary agreements programs are cost-efficient policy instruments. The issue is important, since voluntary agreements in environmental policy are gaining in popularity. The authors provide an analytical framework to explore the welfare effect of voluntary agreements. In order to perform a formal efficiency analysis of voluntary agreements the authors make use of a CGE approach where voluntary agreements are represented as a system of grandfathered permits that work as subsidies on the output side. In that framework they demonstrate that voluntary agreements programs can induce significant excess costs due to distortions on the output side of the economy, particularly in industries characterized by increasing returns and oligopolistic competition.

Part IV: Pension reform

PAYG pension systems have come under mounting pressure due to the demographic crisis. CGE-models are the appropriate framework within which to deal with policy reform proposals involving a full or partial switch to a funded system, or to evaluate the intergenerational and intragenerational distributional effects, as well as the efficiency implications, of different reform scenarios. The papers presented here deal with the problem of an ageing population within the ambit of overlapping generations models in the Auerbach and Kotlikoff tradition. Philippe Liègeois, in Chapter 11 *The ageing of the population and justice between generations: A CGE and generational accounting approach for Belgium*, derives generational accounts specific to each future generation in the general equilibrium framework. He develops a CGE-model with overlapping generations in which lifespan is uncertain and the labour supply is endogenous. The model has been calibrated to fit the Belgian data and focuses on its demographic structure. It shows that the forthcoming ageing of the population in Belgium will induce a substantial increase in the tax rate on wages during the coming decades. The government may wish to restore equity between the generations: this goal is reached in the paper because the government imposes complementary lump-sum transfers – one per year – identical for all the individuals alive in that year.

Barbara Cavalletti and Eckhard Lübke in Chapter 12 *Ageing population and pension reform in Italy*, are also interested in effects of the ageing process of the population on pension systems: their attention, however, is addressed to pension reform schemes in Italy. Cavalletti and Lübke use a life-cycle model augmented to include both a detailed population model (expanded to take account of the first-degree family relationship), and an applied general equilibrium model. Their purpose is twofold: first, to test the transition costs of the present reformed pension system, and second, to explore possible alternative transition paths from the existing pay-as-you-go scheme to a partially funded scheme. Both the simulations presented are steady state equilibrium, not intended to forecast the economic evolution of the Italian economy, but simply to highlight the distribution of the transition costs implied by the two scenarios.

In Chapter 13, *Pension funding reforms in a small open welfare state*, Hans Fehr and Erling Steigum use a calibrated Auerbach-Kotlikoff model of the Norwegian economy, extended by five intragenerational income groups to simulate the distribution consequences of alternative pension and tax reforms. First of all, the model presents a realistic demographic transition, that is, since the starting point is not an initial steady-state situation with regard to population and labour supply, it represents the expected ageing of the Norwegian population. Secondly, it outlines the Norwegian piecewise linear income tax and pension benefit schedules involving jumps in marginal tax rates. Finally, the model isolates the efficiency effects from the welfare effects, in order to pinpoint which generations will enjoy the fruits of the reductions in dead-weight loss generated by the reforms analysed.

In Chapter 14, *Social security in an ageing society: an applied general equilibrium analysis*, Peter Broer studies the effects of the imminent ageing of the population on the social security and health care system in the Netherlands. The chapter attempts to measure the distortionary burden of these systems and their effects on growth and welfare in the Dutch economy within an Auerbach-Kotlikoff overlapping generation model. Broer reveals that under the current system ageing leads to considerable welfare losses for future generations. This baseline solution assumes that world interest rates are constant and that domestic exogenous variables are either constant, or grow at constant rates, except for population, which follows an expected demographic path based on the projections of the Dutch Central Statistical Office.

Part V: Miscellaneous

In the final section of the book, John Hutton and Anna Ruocco, in Chapter 15 *Can tax progression raise employment? a study of four European economies*, examine the traditional view that progressive income taxation reduces economic efficiency, when non-clearing labour markets are introduced. They develop a multi-country, multi-sector CGE-model, which is characterized by a variety of types of labour (full and part-time, male and female), various direct and indirect taxes and terms of trade effects. Using such a model, calibrated to national data, increased progression in four European countries would raise employment and welfare. The more generous the benefit system, the more unemployment and the more effective progression in raising employment. If unemployment benefit is sufficiently low, greater progression will reduce employment and welfare, but from a higher level.

Chapter 16 *Introducing idiosyncratic uncertainty in a life-cycle CGE model*, is the work of Toke W. Petersen, who is chiefly interested in a methodological issue, that is, in investigating the effects of introducing uncertainty in life-cycle CGE models. He compares the results obtained in a model with idiosyncratic earnings uncertainty to the results obtained using a model without uncertainty, that is, a classical Auerbach-Kotlikoff model. The chapter then presents a large-scale dynamic computable general equilibrium model, with overlapping generations of consumers, where consumers are subject to uninsurable idiosyncratic earnings uncertainty, borrowing-constraints and face an endogenous labour supply decision. The model is used to analyse the welfare gains when switching from progressive to proportional taxation of labour income. Petersen's analysis shows that the benefits from removing progressive taxation are greater with uncertainty.

In Chapter 17 *International spillover effects of a demographic shock when fiscal policy is politically responsive*, Mehmet Serkan Tosun examines the international spillover effects of a demographic shock, that is, a decrease in the population growth rate in one period in one of the countries considered. The author uses a median voter framework built into a two-country model with overlapping generations. Unlike recent empirical studies on population ageing, fiscal policy is endogenously determined through a political process in which elderly voters are weighed against younger voters to determine the level of government spending. Interest focuses on the degree to which a more elderly population will support public spending on education, or human capital formation more generally.

Daniel Piazolo is the author of Chapter 18 *An intertemporal evaluation of accession to the European Union*. His contribution discusses the various changes for the Polish economy arising from accession to the European Union. An intertemporal CGE model is used, whose main features are that it is of the small open-economy Ramsey type with intertemporal consumer as well as producer optimisation, and intra-industry trade. Two produced goods (exports and domestic) and two consumer goods (imports and domestic) are considered, and there are three types of imports (each with a separate import duty), that is, capital, intermediate and final imports. The model is used to evaluate the consequences of Poland's integration into the European Union stemming from, (i) tariff reduction, (ii) border–cost reduction, (iii) reduction of the technical barriers to trade, and (iv) increased net EU-transfers from Brussels.

Part I
Methodology

1 Studying the past and future with infinite-horizon simulation models*

Charles Ballard

1 Introduction

By their very nature, economic models abstract from important aspects of reality. (If models did not employ a degree of abstraction, they would not be models.) And yet, if economists hope to have credibility with each other and with the non-economist majority of the population, it is important that our models not be too far-fetched. The problem of credibility is especially acute for applied general-equilibrium modellers. This is because, by definition, we are dealing with models that are sufficiently complex that they are not amenable to analytical solutions. Thus, we produce results that cannot easily be replicated by other researchers. To the rest of the economics profession and to the rest of the world, it may appear that our results come from a mysterious 'black box'. Some may take the output of the black box on faith, but others may not. Faith, once lost, is not easily restored. Over the last generation, economists have used a great variety of general-equilibrium simulation models to analyse the effects of tax-policy changes. These include static models, models with overlapping generations of life-cycle consumers, and models in which the consumers have an infinite horizon.

Regardless of the type of model that is used, the goal of virtually all of this research has been to learn about what might occur in the future, if a particular policy change were implemented. This provides the researcher with the comfortable knowledge that he or she is unlikely ever to be proven wrong. In most cases, the authorities never actually implement the exact policy that is considered by the researcher.[1] Even if a given policy is implemented, the tendency of many researchers is to move on to the next paper, without ever asking whether the simulation results conformed to the facts.[2] It is true that most researchers calibrate their models so that they replicate the original data set, before any policy changes are considered. This does impose a certain amount of

*I am grateful to Brian Hannon for fine research assistance, and to Ken Boyer, Christoph Böhringer, Peter Broer, Glenn Harrison, Brian Parmenter, Tarmo Valkonen, and Wolfgang Wiegard for helpful comments. Any errors are my responsibility.

discipline on the research. However, in most cases, no attempt is made to validate the results of the model, to see whether it will generate reasonable responses to changes in policy.[3]

The purpose of this chapter is to explore a different approach to validation and testing of the model. This different approach involves looking into the past, and using the model to analyse the effects of an actual policy change. This new approach could be applied to any kind of model. However, in this chapter, I will focus on the infinite-horizon model. Infinite-horizon models have retained a great deal of popularity, despite their inability to assess issues relating to the inter-generational distribution of wealth. For example, see Judd (1985), Jorgenson and Yun (1990), Lucas (1990), Greenwood and Huffman (1991), Jorgenson and Wilcoxen (1998), Mendoza and Tesar (1998) and many others.

I use an infinite-horizon model to study the effects of the tax-policy changes that were adopted in the United States in 1964–6. To the greatest extent possible, I try to build a model in the way in which one might have been built in 1963, looking forward to the tax-policy changes that would occur in the next few years. I use data for 1962, which became available in the summer of 1963.

The results are somewhat mixed. For some combinations of parameters, the model generates results that are not out of line. However, on the basis of the results presented here, it is not yet possible to draw a truly definitive conclusion regarding the efficacy of infinite-horizon simulation models. This chapter only represents the beginning of an extended research agenda. In future work, it will be necessary to delve more deeply into the problem, by considering, (1) other policy scenarios, (2) other calibration techniques, and (3) different parameter combinations.[4] However, even at this early stage of the analysis, I believe the results suggest that the economics profession should use caution when interpreting the results of infinite-horizon simulation models.[5] Researchers who use infinite-horizon models should take great care in specifying the details of the model structure and parameters. My own preference is for the profession to reduce its use of infinite-horizon models, in favour of overlapping-generations models.[6]

2   Tax policy in the United States in the early and mid-1960s

In 1960, John F. Kennedy ran for President on a platform that emphasized the need to revitalize the American economy and society, in order to meet the challenge of global communism. As part of this programme, he eventually submitted to the Congress a package of tax-policy proposals. These proposals led to the passage of a series of changes in tax rates, which were phased in beginning in 1964.[7]

From 1954 to 1963, the marginal tax rates in the Federal individual income tax ranged from 20 to 91 per cent. The rates were then lowered in 1964 and again in 1965. By 1965, the marginal rates ranged from 14 to 70 per cent. Barro and Sahasakul (1983, 1986) estimate that this led to a reduction in the average marginal rate, from 24.7 per cent in 1963 to 21.2 per cent in 1965.

At the same time, the marginal rates in the Federal corporation income tax were also reduced. In 1963, the corporation income tax was levied at a rate of 30 per cent on the first $25,000 of taxable corporate income, and at a rate of 52 per cent on taxable corporate income above $25,000. By 1965, these rates had been reduced to 22 per cent on the first $25,000, and 48 per cent on higher incomes.

While the individual and corporate income-tax rates were being reduced, the Social Security payroll tax was being raised. The combined rates on employers and employees were increased from 6.25 per cent in 1962 to 8.4 per cent in 1966, and the maximum taxable earnings level was raised from $4,800 in 1965 to $6,600 in 1966.

Thus, very roughly, the tax-policy changes of the early and mid-1960s can be viewed as a revenue-neutral set of changes, in which reductions in individual income taxes and corporate income taxes were offset by increases in payroll taxes. In fact, in this chapter, this is the way in which the policy changes will be modelled.

Of course, the tax system is sufficiently complicated that it is never possible to capture every single policy change in a model. For one thing, this chapter will only consider changes in Federal tax policies. We abstract from changes in tax policy at the State and local levels, as well as from changes in the policies of other countries.

Even at the Federal level, we focus only on an important subset of tax-policy changes. For example, after 1963, Federal excise taxes were eliminated on a number of commodities, including excises on automobiles and automobile accessories, cameras, electric appliances, furs, luggage, marijuana, musical instruments, opium, playing cards, phonograph records, photographic film, pool tables, radios, refrigerators and sporting goods other than fishing equipment. We do not consider these tax-policy changes. However, it seems unlikely that these excise-tax reductions would have any substantial effect on the results, because most of these excises raised insignificant amounts of tax revenue. The excise taxes on alcohol, tobacco and gasoline are the ones that raised the largest amounts of revenue in the 1960s, and they remain in effect to this day.

We also abstract from the investment tax credit, which was instituted on 1 January 1962, at a rate of 7 per cent. The investment tax credit was suspended for about 5 months in 1966–67, and for about 28 months in 1969–71. Also in 1962, the Internal Revenue Service issued a new set of depreciation guidelines, which were somewhat more liberal than those used previously. It will be interesting to consider these policy changes in future work, but they are not considered explicitly here.

Finally, it is important to remember that tax policies rarely remain unchanged for very long. After the individual income-tax rates were reduced in 1964 and 1965, they remained the same for only 3 years. Individual income-tax rates were raised in 1968, and again in 1969. The rates were then lowered in 1970, and again in 1971. The same pattern of increases and decreases was seen in the corporation income-tax rates. Nevertheless, in this chapter, our simulation experiments involve changing the personal income-tax rate and the capital tax rate once and for all. This is necessary because our goal is to perform a simulation exercise as it might have been performed in 1963. Clearly, if we were to have run these simulations in 1963, it would have been extremely problematic to model the entire time path of future tax-policy changes. In 1963, only a wizard with a crystal ball would have been able to predict that the Vietnam War would lead to tax increases 5 years later.

Therefore, if we claim that infinite-horizon models behave in a fashion that is peculiar in some way, and if we suggest caution in using infinite-horizon models as a result, it is always possible to reach the alternate conclusion that the model is really fine, and that the results are driven by some other forces that have been excluded from the model. At the very least, however, this should remind us that computational general-equilibrium simulation models are not especially well suited for making forecasts. Rather, the strength of these models lies in their ability to shed light on complicated policy questions (even if they do not give us the ability to predict the future).

3   The production side of the model

The goal of this chapter is to represent these tax-policy changes from the 1960s in an economic model. I begin by choosing data for the United States economy for 1962, taken from the July 1963, *Survey of Current Business* (US Department of Commerce 1963).[8] On the production side, the model used here is a slightly modified version of the GEMTAP model, developed by Fullerton, Shoven, Whalley and their colleagues. (For a detailed description of the model, see Ballard *et al.* 1985.) In this model, capital and labour are combined to produce value added, according to constant-elasticity-of-substitution production functions. Corporate taxes and property taxes are treated as *ad-valorem* taxes on the use of capital. Payroll taxes are treated as *ad-valorem* taxes on the use of labour. General retail sales taxes and specific excise taxes are treated as *ad-valorem* taxes on consumption. The model also includes an individual income tax, which is modelled as a linear function with a negative intercept, in order to capture the fact that marginal income-tax rates are greater than average rates. Even though imports and exports are included, the model is basically that of a closed economy. It is assumed that the current account is always balanced, and there are no international flows of capital.

The standard version of the GEMTAP model has been calibrated to data sets for 1973 and 1983. Those data sets had nineteen production sectors, and indeed the methodology can be extended to an unlimited number of sectors.[9] However, the goal of this research is to focus on the consumer dynamics, as represented by an infinite-horizon model. Therefore, the model used here is a one-sector model: the data set for 1962 is based on aggregated data. In future work, it will be valuable to extend the ideas of this chapter to a disaggregated data set.

4   The model of the infinite-horizon consumer

In this chapter, I change the standard version of the GEMTAP model in one important way. In the original GEMTAP model, consumers make their savings decisions on the basis of a current income constraint, rather than an intertemporal wealth constraint. Here, however, the infinitely lived consumer makes savings decisions on the basis of an intertemporal wealth constraint. This combination of the GEMTAP production structure with an infinite-horizon consumer was first explored in Ballard and Goulder (1985).

As in most infinite-horizon models, utility is assumed to be additively separable over time. Below, I shall discuss a version of the model in which the consumer faces a labour/leisure decision. However, I begin with the simplest version of the model, in which labour supply is specified exogenously. In this version, leisure does not have an effect on utility and the utility functional depends only on consumption. Following Starrett (1982) and Ballard and Goulder (1985), I allow for the possibility that a portion of consumption is non-discretionary. The required minimum level of consumption in period t is denoted by C_t^*. (Note, however, that C_t^* can be zero.) The utility functional is:

$$U = \sum_{t=1}^{\infty} \frac{1}{(1+\rho)^{t-1}} \frac{(C_t - C_t^*)^{1-\gamma}}{1-\gamma},$$ (1)

where γ is the inverse of the intertemporal elasticity of substitution, ρ is the rate of time preference, and C_t is consumption in period t. When γ is 1.0, this becomes

$$U = \sum_{t=1}^{\infty} \frac{1}{(1+\rho)^{t-1}} \ln(C_t - C_t^*).$$ (1′)

The consumer is assumed to maximize equation (1) or (1′), subject to a wealth constraint:

$$\sum_{t=1}^{\infty} \frac{P_t C_t}{\prod_{s=1}^{t}(1+r_s)} = K_1 + \sum_{t=1}^{\infty} \frac{W_t H_t + Y_t}{\prod_{s=1}^{t}(1+r_s)},$$ (2)

where P_t is the price of consumption goods in period t, K_1 is the value of initial capital, W_t is the net-of-tax wage rate in period t, H_t is the quantity of labour supplied in period t, Y_t is the value of transfers received in period t, $r_1 \equiv 0$, and r_s is the rate of return in period s, for $s > 1$. This wealth constraint states that the present discounted value of consumption expenditure must be equal to the present discounted value of resources.

Equations (1) and (2) can be combined to form a Lagrangean function. When we differentiate this function with respect to C_t, we obtain the first-order conditions. Combining the first-order conditions for two adjacent periods gives us an equation of motion:

$$C_t - C_t^* = (C_{t-1} - C_{t-1}^*)\left(\frac{P_{t-1}}{P_t}\right)\left(\frac{1+r_t}{1+\rho}\right)^{1/\gamma}. \tag{3}$$

The interpretation of equation (3) is intuitive: the growth rate of discretionary consumption between two adjacent periods is inversely related to the growth rate of prices and the rate of time preference and positively related to the rate of return. The magnitude of the effect of these parameters on the growth rate of discretionary consumption is controlled by the intertemporal substitution elasticity, $1/\gamma$.

The model is calibrated to generate a steady-state growth path in the base case. In the steady state, prices are unchanging. In this case, equation (3) implies that, for any two adjacent periods,

$$\frac{C_t - C_t^*}{C_{t-1} - C_{t-1}^*} = \left(\frac{1+r}{1+\rho}\right)^{1/\gamma}. \tag{4}$$

In equation (4), there is no subscript on the rate of return, r, to indicate the fact that the rate of return is unchanging in the base case, because it is assumed that the base-case sequence of equilibria is on a steady-state growth path.

The left-hand side of equation (4) is one plus the steady-state growth rate of the economy in the base case. If the base-case growth rate in the model is specified on the basis of the data on saving and the initial capital stock, then equation (4) implies stringent restrictions on the possible combinations of r, ρ and γ. (See below for further discussion.)

A somewhat more complicated model involves a labour/leisure decision. In this case, leisure enters the utility function:

$$U = \sum_{t=1}^{\infty} \frac{1}{(1+\rho)^{t-1}} \frac{[(C_t - C_t^*)^\alpha \ell_t^{1-\alpha}]^{1-\gamma}}{1-\gamma}, \tag{5}$$

where the parameter α is used in the calibration process, and ℓ_t is leisure in period t. The wealth constraint is the same as in equation (2). If we use (5) and (2) to form a Lagrangean function, and then take the first-order conditions with respect to consumption and leisure, we can derive an expression that shows the relationship between leisure and discretionary consumption in any period:

$$\ell_t = (C_t - C_t^*)\frac{1-\alpha}{\alpha}\frac{P_t}{W_t}. \tag{6}$$

Substituting equation (6) into the first-order condition for consumption, and recursively calulating the ratio between adjacent periods, we generate an equation that relates discretionary consumption in period t to discretionary consumption in period 1:

$$C_t - C_t^* = (C_1 - C_1^*)\Omega_t^{1/\gamma}\Psi_t^{(\gamma-1)(1-\alpha)/\gamma}, \tag{7}$$

where

$$\Omega_t = \left(\frac{P_1}{P_t}\right)\frac{\prod_{s=1}^{t}(1+r_s)}{(1+\rho)^{t-1}} \tag{8}$$

and

$$\Psi_t = \left(\frac{W_t}{P_t}\right)\left(\frac{P_1}{W_1}\right). \tag{9}$$

As in the model with exogenous labour supply, equations (7) and (8) show that consumption will grow more rapidly when the difference between the rate of return and the rate of time preference is larger and that the rate of growth is also influenced by the intertemporal substitution elasticity.

After some further manipulations, we can derive an expression for first-period discretionary consumption in terms of all of the parameters of the problem:

$$C_1 - C_1^* = \frac{\sum_{t-1}^{\infty}\left[(W_t E_t + Y_t - P_t C_t^*)\prod_{s=1}^{t}1/(1+r_s)\right] + K_1}{\frac{1}{\gamma}\sum_{t=1}^{\infty}\left[P_t\Omega_t^{1/\gamma}\Psi_t^{(y-1)(1-\alpha)}\prod_{s=1}^{t}1/(1+r_s)\right]}. \tag{10}$$

Equation (10) reveals a very important property of intertemporal models such as this one. The numerator of the right-hand side of the equation contains the present discounted value of the consumer's lifetime resources, less the present discounted value of the consumer's lifetime stream of expenditure on required consumption. Since every period's consumption is a normal good and every period's leisure is also a normal good, anything that changes the present discounted value of lifetime resources less the required consumption expenditure will have a direct impact on first-period consumption and leisure. Holding constant the present value of required consumption expenditure, if there is an increase in the present value of lifetime resources, the consumer will want to consume more goods and more leisure in the first period. Similarly, if there is a decrease in the present value of lifetime resources, the consumer will desire to consume fewer goods and less leisure in the first period.

Even modest changes in consumption and leisure can lead to dramatic changes in saving. Starrett (1981) was among the first to appreciate what really happens in this type of intertemporal model. Starrett suggests the introduction of a consumption floor, which introduces an element of complementarity across time. This element is otherwise totally absent from additively separable models of this type. As Starrett puts it:

> Without complementarity, substitution effects 'compound' across time; the rate at which a consumer can trade consumption many periods hence for

consumption now is very sensitive to the rate of interest and (in the absence of complementarity) all consumers will engage in a lot of substitution unless [the intertemporal substitution elasticity is extremely small].

Starrett's analysis was directed specifically at the overlapping-generations work of Summers (1981). However, his comments are even more appropriate for the analysis of an infinite-horizon model, because the infinite horizon means that the effects on the present value of lifetime resources can be even larger than they are in an overlapping-generations framework.

The size of these effects will be determined by a number of parameters, including the intertemporal substitution elasticity, the base-case rate of return, the rate of time preference, and the amount of minimum required consumption. In versions of the model with a labour/leisure choice, the size of the total endowment of time can also play an important role, for two reasons. First, the time endowment places an upper bound on the amount by which labour supply can increase. Second, the time endowment has an important effect on the present discounted value of lifetime resources.[10]

5   Simulation results

5.1   *An analysis of the policy changes in the 1960s*

In this section, I simulate the effects of the Federal tax-policy changes that were passed into law in the mid-1960s. As discussed in Section II, three important tax-policy changes were undertaken from 1964 to 1966. Individual income-tax rates were reduced and corporate income-tax rates were reduced as well, but payroll-tax rates were increased. The reduction in individual income-tax rates is modelled as a reduction in the marginal-tax rate in the model's individual income tax from 30 to 27 per cent.

The reduction in the corporate-tax rate is represented in the model as a reduction in the tax rate on the use of capital in production. As mentioned above, the marginal corporate rate was decreased from 52 to 48 per cent. However, it should be remembered that the Federal corporate tax is only slightly more than one-half of the total tax on capital in the base case. (Property taxes were an important source of capital taxation in 1962, as they are today.) Thus, a reduction in corporate-tax rates should be associated with a proportionally smaller reduction in the overall tax rate on capital. According to the base-case data, the tax rate on capital at the industry level in 1962 was about 53.3 per cent, when expressed as a percentage of gross capital income. I model the policy change as leading to a tax rate of 51 per cent.

The 1964 tax cuts are sometimes presented as a classic example of Keynesian stimulus.[11] However, the tax cuts did not actually lead to a significant expansion of the Federal budget deficit. Both Federal revenues and the deficit remained within a fairly narrow range until 1968, when, as a result of the Vietnam War and increased spending on domestic programmes, Federal expenditure surged sufficiently to increase the deficit to 2.9 per cent of GDP. Consequently, I do not explicitly model debt and deficits. Instead, I use traditional differential-incidence techniques to study these policy changes. I assume that the budget is balanced in every period. With individual income taxes and capital taxes decreasing, it is necessary to increase some other tax to achieve budget balance for the government. The tax chosen for this purpose is the tax on the use of labour at the industry level, which includes the payroll tax.

I assume that, in the absence of taxes, the rate of return to capital is 4 per cent. Following Fullerton *et al.* (1983), I assume that 30 per cent of financial saving is already exempt from saving in the base case. This means that the effective rate of return in the base case is about 4.4 per cent. I use 0.5 for the base-case ratio of C_t^*/C_t.[12] Finally, I begin by using an intertemporal substitution elasticity, $1/\gamma$ of 1/3. The base-case growth rate of the economy is calculated from the data on saving and on the capital stock. These imply a steady-state growth rate of approximately 2.59 per cent.

This immediately raises some problems. The steady-state growth rate has a powerful effect on the long-run shape of the economy. This is because, in a model of this type, the economy must eventually return to the base-case steady-state growth rate (although the approach is asymptotic, and can take many years). Thus, if the steady-state growth rate assumed in the model is substantially different from the growth rate that actually occurred, the results will necessarily miss at least some aspects of the dynamic development of the economy. In fact, over the 10-year period from 1962 to 1972, business-sector productivity rose at an average rate of about 3.27 per cent, and total output rose at an average rate of about 4.46 per cent, in contrast to the calibrated growth rate of about 2.59 per cent. The calibration of the steady state also creates another difficulty. In the procedure outlined above, the intertemporal substitution elasticity is assumed exogenously, based on the econometric literature. The rate of return is also essentially exogenous, and the growth rate of the economy is inferred from information on investment and capital income. This leaves the rate of time preference, ρ, to be calculated as a residual. For the values of the intertemporal substitution elasticity, the growth rate and the rate of return that are described in the previous paragraph, the implied value for the rate of time preference is about -3.32 per cent. Some researchers may feel uncomfortable with a negative rate of time preference. Regardless of one's reaction to any particular value for the rate of time preference, it is still true that not all of the parameters of this model can be chosen independently. In future work, it may be interesting to consider different techniques for choosing the parameters.

I begin by reporting simulation results for a model in which the intertemporal substitution elasticity is 0.333, the base-case ratio of C_t^*/C_t is 0.5, and there is no labour/leisure choice. In other words, I begin by assuming that labour supply is exogenous. (See equation (1).) In this simulation, the rate of return increases over its base-case value, but the increase is quite small: in the first few periods of the simulation, the rate of return rises by only about seventeen basis points. It is important to understand why the rate of return increases by such a small amount.

The decrease in the corporate tax tends to increase the rate of return, but the decrease in the individual income tax has an effect in the opposite direction. When the individual income-tax rate falls, the value of the subsidy to saving decreases, so that the effective price of investment increases. As a result of the modest size of the change in the rate of return, this policy does not have the kind of intertemporal effects that might occur under other policy scenarios.

In the first few periods, in order to maintain government budget balance, it is necessary for payroll-tax rates to rise by about six percentage points. (As the economy grows more rapidly, there is a decrease in the tax rate necessary for government budget balance, to about 4.5 percentage points.) This is at least somewhat consistent with the actual path of payroll-tax rates. However, much of that increase was the result of continued increases in spending on Social Security and Medicare, which are not fully captured in the simulation model. In the late 1960s and 1970s, the rate of growth of domestic spending was actually much more rapid than the steady-state growth rate of the model (and much more rapid than the actual growth rate of the economy).

As a result of the increase in the rate of return, the simulated economy exhibits an increase in investment. However, the surge in investment is relatively modest, because the rate of return increases by such a small amount. Also, the minimum required consumption level reduces the amount by which consumption can be reallocated. With an intertemporal substitution elasticity of 0.333, a required consumption ratio of 0.5, and no labour/leisure choice, aggregate investment in the first 5 years is only about 2.8 per cent larger than in the base case. This is certainly not out of line, since actual investment grew strongly in the mid- and late 1960s.

The minimum consumption requirement has a significant effect on the path of investment. If we keep the intertemporal substitution elasticity at 0.333, and if we continue to assume that labour supply is exogenous, but remove the minimum consumption requirement, the increase in aggregate investment in the first 5 years is about 9.2 per cent.

Now, what happens if we simulate the same policy changes, with an intertemporal substitution elasticity of one-fourth? Once again, it is important to emphasize that the substitution elasticity cannot be changed, without making at least one other change to the model. I continue to use the same data and to assume the same net rate of return in the base case. This means that, if the intertemporal substitution elasticity is changed, the steady-state assumption can only be maintained if we also change the rate of time preference. When the intertemporal substitution elasticity is 0.25, the rate of time preference falls to about -5.77 per cent. While the lower intertemporal substitution elasticity will tend to reduce the possibilities for a savings response, the lower rate of time preference will tend to move in the opposite direction. This illustrates the difficulty of performing sensitivity analysis in an infinite-horizon model. If we desire to perform sensitivity analysis with respect to the static elasticity of substitution between capital and labour in production, it is possible to do so without altering the factor shares. However, calibration of a dynamic system is a much more challenging task, because it involves specifying the entire path of consumption. Thus, in the context of an infinite-horizon model, the results of any 'sensitivity analysis' must be approached with caution.

The net effect is that the intertemporal substitution elasticity is more powerful than the rate of time preference, because a decrease in the intertemporal substitution elasticity is associated with a decrease in the investment response. With an intertemporal substitution elasticity of 0.25 and a required-consumption ratio of 0.50, the increase in investment in the first 5 years is only about 0.46 per cent, relative to the base case. With an intertemporal substitution elasticity of 0.25 and no minimum consumption requirement, however, investment in the first 5 years is about 6.26 per cent larger than in the base case.

Next, we consider the case in which the intertemporal substitution elasticity remains at one-third, but a labour/leisure choice is allowed. As noted earlier, when the rate of return is increased, the present value of lifetime resources is decreased. In the simulations reported here, this makes the consumer 'poorer,' and this leads to a decrease in consumption. Since the instantaneous felicity function consists of both consumption and leisure, the increase in the rate of return will also lead to a decrease in leisure. In other words, the consumer will work more. The increase in labour supply will tend to increase the investment response. When the intertemporal substitution elasticity is one-third, the required consumption ratio is 0.5, and there is no labour/leisure choice, we have seen that the aggregate response of investment in the first 5 years is an increase of about 2.8 per cent. If a labour/leisure choice is allowed, and if the ratio of time endowment to base-case labour is 1.25, then labour supply increases by more than 1 per cent (relative to the base case) for most years in the first decade. This increases disposable income. When combined with the decrease in consumption, the result is an investment increase of about 4.7 per cent in the first 5 years. If the ratio of time endowment to base-case labour is 1.50, the investment response rises to 6.4 per cent.

This chapter began with strong warnings about the problems of infinite-horizon models. At this point, however, the case for the weakness of the infinite-horizon model has not been made very convincingly, because the results presented in the last few paragraphs have not been especially strange. For the parameter combinations discussed above, the model has not produced results that are particularly bizarre. Still, it is hoped that the reader will maintain a healthy skepticism toward infinite-horizon models in general. As explained earlier, computational difficulties have prevented the investigation of some parameter combinations. The parameter combinations that have been investigated here are precisely those that are least likely to cause problems.[13] As we choose higher values of the intertemporal substitution elasticity, combined with lower values of the required-consumption ratio and higher values of the ratio of time endowment to base-case labour supply, a model of this type may tend to produce odd results.[14] In the next section, we perform an analysis in the traditional style, in which a simulation is performed for a tax-policy change that was not enacted.

5.2   An analysis in the traditional style

As stated above, the main purpose of this chapter is to use the model for the United States economy for 1962 to simulate the effects of the policy changes of the mid-1960s. However, to place the results in a context that will be more familiar for many simulation modellers, I will now also report the effects of a policy change that was not implemented in the 1960s. The policy investigated here involves a move toward greater reliance on consumption taxation, in which tax-deferred status is extended to all financial saving. In order to achieve equal tax-revenue yield for the government, the consumer's marginal income-tax rate is increased. For more details on this policy proposal, see Fullerton *et al.* (1983), Ballard *et al.* (1985, especially Chapter 9), Ballard and Goulder (1985) and Ballard (1987).

I begin by reporting the results for the move toward a consumption tax, from the infinite-horizon model with no labour/leisure choice, with an intertemporal substitution elasticity of one-third, and with a required consumption ratio of 0.5. When these parameters are used, the impact effect of the policy change is to increase the rate of return by about 100 basis points. This is a much larger increase than that which occurred as a result of the simulated policy changes for the 1960s. Consequently, this policy change generates much larger effects in the model. In the first 5 years, investment increases by nearly 30 per cent, relative to the base case.

At first, the burst of additional tax-preferred saving makes it necessary to increase the income-tax rate by about 2.6 percentage points, in order to balance the government's budget while paying for the additional subsidy to saving. However, the additional saving causes increased economic growth. Over time, there is a decrease in the tax rate necessary to meet the government's revenue requirement. By 34 years after the policy change, the tax rate is actually lower than it had been in the base case. In the long run, the income-tax rate falls to about 28.6 per cent, compared with the base-case rate of 30 per cent. On the whole, the growth of the economy is quite impressive. In the long run, the capital stock is about 26 per cent larger than in the base case.

What would have happened (according to the model) if the same policy had been instituted, but if the intertemporal substitution elasticity were only one-fourth? By itself, the decrease in the intertemporal substitution elasticity would tend to make the consumer less responsive to the increased rate of return. However, as mentioned in the previous section, calibration of the steady state leads to a simultaneous decrease in the assumed rate of time preference. The decrease in the rate of time preference works to make the consumer more responsive. Thus, the results that emerge from the model are likely to be at least somewhat similar, even when the substitution elasticity is decreased. In the first five periods, investment increases by about 23.7 per cent, relative to the base-case sequence of equilibria. In the long run, the capital stock is more than one-fourth larger under this policy change than under the base case, regardless of the value of the intertemporal substitution elasticity. However, I find the results to be more believable in the case with the lower substitution elasticity, because the short-run burst in saving is not as pronounced. Nevertheless, since the policy was not actually implemented, there is no historical experience against which to judge the simulation results.

The results reported above are for the case of the model with an exogenous path of labour supply. What happens if we allow the consumer to choose the amount of labour, as in equation (5)? The results depend on the total amount of time that is available to be allocated between labour and leisure. If the time endowment is not much greater than the amount of labour supplied in the base case, then labour supply has little room to change, and the results are very similar to those that are generated by the model with exogenous labour supply. When the time endowment is larger, the labour-supply decision begins to have a more substantial effect on the results. For example, the standard assumption in the GEMTAP model was that the time endowment is 1.75 times as great as the amount of labour supplied in the base case. If we impose this assumption on the model used here, the move toward a consumption tax has an effect on labour supply. The increased subsidy to saving leads to an increase in the net rate of return. As a result, the present value of lifetime wealth falls, and the consumer desires to reduce consumption of both goods and leisure. Therefore, there is an increase in labour supply. In the first period, when the intertemporal substitution elasticity is one-fourth and when the required consumption ratio is 0.5, labour supply increases by 1.8 per cent, relative to its base-case value. This gives an added boost to saving. In the first 5 periods, investment soars by nearly 40 per cent, relative to its base-case path. The additional labour supply leads to an increase in taxable labour income and this means that the tax rate necessary to achieve government budget balance is not as high as it was in the first period of the simulation with exogenous labour supply. Over time, both labour supply and the saving rate fall back in the direction of their base-case values, as they did in the simulation with exogenous labour supply.

Of course, many objections can be levelled at these simulations. As mentioned before, the model used here does not include adjustment costs. The inclusion of adjustment costs is an important item on the agenda for future research. In addition, the intratemporal model of the labour/leisure choice in this model takes the Cobb–Douglas form. It is likely that this leads to an exaggeration of the labour-supply response. Therefore, another subject of future research is to change the intratemporal utility function to the constant-elasticity-of-substitution form, and to consider lower values of the instantaneous elasticity of substitution between consumption and leisure. Finally, and most important of all, it is appropriate to do much more sensitivity analysis, considering a wide range of other values for the intertemporal substitution elasticity, the minimum amount of required consumption, the time endowment, and other parameters.

However, it is hoped that the obvious need for further sensitivity analysis does not obscure the central message of this chapter. The message is that simulation modellers need to devote more attention to validation of their models. Calibration is an important first step in the validation process. But it is also valuable to test the models against actual historical experiences, to judge whether they are capable of producing sensible results. In this chapter, I have performed this type of valida-tion exercise for an infinite-horizon model. The results suggest that these models are capable of providing unobjectionable results, at least for certain combinations of parameters. However, at this early stage of the investigation, it still seems appropriate to suggest that these models ought to be approached with caution. The danger that the model may produce strange results is increased when larger values of the intertemporal substitution elasticity are used, or when small values of minimum required consumption are used, or when an elastic labour-supply formulation is used.

6   Conclusion

Among researchers who use economic simulation models, the tradition is to simulate the ways in which the economy might respond to a policy change in the future. Most researchers do not attempt to validate their models by testing them against past historical experiences. In this chapter, I have constructed a compu-tational general-equilibrium model of the United States economy and tax system, based on data for 1962. I then use the model to simulate the effects of the tax-policy changes that occurred during the mid-1960s, including decreases in the marginal-tax rates in the individual income tax and the corporate income tax, as well as increases in the payroll-tax rate.

The model of production used here is similar to that of the GEMTAP model of Ballard et al. (1985), while the demand model is that of an infinitely lived consumer. The results suggest that, for certain combinations of parameters, the infinite-horizon model may do a reasonable job. In particular, a required mini-mum level of consumption can help to reduce the intertemporal sensitivity of the model, as can choice of a modest value for the intertemporal substitution elasticity. Also, the intertemporal responsiveness of the model can be kept within reasonable bounds by adopting a specification that limits labour-supply responses. If steps like these are not taken, the model may be susceptible to quite large swings of saving and investment.

There may be many sets of parameters within the infinite-horizon model that give plausible results. However, in my opinion, the economics profession should approach infinite-horizon models with caution. In future work, I intend to do more sensitivity analysis, with respect to a variety of parameters, to learn more about the combinations of parameters under which an infinite-horizon model does, and does not, perform in a sensible fashion. My most important conclusion is that simulation modellers need to pay more attention to the issues raised here. It is hoped that this will not be the last study that attempts to consider the behaviour of a model with reference to actual historical experience. If we can develop models that give meaningful results, when tested against actual historical episodes, then we can have greater confidence in the results and we can make a stronger case to the rest of the economics profession and the rest of the world.

Notes

1 In some cases, the policy considered by the researchers has special features, so that it would be extremely unlikely for the policy ever to be passed into law. For example, see the papers collected in Joint Committee on Taxation (1997).

2 One notable exception is the paper by Kehoe *et al.* (1995).

3 In the interest of full disclosure, I should make it clear that much of my own work has followed in this tradition. Thus, when I criticize this procedure, I am not merely criticizing others. Instead, I am criticizing a technique that is extremely widespread, throughout the community of researchers who use simulation models.

4 In this paper, I use a combination of algorithms to solve for the dynamic equilibrium path of the economy. The 'inner algorithm' calculates the equilibrium prices in any one period, under an exogenously specified path of expected future prices. The 'outer algorithm' calculates a set of prices that is consistent intertemporally, in that expectations of future prices are in fact realized. The inner algorithm used here is based on the tatonnement algorithm of Kimbell and Harrison (1986). The outer algorithm used here is a modified version of the Gauss-Seidel algorithm of Ballard and Goulder (1985). For some configurations of parameters, these algorithms work reasonably well. In particular, they tend to work well for parameter combinations under which there are limits on the consumer's ability to substitute consumption and leisure across time periods. For example, the algorithms tend to calculate equilibrium prices in reasonable amounts of time for lower values of the intertemporal substitution elasticity, or for parameters that lead to a less-responsive labour-supply choice. However, for higher values of the intertemporal substitution elasticity, or when we allow for a more-responsive labour-supply decision, these algorithms tend to become very inefficient. This has limited the possibilities for performing sensitivity analysis over the full range of parameters. Because of this, the results presented in this paper are somewhat biased in the direction of making the infinite-horizon model look good. For the less-sensitive parameter sets reported here, the model is less likely to generate absurd results. In future work, I intend to adopt other solution algorithms, which will allow for fuller consideration of a wider range of parameters.

5 I recognize that even the new approach outlined in this paper cannot give a rigorous proof of the flaws of the infinite-horizon model. It is always possible to speculate that the model is correct, in and of itself, and that the observed trajectory of the economy is the result of some feature that is left out of the model.

6 Of course, overlapping-generations models are not immune to the problems discussed here. (See Ballard 1990 for discussion.) However, those problems are likely to be somewhat reduced in the context of a model with finite lives. In addition, overlapping-generations models have the advantage of being able to consider inter-generational issues.

7 The data on tax rates presented here are summarized conveniently in Pechman (1987).

8 Of course, although these data are similar to the data one would find in today's National Income and Product Accounts (NIPA), they are not identical, because the original data have been revised. Again, it is important to emphasize that our goal is to perform a simulation as it would have been performed in 1963. In 1963, economists did not have access to the NIPA revisions that were made years later.

9 Some of the most important studies to emerge from this model have taken advantage of the high degree of sectoral disaggregation, by dealing with the tax-induced mis-allocation of capital across sectors. For example, see Fullerton *et al.* (1981).

10 For more discussion, see Ballard (1999).

11 In fact, in some circles, the Kennedy-Johnson tax cuts have acquired nearly mythic status. However, as suggested by Prachowny (2000), the reality of the decision-making process that led to these tax cuts is probably considerably less impressive than the myth.

12 See Ballard (1983) for discussion of some econometric studies that would support values of C_t^* such as these. As C_t^* increases, all else equal, the consumer's responses to policy shocks will become smaller. Note that the present model does not include adjustment costs in the investment process, which are another way of slowing down the economy's responses to tax-policy changes. (See Bovenberg and Goulder 1997 for a model with adjustment costs.) In future research, a high priority will be to incorporate adjustment costs in the investment process and to perform sensitivity analysis with respect to the adjustment-cost parameters, as well as to perform sensitivity analysis with respect to the value of C_t^*.

13 The simulations produce a great deal of information regarding factor supplies, prices and incomes, investment, saving, capital stock, etc. More detailed information is available on request. In addition, several other parameter combinations were simulated, in addition to those reported above. However, all of the combinations involve at least one of the following: (1) a relatively high required-consumption ratio, (2) a relatively low intertemporal substitution elasticity, or (3) a small ratio of time endowment to base-case labour supply.

14 Ballard and Goulder (1985) use an infinite-horizon model to compare the results from, (a) sequences of equilibria with foresight, and (b) sequences of equilibria with myopic expectations. They find that the long-run steady state is the same in each case, but the economy approaches the new steady state more quickly when expectations are myopic. The same kinds of results are found here. The differences between the myopic path and the path with foresight are greater when the parameters allow for greater intertemporal responsiveness. Over the limited range of parameters for which it has been possible to calculate both a myopic equilibrium and a perfect-foresight equilibrium, the responses of the model become more and more dramatic, both in the case of myopia and in the case of perfect foresight, as any of the following occurs: (1) the required-consumption ratio is reduced, or (2) the intertemporal substitution elasticity is increased, or (3) the time endowment is increased. The computational difficulties are considerably smaller when expectations are myopic. Consequently, it has been possible to run myopic simulations for a wider range of parameters than could be used with perfect foresight. For those parameter combinations for which it has only been possible to calculate a myopic equilibrium, the model results are sometimes very bizarre, with exceedingly large bursts of labour supply and investment in the first few periods. If the same pattern were to occur with perfect foresight, the model would certainly generate some bizarre results. However, since it has not yet been possible to run the perfect-foresight simulations with these parameters, the relationship can only be considered to be suggestive at this time.

References

Ballard, C. L. (1983) 'Evaluation of the consumption tax with dynamic general equilibrium models', Unpublished Ph.D. dissertation, Stanford University.

Ballard, C. L. (1987) 'Tax policy and consumer foresight: a general equilibrium simulation study', *Economic Inquiry*, 25 (April), 267–84.

Ballard, C. L. (1990) 'On the specification of simulation models for evaluating income and consumption taxes', in: Rose, M. (ed.) *Heidelberg Congress on Taxing Consumption*, Berlin: Springer-Verlag, 147–77.

Ballard, C. L. (1999) 'How many hours are in a simulated day? The effects of time endowment on the results of tax-policy simulation models', Michigan State University *Mimeo* (October 22).

Ballard, C. L., Fullerton, D., Shoven, J. B. and Whalley, J. (1985) *A General Equilibrium Model for Tax Policy Evaluation*, Chicago: University of Chicago Press.

Ballard, C. L. and Goulder, L. H. (1985) 'Consumption taxes, foresight, and welfare: A computable general equilibrium analysis', in: Piggott, J. and Whalley, J. (eds) *New Developments in Applied General Equilibrium Analysis*, Cambridge: Cambridge University Press, 253–82.

Barro, R. J. and Sahasakul, C. (1983) 'Measuring the average marginal tax rate from the individual income tax', *Journal of Business*, 56 (October), 419–52.

Barro, R. J. and Sahasakul, C. (1986) 'Average marginal tax rates from social security and the individual income tax', *Journal of Business*, 59 (October), 555–66.

Bovenberg, A. L. and Goulder, L. H. (1997) 'Costs of environmentally motivated taxes in the presence of other taxes: General equilibrium analyses', *National Tax Journal*, 50 (March), 59–87.

Fullerton, D., King, A. T., Shoven, J. B. and Whalley, J. (1981) 'Corporate tax integration in the United States: A general equilibrium approach', *American Economic Review*, 71 (September), 677–91.

Fullerton, D., Shoven, J. B. and Whalley, J. (1983) 'Replacing the U.S. income tax with a progressive consumption tax', *Journal of Public Economics*, 20 (February), 3–23.

Greenwood, J. and Huffman, G. W. (1991) 'Tax analysis in a real-business-cycle model', *Journal of Monetary Economics*, 27, 167–90.

'Joint Committee on Taxation' (1997) *Joint Committee on Taxation Tax Modeling Project and 1997 Tax Symposium Papers*, Washington, D.C.: USGPO (November 20).

Jorgenson, D. W. and Wilcoxen, P. J. (1998) 'The economic impact of fundamental tax reform', *Paper Presented at the Fourth Annual Conference of the James A. Baker III Institute for Public Policy*, November 5, Rice University.

Jorgenson, D. W. and Kun-Young Yun (1990) 'Tax reform and U.S. economic growth', *Journal of Political Economy*, 98 (October), S151–93.

Judd, K. L. (1985) 'Short-run analysis of fiscal policy in a simple perfect foresight model', *Journal of Political Economy*, 93 (April), 298–319.

Kehoe, T. J., Polo, C. and Sancho, F. (1995) 'An evaluation of the performance of an applied general equilibrium model of the Spanish economy', *Economic Theory*, 6 (June), 115–41.

Kimbell, L. J. and Harrison, G. W. (1986) 'On the solution of general equilibrium models', *Economic Modeling*, 3 (July), 197–212.

Lucas, R. (1990) 'Supply-side economics: An analytical review', *Oxford Economic Papers*, 42, 293–316.

Mendoza, E. and Tesar, L. (1998) 'The international ramifications of tax reforms: Supply-side economics in a global economy', *American Economic Review*, 88 (March), 226–45.

Pechman, J. A. (1987) *Federal Tax Policy* 5th edn. Washington, D.C.: The Brookings Institution.

Prachowny, M. F. J. (2000) *The Kennedy-Johnson Tax Cut: A Revisionist History*, Cheltenham: Edward Elgar Publishing.

Starrett, D. A. (1982) 'Long run savings elasticities in the life cycle model', *Factor Markets Workshop Research Paper No. 24*, August, Stanford University.

Summers, L. H. (1981) 'Capital taxation and accumulation in a life cycle growth model', *American Economic Review*, 71 (September), 533–44.

U.S. Department of Commerce, Office of Business Economics (1963) 'National Income and Product in 1962', *Survey of Current Business*, 43 (July), 11–40.

2 Policy reform without tears*

Glenn W. Harrison, Jesper Jensen, Morten I. Lau and Thomas F. Rutherford

1. Introduction

Most of the major policy reforms being considered result in winners and losers. It would be nice if this were not so, and one could devise reforms that were 'win–win' propositions when one digs beneath the public rhetoric. Unfortunately, life does not often present reforms that meet the Pareto criterion of economists that nobody be worse off after the reform than they were before it.

We illustrate how one can use a quantitative model of the Danish economy to determine what reforms could be Pareto improvements if one allowed compensation of losers. This approach to 'policy reform without tears' is possible with a quantitative model, even if it is not possible using only theory. The reason is that one must take into account the effects of sidepayments on relative prices and hence on the basis for the welfare evaluation made prior to the sidepayments. This loop raises interminable difficulties if one does not have information on expenditure patterns of different households, as well as the rest of the structure of the economy. One can either assume this problem away (e.g. by assuming community indifference curves or hypothetical sidepayments) or one can attempt to take it into account. We do the latter.

The way in which compensation is undertaken can also have efficiency effects. If distortionary subsidies are used to compensate losers, then there may be an efficiency cost from the very act of compensation which must also be taken into account. Thus, the overall pie may be diminished by the way in which it is sliced up. Of course, it is also possible that 'second-best' interactions with pre-existing distortions result in an efficiency gain from the use of a distortionary compensation scheme.

In addition, the way in which the funds for compensation are raised by the government can have efficiency effects. There is a marginal excess burden from any attempt to raise extra government revenue, whether or not that revenue is being used to finance government expenditures or compensate private households.

*At the time that this research was undertaken we were all members of the *MobiDK* Project, Danish Ministry of Trade and Industry, Copenhagen, Denmark. We are grateful to Tim Folke of *Denmarks Statistics* for extensive discussions about the official input–output database for Denmark.

Again, second-best considerations mean that one must evaluate specific proposals to see if the marginal excess burden is positive or negative.

Compensation schemes are well known in theory, but are often neglected in practical efforts to evaluate policy reforms. We take all of the potential costs and second-best interactions from compensation into account in our calculations. To illustrate our approach we consider the reform of excise taxes on consumption in Denmark. Our illustrative purposes will be served by using a simple, static computable general equilibrium (CGE) model we have constructed to represent the Danish economy in 1992. We use a GE model because we need to trace through the effects of changes in taxes and income on the relative prices of goods and services that households consume, both for the first-round effects of the tax reforms and for the second-round effects of the sidepayments. We use a CGE model because we need to keep arithmetic track of the size of the welfare gains or losses that each household experiences due to the policies and sidepayments. We use a static CGE model because there is nothing essential in the logic of our illustration that requires a dynamic model, although we accept that a dynamic analysis is needed in the end to be able to propose defensible policy reforms (e.g. Jensen 2000; Rutherford 2000). Finally, we use a simple, static CGE model because we do not want to have the elementary logic of our approach blurred by having too many imperfections and '*ad hoc*' assumptions in an effort to make the model appear to be a more realistic representation of the Danish economy. We shall see that simple does not mean small, however.

Our model is intended to be illustrative of the type of policy analysis that can be undertaken with CGE models. With obvious caveats for the current, evolving state of our model and the confidence we place in specific numbers, we are prepared to draw four general conclusions.

- It is feasible to evaluate the types of compensatory schemes needed to ensure that policy reforms are 'win–win' reforms for all households. This is not to say that such reforms always exist, since it is possible that the aggregate pie is insufficient to effect compensation. But the Danish economy, as currently modelled here, provides many opportunities for positive reforms in this sense.
- The compensation schemes are sensitive to undertaking a complete general equilibrium accounting for the 'secondary' effects of the sidepayments themselves. In other words, a naïve analysis that simply drew up a list of winners and losers from some reform and effected sidepayments without checking for further effects on welfare could lead to dangerous policy. The policy would be dangerous because it would get the signs wrong (some households would be making compensation when in fact they ought to be receiving compensation) and it would get the amounts of compensation wrong (some households would receive significantly less compensation than they actually needed).
- Removal of excise taxes is not as important as removing the distortions of the taxes. Virtually all of the welfare gains from complete excise tax removal can be obtained from a policy of strict uniformity across all goods

and with none of the significant equity problems that removal entails (prior to compensation).

- Just as it is feasible to ensure that there are no losers from policy reforms, if the aggregate pie is big enough, it is also feasible to ensure that no household experience a welfare gain less than some prescribed positive threshold amount. This enables one to design policy reforms that can be 'sold' to all segments of the population, rather than just to a select sub-group of winners.

2   A small open economy model

2.1   *General model structure*

Our small open economy (SOE) model is designed for policy analysis with a large number of sectors. The model is a 'generic' GE model of a single economy along the lines of Melo and Tarr (1992), Harrison *et al.* (1993) and Rutherford *et al.* (1994). We describe here the general features of the base model, adding details about the version for Denmark below. The complete database and model is available in machine-readable form via web page http://dmsweb.badm.sc.edu/ glenn/MobiDK.htm. This web page also provides the facility to completely replicate our results.

Goods are produced using primary factors and intermediate inputs. Primary factors include capital and labour. Production exhibits constant returns to scale and individual firms behave competitively, selecting output levels such that marginal cost at those output levels equals the given market price. Output is differentiated between goods destined for the domestic and export markets. Composite output is an aggregate of domestic output and exports.

Final demand by private households arises from nested constant elasticity of substitution (CES) utility functions. This allows consumer decision-making to occur in the form of multi-stage budgeting. At the top level the consumer trades off a composite bundle of consumer goods with leisure (the own-consumption of the consumer's labour endowment). At the second level goods from different sectors compete subject to the budget constraint of the consumer, and all income elasticities are unity. In the third stage the consumer decides how much to spend on domestic or imported goods in each sector, subject to income allocated to spending in that sector in the second stage. Each allocation decision is modelled as a CES function.

There are several private households in our model. They are distinguished by one or other socio-demographic characteristic, such as income or employment status. Each household type has a different expenditure pattern, a different income tax rate, and different factor endowments.

Government expenditures and investment demand are exogenous. Funding of government expenditures is provided by tax revenues minus subsidy payments. Unless otherwise specified the government recovers any lost revenues by increasing 'lump-sum' taxes on each household.[1] Similarly, it provides lump-sum subsidies for any increase in revenue due to a counter-factual scenario.

Since private consumption equals income from primary factors plus net transfers to consumers by the government, Walras law is satisfied. Changes in public consumption are balanced with endogenous changes in revenue, so that the public deficit in the base year is effectively exogenous. It is not zero, but constant, so that it is the change in the public deficit that is held zero.[2]

World market import and export prices are fixed, so there are no endogenous changes in the terms of trade. In other words, import supplies and export demands are infinitely elastic at given world prices. The current account imbalance in the base year is assumed to be matched by an exogenous capital inflow or outflow. These capital flows have no effect on the stock of domestic capital, nor on interest payments to foreigners. Domestic prices change to ensure that the change in the current account is zero. The fixed world prices that Denmark is assumed to face may be changed parametrically.

The aggregate stock of capital in Denmark is fixed in this static model. The aggregate endowment of labour is also fixed, although we include a labour-leisure trade-off such that the amount of that endowment which is allocated to (official) employment is endogenous. In effect we model the consumption of leisure as the decision by the private household to 'buy back' some of its own labour endowment. Hence the supply of labour to industries is endogenous, but the aggregate endowment of labour is exogenous.

2.2 Empirical implementation of the model

Based on 1992 input–output data for Denmark, the model identifies 117 sectors. These are listed in Table 2.1, along with their model acronym. This is the level of disaggregation available to the public through the input–output statistics provided by *Denmarks Statistics*, and provides excellent detail for our purposes. It is possible to aggregate to a smaller number of sectors, but there seems little advantage in doing so in the present exercise and some potential for misleading analysis.[3] Moreover, it is always possible to assess the information loss of employing specific aggregations if the model is fully disaggregated, while the reverse is obviously not true.

The household disaggregation is based on the 1987 Household Expenditure Survey conducted by *Denmarks Statistics*. It provides detailed information on expenditure patterns of seven groups of households. The households are differentiated by various characteristics and we use the characteristic 'total income' in the present analysis. These household types are defined as follows: TI1, Total household income less than 50,000 kroner; TI2, Total household income between 50,000 and 99,999 kroner; TI3, Total household income between 100,000 and 199,999 kroner; TI4, Total household income between 200,000 and 299,999 kroner; TI5, Total household income between 300,000 and 399,999 kroner; TI6, Total household income between 400,000 and 499,999 kroner;

Table 2.1 Sectors in the Danish model

AGR	Agriculture
HOR	Horticulture
FUR	Fur farming and related activities
AGS	Agricultural services
FRS	Forestry and logging
FIS	Fishing
EXT	Extraction of coal, oil and gas
OMI	Other mining
MEA	Slaughtering and processing of pigs and cattle
POU	Poultry killing, dressing and packing
DAI	Dairies
MIL	Processed cheese and condensed milk
ICR	Ice cream manufacturing
FRV	Processing of fruit and vegetables
FSP	Processing of fish
OML	Oil mills
MAR	Margarine manufacturing
FSM	Fish meal manufacturing
GRA	Grain mill products
BRE	Bread factories
CAK	Cake factories
BAK	Bakeries
SUG	Sugar factories and refineries
CHO	Chocolate and sugar confectionery
OFP	Manufacture of food products NEC
ANF	Manufacture of prepared animal feeds
DST	Distilling and blending spirits
BEE	Breweries
TOB	Tobacco manufactures
TXW	Spinning and weaving of textiles
TXM	Manufacture of made-up textile goods
KNI	Knitting mills
ROP	Cordage, rope and twine industries
WAP	Manufacture of wearing apparel
LEA	Manufacture of leather products
FOO	Manufacture of footwear
WOO	Manufacture of wood products exc. furniture
WOF	Manufacture of wooden furniture and related goods
PPP	Manufacture of pulp, paper and paperboard
PAP	Manufacture of paper containers and wallpaper
REP	Reproducing and composing services
BOO	Book printing
PRO	Offset printing
PRI	Other printing
BBI	Bookbinding
PRN	Newspaper printing and publishing
PUB	Book and art publishing
PUM	Magazine publishing
PUO	Other publishing
ICH	Manufacture of basic industrial chemicals
FRT	Manufacture of fertilizers and pesticides

Table 2.1 (Continued)

PLM	Manufacture of basic plastic materials
PAI	Manufacture of paints and varnishes
DRG	Manufacture of drugs and medicines
CSM	Manufacture of soap and cosmetics
CHM	Manufacture of chemical products NEC
PET	Petroleum refineries
ASP	Manufacture of asphalt and roofing materials
TYR	Tyre and tube industries
RUB	Manufacture of rubber products NEC
PLS	Manufacture of plastic products NEC
POT	Manufacture of earthenware and pottery
GLS	Manufacture of glass and glass products
CLY	Manufacture of structural clay products
CEM	Manufacture of cement, lime and plaster
CNC	Concrete products and stone cutting
NMM	Non-metallic mineral products NEC
ISW	Iron and steel works
ISC	Iron and steel casting
NFW	Non-ferrous metal works
NFC	Non-ferrous metal casting
MFU	Manufacture of metal furniture
SMP	Manufacture of structural metal products
MCA	Manufacture of metal cans and containers
MOM	Manufacture of other fabr. metal products
AGM	Manufacture of agricultural machinery
IDM	Manufacture of industrial machinery
REM	Repair of machinery
HOM	Manufacture of household machinery
RFR	Manufacture of refrigerators and accessories
TEL	Manufacture of telecommunication equipment
EHA	Manufacture of electrical home appliances
BAT	Manufacture of accumulators and batteries
MEL	Manufacture of other electrical supplies
SHP	Ship building and repairing
RAI	Railroad and automobile equipment
CYC	Manufacture of cycles, mopeds and related goods
PEQ	Professional and measuring equipment
JEW	Manufacture of jewellery and related goods
TOY	Manufacture of toys, sporting goods and related goods
ELE	Electric light and power
GAS	Gas manufacture and distribution
STE	Steam and hot water supply
WAT	Water works and supply
CON	Construction
WTR	Wholesale trade
RTR	Retail trade
RES	Restaurants and hotels
TRR	Railway and bus transport
TRL	Other land transport
TRW	Ocean and coastal water transport
TRS	Supporting services to water transport

Table 2.1 (*Continued*)

TRA	Air transport
TRT	Services allied to transport
COM	Communication
FIN	Financial institutions
INS	Insurance
DWE	Dwellings
BUS	Business services
EDU	Markets services of education
HEA	Health market services
REC	Recreational and cultural services
MVR	Repair of motor vehicles
HSE	Household services
DSE	Domestic services
PNP	Private non-profit institutions
GOV	Producers of government services

and TI7, Total household income greater than 500,000 kroner. In August 1999 one US dollar was worth approximately 7 Danish kroner.

Each sector produces output using intermediate inputs and a value added composite of the primary factors. Although the natural assumption might be to model the substitutability of the intermediate inputs by assuming a Leontief technology,[4] we use instead a CES function with a low elasticity of substitution (0.25) across all sectors. The value added composite is produced using a CES production function and consists of two inputs: labour and capital. In many cases we have assumed elasticities that are uniform across sectors or consumption goods. In particular, we assume that the elasticity of substitution between consumer goods in each household utility function is one (i.e. Cobb–Douglas), that the uncompensated labour supply elasticity is 0.1 for all households,[5] and that the elasticity of substitution between intermediate inputs and the value added composite in each sector is 0.25 in all sectors (reflecting an approximation to the Leontief tradition for intermediate input substitutability). In some cases we employ elasticities that have been used in many other studies, anticipating refinement to Danish estimates as they become available. For example, for the elasticity of substitution between capital and labour in each sector we employ point estimates from Harrison et al. (1993) which in turn derive from estimates generated for the United States by Harrison et al. (1993). Similarly, the elasticity of substitution by consumers between domestic production and imports varies by sector. The trade elasticities assumed reflect the best econometric estimates currently available (Reinert and Shiells (1991); Reinert and Roland-Holst (1992)). Although they are low in relation to elasticity estimates used in some modelling exercises (e.g. Harrison et al. 1996, 1997), it is important to stress that they are, (a) based on explicit econometric estimates, and (b) used in a model that rules out any 'terms of trade effects' by assumption.[6]

The SOE model is generated with the GAMS/MPSGE software developed by Brooke et al. (1992) and Rutherford (1995, 1999). It is then solved using the

PATH algorithm developed by Dirkse and Ferris (1995). Our model runs on standard laptop computers, solving in about 1 min per simulation. Readers that do not want to download the model and data, or do not have the necessary GAMS/MPSGE/PATH software, can access the model to conduct their own simulations at http://dmsweb.badm.sc.edu/glenn/MobiDK.htm.

3 Reform of excise taxes

Consider the effects of reform of excise taxes on consumption in Denmark. These taxes are relatively distortionary, certainly in comparison to the value added tax and even to income taxes on labour. We calculate the marginal cost of funds (MCF) of the VAT at 12 per cent, and the MCF of excise taxes at 61 per cent. Although these estimates are sensitive to model specification, they do point to a costly excise tax system from an efficiency perspective. The MCF is defined as the percentage efficiency cost of a marginal transfer of funds from private consumers to the government using the specified tax instrument. Thus, for every 100 Danish kroner raised by the government through excise taxes, Danish consumers effectively pay 61 kroner in addition to the 100 kroner that they transfer to the government. The extra costs are not paid literally to the government, but reflect lower standards of living due to higher prices and resource mis-allocation induced by the increase in taxes.

We evaluate the effects of movements toward abolition of the excise taxes. These taxes could be abolished by simple scalar reductions applied across-the-board to the benchmark legal rates and we consider 25 per cent decrements in scenarios TC75, TC50, TC25 and TC0 respectively. These taxes could also be abolished as distortionary wedges by making them uniform, as we do in scenario U_TC. Ignoring second-best considerations for the moment, making excise taxes uniform would remove most of their efficiency costs and would not be as dramatic a reform in some administrative respects.

3.1 Welfare effects of excise tax reductions

The detailed pattern of excise taxes at the industry level is very distortionary and clearly 'hits' luxury goods. Table 2.2 lists the rates at the industry level, as well as the base level of consumption expenditures in billions of kroner. It also lists the percentage changes in the quantity of consumption for scenarios TC0 and U_TC.

The highest rates do indeed hit the 'usual suspects'. Up in the stratosphere above 100 per cent, we have Spirits (DST), Tobacco (TOB) and Petrol (PET). Rates in excess of 40 per cent apply to automobiles (in RAI), Breweries (BEE) and Electricity (ELE). Excise taxes in our model are differentiated by the sector of sale for intermediate input purposes and by the category of final demand. Hence the distortions in the model and the Danish economy, are greater than suggested by the average rates reported in Table 2.2. There are no surprises here in these rates apart from the general height.

The reform TC0 generates the expected changes in quantities consumed towards those goods that are relatively heavily taxed and away from those goods

Table 2.2 Excise tax rates and expenditures at the industry level

Sector	Rate%	Bench	TC0	U_TC
AGR	−0.9	1.8	−7.1	−13.7
HOR		3.1	−2.2	−5.0
FUR		0.1	−16.2	−21.1
AGS			−6.7	−13.4
FRS		0.2	2.6	0.4
FIS	−0.3	0.1	−1.5	−24.4
EXT	7.1		32.3	26.6
OMI	6.4	0.2	2.5	−1.1
MEA	−3.1	10.0	−7.7	−11.6
POU		0.9	−12.5	−16.3
DAI	−0.8	5.3	−5.7	−11.7
MIL	−6.4	0.7	−7.2	−12.2
ICR	17.0	0.9		−3.3
FRV	27.6	3.0	18.4	13.1
FSP		0.6	−1.8	−21.4
OML	−2.8	0.2	−12.9	−20.2
MAR	0.1	0.4	−7.7	−12.6
FSM	−3.8	0.1	−11.9	−20.3
GRA		0.5	−3.7	−8.7
BRE	0.1	1.0	−5.0	−8.6
CAK	0.9	0.9	−3.9	−7.8
BAK		2.5	−4.3	−7.3
SUG	3.1	0.2	11.1	3.5
CHO	22.8	3.0	0.5	−3.2
OFP	0.6	2.1	−1.2	−5.7
ANF	−6.9	0.5	−13.7	−20.1
DST	222.2	0.3	88.2	78.1
BEE	45.6	4.0	34.8	30.8
TOB	451.4	1.5	251.6	246.9
TXW		1.1	0.2	−5.6
TXM		1.1	−2.3	−5.3
KNI		2.9	−3.7	−8.0
ROP		0.1	0.9	−3.3
WAP		6.1	−3.7	−7.6
LEA		0.5	−0.2	−6.1
FOO		1.7	−7.3	−8.0
WOO		0.3	1.4	−2.4
WOF		2.0	−0.9	−3.0
PPP		0.4	4.1	−0.8
PAP	3.1	0.5	9.5	3.9
REP		0.1	3.1	−0.4
BOO		0.2	2.5	−1.3
PRO		0.2	2.3	−1.4
PRI		0.1	7.6	3.3
BBI			2.7	−1.4
PRN		1.7	0.6	−2.0
PUB		0.8	−5.5	−5.3
PUM		1.3	−5.7	−5.9
PUO		0.1	3.5	−0.9
ICH	0.1	0.1	2.8	−2.0

Table 2.2. (*Continued*)

Sector	Rate%	Bench	TC0	U_TC
FRT	0.1		−4.3	−11.5
PLM	0.1	0.2	3.2	−1.9
PAI			4.1	−0.7
DRG	−0.2	1.4	−2.4	−3.0
CSM		1.8	−3.1	−5.5
CHM		0.5	3.0	−1.5
PET	108.6	3.2	33.4	27.9
ASP	0.1	0.1	1.9	−2.2
TYR		0.1	8.8	4.1
RUB		0.4	7.0	2.7
PLS	0.6	0.9	2.2	−1.7
POT		0.4	−2.7	−4.6
GLS	8.5	0.2	16.3	11.7
CLY			0.4	−2.2
CEM	0.3		1.1	−1.9
CNC			0.5	−2.1
NMM	0.1		1.7	−1.3
ISW			4.7	−0.2
ISC			4.4	0.5
NFW			4.5	−0.2
NFC			3.5	−0.1
MFU		0.4	1.6	−0.4
SMP		0.2	2.6	−1.0
MCA	0.1		7.6	−0.2
MOM	0.1	1.3	2.2	−1.0
AGM			2.5	0.7
IDM		0.3	1.2	−0.4
REM			−0.7	−6.7
HOM	0.4	1.0	−0.9	−3.6
RFR		1.4	2.6	−0.1
TEL	1.0	2.2	1.7	−1.4
EHA		0.3	−0.5	−3.6
BAT			6.0	2.3
MEL	1.3	0.3	4.0	0.5
SHP	0.8	0.1	1.9	−0.7
RAI	69.6	5.6	34.9	29.7
CYC	1.9	0.6	7.9	5.3
PEQ	0.9	1.2	−0.8	
JEW		0.7		−6.3
TOY		2.3	−1.4	−4.0
ELE	40.0	4.9	23.6	21.0
GAS	0.1	2.1	17.6	16.4
STE		6.0	25.8	25.0
WAT		0.6	−1.6	−4.6
CON	−0.7		−0.2	−1.5
WTR		18.2	3.1	−0.1
RTR		40.2	4.3	1.7
RES		19.5	3.9	−1.4
TRR		4.5	−0.1	−3.4
TRL		3.4	2.9	

Table 2.2 (*Continued*)

Sector	Rate%	Bench	TC0	U_TC
TRW		1.1	3.8	3.4
TRS		0.5	1.5	−1.6
TRA	2.2	3.0	1.9	−2.0
TRT		1.7	4.4	−2.0
COM		7.4	−1.7	−3.0
FIN		4.3	1.1	−3.0
INS	16.6	3.6	4.6	0.9
DWE		97.1	−5.5	−6.8
BUS	5.9	3.8	5.2	2.4
EDU		0.8	8.2	4.6
HEA		3.7	−1.3	−3.3
REC	1.1	8.1	−3.1	−5.2
MVR		12.3	10.7	6.8
HSE	2.9	6.1	0.5	−2.4
DSE		1.0	2.9	−6.5
PNP		5.6	−3.5	−3.3
GOV		14.2		−0.4

that are lightly taxed. To the extent that there are external costs of increased consumption of some of these goods, we need to be precise about what our welfare measures are capturing.[7] Our task here is just to display the *direct* economic cost of certain tax policies; a more complete analysis would try to take into account the externalities that might be generated.

The welfare effects of these scenarios on households differentiated by total income are shown in Table 2.3. Each column shows the welfare effects for one of the scenarios. We focus just now on the tax reduction scenarios and examine the uniformity scenario later. The welfare variables are the percentage change in welfare, the welfare change for the aggregate household type in billions of Danish kroner and the welfare change for the typical household in each household type in Danish kroner. All three are needed to get an overall picture of the welfare effects of the reform. The first measure provides an index of the change in the (real) cost of living for households in each type. The second measure portrays the size of the overall pie that goes to each household type, which can be critical to see if there is enough 'positive pie' created to offset the 'negative pie' for household types that lose. It is quite possible that some households experience a large welfare gain in percentage terms, but that they account for so little of the overall pie that their gains are insufficient to compensate the losers. This is what the second welfare measure allows one to determine quickly. The third measure relates the actual changes to some easily understood level, the individual household and Danish kroner. All welfare changes refer to annual changes that are recurring in the absence of any other change in the economy.

Finally, we show the same three welfare change measures in aggregate form. All that we do here is aggregate over the households listed. Although one could

Table 2.3 Welfare effects of excise tax reform on households differentiated by total income

	TC75	TC50	TC25	TC0	U_TC
A. Hicksian equivalent variation (%)					
TI1	−5.1	−11.5	−19.6	−31.6	0.7
TI2	−2.5	−5.7	−10.0	−16.6	2.4
TI3	−0.6	−1.6	−3.0	−5.6	2.8
TI4	1.0	2.0	2.9	3.6	3.5
TI5	1.6	3.3	5.2	7.2	3.4
TI6	2.0	4.1	6.5	9.2	3.3
TI7	3.0	6.3	10.0	14.5	4.5
B. Hicksian equivalent variation – billion DK					
TI1	−0.28	−0.63	−1.08	−1.74	0.04
TI2	−0.83	−1.90	−3.34	−5.56	0.80
TI3	−0.41	−1.03	−1.98	−3.65	1.82
TI4	0.92	1.83	2.70	3.35	3.20
TI5	2.14	4.44	6.96	9.73	4.58
TI6	1.81	3.78	5.97	8.44	3.05
TI7	2.32	4.90	7.86	11.35	3.54
C. Hicksian equivalent variation – DK per household					
TI1	−3292	−7357	−12615	−20277	462
TI2	−2163	−4950	−8715	−14513	2086
TI3	−796	−1990	−3819	−7046	3513
TI4	2113	4199	6190	7674	7345
TI5	5122	10639	16694	23342	10989
TI6	8333	17419	27525	38907	14049
TI7	15889	33594	53819	77772	24241
D. Aggregate welfare impact					
Per cent	1.1	2.3	3.4	4.4	3.4
Billions DK	5.7	11.4	17.1	21.9	17.0
DK per household	2569.5	5171.5	7757.5	9952.3	7730.7

Note: TI1 Total household income less than 50,000 kr. TI2 Total household income 50,000–99,999 kr. TI3 Total household income 100,000–199,999 kr. TI4 Total household income 200,000–299,999 kr. TI5 Total household income 300,000–399,999 kr. TI6 Total household income 400,000–499,999 kr. TI7 Total household income more than 500,000 kr.

interpret these as measures from a classical utilitarian social welfare function (SWF), we prefer to just think of them as summary measures of overall change. Given our focus on the size of the overall pie, in anticipation of the need to effect sidepayments, we are particularly interested in the sign of these measures.

Turning to the specific results in Table 2.3, there are some clear winners and losers. The scalar-reduction reforms generate substantial welfare losses for the poorest households (TI1, TI2 and TI3). Welfare losses decrease and welfare benefits increase, with household income. The biggest winners from these reforms are the richest households, who each stand to gain as much as 77,772 kroner per year from the abolition of excise taxes.

It appears that the aggregate pie is also likely to be large enough that the winners can compensate the losers. The richest household gains more than enough (11.35 billion kroner) by itself to compensate all of the losers (who lose $1.74 + 5.56 + 3.65 = 10.95$ billion kroner), if we ignore general equilibrium effects of those sidepayments. The overall picture that emerges from these equity effects is that the excise taxes do appear to be very progressive in incidence.

3.2 Welfare effects of excise tax

The most important feature of the U_TC scenario, for present purposes, is that it generates substantial welfare gains for virtually all household types. Although some distributional effects persist, they are of an order of magnitude less than when we abolish excise taxes. Contrast the U_TC and TC0 scenarios in terms of the effects on sectoral consumption in Table 2.2. By and large the changes are identical in U_TC and TC0, reflecting the fact that we are primarily seeing substitution effects at work here. That is, the TC0 scenario can be viewed as both reducing the overall level of excise taxes and making them more uniform. The U_TC scenario just does the latter. The fact that they generate almost the same quantity changes indicates that it is the uniformity of excise taxes that is driving these sectoral results, in conjunction with the low MEB of the VAT.

3.3 Compensating losers

For the excise tax reduction scenarios there appears to be a serious problem recommending policy reform if we stick to the simple application of the Pareto criterion to the results in Table 2.3. Since some households lose and the losses appear to be quite significant in both percentage and absolute terms, the reforms could not be advocated using that criterion. One alternative is to extend the applicability of the criterion so as to allow sidepayments to losers be a part of the reform. We calculate the smallest set of sidepayments such that no household lose, taking into account the effects of these sidepayments on the underlying general equilibrium.

The results are shown in Table 2.4, and contain some surprises. The first 'result,' in a sense, is that we are able to compute these solutions at all! This might appear to be stating the obvious, but it is noteworthy since we are only aware of one other policy analysis that implements such calculations.[8]

The second result is that the naïve expectations of who should compensate whom would be qualitatively wrong. Consider scenario TC0 to be specific. Those expectations from Table 2.3 might have been that households TI4, TI5, TI6 and TI7 would have been making sidepayments and that only households TI1, TI2 and TI3 would need to receive them. In fact household TI4 ends up having to receive sidepayments as well, rather than making them. The reason is that the general equilibrium effects of the changes in income occasioned by the 'initial' round of sidepayments affect welfare. Hence the qualitative pattern of compensations is different when one takes into account the real effects of effecting them.

The third result is that the quantitative size of the compensation amounts differs from the naïve analysis. From Table 2.3 one might be tempted to conclude that households in the TI1, TI2 and TI3 groups would need to receive 10.95 billion kroner in compensation. In fact, the amounts required from panel E of Table 2.4

Table 2.4 Effecting compensation to losers

	TC75	TC50	TC25	TC0
A. Hicksian equivalent variation (%)				
TI1	0.0	0.0	0.0	0.0
TI2	0.0	0.0	0.0	0.0
TI3	0.0	0.0	0.0	0.0
TI4	0.4	0.7	0.5	0.0
TI5	1.2	2.4	3.6	4.4
TI6	1.7	3.5	5.3	7.1
TI7	2.7	5.7	9.1	12.8
B. Hicksian equivalent variation – billions of DK				
TI1	0.0	0.0	0.0	0.0
TI2	0.0	0.0	0.0	0.0
TI3	0.0	0.0	0.0	0.0
TI4	0.39	0.60	0.49	0.00
TI5	1.63	3.27	4.86	5.91
TI6	1.55	3.17	4.88	6.45
TI7	2.14	4.49	7.11	10.00
C. Hicksian equivalent variation – DK per household				
TI1	0.0	0.0	0.0	0.0
TI2	0.0	0.0	0.0	0.0
TI3	0.0	0.0	0.0	0.0
TI4	906	1382	1126	0
TI5	3918	7830	11646	14161
TI6	7130	14611	22478	29736
TI7	14671	30749	48701	68467
D. Sidepayments as a per cent of expenditure				
TI1	7.0	15.8	27.5	45.7
TI2	3.9	8.9	15.7	27.1
TI3	1.6	3.8	7.1	13.0
TI4	0.0	0.0	0.0	0.7
TI5	0.0	0.0	0.0	0.0
TI6	0.0	0.0	0.0	0.0
TI7	0.0	0.0	0.0	0.0
E. Total sidepayments – billions of DK				
TI1	0.4	0.8	1.4	2.3
TI2	1.3	2.8	4.9	8.1
TI3	1.0	2.4	4.3	7.5
TI4	0.0	0.0	0.0	0.6
TI5	0.0	0.0	0.0	0.0
TI6	0.0	0.0	0.0	0.0
TI7	0.0	0.0	0.0	0.0
F. Aggregate welfare impacts				
Percent	1.1	2.3	3.5	4.5
BillionsDK	5.7	11.5	17.3	22.4
DK per household	2595.4	5232.6	7869.0	10147.1

are calculated to be much larger: $2.3 + 8.1 + 7.5 + 0.6 = 18.5$ billion kroner. Thus a naïve analysis that ignored the general equilibrium effects would dramatically understate the required amounts of compensation and would in fact leave some losers from the reform. Again, the reason for the difference is that our CGE analysis takes into account the real effects of actually making the sidepayments.

3.4   Can everyone win?

Without delving into the psychology of voters or politicians too deeply, it is apparent that it would be desirable to be able to design policy reforms in which all households gained something, rather than just being non-losers. That is, can we design compensation schemes such that each household is guaranteed to get a certain positive threshold gain in welfare? This question is, of course, just a logical extension of the previous compensation exercises where the minimum threshold is positive rather than zero. Hence the same common-sense caveats apply: such compensation assumes that the underlying reform generates enough aggregate pie to enable sidepayments to be undertaken without diminishing the 'goose laying the golden egg.'

To illustrate the feasibility of this extension, we considered the TC0 scenario again. As we constrain each household to receive a specified positive percentage welfare gain, ranging from 1 per cent up to 3 per cent in increments of 1 per cent, we find that aggregate welfare is reduced. The average Danish household gives up 21 kroner per year[9] to ensure that all households gain by at least 1 per cent and this cost grows to 42 kroner and 54 kroner per year to ensure welfare gains of 2 per cent and 3 per cent, respectively. However, this is just the price tag for undertaking a policy reform that is more likely to be accepted by all parties. In other words, there is a political trade-off between efficiency and equity which translates into less-efficient reforms having a greater chance of being politically palatable since they are more equitable.

The winners of some initial reform package, in which there are losers, face a simple choice. Either push for the original reform (with a relatively high payoff but a relatively low probability of acceptance) or accept a modified reform package that effects compensation (and hence offers a lower payoff, but with a higher probability of acceptance). Our task is to guide citizens in making these trade-offs by indicating the amounts of compensation that would be required, and the reduction in payoffs associated with that modification.

4   Extensions

For the purposes of offering specific policy recommendations in Denmark, there are many possible extensions to our underlying model. These extensions are, however, not important for the general methodological point we are making here.

Two extensions are, however, germane to the simple point we are making here about the feasibility of designing policy reforms without tears. One has to do with the willingness of households to share their potential welfare gains and the other has to do with the costliness of effecting sidepayments.

4.1 Willingness to compensate

An extension of our present approach is to recognize that some households might be more willing than others to undertake compensation if needed. We have implicitly assumed here that any household would be willing to transfer up to 100 per cent of it's welfare gain in order to effect sidepayments.[10]

One could use survey methods to elicit the *ex ante* willingness of each household to effect compensation if necessary for policy reform. Specifically, consider a question of the following form: 'If you were to gain from this policy reform, what percentage of your gains would you be willing to give up each year to compensate losers from the reforms?' Why would households ever reveal some positive percentage? Because they would realize, and we would tell them in the survey, that in the absence of sufficient compensation it is possible that the reforms would be politically infeasible. Households would be told that we would not take any greater percentage than they specified, so there would be no chance that they would lose from the reform, at least to the extent that they are correctly represented in the model.

This extension raises the possibility of strategic misrepresentations from households when confronted with the possibility that their response could affect the extent of their consumer surplus. This issue has been neglected in the older welfare economics literature on the use of the compensation criteria, probably because of a belief that the criteria suffered from other more serious problems (e.g. inconsistency, and indeterminacy if compensation were actually effected). Hammond and Sempere (1995) consider the problem, but only by way of a critique of casual attempts to infer sidepayments necessary for policy reform 'without tears'. This type of strategic misrepresentation is a general one facing surveys of this kind, and techniques for dealing with it have been proposed (e.g. see Blackburn *et al.* 1994). We are optimistic that this problem can be solved, or at least mitigated, but it remains an open one for future investigation.

Once elicited and assuming them to be true reports, these percentages would be used to constrain further the computation of sidepayments. Since that calculation assumed these percentages to be up to 100 per cent for each and every household, as noted above, we would just add in these constraints as a tightening of the sidepayments constraints applying to each household type. Of course, this could make the possibility of Pareto-ensuring side-payments infeasible, but that would likely be a signal that the reform may also be politically infeasible.

4.2 The leaky bucket

We model the compensations from winners to losers by having the government agent make lump-sum sidepayments to losers and collect extra revenues from all households in a lump-sum manner. Since some households receive, on balance, more from the government than they pay, we are in effect transferring income from winners to losers.

It is possible that if the government does not have access to a lump-sum tax and subsidy instrument that it would use costly instruments to redistribute income. In other words, it is possible that the simple act of merely transferring one kroner amongst private households could impose some efficiency costs (see Ballard 1988).

These costs could arise on the 'taking' end, as the government uses a distortionary tax instrument to raise revenues, and/or it could occur on the 'giving' end as the government uses a distortionary subsidy instrument to disburse the revenues. Of course, second best considerations could result in these instruments generating efficiency gains even if they are distortionary in a partial equilibrium sense. To illustrate the nature of the problem, imagine that the government used the VAT to raise the revenues needed for these compensations. We know that there is a positive MEB from this use of the VAT, so the aggregate pie would likely be smaller due to the very act of redistribution. In the public finance literature this is referred to as 'Okun's leaky bucket,' to reflect the idea that just carrying water from one household to another may result in the loss of some water for all. An evaluation of the feasibility of policy reform without tears in Denmark must take into account the leaks in the Danish welfare state bucket.

Notes

1 We have several household types in the model, distinguished by some socio-demographic characteristic. These lump-sum taxes are assigned to household types in proportion to the number of actual households in that household type. Thus, if the first household type has 11 per cent of the households in Denmark, we assign it 11 per cent of the required aggregate payment of lump-sum taxes. Our lump-sum taxes can then be correctly interpreted as applying equally to each household in Denmark. This distinction only arises because we do not have one household type for every distinct household in Denmark.

2 The model can also be simulated with this 'revenue replacement' option off, in which case government expenditures expand or contract to ensure constancy of the benchmark public deficit.

3 With respect to the use of a priori judgements, our belief is that it is much easier to apply serious priors to detailed sectors than it is to synthetic aggregates. In any event, if the priors in question are essentially held in a diffuse manner over a range of sectors, then nothing is lost if one so applies them in our disaggregated model. Providing the reader knows when such uniform assumptions are being applied and is not dazzled by the fake detail of the analysis, it is foolish to 'hardwire' in the level of application of priors by aggregation. The primary argument for aggregation, given the ready availability of powerful software and hardware for these models, has to do with the 'reliability' of data and priors at the proposed level of aggregation. Several of the data items required for our analysis are only available at an aggregated level of about 20 or 30 sectors, although far fewer than one would think. Aggregation is, however, likely to become important and appropriate as one moves to explicit inter-temporal models because of the computational burden of solving models with too many sectors.

4 Since the matter continues to be confused by commentators that should know better (e.g. Jorgenson and Wilcoxen 1995: 176), we stress that the assumption of a Leontief technology is not mandated by our use of the calibration approach to estimation, nor by computational constraints. In general, we do restrict ourselves to nested-CES functions, although they can be used to represent globally regular functional forms in a locally flexible manner (see Perroni and Rutherford 1995a,1995b).

5 In conjunction with an assumption that the ratio of leisure to labour endowment is 0.25, this implies calibrated elasticities of substitution that vary across households. For example, these elasticities range from 1.9 for the poorest households to 0.6 for the richest households.

6 The popular reason for using higher trade elasticities is that one can thereby avoid these effects, which are deemed unlikely a priori for a country as small in international trade terms as Denmark. Although the specification of trade elasticities that mitigate these effects is more involved than just assuming 'large' or 'small' values (e.g. see Harrison *et al.* 1996), these are not debates which are relevant here.

7 For example, we estimate that there would be a substantial increase in the quantity of Spirits consumption, Beer consumption, and Tobacco consumption under the TC0 reform. To some Danes this would represent a reduction in their welfare, even if they do not drink alcohol or smoke: they just dislike having drunks out on the street or cancer-ridden smokers using up hospitals, and believe that these externalities are positively correlated with aggregate consumption. As a drinker or smoker one may disagree with their assessment of internal or external net costs, but that is irrelevant here.

8 Due to Harrison *et al.* (1995).

9 We calculate that the average Danish household gains by 10,147 kroner per year when the Pareto criterion is applied to ensure that no household loses, and that the gain is only 10,168 kroner per year when the criterion is applied to ensure that no household gain less than 1 per cent in welfare terms. Hence the difference is $21 = 10, 147 - 10,168$ per year.

10 This 100 per cent refers to the simulations in which we required that no household lose. The percentage would be less than 100 per cent for the simulations in which we require that each household have a positive welfare gain, of course.

References

Ballard, C. L. (1988) 'The marginal efficiency cost of redistribution', *American Economic Review*, 78(5), December, 1019–33.

Blackburn, Mc., Harrison, G. W. and Rutström, E. E. (1994) 'Statistical bias functions and informative hypothetical surveys', *American Journal of Agricultural Economics*, 76(5), December, 1084–88.

Brooke, A., Kendrick, D. and Meeraus, A. (1992) *GAMS: A User's Guide, Release 2.25* Danvers, MA.: Boyd & Fraser.

Dirkse, S. P. and Ferris, M. C. (1995) 'The PATH solver: a non-monotone stabilization scheme for mixed complementarity problems', *Optimization Methods and Software*, 5, 123–56.

Hammond, P. J. and Sempere, J. (1995) 'Limits to the potential gains from economic integration and other supply side policies', *Economic Journal*, 105, September, 1180–204.

Harrison, G. W., Jones, R., Kimbell, L. J. and Wigle, R. (1993) 'How robust is applied general equilibrium analysis?', *Journal of Policy Modeling*, 15(1), 99–115.

Harrison, G. W., Rutherford, T. F. and Tarr, D. G. (1993) 'Piecemeal trade reform in the partially liberalized economy of Turkey', *World Bank Economic Review*, 7, May, 191–217.

Harrison, G. W., Rutherford, T. F. and Tarr, D. G. (1996) 'Increased competition and completion of the market in the European union: static and steady state effects', *Journal of Economic Integration*, 11(3), September, 332–65.

Harrison, G. W., Rutherford, T. F. and Tarr, D. G. (1997) 'Quantifying the Uruguay round', *Economic Journal*, 107, September, 1405–30.

Harrison, G. W., Rutherford, T. F. and Wooton, I. (1995) 'Liberalizing agriculture in the European community', *Journal of Policy Modeling*, 17, 223–255.

Jensen, J. (2000) 'How valuable are delayed cutbacks in Danish carbon emissions?', in: Harrison, G. W., Jensen, S. E. H., Pedersen, L. H and Rutherford, T. F. (eds) *Using Dynamic General Equilibrium Models for Policy Analysis*, Amsterdam: North-Holland.

Jorgenson, D. W. and Wilcoxen, P. J. (1995) 'Intertemporal equilibrium modeling of energy and environmental policies', in: Johansson, P-O, Kriström, B. and Mäler, K-G (eds) *Current Issues in Environmental Economics*, New York: Manchester University Press.

Melo, Jaime de and Tarr, D. (1992) *General Equilibrium Analysis of U.S. Foreign Trade Policy*, Cambridge, MA: MIT Press.

Perroni, C. and Rutherford, T. F. (1995a) 'Regular flexibility of nested CES functions', *European Economic Review*, 39, 335–43.

Perroni, C. and Rutherford, T. F. (1995b) 'A Comparison of the performance of flexible functional forms for use in applied general equilibrium analysis', *Discussion Paper* 95–6, Department of Economics, University of Colorado.

Reinert, K. A. and Roland-Holst, D. W. (1992) 'Armington elasticities for the manufacturing sectors of the united states', *Journal of Policy Modeling*, 14(5), 631–9.

Reinert, K. A. and Shiells, C. R. (1991) 'Trade substitution elasticities for analysis of a North American free trade area', Unpublished Manuscript, Office of Economics, U.S. International Trade Commission, January.

Rutherford, T. F. (1995) 'Extensions of GAMS for complementarity and variational problems arising in applied economics', *Journal of Economic Dynamics and Control*, 19(8), November, 1299–324.

Rutherford, T. F. (1999) 'Applied general equilibrium modeling with MPSGE as a GAMS subsystem: an overview of the modeling framework and syntax', *Computational Economic*, 14 (1/2), October, 1–46.

Rutherford, T. F. (2000) 'Carbon abatement in Denmark: technical change and intergenerational burden sharing', in: Harrison, G. W., Jensen, S. E. H., Pedersen, L. H. and Rutherford, T. F. (eds) *Using Dynamic General Equilibrium Models for Policy Analysis*, Amsterdam: North-Holland.

Rutherford, T. F., Rutström, E. E. and Tarr, D. G. (1994) 'L'Accord de Libre Echange entre le Maroc et la CEE: Une Evaluation Quantitative', *Revue d'Economie du Developpement*, 2, 97–133.

3   The marginal cost of public funds in developing countries

Shantayanan Devarajan, Karen E. Thierfelder
and Sethaput Suthiwart-Narueput

1   Introduction

The notion that raising a dollar of taxes could cost society more than a dollar is one of the most powerful ideas in economics. The reasoning is simple. By causing agents to alter their behaviour as a result of the tax – consumers buy less, for example – the tax lowers welfare by more than it collects in revenue. The difference, often referred to as a 'deadweight loss', leads to the marginal cost of raising a dollar of public funds being higher than a dollar.

The power of this idea derives from its implications. One is that the higher the marginal cost of funds (MCF) is, the fewer public goods will be provided. Another is that, if the MCF across different tax instruments varies greatly, directions for revenue-neutral tax reform are readily apparent.

Given the power and implications behind the idea, the marginal cost of public funds has spawned a modest literature on its theoretical properties and empirical magnitudes. That literature has highlighted several issues. First, the size of the deadweight loss depends on the elasticities of response to the tax. In the limiting case when the elasticity is zero, the tax is equivalent to a lump-sum tax and there is no deadweight loss. Second, the MCF of a tax rises with the tax rate – the deadweight loss is convex in the tax rate. Third, the MCF depends not just on the tax being raised, but also on other distortions in the economy – and whether they increase or decrease in response to the tax increase. For instance, in an economy with a very high tax on coffee, the MCF raised by taxing tea may be quite low, since the tax would induce consumers at the margin to buy more coffee, reducing the distortion associated with the coffee tax.

From this perspective, it is curious that there have been so few estimates of the MCF for developing countries. For one thing, tax reform and the evaluation of public projects are the bread-and-butter of policymakers in developing countries. For another, the issues mentioned above are particularly salient in these countries. The presence of an informal sector means that some elasticities could be quite high; tax rates tend to be high because the taxable base is so small; and developing countries are replete with distortionary taxes, including taxes on trade, sales and income.

In this chapter, we attempt to partially remedy the situation by providing estimates of the MCF for three developing countries – Cameroon, Bangladesh and Indonesia. The rest of this introduction briefly surveys the literature and places our chapter in it. In Section 2, after describing our model, we present our results. Section 3 represents an attempt to decompose those results into heuristic, partial-equilibrium calculations to get a better understanding of what is driving our estimates. Section 4 concludes.

1.1   *Relationship to existing literature*

While there has been an extensive literature on MCF, much of the literature has focussed on resolving conceptual issues regarding the MCF rather than providing estimates. Where estimates do exist, they are almost exclusively for developed rather than developing countries.

Much of the MCF literature has focussed on whether the Samuelson (1954) condition for the optimal provision of public goods, $\sum \text{MRS} = \text{MRT}$, (where $\sum \text{MRS}$ is the sum across households of the benefits of an extra unit of a public good and MRT is the cost of the resources used to provide it) leads to excess provision given financing from distortionary rather than lump-sum taxes, that is, whether the MCF is necessarily greater than one. If so, this would lead to a modified cost-benefit analysis for public projects. If the welfare loss from raising a dollar of revenue through distortionary taxation were 20 cents, for example, then a public project would need to generate marginal benefits of more than $1.20 per dollar of cost to be justified.

These conceptual issues are well surveyed in Fullerton (1991) and Ballard and Fullerton (1992). Pigou (1920), Harberger (1964) and Browning (1987) implicitly compare distortionary taxes with equal revenue lump-sum taxes. Since income effects are equal by construction, their analysis involves only substitution effects and depends upon compensated demand and supply elasticities. Because these substitution effects are distortionary, the MCF is necessarily (weakly) greater than one. By contrast, in Stiglitz and Dasgupta (1971) and Atkinson and Stern (1974), taxes are raised to spend on a public project. Since the taxes generate income effects, their analyses depend upon uncompensated demand and supply elasticities. Because these income effects offset the (distortionary) substitution effects, the MCF is not necessarily greater than one. If public spending is not separable in utility, the MCF will also depend upon the effect of that spending. The difference between these approaches was noted in Wildasin (1984).

On empirical magnitudes there are two approaches to estimating the MCF: via analytical formulae and numerical simulations. Browning (1987) uses an analytical, partial-equilibrium formula to estimate the marginal excess burden (MEB) of labour taxes in the United States. Ahmad and Stern (1987) use a simplified analytical formula based on effective taxes (the amount by which government revenue would increase if there were a unit increase in final demand for a good) to calculate the welfare cost of various taxes in India. Ahmed and Croushore (1996)

Table 3.1 Some previous MCF estimates

Country	Tax type	Estimate	Source
United States	Surcharge	1.17–1.56	Ballard *et al.* (1985)
	Labour	1.21–1.24	Stuart (1984)
	Labour	1.32–1.47	Browning (1987)
	Labour	1.08–1.14	Ahmed and Croushore (1996)
Sweden	Surcharge	0.67–4.51	Hansson and Stuart (1985)
New Zealand	Labour	1.18	Diewert and Lawrence (1994)
India	Excise	1.66–2.15	Ahmad and Stern (1987)
	Sales	1.59–2.12	
	Import	1.54–2.17	

derive MCF estimates for the US when public spending is non-separable in utility. Snow and Warren (1996) derive a more general analytical formula to reconcile a variety of previous MCF estimates.

Other estimates rely upon simulation models. Stuart (1984) and Ballard *et al.* (1985) use computable general equilibrium (CGE) models of the US to estimate the MCF. Hansson and Stuart (1985) use a CGE model of Sweden to estimate a MCF which is sensitive to both the type of tax and spending. Estimates from these previous studies are presented in Table 3.1. As noted in Fullerton (1991) and Snow and Warren (1996), it should be emphasised that these studies encompass myriad approaches and definitions. With the exception of Ahmad and Stern (1987), all the estimates are for developed countries.

Both approaches have their drawbacks and advantages. By their nature, the analytical papers have to make many simplifying assumptions and abstract from many features of the economic landscape (other distortions, for example) to arrive at tractable formulae. In light of the wide variety of definitions and approaches to calculating the MCF, the emphasis seems to be more on explaining and reconciling previous approaches and estimates rather than providing estimates which take into account specific details and important second-best effects. A recent example is Snow and Warren (1996). By contrast, estimates obtained from CGE simulations tend to have a 'black box' feel, because the models themselves may be quite complicated. It is sometimes difficult to understand precisely what drives the estimates obtained.

In this chapter, we try to strike a balance between these two approaches. Since the objective is to obtain particular MCF estimates for various developing countries, we use CGE models which capture salient features of the economies (e.g. distorted factor markets, other taxes). However, a strong attempt is made to decompose the results and trace through step-by-step precisely what is driving the estimates obtained. As will be seen, taking into account other distortions is extremely important because second-best effects play a very important role in driving the MCF. This suggests that estimates obtained using analytical formulae which abstract from other distortions are not likely to be accurate, particularly for developing countries where such distortions could be large.

2   Methodology

2.1   *Model overview*

We use a CGE model to measure the MCF. Policy shocks, such as a tax increase in one sector, affect other sectors in the economy through sectoral and factor market linkages. Sectors are linked directly through intermediate demands as described in each country's input-output table. As one sector expands, the demand for intermediate goods used in that sector increases.[1] Sectors also are linked through factor markets as producers compete for resources which are in fixed supply. Factors are imperfect substitutes in production. As the cost of one input increases, producers can substitute the cheaper inputs.

Imports are imperfect substitutes for the domestic variety. A policy shock that affects imported goods will have spillover effects on domestic production as well. Likewise, exports and domestic goods are imperfect substitutes. Each country is treated as a small country in world markets. The world prices of import and export goods are constant. There are no terms of trade effects of a policy shock.

Households receive income from factors returns and transfers. This income is spent on taxes, savings and consumer goods. Consumer demand is derived from a Cobb–Douglas utility function with fixed expenditure shares of each commodity which is a composite of the imported and the domestic variety of the good.

The government receives revenue from taxes such as indirect business taxes, value added taxes, tariffs, enterprise taxes and household taxes. It spends its income on commodities and transfer payments. Government consumption shares are fixed.

Closure rules

In the model, savings equals investment. We close the model by assuming investment is constant. Savings must adjust following a policy shock to generate the revenue needed for investment expenditure. Total savings is comprised of household savings, government savings and foreign savings. Real government spending is constant and government savings (the budget deficit) is endogenous. It changes as tax revenue from various sources change, as well as in response to changes in prices of goods for government consumption. Foreign savings is constant. The relative price of traded to non-traded goods adjusts to maintain the current account balance. We assume a uniform adjustment to the savings rate for each household to insure that savings equals investment. A policy shock that reduces tariff revenue, for example, can force an increase in household savings to meet the investment requirement. In essence there is a lump-sum tax on the households. Likewise, a policy that generates government savings can reduce household savings and increase household consumption.

In the factor markets, we assume a fixed supply of each input. Factors are perfectly mobile across sectors. However, there are sector-specific factor productivity differences.

Measuring the marginal cost of funds

To calculate the MCF, we describe the welfare change following the tax increase necessary to generate one unit of real government revenue. We use equivalent variation to measure welfare. It is the amount a consumer would be willing to pay to avoid a tax increase. First, we calculate the consumer's utility following a policy shock.[2] Then we determine the income necessary to attain this utility level at the prices the consumer faced before the policy shock. Equivalent variation is the base level income minus this hypothetical income. A negative number indicates a welfare gain because at the original prices, the consumer needs more income to attain the level of utility observed after the policy shock. In essence, his pre-policy shock budget line has shifted out. Equivalent variation is thus a dollar measure of the change in utility following a policy shock.

Consider on Figure 3.1 the elimination of tariffs on good x. Point A is the original consumption point with the tariff inclusive price of good x. When tariffs are eliminated, the budget line rotates to point F and consumption occurs on a higher indifference curve, point B. At the original prices, the consumer would be at point C on the new indifference curve. Equivalent variation is the difference between the original budget line, DE and the hypothetical budget line GH: (DE − GH). In this example, equivalent variation is negative as the consumer is better off under trade liberalization. A general equilibrium model captures both the direct effect of increasing the distortion in the taxed sector as well as the second-best effects as output in other sectors, with their own distortions, adjusts. For example, the model includes factor market distortions – when there are factor market productivity differences between sectors, the value of the marginal product of labour (or other factors) is not equal across sectors. There are welfare gains when high-productivity sectors expand and low-productivity sectors contract. The model also includes tariff distortions. Domestic production is too high in sectors with tariffs. A policy shock that induces a decline in the output of these sectors will improve welfare. One indication of such a change is that imports and

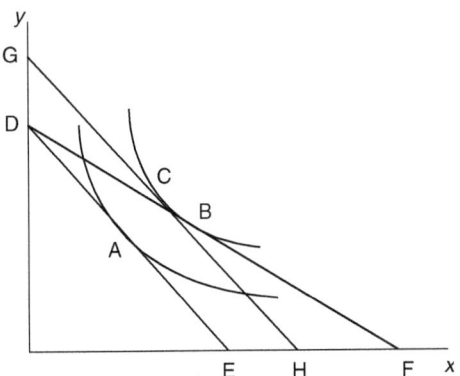

Figure 3.1 Tariff elimination and welfare.

therefore observed tariff revenue, rise. Other taxes in the model keep domestic production too low. For example, indirect taxes and value added taxes discourage production so a policy that expands these taxed sectors will be welfare improving.

Raising a dollar of revenue in a distorted economy can generate welfare gains. In this case, a public project would need to generate a marginal benefit of less than one dollar of cost to be justified.

2.2   MCF for Bangladesh, Cameroon and Indonesia

We calculate the MCF for three developing countries, Bangladesh, Cameroon and Indonesia. While the three countries were chosen primarily because of the availability of suitable CGE models of their economies, they also illustrate many of the salient features in an analysis of the marginal cost of public funds. Cameroon, like many African countries, has a high export tax on selected commodities, coffee and cocoa. It also has a distorted factor market with large productivity differences by sector. Bangladesh has high taxes, particularly tariffs, in certain sectors making its tax structure uneven across sectors. In contrast, Indonesia is an economy that appears to have lowered many of the distortions associated with *ad valorem* taxes and tariffs. It has a fairly uniform tax structure.

We consider a variety of instruments to generate an increase in public funds. First we consider an increase in the indirect tax rate by sector. Then we consider a uniform increase in indirect taxes.[3] Finally, we consider an increase in individual tariff rates and a uniform tariff rate.

Table 3.2 presents selected results.

Table 3.2 Marginal cost of public funds for selected sectors

	Indirect tax			Import tax		
	Sector with highest tax rate	Sector with lowest tax rate	Uniform adjustment	Sector with highest tariff	Sector with lowest tariff	Uniform adjustment
Bangladesh	1.07 Tobacco	0.95 Fisheries	1.05	2.18 Sugar	1.17 Livestock	1.20
Cameroon	0.48 Cash crops	0.96 Food and forestry	0.90	1.37 Food and consumption	1.05 Intermediate goods	1.05
Indonesia	0.97 Liquid natural gas	1.11 Electricity and gas	1.04	1.18 Other industries	0.99 Business services	0.99

Note: See Tables 3.3, 3.4 and 3.5 for a complete list of results for all sectors in each country. The sectors for each country depend on the model detail available. For Bangladesh there are thirty-five sectors (Devarajan *et al.* 1998), for Cameroon there are six sectors (Benjamin *et al.* 1991) and for Indonesia, there are thirty sectors (Lewis 1991).

The numbers indicate the marginal benefit needed to justify a dollar's increase in real revenue by the particular instrument. In the absence of other distortions, one anticipates that a policy which increases the highest tax rate will generate a welfare loss, raising the MCF. We find this holds for the highest indirect tax in Bangladesh and the highest tariff in all countries. The MCF is highest when the sugar tariff in Bangladesh, the country with the widest tariff range (see Table 3.3), is used to generate a one unit increase in real government revenue. The tariff increases from 254 to 509 per cent.

In contrast, a policy which increases the lowest tax rate, in the absence of other distortions, will reduce the MCF as the tax structure becomes more uniform.

Table 3.3 Detailed MCF results for Bangladesh

Sector	Old rate	New rate	MCF
Indirect tax instrument			
Tea	0.01	0.28	1.01
Fisheries	0.00	0.04	0.95
Sugar	0.01	0.07	0.97
Tobacco	0.41	0.52	1.07
Other food	0.01	0.06	1.00
Cotton yarn	0.01	0.23	0.88
Cloth	0.00	0.05	1.04
Jute textile	0.02	1.14	1.10
Paper	0.03	0.24	1.00
Leather	0.03	0.46	0.91
Pharmaceuticals	0.02	0.06	1.02
Cement	0.05	1.40	1.23
Basic metals	0.01	0.13	1.10
Metal products	0.01	0.04	1.18
Wood and misc. industries	0.01	0.04	1.01
Petroleum	0.03	0.10	1.15
Electricity and gas	0.20	0.32	1.09
Transport service	0.00	0.02	0.97
Trade and other services	0.00	0.02	1.02
Across the board	1.00	1.11	1.05
Tariff instrument			
Livestock	0.17	0.47	1.17
Sugar	2.54	5.09	2.18
Edible oil	0.79	1.25	1.38
Cotton yarn	2.30	3.82	1.86
Cloth	0.83	1.89	1.57
Paper	1.31	2.62	1.58
Pharmaceuticals	0.72	0.99	1.41
Cement	0.41	1.04	1.22
Basic metals	0.56	0.84	1.37
Metal products	0.43	0.47	0.82
Wood and misc. industries	1.34	1.97	1.79
Petroleum	0.41	0.61	1.06
Across the board	1.00	1.03	1.20

When the lowest tax is raised, the MCF is less than one for indirect taxes in Bangladesh and Cameroon and tariffs in Indonesia.

Interestingly, in Cameroon and Indonesia, there are welfare gains when the indirect tax increases in the sectors with the highest rate. Indeed, for Cameroon the gains are higher when the highest indirect tax increases, compared to an increase in the lowest tax. The indirect tax on cash crops in Cameroon increases from 19 to 20 per cent while in Indonesia the indirect tax on liquid natural gas increases from 24 to 33 per cent (see Tables 3.4 and 3.5). This is due to second-best effects, primarily from labour market distortions, which dominate the distortionary effects of the policy change on the tax structure.[4]

In Cameroon the output of cash crops declines 1.5 per cent while output of all other sectors increases following an increase in the indirect tax on cash crops, the sector with the highest indirect tax rate. Cash crops has the lowest labour productivity of the six sectors in the economy; there are welfare gains as labour moves into more productive uses.[5] Furthermore, changes in the structure of production reflect changes in the real exchange rate. Cash crops is primarily an export commodity so a tax on production is in essence an export tax. Since the current account balance is fixed, the real exchange rate, or the relative price of tradeables to non-tradeables must adjust to reduce imports and increase exports in other sectors. Sectors with high export shares will expand. Following cash crops, intermediate goods has the highest export share of production. It also has the most productive labour. For Indonesia, there is a slight welfare gain when the highest indirect tax rate is raised. The model has more sectors so the explanation is more complex. Unlike Cameroon, the taxed sector in Indonesia, liquid natural gas, has labour that is more productive than average. However, other sectors with high labour productivity expand as the liquid natural gas sector contracts slightly. The sectors with the lowest labour productivity (farming, wood furniture and textiles) contract.

Table 3.4 Detailed MCF results for Cameroon

Sector	Old Rate	New Rate	MCF
Indirect tax instrument			
Food and forestry	0.01	0.01	0.96
Cash crops	0.19	0.20	0.48
Food and consumption	0.07	0.08	0.95
Intermediate	0.02	0.03	1.32
Capital and construction	0.03	0.04	1.07
Services	0.06	0.06	1.00
Across the board	1.00	1.01	0.90
Tariff instrument			
Cash crop	0.23	0.43	1.13
Food and consumption	0.37	0.43	1.37
Intermediate	0.20	0.21	1.05
Capital and construction	0.27	0.28	0.97
Across the board	1.00	1.02	1.05

Table 3.5 Detailed MCF results for Indonesia

Sector	Old Rate	New Rate	MCF
Indirect tax instrument			
Farm food crops	0.00	0.00	0.74
Farm non-food crops	0.00	0.00	1.00
Livestock	0.00	0.00	1.02
Forestry	0.01	0.01	0.97
Fishery	0.00	0.00	0.94
Coal mining	0.01	0.03	1.12
Oil and gas mining	0.00	0.00	1.08
Other mining	0.01	0.01	1.04
Liquid natural gas	0.24	0.33	0.97
Electricity and gas	0.00	0.00	1.11
Water	0.00	0.01	1.18
Trade and storage	0.04	0.04	1.06
Restaurants and hotels	0.02	0.02	1.03
Land transportation	0.01	0.01	1.06
Other transportation	0.00	0.00	1.17
Financial services	0.00	0.01	1.23
Business services	0.02	0.02	1.08
Other services	0.01	0.01	1.03
Across the board	1.00	1.00	1.04
Tariff instrument			
Farm food crops	0.01	0.02	1.14
Farm non-food crops	0.01	0.02	0.85
Livestock	0.03	0.17	1.12
Forestry	0.05	0.56	1.09
Coal mining	0.04	0.41	1.02
Oil and gas mining	0.01	0.01	1.07
Other mining	0.00	0.01	0.70
Processed foods	0.06	0.07	1.12
Textiles	0.08	0.09	1.16
Wood and furniture	0.12	1.17	1.91
Paper and printing	0.07	0.07	1.00
Chemicals and fertilizer	0.04	0.05	1.01
Oil refining	0.07	0.08	1.05
Non-metallic minerals	0.03	0.04	0.94
Basic minerals	0.04	0.04	0.95
Machines	0.06	0.06	0.98
Other industry	0.16	0.22	1.18
Business services	0.00	0.00	0.99
Other services	0.00	0.00	0.99
Across the board	1.00	1.00	0.99

In Indonesia, an indirect tax reduces domestic sales. An expansion in domestic sales of another sector with an indirect tax will also contribute to the welfare gain observed as the tax on liquid natural gas increases. We find an increase in domestic sales in sectors with the highest indirect tax rates. Interestingly, domestic sales of liquid natural gas increase, despite the slight reduction in output as the tax on domestic sales increases. Liquid natural gas is produced primarily for export (99.8 per cent of production is exported and it accounts for 19 per cent of Indonesia's total exports). An increase in the tax on domestic production creates an incentive to substitute towards exports for a given level of output. Since the current account balance is constant, the real exchange rate must adjust to discourage exports in other sectors and increase imports. We find the price of non-tradeable relative to tradeables in the liquid natural gas sector increases which accounts for the slight increase in domestic sales despite an increase in the tax on domestic sales.

In the model for Bangladesh, there are no labour productivity differences. When indirect taxes are the instrument to generate revenue, the welfare changes reflect the changes in the indirect tax structure – when the highest indirect tax is raised, there are welfare costs and when lowest indirect tax is raised, there are welfare gains.

However, Bangladesh has the highest and the widest range of import tariffs (from 17 per cent in live stock to 254 per cent in sugar). In contrast, the tariffs range from 20 to 37 per cent in Cameroon and 0.02 to 16 per cent in Indonesia (see Tables 3.3, 3.4, and 3.5). When the tariff rate on livestock, the sector with the lowest tariff in Bangladesh, increases, there are welfare losses due to second-best effects. In this scenario, other sectors that have high tariffs expand, exacerbating the distortionary effect of the tariff in those sectors. For example, basic metals (56 per cent tariff), metal products (43 per cent tariff) and wood and other (134 per cent tariff) expand; together these sectors account for 7 per cent of total output in Bangladesh.

3   What drives the MCF estimates?

We estimated the marginal welfare cost of taxation (alternatively, the marginal cost of public funds or MCF) in Cameroon using a CGE model. Not surprisingly, the estimates are quite sensitive to both the sector being taxed as well as the underlying setup of the model. There are six sectors in the model: food and forestry, cash crops, food and consumption, intermediate goods, capital and consumption goods, and services. These sectors have both indirect taxes and tariffs. To illustrate the different factors which affect the MCF, we also ran the model under various scenarios corresponding to different factor market assumptions, that is, the degree of capital mobility and the existence of wage and rental distortions.

These distortions lead to sectoral wage and rental differentials which persist even in the presence of factor mobility. They reflect the observation that factors of a given type may earn different returns in different sectors. Figure 3.2 is drawn for a given factor j, where MVP_j^i denotes the marginal value product of factor j in sector i. The existence of factor market distortions implies that equilibrium occurs at a point such as A, where factor returns are not equalized across sectors in spite of mobility, but continue to vary by a given proportion AC/BC. By contrast, the absence of factor market distortions implies an equilibrium such as D where returns are equalized.

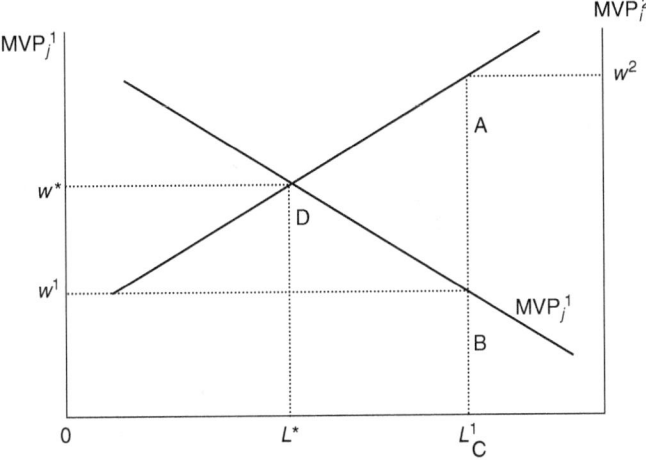

Figure 3.2 Factor market distortions.

Table 3.6 Marginal welfare cost of public funds in Cameroon. Welfare cost per CFA franc raised

	Labour and capital undistorted	Labour undistorted; capital mobile but distorted	Labour distorted; capital mobile but distorted	Labour distorted; capital fixed
Food and forestry	−0.130	−0.100	−0.043	−0.036
Cash crops	1.740	2.688	0.241	−0.521
Food and consumption	−0.091	−0.381	−0.320	−0.048
Intermediate	−0.056	−0.647	−0.338	0.323
Capital and construction	−0.063	−0.192	−0.088	0.070
Services	0.023	0.143	0.132	0.003
Across the board	0.278	0.351	0.020	−0.104

Source: Author calculations.

The results are presented in Table 3.6 for four factor market scenarios and seven tax experiments. Labour is always mobile, but wage distortions may or may not be present. Capital may be either fixed or mobile. Rental distortions are always present in the former case, but may or may not be present in the latter case. The tax experiments comprise six sector-specific and one across-the-board increase in indirect taxes.[6] Welfare is measured as equivalent variation and represents the amount the consumer would be willing to pay to avoid the increase in taxes required to generate a unit increase in real government revenue (units are in one million CFA francs). Because welfare is measured as equivalent variation, negative numbers represent a welfare benefit.

What is immediately striking is the tremendous variation in the MCF estimates across both taxes and scenarios. Under the limiting case with labour and capital undistorted, taxes on cash crops have by far the highest welfare cost (1.74 per CFA franc raised), while several other taxes actually have welfare benefits. By contrast, in the case with labour distorted and capital fixed, cash crop taxes have the lowest welfare cost (or highest benefit at − 0.52 per CFA franc), while taxes on intermediate goods instead have the highest welfare cost.

What accounts for the tremendous variation in estimates? The critical factor driving the MCF appears to be the effect that the tax induces on the key distortions in the economy. In an economy with large distortions, these induced effects will typically outweigh the 'own' effects. Table 3.7 presents base tax rates along with the proportional differences in factor prices across sectors due to the aforementioned factor market distortions.

Differences in the MCF estimates of different taxes can be largely explained by the effects they induce relative to these key distortions in the Cameroonian economy. In the limiting case with undistorted labour and capital, there are no sectoral differences in factor prices and productivity. The critical distortions are the tax rates. With a tax rate of 19 per cent, cash crops are by far the most distorted sector. This suggests that because cash crops are significantly under-produced relative to the optimum, any policy changes which increase the production of cash crops are likely to be beneficial. This is indeed the case.

The percentage change in cash crop production due to increases in the different taxes are cash crops − 4.796; services − 0.033; capital and construction 0.147; food and forestry 0.233; food and consumption 0.337; and intermediate goods 0.435. Comparing these figures with the corresponding MCF estimates under column 1 of Table 3.6, we observe that the sign of the welfare effect is given by the induced effect on cash crop production. If the tax increases (decreases) cash crop production, the tax increases (decreases) welfare. While each tax also has the effect of reducing 'own' production and exacerbating this existing distortion, this is overwhelmed by the induced effect given the dominance of the cash crop distortions.

The above has a rather significant policy implication. The MCF will be high in those sectors where distortions are large. However, the very presence of such large distortions implies the existence of other taxes for which the MCF will be low precisely because they offset the large distortion through substitutability.

Table 3.7 Sample key distortions in Cameroon

	Base tax rate	Capital	Unskilled labour	Skilled labour
Food and forestry	0.007	1.249	0.732	1.923
Cash crops	0.191	0.614	0.348	0.292
Food and consumption	0.074	0.496	0.841	0.699
Intermediate	0.025	0.315	2.347	1.972
Capital and construction	0.034	0.526	2.023	1.686
Services	0.060	2.037	1.121	0.927

Source: Author estimates.

This runs counter to the conventional view that the welfare cost of taxation will be large in highly-distorted economies.

Consider now the effect of introducing additional distortions in the factor markets. We introduce factor distortions 'one-by-one' by considering each scenario in turn. For concreteness, we focus the discussion on two types of taxes, cash crops and intermediate goods. These are of particular interest because they have the highest welfare costs depending upon the scenario considered. As will be seen, since taxes on cash crops may no longer be the critical distortion, welfare effects will now depend on more than induced cash crop production alone. However, inferences regarding welfare effects can still be made by referring to the relative factor market distortions.

Consider first the effect of introducing capital market distortions. From Table 3.6, we see that the welfare cost for cash crop taxes increases sharply from 1.740 to 2.688. Production effects of increasing cash crop taxes under different scenarios are provided in Table 3.8. Just as in the undistorted scenario, there is a large decrease (increase) in the production of cash crops (intermediate goods). Capital and labour flow out of cash crops towards intermediate goods. From Table 3.7, relative to the intermediate sector, cash crops have significantly higher capital productivity and lower labour productivity. With capital market distortions, the cash crop tax means that capital flows from a high to low productivity sector, which raises the welfare cost. (In effect, the height AB in Figure 3.2 is forgone at the margin.)

Next, introduce labour market distortions. The welfare cost of the cash crop tax now drops from 2.688 to 0.241. The tax now means that labour flows from a low- to a high-productivity sector. This counteracts the preceding capital effect, yielding a lower welfare cost.

Lastly, let capital be immobile across sectors. In this case, there is no negative capital effect, only a positive labour effect. This positive effect is sufficient to outweigh the welfare loss from reduced output of cash crops. There is a net welfare benefit from the increase in cash crop taxes.

Table 3.8 Production effects of increase in cash crop tax – percentage change

	Labour and capital undistorted	Labour undistorted; capital mobile but distorted	Labour distorted; capital mobile but distorted	Labour distorted; capital fixed
Food and forestry	0.352	0.326	0.521	0.304
Cash crops	−4.796	−5.261	−3.964	−1.456
Food and consumption	0.494	0.456	0.514	0.200
Intermediate	0.783	0.785	0.694	0.219
Capital and construction	0.301	0.316	0.259	0.097
Services	−0.063	−0.134	−0.009	0.039

Source: Author calculations.

Table 3.9 Production effects of increase in intermediate goods tax – percentage change

	Labour and capital undistorted	Labour undistorted; capital mobile but distorted	Labour distorted; capital mobile but distorted	Labour distorted; capital fixed
Food and forestry	0.039	0.081	0.047	−0.014
Cash crops	0.435	0.416	0.420	0.134
Food and consumption	0.034	0.096	0.066	0.010
Intermediate	−0.487	−0.399	−0.439	−0.323
Capital and construction	−0.052	−0.037	−0.044	−0.025
Services	0.032	0.080	0.061	0.006

Source: Author calculations.

Table 3.9 reports the production effects of increasing taxes on intermediate goods. Since the sector has higher (lower) labour (capital) productivity than cash crops, the effects essentially mirror those discussed above. Note, however, that the correspondence between induced cash crop production and the welfare effect no longer holds. In particular, induced cash crop production is always positive, but in the scenario with distorted labour and fixed capital, the net welfare effect of the tax is negative.

3.1   Marginal cost of funds heuristics

The above results have a straightforward analytical interpretation. Consider an increase in the tax on sector i, from t_i^0 to t_i^1. The own, direct welfare loss from this tax increase is given by the shaded area in the left-hand side of Figure 3.3. However, the tax increase also induces effects in the other sectors, denoted $-i$. In the case of substitutability in production, there is an induced welfare gain given by the shaded area on the right-hand side of Figure 3.3. Note that because the supply curve in sector $-i$ is drawn for a given tax rate t_i, an increase in t_i also shifts this supply curve. Since taxes on cash crops are so much larger than those in other sectors, it is easy to see why induced effects can easily outweigh the direct effect in determining the overall welfare impact of tax changes.

From Figure 3.3, in the case where taxes are the only critical distortions, a first-order approximation for the welfare effect of a tax increase is given by $\Delta W = \sum_i t_i \Delta x_i$, where Δx_i are the output changes.

The calculation of ΔW compares reasonably with the welfare estimates obtained from the full CGE model. As shown in Table 3.10, the ΔW have the correct sign and all but one (cash crops) are accurate to within the first decimal place.[7]

Two points are worth emphasizing. First, because the output changes Δx_i were obtained from the CGE model anyway, it may appear that there is little computational gain from the shortcut calculation ΔW. The point is that if the analyst were somehow able to approximate such output changes (e.g. by estimating certain key elasticities), then there may be relatively little additional gain from constructing a full-blown CGE model for the purposes of estimating the MCF. In

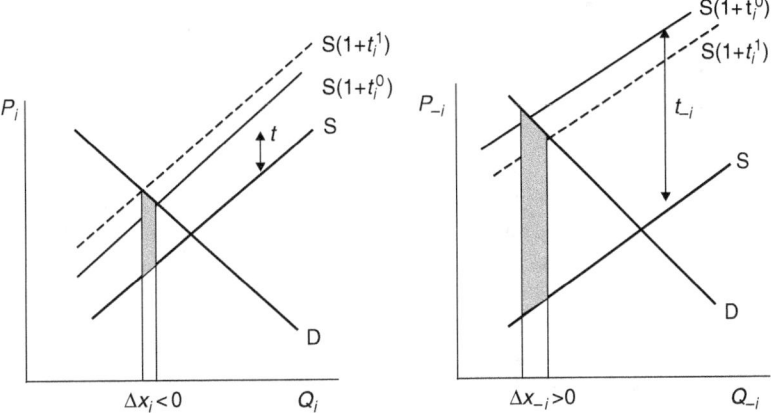

Figure 3.3 Welfare effects of tax changes.

Table 3.10 Full CGE versus heuristic MCF estimates – welfare cost per CFAF raised

	Food and forestry	Cash crops	Food and consumption	Intermediate	Capital and construction	Services
ΔW	0.14	−1.82	0.03	0.06	0.07	−0.02
CGE (−EV)	0.13	−1.70	0.09	0.06	0.06	−0.02

Source: Author calculations.

many cases, for example, it may be reasonable to assume that some of the cross-elasticities are zero. Computational considerations aside, the calculation of ΔW is also useful for expositional purposes as it clarifies what is driving the results behind the full CGE model.

Second, ΔW is only a reasonable approximation for the MCF when taxes are the only critical distortions. Nonetheless, they may provide a useful benchmark even in cases where factor market distortions may be important. If relative productivity differences across sectors are known, then it should be possible to infer whether the ΔW constitute a lower or upper bound for the 'true' MCF. In the preceding section, for example, we showed how the introduction of capital (labour) market distortions raises (lowers) the MCF for cash crops because capital (labour) flowed into a lower (higher) productivity sector with an increase in cash crop taxes. In this case, we could be reasonably comfortable that ΔW represents a lower (upper) bound to the true MCF estimate in the presence of capital (labour) distortions.

4   Concluding remarks

The purpose of this chapter was to derive realistic but transparent estimates of the marginal cost of public funds in developing countries. Not only are these estimates very few, but particular features of developing countries – factor market distortions, a large informal sector, etc. – meant that even the sign, not to mention the magnitude, of the MCF could not be determined a priori.

Our estimates of the MCF for Bangladesh, Cameroon and Indonesia reinforced this point: they range from 0.5 to 2.0. However, we were able to interpret these results in light of the model's assumptions and the features of the underlying economy. For instance, estimates of the MCF were less than one (where a tax leads to a welfare gain) only when the economy had a large, existing distortion which was reduced as a result of the tax change. We found that calculating the revenue losses and gains from these other distortions was a useful way of approximating the overall welfare effect of a tax change.

Two lessons emerge from this exercise. First, the conventional wisdom that the marginal cost of public funds in developing countries is extraordinarily high simply cannot be sustained by our analysis. Our estimates lie within the range of those obtained for developed countries. Furthermore, we can interpret our estimates in terms of the actual data in the countries under study. The same reason why people feel the MCF in developing countries is very high – the presence of large distortions – is the reason why the MCF can be very low: a tax whose substitution effect lowers that large distortion could have a very low (or negative) welfare cost. Second, this same logic points to another policy implication: the marginal cost of taxation is by no means uniform across sectors and instruments. The lesson there is that the potential for revenue-neutral (or even revenue-increasing) tax reforms in developing countries is enormous, and analyses like the one presented here could provide the underpinnings of such reform efforts.

Notes

1 Intermediate demand can be modeled as a fixed share of output or as an imperfect substitute for primary inputs – labour, land and capital. In the country models used in this study, intermediate demand is a fixed share of output in Bangladesh and Cameroon; an aggregate of intermediate inputs is an imperfect substitute for primary inputs in the model of Indonesia.
2 There is a Cobb-Douglas utility function over consumption of final goods. Savings is not part of the utility function.
3 In Cameroon, the indirect taxes are applied to all domestic production (which can go to domestic sales or to exports). In Bangladesh and Indonesia, the indirect taxes are applied to domestic sales only.
4 While both countries also have tariffs which can contribute to second-best effects, the rates are low and are fairly evenly distributed.
5 Capital, the only other input, is sector-specific in the model of Cameroon and Indonesia.
6 The last column, 'Labour distorted capital fixed' corresponds to the factor market conditions used in the scenarios presented in Table 3.1. Hence welfare cost of −0.52 for cashcrops corresponds to a MCF of 0.48 reported in Table 3.1.
7 Recall that because welfare was estimated as equivalent variation, a negative (positive) figure indicates a welfare benefit (cost). By contrast, a negative (positive) figure for ΔW indicates a welfare cost (benefit). For comparison purposes the full model estimates are therefore reported as $-(EV)$ in Table 3.10. Note that the second row in Table 3.10 is the same as the first column of Table 3.6 with the sign changed.

References

Ahmad, E. and Stern, N. (1987) 'Alternative sources of government revenue: illustrations from India, 1979–80', in: Newbery, D. and Stern, N. (eds) *The Theory of Taxation for Developing Countries*, Oxford: Oxford University Press.

Ahmed, S. and Croushore, D. (1996) 'The marginal cost of funds with nonseparable public spending', *Public Finance Quarterly*, 24 (April), 216–36.

Atkinson, A. B. and Stern, N. H. (1974) 'Pigou, Taxation and Public Goods', *Review of Economic Studies*, 41 (January), 119–28.

Ballard, C. L. and Fullerton, D. (1992) 'Distortionary taxation and the provision of public goods', *Journal of Economic Perspectives*, 6, 117–31.

Ballard, C. L., Shoven, J. B. and. Whalley, J. (1985) "General equilibrium computations of the marginal welfare cost of taxes in the United States', *American Economic Review*, 75, 128–38.

Benjamin, N. C., Devarajan, S. and Weiner, R. J. (1989) 'The "Dutch Disease" in a developing country: oil reserves in Cameroon', *Journal of Development Economics*, 30, 71–92.

Browning, E. K. (1987) 'On the marginal welfare cost of taxation', *American Economic Review*, 77 (March), 11–23.

Devarajan, S., Ghanem, H. H. and Thierfelder, K. (1998) 'Labour market regulations, trade liberalization and the distribution of income in Bangladesh', *Journal of Policy Reform*, 1, 1–28.

Diewert, W. E. and Lawrence, D. A. (1994) 'The marginal costs of taxation in New Zealand', Report prepared for the New Zealand Business Roundtable by Swan Consultants Pty. Ltd., Canberra, Australia.

Fullerton, D. (1991) 'Reconciling recent estimates of the marginal welfare cost of taxation', *American Economic Review*, 81 (March), 302–8.

Hansson, I. and Stuart, C. (1985) 'Tax revenue and the marginal cost of public funds in Sweden', *Journal of Public Economics*, 27, 331–353.

Harberger, A. C. (1964) 'The measurement of waste', *American Economic Review*, 54 (May), 58–76.

Lewis, J. D. (1991) 'A Computable General Equilibrium (CGE) Model of Indonesia', *Development Discussion Paper 378*, Institute for International Development, Cambridge, Mass.: Harvard University.

Pigou, A. (1920) The Economics of Welfare, London: MacMillan.

Samuelson, P. A. (1954) 'The pure theory of public expenditure', *Review of Economics and Statistics*, 36 (November), 387–89.

Snow, A. and Warren, R. Jr (1996) 'The marginal welfare cost of public funds: theory and estimates', *Journal of Public Economics*, 61, 289–305.

Stiglitz, J. E. and Dasgupta, P. S. (1971) 'Differential taxation, public goods, and economic efficiency', *Review of Economic Studies*, 38 (April), 151–74.

Stuart, C. (1984) 'Welfare costs per dollar of additional tax revenue in the United States', *American Economic Review*, 74, 352–62.

Wildasin, D. E. (1984) 'On public good provision with distortionary taxation', *Economic Inquiry*, 22 (April), 227–43.

4 CGE models for practical policy analysis

The Australian experience

Peter B. Dixon, Brian R. Parmenter
and Maureen T. Rimmer

1 Introduction

Australia has a long history of using CGE models in the economic policy process. Governments regularly commission modellers to analyse policy issues. Discussion of policy in the news media often focuses on the modellers' results.

Fundamental to the popularity of CGE modelling was the Australian government's decision in 1975 to establish the IMPACT Project. The core of the IMPACT research team has worked continuously since 1975 on the development of CGE models. Government funding and contract research have been the team's main sources of finance. The team has always had affiliations with one or other of Melbourne's main universities. Currently, it forms the Centre of Policy Studies (CoPS) at Monash University. These arrangements have ensured that, as well as remaining focussed on practical issues, the modelling is exposed regularly to review via the academic journals and at academic conferences.

A second factor is the emphasis that the CoPS/IMPACT team has placed on training. A result of this is that there are many model-literate economists in Australia, several holding senior government positions.

The best known of the models developed by the CoPS/IMPACT team is ORANI, a static CGE model (Dixon *et al.* 1982). It represents the economy as a system of optimising agents (producers, investors, households, etc.) operating in competitive markets. The level of disaggregation is high, the standard version distinguishing 112 industries producing 114 commodities. By top-down methods, results are generated for 340 occupations, 56 regions and many households. This detail means that the model can be applied to a wide range of problems. Nevertheless, application-specific versions are created regularly by aggregation or disaggregation of the database and by incorporating detailed sectoral submodels (Meagher *et al.* 1985; Dixon *et al.* 1991; McDougall and Dixon 1996).

More recently, the CoPS/IMPACT team has developed a dynamic model, called MONASH (Dixon and Rimmer 2001). MONASH retains the sectoral, occupational, regional and distributional detail of ORANI. It comprises a series of ORANI-style models, each describing the economy in one of a sequence of years. The annual models are linked by intertemporal equations that describe the accumulation of sector-specific capital. We use MONASH for historical analysis, forecasting and dynamic policy analysis (Dixon *et al.* 2000).

Models in the ORANI–MONASH stable are solved with GEMPACK software (Pearson 1986; Harrison and Pearson 1994), using linearisation techniques pioneered in economics by Johansen (1960). Johansen's techniques implemented in GEMPACK allow modellers to implement very large models and to manipulate them flexibly. Closure changes (i.e. changes to the selection of exogenous variables) are routine and are important in our use of MONASH for a variety of purposes. The software can generate solutions free of linearisation errors using multi-step linear computations.

In this chapter, we review our experience of using CGE models for policy analysis. Section 2 identifies some of the major shortcomings of comparative-static analysis with models like ORANI. In Section 3, we explain how we use MONASH for forecasting and policy analysis. Section 4 provides an example of dynamic policy analysis. Section 5 contains conclusions.

2 Static policy analysis with ORANI

ORANI is used for comparative-static analysis in which the model is interpreted as representing the economy in some target future year. But it is usually calibrated to data for some historical year, not necessarily a plausible base case for the economy in the target year. The model is used to project the effect on the economy in the target year of shocks imposed in some earlier year. The length of the period between the target and shocked years is not explicit but is determined implicitly by the closure of the model and by the values chosen for key response parameters (primary-factor substitution elasticities, for example). One option is short-run assumptions, with capital stocks not allowed to respond to the shocks and with rates of return on capital endogenous. Alternatively, we could use the model to examine long-run responses. For a small country like Australia, we would then assume that rates of return on capital were unaffected by the shocks but that capital stocks adjust.

Comparative-static ORANI simulations are computed and reported as percentage changes in the variables. Their interpretation is shown by Figure 4.1, in which we plot the level of some endogenous variable against time. The target year is T^* and the shock occurs at year 0. The control value for the variable in year $t[V^c(T^*)]$ is its value in the data to which the model is calibrated. Possibly, this is its value in year 0 [$V(0)$], but more likely its value in some historical year for which input–output (IO) accounts are available. With the application of a shock to some exogenous variable(s), the model calculates a new value for the endogenous variable [$V^s(T^*)$]. The percentage change in V (denoted v) is defined by:

$$v(T^*) = 100 \cdot [V^s(T^*) - V^c(T^*)]/V^c(T^*). \tag{1}$$

This is the percentage difference between the shocked and control values of the variable in year T^*.

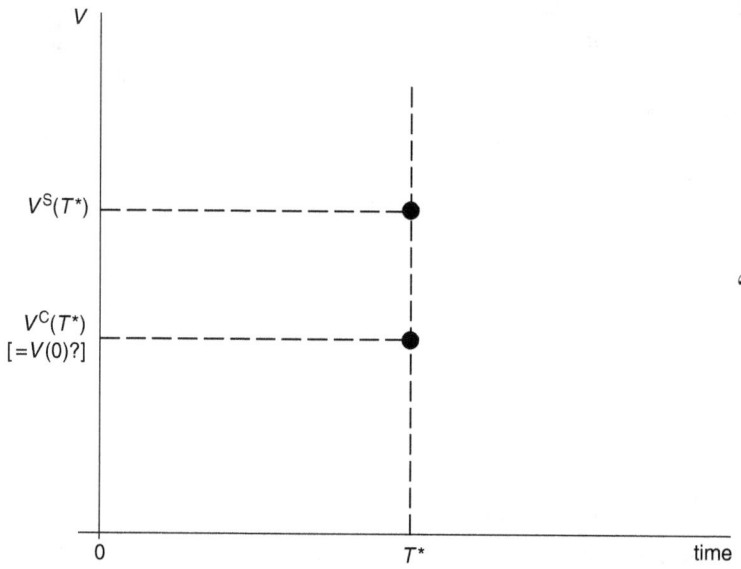

Figure 4.1 Comparative-static percentage changes from ORANI.

This approach has several shortcomings.

- The first follows from using an historical calibration database as a control solution for the (future) target year. To accept v in (1) as a good estimate of the effect of the shock in year T^*, you would have to believe that the effect is not very sensitive to changes in the structure of the economy between the calibration data and year T^*. In dynamic simulations with MONASH (Sections 3 and 4), we attempt to project realistic base cases. In assessing the effects of shocks in year T^*, we first use MONASH to forecast a plausible representation of the economy in year T^* without the shocks. In Section 4, we find that the effects of shocks are sensitive to details of the base case.
- A second problem is that the comparative-static approach is silent on issues of timing, although these are often crucial for policy analysis. Global warming provides one example. The timing of action to reduce greenhouse-gas emissions is crucial both for the benefits and for the costs of action. Global warming depends on the accumulation of the stock of gases in the atmosphere, not just on the annual flows of emission. Hence, early action to reduce emissions is superior to later action in moderating global warming. On the other hand, the prevalence of large sunk costs in emissions-intensive equipment (e.g. coal-fired electricity generation) implies that early action is likely to be more costly than delayed action. It may require the scrapping of a plant that has not reached the end of its economic life.

- A third shortcoming of comparative static analyses is their inability to provide information on structural adjustment. Suppose that our static model indicates that trade liberalisation will reduce employment in protected sectors, or in the occupations employed intensively in those sectors, or in regions in which the protected sectors are important employers. Whether or not this implies structural-adjustment problems for those sectors, occupations or regions depends on base-case employment prospects. Policy-induced reductions in employment in areas with underlying strong growth may just mean that growth will be a little slower than it would have been in the absence of the policy change. The implications of this for structural adjustment differ from cases in which the policy change implies negative employment growth.

In view of these difficulties, there are significant advantages in conducting policy analysis in a dynamic framework, even with very simple dynamic assumptions.

3   Forecasting and dynamic policy analysis with MONASH

3.1   The structure of the model

MONASH consists of a series of ORANI-style static models, one for each of a succession of years, linked by dynamic equations describing the accumulation of sector-specific capital (Dixon and Parmenter 1996). Investors can have static or forward-looking expectations. Static expectations allow the model to be solved recursively. Starting with a solution for some base year (0) and values for exogenous variables in year 1, we obtain a solution for endogenous variables in year 1 without knowing anything about solutions for subsequent years. If we assume that investors are forward-looking, the solution for year 1 is not independent of rates of return on capital in subsequent years. We must then solve for all years in our time horizon simultaneously or adopt an iterative procedure. Our judgement to date has been that the costs of the additional computations are not justified by the additional insights that are yielded by allowing for forward-looking expectations.

In forecasting with MONASH, we project annual growth rates of the variables. This is illustrated in Figure 4.2. We begin with an initial solution (including $V(0)$ in Figure 4.2) for an up-to-date base year (0). We estimate this from an historical simulation with the model (Dixon and McDonald 1992). Then, outside the model, we forecast first-year growth rates for all the exogenous variables and solve for first-year growth rates of the endogenous variables.[1] Hence, we can calculate $V^f(1)$ in Figure 4.2. In fact, using the year-1 solution we can update the entire base-year data. The updated data are used as an initial solution for a year-2 forecast. By a sequence of these annual solutions and data updates, we forecast time paths for the variables, such as $V^f(t)$ in Figure 4.2.

Results from the MONASH forecasts, like the results from ORANI comparative-static simulations (Figure 4.1), are reported as percentage changes in the variables. In MONASH forecasts, however, the percentage changes are annual growth rates. In Figure 4.2 we generate along the path $V^f(t)$, annual

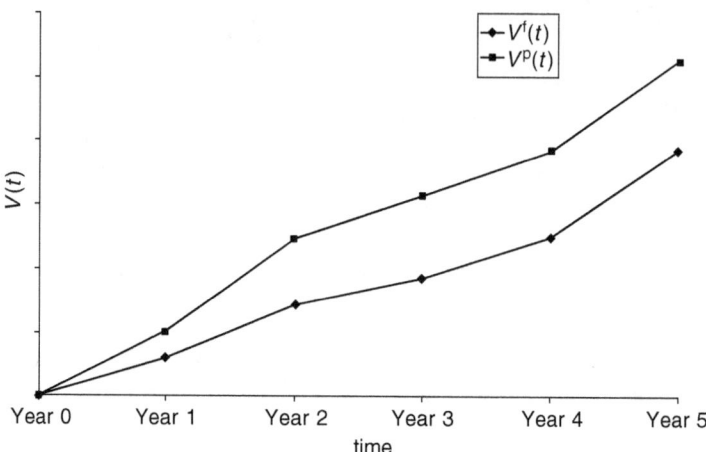

Figure 4.2 Forecast average annual growth rates and policy deviations in MONASH.

growth rates, $v^f(t)$, defined by:

$$v^f(t) = 100 \cdot [V^f(t) - V^f(t-1)]/V^f(t-1). \tag{2}$$

The dynamics underlying MONASH forecasts are illustrated in Figure 4.3. For each year t, including the base year 0, the MONASH solution covers flow variables, such as investment $[I(t)]$ and the return to capital $[R(t)]$, and stock variables, such as the stock of capital available at the beginning of the year $[K(t)]$ and the stock available at the end of the year $[K(t+1)]$. We assume that only $K(t)$ is available for use during year t and that there is a one-year gestation lag so that $K(t+1)$ is related to $K(t)$ by an accumulation relationship:

$$K(t+1) = K(t)D + I(t), \tag{3}$$

where D is one minus the depreciation rate.

From the point of view of year 1, capital available for use, $K(1)$, is pre-determined by the base-year data. In forecasting year-1 growth rates, the appropriate value for the growth rate of capital available for use, $k^f(1)$, is the percentage difference between the stock of capital available at the end of the base year and the stock available at the beginning of that year. That is:

$$k^f(1) = 100 \cdot [K(1) - K(0)]/K(0). \tag{4}$$

An equation to perform this calculation is included in the GEMPACK code for MONASH.

MONASH includes behavioural equations that relate growth of the capital stock through the forecast year to investors' expectations about returns to capital in the next year. For year 1 in Figure 4.3, these can be summarised as:

$$k^f(2) = f(E[R(2)]), \tag{5}$$

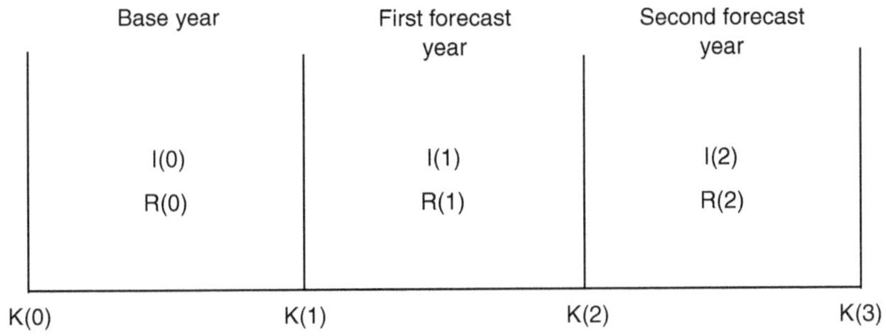

Figure 4.3 Capital accumulation in MONASH.

where $E[R(2)]$ is the expectation in year 1 of the return on capital in year 2. Our alternative rules for determining expected returns are

$$E[R(2)] = R(1), \text{ static expectations,} \tag{6}$$

and

$$E[R(2)] = R(2), \text{ forward-looking expectations.} \tag{7}$$

With $k^f(1)$ predetermined, as shown in equation (4), and with $k^f(2)$ determined by the behavioural equation (5), the accumulation relationship (3) determines the forecast rate of growth of investment for year 1 $[i^f(1)]$. The model calculates how much investment must be made in year 1 to move the capital stock from its (predetermined) level at the beginning of the year to the level that investors wish to have in place at the end of the year.

The forecast for year 2 uses as its initial solution data for year 1, updated from the year-0 data using the results of the year-1 forecasts. The process continues until forecasts for all years of the horizon have been computed. We restrict ourselves to horizons of policy interest, typically 10 and rarely more than 20 years.

3.2   *Closure and shocks for forecasting*

MONASH forecasts have two roles. The first is to project how the structure of the economy might develop. Agencies planning future actions must take views about this. Many find MONASH forecasts helpful. Examples include

- government authorities responsible for resource allocation in the Australian vocational education and training system. These agencies use detailed MONASH forecasts of the occupational structure of employment.
- government authorities planning Australia's response to greenhouse-gas reduction targets. These agencies require forecasts of Australia's greenhouse-gas emissions under business as usual assumptions (Adams and Parmenter 1999).

The second role for MONASH forecasts is as a base case for policy analysis. In all forecasting simulations, we impose on MONASH forecasts determined outside the model for

- macroeconomic variables;
- foreign-currency prices and volumes for most exports;
- planned industry-policy changes; and
- changes in production technologies and households' preferences.

We rely on MONASH to forecast changes in the structure of the economy (output by industry, employment by occupation, etc.) consistent with these externally imposed forecasts.

In the closure adopted for forecasting, all the variables corresponding to the externally forecast items are exogenous. The model then determines values for accommodating variables that would normally be thought of as exogenous. We give two examples.

- The externally supplied macroeconomic forecasts include growth in factor inputs and growth in aggregate output. Hence, the rate of aggregate factor-saving/using technical change is implied.
- The external forecasts include world prices and export volumes. To accommo-date these, the model projects shifts in its export demand and supply schedules.

3.3   *Closure and shocks for policy analysis*

Policy analysis with MONASH is conducted by computing deviations away from base forecasts. The forecasting closure is inappropriate for the policy simu-lations. In these, macroeconomic variables, and export volumes and prices should be free to respond to policy shocks. Hence, we adopt a closure in which these variables are endogenous and the variables that accommodated their settings in the base forecasts are exogenous. In a policy simulation, we set these exogenous variables at the values they took in the corresponding base simulation. For example,

- in the policy simulation real GDP (which was exogenous in forecasting) is endogenous and aggregate factor-saving/using technical change (which was endogenous in forecasting) is exogenous and set to the path projected for it in the base forecasts.
- in the policy simulation export volumes and world prices (which were exogenous in forecasting) are endogenous and the positions of the corresponding export demand and supply schedules (which were endogenous in forecasting) are exogenous. Shifts in the schedules are set to the paths that were necessary to accommodate the exogenous volumes and prices in the base forecasts.

We could reproduce the base forecasts in the policy closure by setting the switched exogenous variables at the values implied for them in the forecast simulation (as described above) and setting all other exogenous variables at the values assigned in the base simulation. This is a useful check on the accuracy of our procedures.

To compute a policy deviation, we run a second simulation in the policy closure. In this, most of the exogenous variables are set at the values they took in reproducing the base forecasts. But we shift key exogenous variables from their base-case paths to reflect the policy shock. In Figure 4.2, we compute revised paths like $V^P(t)$ for the endogenous variables.

We can now compute policy differentials analogous to those in comparative-static simulations (see Section 4.2). In Figure 4.2, the percentage effect of the shock in year 3 $[v^P(3)]$ is:

$$v^P(3) = 100 \cdot [V^P(3) - V^f(3)]/V^f(3). \tag{8}$$

Unlike the differentials from comparative-static simulations, the MONASH policy differentials are from a realistic base case, with explicit calendar timing.

4 An example: the Asian economic crisis and foreign students in Australia

Throughout the 1990s foreign students studying in Australia were a rapidly growing source of foreign exchange. The Asian economic crisis in 1997 threatened to reduce growth of the numbers of foreign students. We used MONASH to examine the economic significance of this possibility.

The modelling required data, actual and projected, on student numbers and on foreign students' expenditure patterns. These data are described in Section 4.1. In Section 4.2, we outline the structure of the MONASH simulations. The results are reported in Sections 4.3 and 4.4.

4.1 Data

(a) Students' expenditure patterns
Table 4.1 is a combination of data from the Australian Commonwealth Department of Education, Training and Youth Affairs (DETYA) and the Morgan Research Centre (MRC). Total expenditure by foreign students in 1996–7 was $3,225 billion. This is about 0.7 per cent of GDP or 3.2 per cent of aggregate exports. More than half of the expenditure goes to course fees and course-related expenses. Housing, and food and groceries are also major items. Together, other items account for less than 25 per cent of total expenditure.

The 14 MRC categories (Table 4.1) were mapped to the 115 MONASH commodity categories. Expenditure in each of the MRC categories was distributed across the corresponding MONASH categories assuming that foreign students' expenditure within an MRC category is allocated between the

Table 4.1 Expenditure of foreign students in Australia, 1996–97

Expenditure category (from MRC survey)	$million	Share in total
1. Housing	500	0.155
2. Utilities	153	0.047
3. Health	35	0.011
4. Food and groceries	312	0.097
5. Alcohol and cigarettes	47	0.014
6. Car costs	41	0.013
7. Daily transport	59	0.018
8. Entertainment	118	0.037
9. Other weekly expenses	29	0.009
10. Clothing and footwear	77	0.024
11. Household goods	53	0.016
12. Overseas travel	100	0.031
13. Course fees	1,583	0.491
14. Course related expenses	118	0.037
Total	3,225	1.000

Note: Morgan Research Centre expenditure categories.

corresponding MONASH categories in the same proportions as domestic households' expenditure.

The MONASH database relies heavily on IO accounts published by the Australian Bureau of Statistics (ABS, Catalogue no. 5209.0). With the exception of course fees (MRC category 13), the IO data fail to distinguish between expenditures made in Australia by foreign students and domestic households. To this extent, the standard MONASH database understated exports and overstated households' spending. In the data used for the present example, all of the estimated expenditures of foreign students are treated as exports.

(b) Foreign-student numbers

Table 4.2 contains DETYA data on the recent history of foreign students studying in Australia and forecasts of student numbers. Student numbers grew rapidly in the mid 1990s, although in 1996–97 growth was slower than in the preceding two years. Our base-case assumption (see columns (1) and (2) of Table 4.2) is that student numbers grow strongly through to 2004–05. We include this assumption in a base-case scenario about the development of the economy that was formulated prior to the Asian crisis (Section 4.2). For the deviation simulation we assume that, in view of the Asian crisis, growth in foreign student numbers would slow for the period 1997–98 to 1999–2000 (columns (3) and (4) of Table 4.2) but recover to the rate assumed in the base case by 2001–02.

The final column of Table 4.2 shows, for each forecast year, the percentage difference between the revised forecast and the base case. From 2001–02 onwards, there are 17.31 percent fewer foreign students studying in Australia under the revised assumptions than in the base-case. Our simulations are designed to project the economic implications of student numbers falling short

Table 4.2 Assumptions about numbers of foreign students, 1997–98 to 2004–5

Year	Base-case		Revised forecasts		
	Number of foreign students (1)	Percentage growth rate (2)	Number of foreign students (3)	Percentage growth rate (4)	Percentage deviation from base-case = 100[(3)/(1)−1] (5)
1993–94[a]	92,319				
1994–95[a]	109,984	19.1			
1995–96[a]	131,856	19.9			
1996–97[a]	147,588	11.9			
1997–98[b]	162,199	9.9	151,833	2.9	−6.39
1998–99[b]	177,446	9.4	154,409	1.7	−12.98
1999–2000[b]	193,239	8.9	161,268	4.4	−16.54
2000–1[b]	209,664	8.5	173,439	7.5	−17.28
2001–2[b]	227,485	8.5	188,108	8.5	−17.31
2002–3[b]	246,822	8.5	204,097	8.5	−17.31
2003–4[b]	267,801	8.5	221,445	8.5	−17.31
2004–5[b]	290,565	8.5	240,268	8.5	−17.31

Note:
a actual.
b forecast.

of those assumed in the base case by the amounts shown in column (5) of Table 4.2.

A regional breakdown of the national data reported in columns 1, 3 and 5 of Table 4.2 is given in Table 4.3. It shows

- base-case assumptions about the numbers of foreign students in each state and territory;
- revised forecasts by state and territory; and
- percentage deviations between the revised base-case assumptions.

According to Table 4.3, Victoria, South Australia, Western Australia and Tasmania all suffer percentage reductions in student numbers larger than the economy-wide reduction. The percentage reductions in the Northern Territory, Queensland, the ACT and NSW are smaller than the economy-wide reduction.

4.2 Simulations

We use MONASH to make a pair of simulations, covering the period 1996–97 to 2004–05.

- a base simulation with foreign-student numbers assumed to grow as in columns (1) and (2) of Table 4.2; and
- a deviation simulation with foreign-student numbers assumed to grow as in columns (3) and (4) of Table 4.2.

Table 4.3 Assumptions about regional distribution of foreign students, 1997–98 to 2004–5

Region		1997/98	1998/99	1999/00	2000/1	2001/2	2002/3	2003/4	2004/5
New South Wales	Base	57,191.23	61,694.41	67,249.21	73,054.03	79,263.47	86,001.14	93,310.93	101,242.68
	Revised forecast	53,559.00	54,030.00	57,104.00	61,890.00	67,262.00	72,979.00	79,181.00	85,911.00
	%dev. from base	−6.35	−12.42	−15.09	−15.28	−15.14	−15.14	−15.14	−15.14
Victoria	Base	43,998.05	49,589.63	54,104.10	58,801.60	63,799.61	69,222.80	75,106.49	81,490.80
	Revised forecast	41,064.00	42,774.00	44,343.00	47,404.00	51,305.00	55,666.00	60,398.00	65,531.00
	%dev. from base	−6.67	−13.74	−18.04	−19.38	−19.58	−19.58	−19.58	−19.58
Queensland	Base	26,069.60	27,881.19	30,164.36	32,499.35	35,261.73	38,259.09	41,510.98	45,039.56
	Revised forecast	24,530.00	24,610.00	25,766.00	27,794.00	30,225.00	32,794.00	35,583.00	38,607.00
	%dev. from base	−5.91	−11.73	−14.58	−14.48	−14.28	−14.28	−14.28	−14.28
Western Australia	Base	21,653.84	23,430.53	25,557.14	27,784.96	30,146.62	32,709.19	35,489.35	38,506.07
	Revised forecast	20,261.00	20,050.00	20,474.00	21,703.00	23,388.00	25,376.00	27,533.00	29,874.00
	%dev. from base	−6.43	−14.43	−19.89	−21.89	−22.42	−22.42	−22.42	−22.42
South Australia	Base	7,881.85	8,757.99	9,525.36	10,318.43	11,195.47	12,147.13	13,179.59	14,299.90
	Revised forecast	7,355.00	7,589.00	7,921.00	8,507.00	9,224.00	10,009.00	10,859.00	11,782.00
	%dev. from base	−6.68	−13.35	−16.84	−17.56	−17.61	−17.60	−17.61	−17.61
ACT	Base	3,169.95	3,648.63	3,988.92	4,335.96	4,704.50	5,104.40	5,538.26	6,009.03
	Revised forecast	2,970.00	3,236.00	3,472.00	3,810.00	4,175.00	4,531.00	4,916.00	5,334.00
	%dev. from base	−6.31	−11.31	−12.96	−12.13	−11.26	−11.23	−11.24	−11.23
Tasmania	Base	1,893.53	2,046.76	2,229.17	2,420.01	2,625.71	2,848.90	3,091.05	3,353.80
	Revised forecast	1,773.00	1,763.00	1,814.00	1,931.00	2,093.00	2,270.00	2,463.00	2,673.00
	%dev. from base	−6.37	−13.86	−18.62	−20.21	−20.29	−20.32	−20.32	−20.30
Northern territory	Base	340.95	396.86	420.75	449.66	487.88	529.35	574.35	623.17
	Revised forecast	321.00	357.00	374.00	400.00	436.00	472.00	512.00	556.00
	%dev. from base	−5.85	−10.04	−11.11	−11.04	−10.63	−10.83	−10.86	−10.78
Australia	Base	162,199.00	177,446.00	193,239.00	209,664.00	227,485.00	246,822.00	267,801.00	290,565.00
	Revised forecast	151,833.00	154,409.00	161,268.00	173,439.00	188,108.00	204,097.00	221,445.00	240,268.00
	%dev. from base	−6.39	−12.98	−16.54	−17.28	−17.31	−17.31	−17.31	−17.31

Each simulation produces year-by-year projections of how the economy would develop over the eight-year period under its particular set of assumptions. By comparing the growth paths of variables in the deviation simulation with their paths in the base simulation, we can deduce the effects on the economy of the change in the growth of foreign-student numbers. We report these effects as percentage deviations, as defined by equation (8).[2]

4.3 National results

(a) Base simulations

In computing the base simulations, we imposed on MONASH the following forecasts determined outside the model

- macroeconomic forecasts supplied by Access Economics;[3]
- forecasts of foreign-currency prices and volumes of agricultural and mineral exports supplied by the Australian Bureau of Agricultural and Resource Economics (ABARE);
- forecasts of international tourist arrivals supplied by the Australian Tourism Forecasting Council (TFC);
- forecasts of industry-policy changes consistent with government plans; and
- forecasts of changes in production technologies and households' preferences based on CoPS' studies of recent history.

Table 4.4 contains the macroeconomic assumptions. These were made prior to the 1997 Asian crisis. In Table 4.5, we report a selection of the corresponding base-case industry projections. They are provided mainly as a point of reference for our discussion of the effects on industries' of changes in foreign-student numbers.

(b) Deviation simulations

In our deviation simulations, we project time paths for variables on the assumption that foreign-student numbers will grow more slowly than is assumed in the base-case simulations. We report the percentage deviations of the levels of variables in the deviation simulations from their levels in the base-case simulations. Percentage deviations for the foreign-student numbers are given in column (5) of Table 4.2. For other national variables, the deviations are plotted in Charts 4.1–4.9.

The explanation of the deviations is in numbered points with italicised headings setting out the main structure.

(1) *The reduction in student numbers is progressively more severe.* Column (5) of Table 4.2 shows that in the deviation simulations foreign-student numbers are assumed to fall progressively further below their base-case levels in the first five years of the projection period. By 2001–02, student numbers are 17.31 per cent below base. In 2001–02, the growth rate of student numbers returns to the base-case rate. Hence, student numbers remain 17.31 per cent below base. Because foreign-student numbers are growing more rapidly than aggregate exports in the base case, and much more rapidly than GDP, absorbing the 17.31 per cent reduction is progressively more difficult through the last four years of the period.

Table 4.4 Base-case forecasts: macroeconomic variables (percentage growth rates)

Variable	1997–98	1998–99	1999–00	2000–1	2001–2	2002–3	2003–4	2004–5	Ave annual 1997–2005
Real GDP	4.30	3.92	3.31	3.83	2.96	2.96	2.96	2.97	3.40
Aggregate employment	3.30	2.40	2.30	3.40	2.00	2.00	2.00	2.00	2.42
Capital stock	1.42	2.18	2.65	2.75	3.02	2.97	2.95	2.95	2.61
Real private consumption	3.60	4.10	3.20	4.10	3.00	3.00	3.00	3.00	3.37
Real private investment	9.40	6.30	3.40	5.80	3.00	3.00	3.00	3.00	4.59
Import volume	8.59	8.12	7.09	8.44	6.28	6.00	6.04	6.09	7.08
Export volume	8.00	8.00	10.00	8.00	7.00	6.52	6.54	6.57	7.57
Real devaluation	0.00	0.00	0.00	0.00	0.00	0.00	0.00	0.00	0.00
Real wage	1.39	−0.73	0.42	1.06	1.00	1.00	1.00	1.00	0.77
Terms of trade	3.49	−1.54	3.35	−2.93	0.00	0.00	0.00	0.00	0.28

Table 4.5 Base-case forecasts: output by selected industry (percentage growth rates)

Industry	1997–98	1998–99	1999–00	2000–1	2001–2	2002–3	2003–4	2004–5	Ave annual 1997–2005
1. Pastoral zone	−7.36	2.42	2.26	2.47	2.32	2.87	2.44	2.38	1.17
2. Wheat-Sheep zone	−6.32	2.01	2.39	3.05	2.64	3.75	4.03	4.00	1.89
3. High-Rainfall zone	−3.18	2.37	1.40	1.12	1.16	1.61	1.53	1.50	0.924
4. Northern beef	0.71	2.49	1.28	1.50	1.13	1.21	1.23	1.21	1.34
5. Milk cattle	4.02	4.64	4.90	4.51	3.65	3.27	3.27	3.25	3.94
6. Other farming export	2.60	3.40	4.91	4.14	2.81	1.86	1.96	2.06	2.96
7. Other farming imp. ctg	4.64	4.20	4.90	4.12	4.05	3.08	3.10	3.02	3.89
8. Poultry	4.56	5.60	4.24	4.48	3.86	3.97	3.96	3.96	4.33
9. Services to agriculture	1.53	2.83	3.52	3.38	2.98	2.79	2.85	2.85	2.84
10. Forestry	4.51	2.91	3.09	2.66	2.58	2.73	2.75	2.76	3.00
11. Fishing	5.39	4.75	2.72	4.02	3.19	2.89	2.91	2.93	3.60
12. Iron ore	1.59	1.50	1.74	2.10	2.96	4.52	4.59	4.66	2.95
13. Non-Ferrous ores	7.02	3.13	5.57	2.58	1.41	5.39	5.38	5.37	4.47
14. Black coal	4.50	5.00	4.45	2.01	3.63	5.83	5.88	5.92	4.64
15. Oil and gas	2.84	3.95	1.71	2.29	4.16	2.43	2.53	2.63	2.82
16. Other minerals	8.05	6.21	7.95	7.21	5.42	4.45	4.42	4.43	6.01
17. Services to mining	−1.22	−2.80	−1.80	−3.30	−3.62	−2.20	−2.15	−2.11	−2.40
18. Meat cattle	4.35	5.93	3.96	4.23	3.45	3.63	3.63	3.63	4.10
23. Bakery products	0.63	0.33	0.49	0.55	−0.12	−0.08	−0.08	−0.07	0.21
25. Seafood and sugar	−0.43	3.96	3.73	4.12	2.88	1.85	1.82	1.80	2.46
26. Soft drinks	3.87	3.34	3.23	3.77	2.53	2.91	2.85	2.79	3.16
27. Beer	1.14	0.46	0.00	0.88	−0.63	−0.90	−1.02	−1.15	−0.16
28. Other alcoholic drinks	9.18	8.14	9.69	9.33	7.79	6.93	6.93	6.95	8.11
29. Tobacco products	−0.32	−0.76	−0.44	−0.65	−1.32	−1.01	−0.96	−0.91	−0.80
30. Fibre processing	7.21	3.24	2.98	0.49	6.58	2.48	2.57	2.09	3.43
31. Synthetic yarn	8.75	7.02	8.13	8.19	7.49	7.21	7.24	7.28	7.66
42. Fittings	6.44	4.13	−0.04	−1.24	1.19	1.17	1.18	1.19	1.73

Table 4.5 (Continued)

Industry	1997–98	1998–99	1999–00	2000–1	2001–2	2002–3	2003–4	2004–5	Ave annual 1997–2005
47. Newspapers and books	1.40	0.68	0.61	0.92	-0.04	-0.06	-0.06	-0.07	0.42
49. Fertilizer	-2.82	-2.11	-1.62	-1.81	-2.43	-2.07	-1.98	-1.92	-2.10
58. Clay products	7.25	4.20	0.58	-1.43	1.50	1.44	1.45	1.45	2.02
59. Cement	6.11	3.25	0.21	0.50	0.67	0.73	0.71	0.68	1.59
60. Readymix concrete	9.00	5.81	1.70	2.03	2.66	2.74	2.73	2.73	3.65
61. Pipes	9.42	6.44	3.05	3.89	3.56	3.71	3.71	3.70	4.67
64. Non-Ferrous metals	5.86	6.08	6.97	6.96	4.16	4.97	4.95	4.92	5.60
73. Electronic equipment	13.43	12.32	13.64	13.49	10.89	10.00	10.02	10.03	11.72
77. Construction machinery	0.47	3.58	10.91	9.52	7.73	5.75	5.91	5.99	6.19
79. Leather products	10.61	9.60	14.70	12.08	9.99	7.95	8.17	8.36	10.16
87. Residential building	12.91	8.51	0.10	-4.34	3.88	3.89	3.90	3.91	3.99
90. Retail trade	3.61	4.00	3.07	4.30	3.02	3.05	3.13	3.20	3.42
95. Water transport	1.62	1.99	2.17	1.00	1.38	2.73	2.86	2.98	2.09
96. Air transport	8.82	7.89	7.64	8.54	6.95	6.98	6.93	6.88	7.58
98. Communication	9.13	8.55	7.89	8.86	7.69	7.70	7.70	7.69	8.15
99. Banking	9.00	8.39	7.90	8.50	7.64	7.56	7.53	7.50	8.00
100. Non-Bank finance	9.54	9.43	8.86	9.14	8.20	7.95	7.90	7.85	8.61
101. Investment services	10.42	9.76	10.05	10.30	9.11	8.93	8.83	8.75	9.52
102. Insurance	9.79	9.66	8.67	9.15	7.48	7.39	7.30	7.19	8.32
104. Ownership of dwellings	2.32	2.76	3.00	2.80	2.39	2.41	2.43	2.45	2.57
108. Education	4.09	3.41	2.30	3.19	3.38	3.39	3.40	3.41	3.32

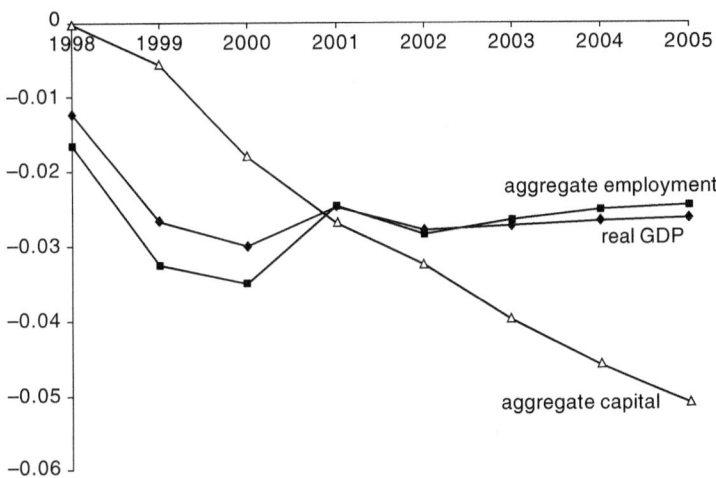

Chart 4.1 Real GDP and factor inputs (% deviation from base-case forecasts).

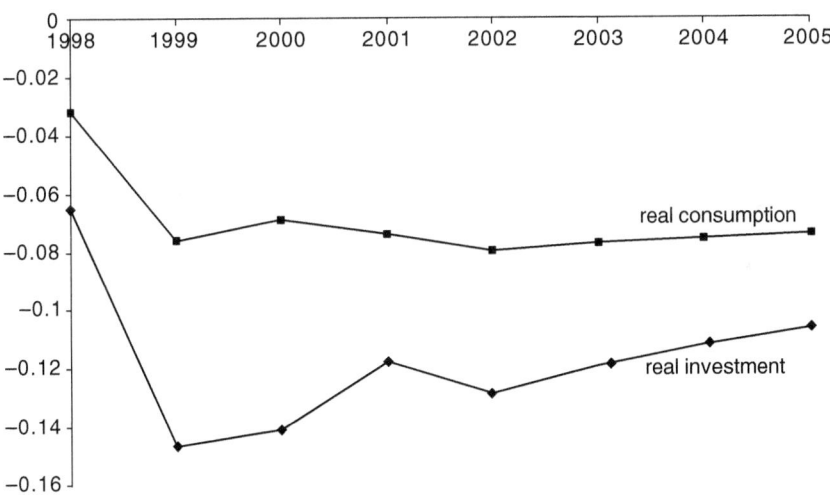

Chart 4.2 Real investment and consumption (% deviation from base-case forecasts).

(2) *The reduction in foreign-student numbers affects the economy mainly via the external accounts.* It reduces foreign-exchange earnings but our macroeconomic assumptions do not allow the balance of trade to make an equivalent move towards deficit. In fact, as is indicated by Charts 4.1 and 4.2, gross national expenditure (GNE) declines relative to GDP (point 3 below), moving the trade balance towards surplus.

(3) *Real GNE declines relative to real GDP.* Chart 4.1 shows that the reduction in student numbers moves GDP below base throughout the projection period and

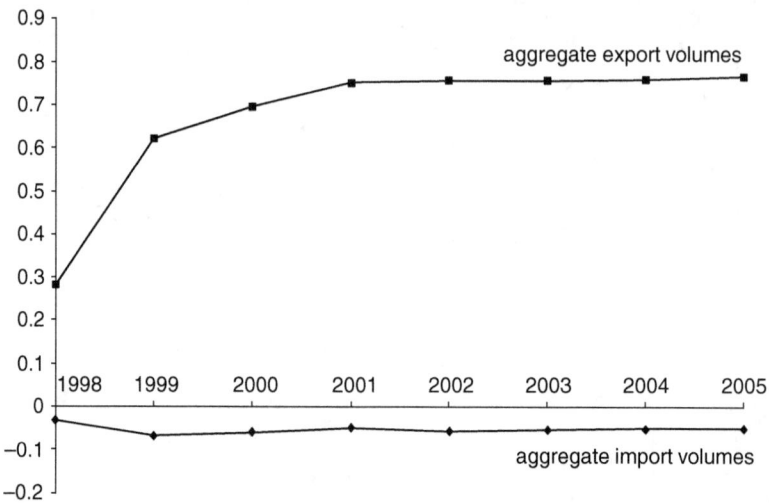

Chart 4.3 Aggregate export and import volumes (% deviation from base-case forecasts).

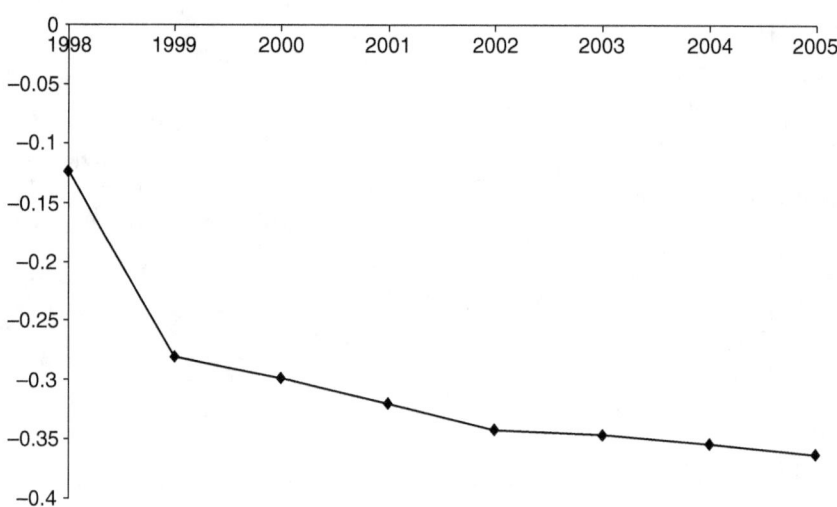

Chart 4.4 Real exchange rate (positive means appreciation) (% deviation from base-case forecasts).

causes the capital stock to fall progressively relative to base (point 7 below.) Aggregate consumption (Chart 4.2) is assumed to move in line with the change (relative to base) in real national income. National income is reduced in the deviation by declines in real GDP and in the terms of trade (Chart 4.6, point 5 below). Hence, the fall in real consumption is larger than the fall in GDP. Real

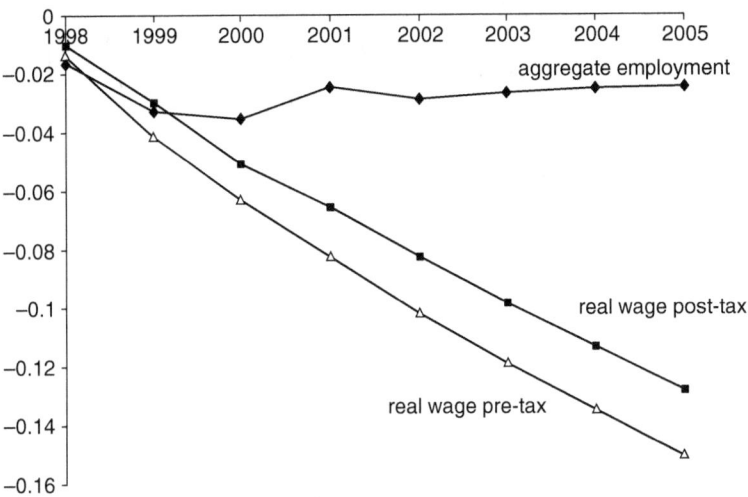

Chart 4.5 Real wage rates and aggregate employment (% deviation from base-case forecasts).

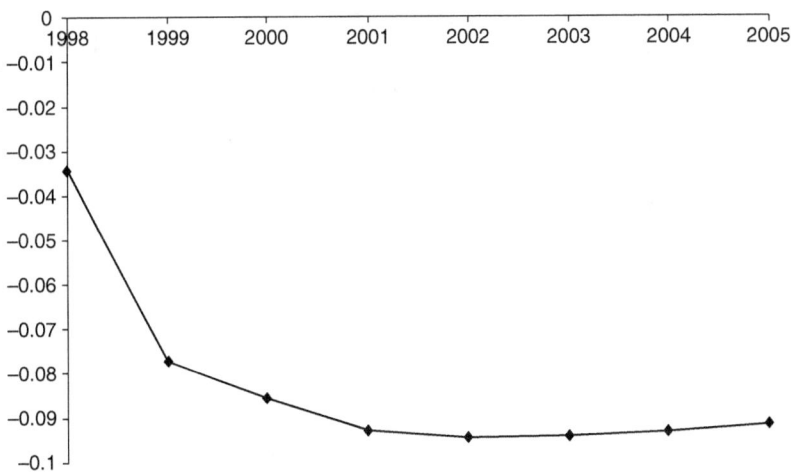

Chart 4.6 Terms of trade (% deviation from base-case forecasts).

investment (Chart 4.2) declines even more sharply, consistent with the decline in the capital stock. Government spending is assumed to be unaffected by the decline in student numbers but the declines in consumption and investment are sufficient to ensure that real GNE declines relative to real GDP.

(4) *Real depreciation moves the balance of trade towards surplus.* The requirement that the trade balance improve relative to base despite the loss of foreign-exchange earnings from foreign students means that the real exchange rate must depreciate

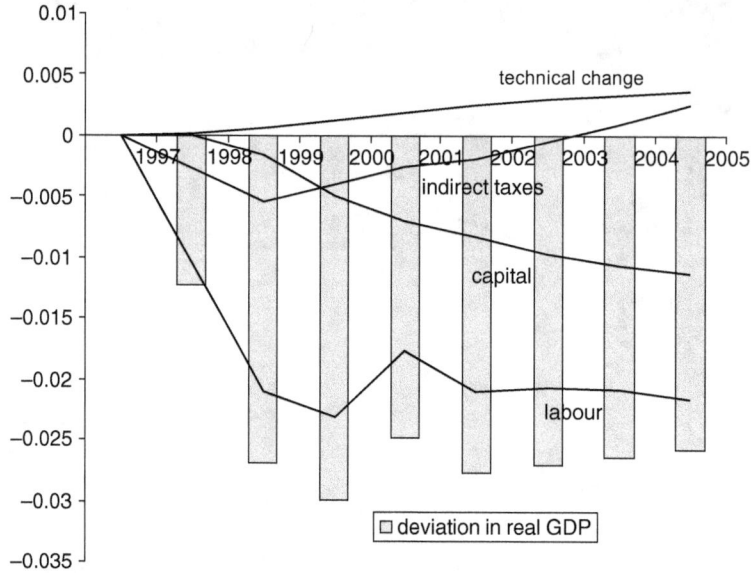

Chart 4.7 Percentage point contributions to the growth in real GDP.

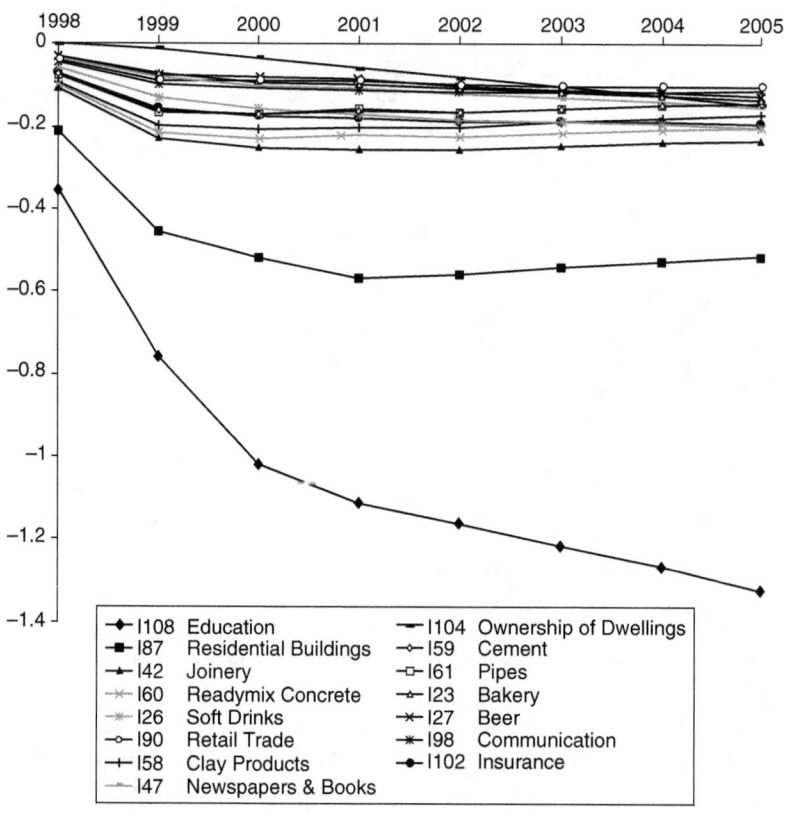

→	I108	Education	— I104 Ownership of Dwellings
▪	I87	Residential Buildings	◇ I59 Cement
▲	I42	Joinery	□ I61 Pipes
✳	I60	Readymix Concrete	▵ I23 Bakery
✳	I26	Soft Drinks	✳ I27 Beer
○	I90	Retail Trade	✳ I98 Communication
+	I58	Clay Products	● I102 Insurance
─	I47	Newspapers & Books	

Chart 4.8 Output of the main losers (% deviation from base-case forecasts).

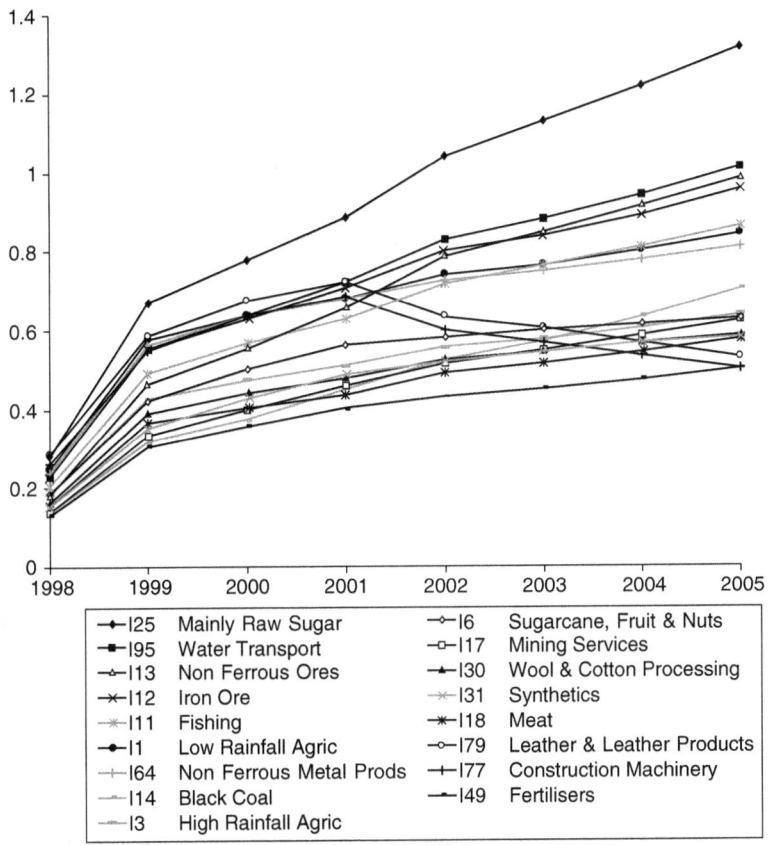

Chart 4.9 Output of the main winners (% deviation from base-case forecasts).

(Chart 4.4). The required depreciation increases throughout the period. For the first five years this is due largely to foreign-student numbers moving further below base. Thereafter, the rate of growth of student numbers returns to base and the continuing increase in the required depreciation reflects the increasing burden of the loss of foreign-student numbers (point 1 above). The real depreciation moves the volumes of non-education exports well above base (Chart 4.3). It also leads to the substitution of domestic supplies for imports. But despite this and despite the marked decline in real GNE, especially its import-intensive investment component, the decline in import volumes relative to base is small. The reason is that the exports that are stimulated by the depreciation, especially manufactured exports, use imports intensively as inputs.

(5) *The terms of trade deteriorate relative to base* (Chart 4.6). This is a counterpart of the expansion in the volumes of non-education exports noted in point 4. MONASH assumes that foreign demand schedules are less than infinitely elastic. Hence to export more, the economy must accept some reduction in the

foreign-currency prices of exports. Another factor is that in the base case, the foreign-currency prices received for educating foreign students grow more rapidly than the foreign-currency prices of non-education exports. Hence, shifting the composition of exports away from education reduces the terms of trade even if no foreign currency prices deviate from their base-case paths. As noted in point 3, the decline in the terms of trade contributes to the decline in real consumption relative to real GDP.

(6) *Employment declines initially leading to reductions in the real-wage and the capital stock.* Educational services are labour-intensive relative to the activities that are stimulated by the decline in foreign-student numbers (point 8 below). Hence, the decline in student numbers initially reduces aggregate employment relative to base (Chart 4.1 or 4.5). In the deviation simulation, we assume that so long as employment is below base, workers accept reductions in post-tax real wage rates (Chart 4.5). This allows aggregate employment to revert towards base later in the projection period. However, the reversion is never complete because the employment-reducing pressure continually increases, reflecting the increasing burden of the loss in student numbers (point 1). In accepting wage reductions, workers are assumed not to anticipate this, just to react to the current reduction in employment. The decline in real wage rates causes all industries to move to lower capital/labour ratios. Hence, the aggregate capital stock declines (Chart 4.1). In Chart 4.5 the real pre-tax wage deviates further from base than does the real post-tax wage. The cut in student numbers allows a reduction in the income tax rate because indirect tax revenue rises. This is a consequence of the induced depreciation of the real exchange rate, which raises the prices of imports and domestically produced import-competing goods, increasing the revenue raised from the *ad valorem* taxes levied on them.

(7) *Real GDP falls below base throughout the period.* The reduction in foreign-student numbers causes the economy to employ less labour and less capital (point 6). This is accompanied by a reduction in real GDP at market prices (Chart 4.1). The percentage reduction in real GDP is greater than the percentage reduction in the aggregate factor input early in the period but smaller than it in the last few years. Two mechanisms underlie the differences, both of which follow from structural changes in the economy induced by the fall in foreign-student numbers (point 8).

The first is that total factor productivity increases. This occurs because structural change favours industries experiencing rapid factor-saving technical change at the expense of industries experiencing slow factor-saving technical change. Note that each industry's rate of factor-saving technical change is assumed to be the same in the deviation simulation as it was in the base case. By the end of the period, this productivity effect dominates.

The second mechanism is that real GDP (market prices) diverges from real GDP (factor cost) because structural change favours industries producing lightly taxed commodities. Real GDP (market prices) decreases when factors switch from heavily taxed to lightly taxed items because the switch reduces the value of output from the consumers' point of view. At the beginning of the period, this tax effect dominates.

Chart 4.7 shows contributions to the deviation in real GDP (market prices) in each year of the projection period. The contribution of the technology term is positive, partially offsetting the negative effects on real GDP of the declines in primary-factor inputs. The contribution of the tax term is negative in the early part of the period, reinforcing the negative effects of the declines in primary-factor inputs.

(8) *Some industries lose but others gain.* Chart 4.8 shows the industries whose output levels are most severely depressed (relative to base) by the decline in student numbers. The industry that is most adversely affected is industry 108 (Education). This is the industry for which foreign students' expenditure accounts for the largest share of total sales. Industry 87 (Residential building) shrinks relative to base because the decline in foreign students' demand for housing reduces investment in the housing sector. Many of the other industries shown as losers in Chart 4.8 depend heavily on Education (47 and 98) or Residential building (42, 60, 61, 58 and 59).

Chart 4.9 shows the industries that have most to gain from the decline in foreign-student numbers. Most of the gains derive from the exchange-rate effects on non-education exports (point 4). The extent to which exchange-rate depreciation stimulates exports depends, in part, on the extent to which the exporters use imported inputs. Manufactured exports typically require more imported inputs than traditional agricultural and mineral exports. This explains why the pattern of stimulation of manufacturing industries (79 and 77) differs from the pattern experienced by the mineral industries (13, 12, 64, 14 and 17) and the agricultural industries (25, 1, 3, 6 and 18).

To assess the significance of the industry results for structural adjustment in the economy, we can compare the deviations in Charts 4.8 and 4.9 with the base-case projections in Table 4.5. Of particular interest is whether any of the industries affected adversely by the decline in foreign-student numbers (Chart 4.8) are slow-growing in the base case. The two most adversely affected industries (108 Education and 87 Residential building) both have base-case growth projections close to the GDP growth rate and should be able to accommodate the fall in student numbers without extreme adjustment problems. Education, for example, would experience a reduction in its average annual growth rate from about 3.3 to about 3.15 per cent. There are some industries in Chart 4.8 that have slow growth rates in the base case, for example, 42, 47, 23, 27 and 59. But the adverse effects on them of the decline in foreign-student numbers are small. The list in Chart 4.9 of industries favourably affected by the decline in student numbers includes several industries (13, 64, 14, 18, 31, 79, 69 and 77) which have growth rates in the base case well above the GDP growth rate.

4.4 *Regional results*

We use a top-down method to infer from our economy-wide results the likely effects of the reduction in foreign-student numbers on each of the states and territories.[4] It requires a distinction between goods that can readily be traded between regions (called national commodities) and goods (mainly services) for which there is no inter-regional trade (called local commodities).

For national commodities, we assume that the regional distribution of output is independent of the regional distribution of demand. For each national commodity, the percentage change in output at the regional level induced by the reduction in student numbers is assumed to be the same as the percentage change in output induced at the economy-wide level. Included in the top-down method is the assumption that the demand in each region for local commodities must be satisfied by output within the region. Hence, the regional distribution of changes in foreign-student numbers is important in determining the regional distribution of the corresponding output changes for local commodities. Education and housing expenses are both classified as local commodities.

Chart 4.10 shows the percentage deviations from base of real gross regional products (GRP) generated by the slowdowns in foreign-student numbers reported in Table 4.3. The slowdowns generate increases in real GRP relative to base in some regions even though at the national level they cause a reduction in real GDP (Charts 4.1 and 4.7). Table 4.6 provides the key to understanding the results. A region is likely to do relatively well (poorly) from the decline in student numbers if

- foreign students' expenditure accounts for a relatively low (high) share of its GRP (first column of Table 4.6); or
- industries favourably affected by the reduction in student numbers (Chart 4.9) account for a relatively high (low) share of its GRP (second column of Table 4.6); or
- the slowdown in student numbers in the region is small (large) relative to the economy-wide average slowdown (final column of Table 4.6).

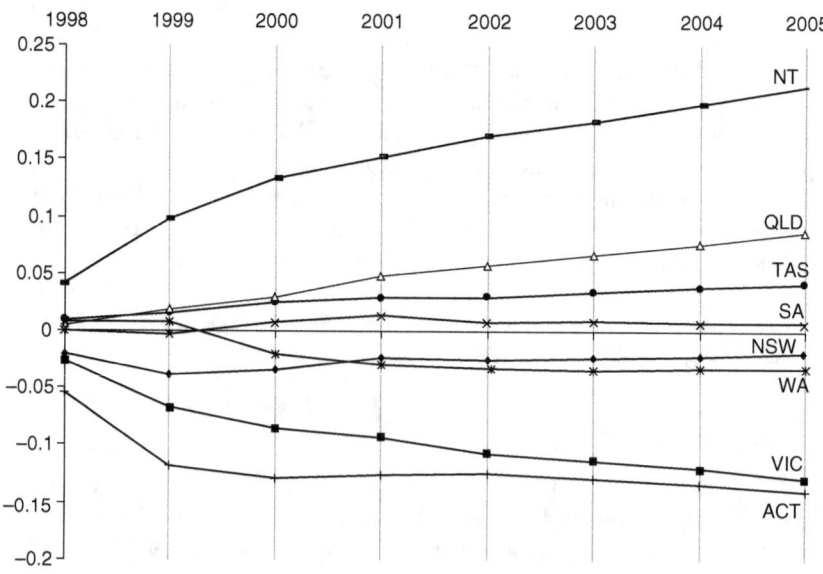

Chart 4.10 Gross regional state product (% deviation from base-case forecasts).

Table 4.6 Selected regional data

Region	Percentage shares in GRP in 1997–98 data of		Severity of slowdown in foreign-student numbers (Table 4.3)
	Foreign students' expenditure	Main winners (Chart 4.9)	
NSW	0.751	0.041	Below average
Victoria	0.653	0.044	Above average
Queensland	0.678	0.081	Below average
WA	0.902	0.131	Above average
SA	0.364	0.048	Slightly above average
ACT	0.689	0.001	Below average
Tasmania	0.321	0.051	Above average
NT	0.128	0.065	Below average
Australia	0.677	0.058	Average

According to Chart 4.10, the Northern Territory (NT) is the region most favourably affected. For the NT, all three of the factors identified in Table 4.6 exert favourable influences. Queensland is the second most favourably affected region. The share of foreign students' expenditure in its GRP is close to the economy-wide average, but the share of industries favourably affected by the reduction in student numbers is relatively high and the slowdown in student numbers in the region is relatively small. For Tasmania and South Australia, the shares of foreign students' expenditure in GRP are relatively low. This favourable factor is enough to outweigh the fact that the slowdowns in student numbers in Tasmania and SA are more rapid than the average slowdown and the fact that the shares of industries favourably affected by the reduction in student numbers are a little below the economy-wide average.

Both the Australian Capital Territory (ACT) and Victoria experience more severe percentage declines in real GRP (relative to base) than the corresponding percentage decline in real GDP. The ACT is the region most adversely affected. The reason is that the share of industries favourably affected by the reduction in student numbers in the ACT's GRP is very low. For Victoria, the share of foreign students' expenditure in GRP is close to the economy-wide average. However, the share of industries favourably affected by the reduction in student numbers is below average and the slowdown in student numbers is relatively large.

Western Australia (WA) and New South Wales (NSW) both experience percentage declines in real GRP (relative to base) that are close to the corresponding percentage decline in real GDP. The share of industries favourably affected by the reduction in student numbers in the WA's GRP is very high, a favourable factor, but the share of foreign students' expenditure is also high and the slowdown in student numbers in WA exceeds the economy-wide average. The share of industries favourably affected by the reduction in student numbers in the GRP of NSW is below the economy-wide average and the share of foreign students' expenditure in GRP is a little above the economy-wide average. Off-setting these adverse factors is the fact that the decline in student numbers is slightly below average.

5   Conclusion: relationship to dynamic CGE analysis based on steady states

Much of the current work on dynamic CGE modelling, especially in the North American literature, emphasises what-if policy analysis using steady-state base solutions. Under this approach, the first step is to construct a steady-state solution. The time path(s) for some variable(s) are then disturbed from their steady-state values and the model is re-solved, eventually achieving a new steady state. Results are presented as deviations from the initial steady state.

In contrast, our approach pays no attention to steady-state properties. Our base-year data always exhibit features confirming that in the base year, the economy was far from a steady state or a balanced growth path. For example, ratios of net investment to capital stocks vary widely across sectors, as do rates of return on capital. Moreover, we recognise realistic phenomena such as non-homothetic preferences, and export demand elasticities that vary across com-modities. We could design simulations in which we set exogenous variables to reflect balanced growth and then allow the model to run out to a balanced growth path. But it would take many periods to do so. While this might be of theoretical interest, our view is that it has very little relevance to practical policy issues. In our experience, even for long-term policy issues such as greenhouse, policy makers are concerned with time horizons far shorter than are relevant to the re-establishment of steady states in CGE models.

Our work suggests that specific features of the base-case assumptions do matter in assessing the effects of shocks within horizons of policy interest. If this is true, it is important to use as a base case a realistic forecast of how the economy might develop in the absence of the shock. In general, such realistic forecasts will not show the economy on a steady-state or balanced-growth path, or on a smooth transition towards one. Another reason to use realistic forecasts as base cases for policy analysis is that they allow issues of structural adjustment to be addressed.

The policy analysis presented in Section 4.4 provides some examples of these points.

- Several aspects of the results depend on the export of education services growing rapidly in the base case (column 2 of Table 4.2). Because of this, the reduction in foreign-student numbers represents a larger shock for the economy in each successive year, even after 2001–02 when the percentage loss of foreign students has plateaued (column 5 of Table 4.2). For example, this accounts for the failure of employment to return to base (Chart 4.1 or Chart 4.5) despite the operation of a wage-adjustment mechanism (point 6 of Section 4.4.3). It accounts also for the fact that the required exchange-rate depreciation increases throughout the period (Chart 4.4 and point 4 of Section 4.4.3).

- Part of the reason for the terms-of-trade loss shown in Chart 4.6 is our assumption that the foreign-currency prices received for educating foreign students are rising more rapidly in the base forecasts than are the prices of the non-education exports that are stimulated when foreign-student numbers decline.
- The technical-change contribution to our decomposition of the change in real GDP (Chart 4.7) depends on a reallocation of activity from industries that are assumed to experience relatively slow input-saving technical change to industries assumed to experience relatively rapid technical change.
- Because we have explicit assumptions about the growth prospects of industries in the base forecasts (Table 4.5), we were able to conclude that the adverse effects of the slowdown in foreign-student numbers on the growth prospects of the Education and Residential building industries are unlikely to present structural-adjustment problems.

We are not persuaded that it is necessary to base dynamic CGE calculations on steady-state or balanced-growth paths. But if we were to become convinced of this, we would favour a three-part procedure for policy analysis. First, we would generate such a path by making appropriate assumptions about exogenous variables. Then we would shock the model away from this path to produce a realistic forecast over the period of policy interest. This would involve shocks to exogenous variables through the policy-relevant period that are very different from those required for steady states or balanced growth. For the very long run (usually beyond much policy interest) the shocks could evolve to be consistent with re-establishment of a steady state or a balanced growth path. Shocks through the policy-relevant period would include, for example,

- patterns of input-saving/using technical change that are non-uniform across inputs and users;
- shifts in export-demand and import-supply schedules that are non-uniform among commodities;
- changes in government policy instruments that alter the structure of the economy; and
- commodity-biased shifts in household preferences.

In the final part of the three-part procedure, we would conduct our policy analysis as a deviation from the realistic base forecast, not from the steady state.

Notes

1 Note that this calculation is identical to a comparative-static simulation in which we take the solution for the base year (0) as the base solution for year 1 and impose year-1 shocks calculated as the percentage differences between the values of the exogenous variables forecast for year 1 and their base-year values.

2 In the simulations, we assumed that all of the fees paid by the students (i.e. their entire expenditure on category 13 in Table 4.1) are absorbed by the cost of the resources required to provide the corresponding educational services. An alternative assumption that we explored in an earlier version (Dixon *et al.* 1998) is that the resource cost of providing the services is less than the fees that the students pay. This assumption would be appropriate if there are large economies of scale in the *Education* industry.

3 Access Economics is a prominent macroeconomic forecasting agency in Australia.

4 The method is described in detail in Dixon *et al.*, 1982 (chapter 6). ORANI: a Multi-sectoral Model of the Australian Economy, North Holland Publishing Company.

References

Adams, P. D. and Parmenter, B. R. (1999) 'Revised projections of future greenhouse gas emissions', report prepared for the Australian Greenhouse Office, July, pp. 23.

Dixon, P. B., Horridge, J. M. and Johnson, D. T. (1991) 'ORANI projections for the Australian economy for 1989 to 2020 with special reference to the Land Freight Industry', *Empirical Economics*, 16(1), 3–24.

Dixon, P. B. and McDonald, D. (1992) 'Creating 1990–91 input–output tables for Australia by ORANI simulation', paper presented to the 16th Annual Conference of the Australian Regional Science Association, Ballarat University College, December.

Dixon, P. B. and Parmenter, B. R. (1996) 'Computable general equilibrium modelling for policy analysis and forecasting', in: Amman, H. M., Kendrick, D. A. and Rust, J. (eds), *Handbook of Computational Economics, Volume 1*, Amsterdam: North-Holland, pp. 4–85.

Dixon, P. B., Parmenter, B. R. and Rimmer, M. T. (1998) 'The effects of foreign students on the Australian economy and its regions', paper presented at the 27th Conference of Economists, University of Sydney, September, pp. 42.

Dixon, P. B., Parmenter, B. R. and Rimmer, M. T. (2000) 'Forecasting and policy analysis with a dynamic CGE model of Australia', in Harrison, G. W., Hougaard Jensen, S. E., Pedersen, L. H. and Rutherford, T. F. (eds) 'Using Dynamic General Equilibrium Models for Policy Analysis', North Holland Publishing Company, pp. 363–405.

Dixon, P. B., Parmenter, B. R., Sutton, J. and Vincent, D. P. (1982) *ORANI: A Multisectoral Model of the Australian Economy*, Amsterdam: North Holland Publishing Co.

Dixon, P. B. and Rimmer, M. T. (2001) 'Dynamic general equilibrium modelling: A practical guide and documentation of MONASH', Centre of Policy Studies, Monash University, pp. 549.

Harrison, J. and Pearson, K. R. (1994) 'An Introduction to Gempack, Second Edition', *GEMPACK Document No. 1*, CoPS/IMPACT Project, Monash University, April.

Johansen, L. (1960) *A Multisectoral Model of Economic Growth*, Amsterdam: North Holland Publishing Company (2nd edn 1974).

McDougall, R. A. and Dixon, P. B. (1996) 'Analysing the economy-wide effects of an energy tax: Results for Australia from the ORANI-E Model', in Bouma, W. J., Pearman, G. I. and Manning, M. M. (eds) 'Greenhouse: coping with climate change', CSIRO, Australia, pp. 607–619.

Meagher, G. A., Parmenter, B. R., Rimmer, R. J. and Clements, K. W. (1985) 'ORANI-WINE: Tax issues and the Australian wine industry', *Review of Marketing and Agricultural Economics*, 53, 47–62.

Parliament of the Commonwealth of Australia (1999) *Senate Select Committee on a New Tax System: First Report*, Parliament House, Canberra, February.

Pearson, K. R. (1986) 'Automating the computation of solutions of large economic models', *Economic Modelling*, 7, 385–95.

Part II

Imperfect competition

5 An applied intertemporal general equilibrium model of trade and production with scale economies, product differentiation and imperfect competition*

Jean Mercenier

1 Introduction

This paper provides an investigation of the potential welfare and employment effects of Europe's move to a single market, using a state-of-the-art large-scale applied general equilibrium model of trade and production. The model is intertemporal, multicountry and multisectoral. Increasing returns to scale are introduced in some production activities, with firms behaving as oligopolies. There is, furthermore, product differentiation at the individual producer level. Competition is either of Bertrand or of Cournot type: the oligopolistic game between firms is Nash in prices or in output.[1] In the short run, the market structure is fixed (i.e. the number of oligopolists remains constant) and imperfections such as oligopolistic profits and wage rigidities may exist. These imperfections vanish in the long run, the last period being characterized by stock-flow equilibrium consistent with steady-state growth and Chamberlinian entry and exit of firms in the industry.

In the initial equilibrium, national markets within Europe are segmented: because of non-tariff barriers that prevent consumers from cross-border arbitraging, non-competitive firms are modelled as price-discriminating oligopolists. The policy experiment – the completion of the European Single Market – is modelled as the elimination of the possibility for oligopolistic firms to price discriminate between client countries within Europe. The analysis is performed under two alternative labour market assumptions. Wages are either assumed flexible so that the labour market continuously clears at the initial level of employment, or alternatively, they are held fixed in terms of the consumer price index in the short run so that aggregate short-term employment is demand

*A first version of this paper was written while I was at the CRDE and the Département de sciences économiques, Université de Montréal. Financial support from the FCAR of the Government of Québec and the SSHRC of the Government of Canada is gratefully acknowledged.

determined; long-term employment is also affected by this rigidity because of labour market hysteresis. None of these two extreme scenarios is meant to be realistic; they nevertheless provide a range of estimates that would presumably include the predictions made with a more realistic assumption.

Though the paper provides results on an important real world policy problem, these are only very briefly discussed here, the emphasis being on the description of the mathematical structure of the model, on calibration techniques, on temporal aggregation issues and on computational considerations. For other policy applications, see Mercenier and Yeldan (1997, 1999).

The paper is organised as follows. A formal presentation of the model is made in the next section. Section 3 introduces the trade policy experiment and presents the welfare criterion by which this policy is to be evaluated. Calibration and computational considerations are made in Section 4. The results are presented and discussed in Section 5.

2   The model

2.1   *Dynamic structure*

In each country[2], there is a single representative household, competitive, infinitely lived and utility maximizing. The domestic household owns all the countries' primary factors, namely labour and physical capital, which it rents to domestic firms only, at competitive prices w and r respectively (for notational convenience, I neglect the country subscript in this subsection). Labour is in fixed supply L. The decision variables of the household are consumption (C) and investment (I). In making these optimal decisions, it has access to international financial markets on which it can borrow or lend. Its intertemporal decision problem is to maximize

$$\int_0^\infty e^{-\rho t} \frac{C(t)^{1-\gamma}}{1-\gamma}\, dt, \tag{1}$$

subject to

$$\dot{K}(t) = I(t) - \delta K(t), \tag{2}$$

$$\int_0^\infty e^{-\rho t} \left[p_c(t) C(t) + p_I(t) I(t) \right] dt \leq$$
$$\int_0^\infty e^{-\rho t} \left[w(t) L(t) + r(t) K(t) + \sum_s \pi_s(t) + G(t) \right] dt + F(0), \tag{3}$$

$K(0)$, $F(0)$ given. Equation (2) accounts for capital accumulation with exponential depreciation. Equation (3) is the household's intertemporal budget constraint. It specifies that the sum of discounted stream of consumption and investment expenditures (for convenience, all prices are defined as undiscounted) cannot exceed the discounted sum of revenues earned from primary factor ownership and government transfers $G(t)$, plus initial holding of foreign assets $F(0)$. The term $\sum_s \pi_s(t)$ in the budget constraint accounts for the possibility that, in the short run, because of unexpected shocks to imperfectly competitive industries, supranormal profits may add to capital rental earnings. All countries have the same constant discount rates ρ.

2.2   Instantaneous equilibrium structure

I now neglect the time index. I identify sectors of activity by indices s and t, with S representing the set of all industries, so that $s, t = 1, \ldots, S$. The set S is partitioned into the subset of competitive, constant return-to-scale sectors, denoted C, and the subset of non-competitive, increasing return-to-scale industries, denoted $\bar{C}$.[3] Countries are identified by indices i and j, with $i, j = 1, \ldots, W$ and $W = EU \cup ROW$, where the first subset represents the European Union, and ROW represents the Rest of the World. To keep track of the trade flows, I follow the usual practice which identifies the first two indices with, respectively, the country and the industry supplying the good and, when appropriate, the next two with the client country and industry.[4]

Households

For exposition ease, I break the household i's static decision making into a 'consumer' and an 'investor' choice problem; this is innocuous, given my separability assumptions on preferences and investment technologies. The domestic consumer values products of competitive industries from different countries as imperfect substitutes (the Armington 1969 assumption), while the consumer treats as specific each good produced by individual firms operating in the non-competitive industries (the Dixit–Stiglitz 1977 specification). This is represented by a two-level utility function. The first level combines consumption goods ($c_{.si}$), assuming constant expenditure shares (ρ_{si}). The second level determines the optimal composition of the consumption aggregates in terms of geographical origin for competitive industries or in terms of the individual firm's product for the non-competitive sectors. Formally, the consumer's preferences are

$$\log C_i = \sum_{s \in S} \rho_{si} \log c_{.si}, \qquad \sum_{s \in S} \rho_{si} = 1, \tag{4}$$

$$c_{.si} = \left[\sum_{j \in W} n_{js} \delta^c_{jsi} c_{jsi}^{(\sigma^f_s - 1)/\sigma^f_s} \right]^{\sigma^f_s/(\sigma^f_s - 1)} \qquad \text{(with } n_{js} = 1 \text{ for } s \in C),$$

where δ^c_{jsi} are share parameters, σ^f_s the substitution elasticities, and n_{js} denotes the number of symmetric firms operating in country j, sector s.[5] Observe that when $s \in C$, c_{jsi} denotes the sales to the consumer of the whole industry s of country j, whereas when $s \in \bar{C}$, it represents the sales of a single representative oligopolist. For goods that are non-traded, $\delta_{jsi}^c = 0$, $\forall j \neq i$.

The consumer maximizes (4) with respect to c_{jsi}, subject to:

$$p_{ci} C_i \geq \sum_{j \in W} \sum_{s \in S} (1 + \tau_{jsi}) p_{jsi} n_{js} c_{jsi} \quad \text{(with } n_{js} = 1 \text{ for } s \in C\text{)}, \tag{5}$$

where τ_{jsi} are tariff rates, p_{jsi} prices on which consumers have no influence and the term on the left side, aggregate consumption expenditures at current prices, results from the intertemporal decision of the household.

The investor's problem is to determine the optimal composition of the domestic investment good; for this, the investor maximises (6) with respect to I_{jsi}:

$$\log I_i = \sum_{s \in S} \omega_{si} \log I_{si}, \qquad \sum_{s \in S} \omega_{si} = 1, \tag{6}$$

$$I_{si} = \left[\sum_{j \in W} n_{js} \delta_{jsi}^I I_{jsi}^{(\sigma_s^f - 1)/\sigma_s^f} \right]^{\sigma_s^f/(\sigma_s^f - 1)} \quad \text{(with } n_{js} = 1 \text{ for } s \in C\text{)},$$

subject to

$$p_{Ii} I_i \geq \sum_{j \in W} \sum_{s \in S} (1 + \tau_{jsi}) p_{jsi} n_{js} I_{jsi}, \tag{7}$$

where again τ_{jsi} are tariff rates, p_{jsi} prices that investors take as given, and the term on the left side of the inequality results from the intertemporal decision of the household (i.e. aggregate investment expenditures at current prices). Observe that the share parameters δ_{jsi}^c and δ_{jsi}^I in (4) and (6) are specific to each decision problem, so that price responsiveness of the two final demand components will differ, even though the 'consumer' and the 'investor' are assumed to have the same substitution elasticities (σ_s^f) since no econometric information is available on potential differences.

Firms

Competitive industries   In competitive industries, the representative firms of country i, sector s, operate with constant return-to-scale technologies, combining variable capital (K_{is}^ν) and labour (L_{is}^ν) as well as intermediate inputs (x_{jtis}). Material inputs are introduced in the production function in a manner similar to the way consumption goods are treated in the preferences of households: with an Armington specification for goods produced by competitive industries and with an Ethier (1982) specification (i.e. with product differentiation at the firm level) in the imperfectly competitive sectors. Input demands by country i's representative producer of sector $s \in C$ result from minimization of the variable unit cost ν_{is}

$$\nu_{is} Q_{is} = \sum_{j \in W} \sum_{t \in S} (1 + \tau_{jti}) p_{jti} n_{ji} x_{jtis} + w_i L_{is}^{\nu} + r_i K_{is}^{\nu} \quad \text{(with } n_{jt} = 1 \text{ for } s \in C\text{)},$$

(8)

for a given level of output Q_{is}, such that

$$\log Q_{is} \leq \alpha_{Lis} \log L_{is}^{\nu} + \alpha_{Kis} \log K_{is}^{\nu} + \sum_{t \in S} \alpha_{tis} \log x_{.tis} \tag{9}$$

$$x_{.tis} = \left[\sum_{j \in W} n_{jt} \beta_{jtis} x_{jtis}^{(\sigma_t^x - 1)/\sigma_t^x} \right]^{\sigma_t^x/(\sigma_t^x - 1)} \quad \text{(with } n_{js} = 1 \text{ for } s \in C\text{)},$$

where the α and β are share parameters with

$$\alpha_{Lis} + \alpha_{Kis} + \sum_{t \in S} \alpha_{tis} = 1,$$

$\beta_{jtis} = 0 \ \forall j \neq i$ if t is non-traded and σ_t^x has the same interpretation as σ_s^f in (4) and (6).

Cost minimization implies marginal cost pricing ($p_{isj} = \nu_{is}$) and zero profits ($\pi_{is} = 0$) in the competitive sectors.

Noncompetitive industries   Noncompetitive industries have increasing returns to scale in production. I model this by assuming that in addition to variable costs associated with technological constraints similar to (8), (9), the individual firm in country i sector s, faces fixed primary factor costs. This introduces a wedge between total unit costs V_{is} and marginal costs ν_{is}:

$$V_{is} = \nu_{is} + \frac{w_i L_{is}^F + r_i K_{is}^F}{Q_{is}}, \quad s \in \bar{C}, \tag{10}$$

where $Q_{is}, L_{is}^F, K_{is}^F$, denote, respectively, the individual firm's output, fixed labour and fixed capital.

Because of the presence of various forms of non-tariff barriers that prevent cross-border price arbitraging, national economies are treated as segmented markets. Consequently, the non-competitive firm facing demand segmentation takes advantage of the monopoly power it has on each individual country market. For this purpose, the firm is endowed with the knowledge of preferences (4) and technologies (6), (9) of its clients. It then performs a partial equilibrium profit maximization calculation assuming that in each country, each individual client's current-price expenditure on the whole industry is unaffected by its own strategic action z_{isj}, so that[6]

$$\frac{\partial p_{cj} C_j}{\partial z_{isj}} = 0, \quad \frac{\partial p_{Ij} I_j}{\partial z_{isj}} = 0, \quad \frac{\partial \nu_{jt} Q_{jt}}{\partial z_{isj}} = 0, \quad j \in W, \quad t \in S. \tag{11}$$

In the Bertrand case of non-cooperative behaviour with prices charged to segmented markets as the strategic variables p_{isj}, profit maximization yields:

$$\frac{p_{isj} - v_{is}}{p_{isj}} = -\frac{\partial \log z_{isj}}{\partial \log p_{isj}}, \quad s \in \bar{C}, \; j \in W; \tag{12a}$$

alternatively, if we make the Cournot assumption of non-cooperative behaviour with sales to each individual market as the strategic variables z_{isj}, the profit-maximization equation – also known as Lerner's equation – becomes:

$$\frac{p_{isj} - v_{is}}{p_{isj}} = -\frac{\partial \log p_{isj}}{\partial \log z_{isj}}, \quad s \in \bar{C}, \; j \in W; \tag{12b}$$

with

$$Q_{is} = \sum_{j \in W} z_{isj}. \tag{13}$$

The computation of the elasticities on the right side of (12) requires inverting log-linearized aggregate demand systems. See the next subsection for further elaboration on the determination of the oligopolistic markups.[7]

The definition of oligopolistic industry profits then immediately follows:

$$\pi_{is} = n_{is} \left(\sum_{j \in W} p_{isj} z_{isj} - V_{is} Q_{is} \right), \quad s \in \bar{C}. \tag{14}$$

Static equilibrium conditions

The instantaneous general equilibrium is defined as a static allocation, supported by a vector of prices (p_{isj}, w_i, r_i), $s \in S$, $i, j \in W$, consistent with the intertemporal constraints and choices (1)–(3) and such that

- Tariff revenues are rebated to consumers lump sum:

$$G_i = \sum_{j \in W} \sum_{s \in S} \tau_{jsi} p_{jsi} n_{js} \left(c_{jsi} + I_{jsi} + \sum_{t \in S} x_{jsit} \right) \quad \text{(with } n_{js} = 1 \text{ for } s \in C); \tag{15}$$

- Consumers maximize (4) subject to (5);
- Investors maximize (6) subject to (7);
- Firms minimize (8) subject to (9);
- Oligopolistic firms set prices according to (12) and satisfy the resulting demand so that

$$z_{isj} = c_{isj} + I_{isj} + \sum_{t \in S} x_{isjt}, \quad s \in \bar{C}, \; i, j \in W, \tag{16}$$

and (13) holds;

- Supply equals demand on each competitive market:

$$Q_{is} = \sum_{j \in W} \left[c_{isj} + I_{isj} + \sum_{t \in S} x_{isjt} \right], \qquad s \in C, \quad i \in W; \tag{17}$$

$$K_i = \sum_{s \in C} K_{is}^{\nu} + \sum_{s \in \bar{C}} n_{is} [K_{is}^{\nu} + K_{is}^{F}], \qquad i, j \in W; \tag{18}$$

$$L_i = \sum_{s \in C} L_{is}^{\nu} + \sum_{s \in \bar{C}} n_{is} [L_{is}^{\nu} + L_{is}^{F}], \qquad i, j \in W; \tag{19}$$

- Industry concentration $n_{is} > 1, s \in \bar{C}, i \in W$ adjusts with inertia to the existence of non-negative oligopoly rents so that, in the long run, these rents are null. The process of entry and exit of firms is implemented in the following way:[8]

$$n_{is}(0) \text{ given}, \ n_{is}(\infty) \text{ such that } \pi_{is}(\infty) = 0,$$
$$\dot{n}_{is}(t) = \theta[n_{is}(\infty) - n_{is}(0)], \quad 0 < \theta < 1. \tag{20}$$

The first period *ROW* wage rate is chosen as the numéraire.[9]

2.3   The oligopolistic markups (the Cournot case)

The difficulty here is keeping track of individual firms' variables. Define $\mathbf{P}_j$ as the vector of prices on market j:

$$\mathbf{P}'_j = [p_{1j}^1, \dots, p_{1j}^{n_1}, \ \dots, p_{ij}^1, \ \dots, p_{ij}^f, \ \dots, p_{ij}^{n_i}, p_{Wj}^1, \dots, p_{Wj}^{n_W}],$$

where p_{ij}^f, is the price charged by firm f of country i on market j. (For notational convenience, I neglect the subscript s.) Define in a similar way $\mathbf{Z}_j$, $\mathbf{C}_j$, $\mathbf{I}_j$, $\mathbf{X}_{jt}$ as the vectors of sales (z_{ij}^f), consumption (c_{ij}^f), investment (I_{ij}^f), and input demands by sector t (x_{ijt}^f). In market j, firms face a demand system that, according to assumptions (11), is of the form

$$\mathbf{Z}_j = \mathbf{C}_j(\mathbf{P}_j(\mathbf{Z}_j)) + \mathbf{I}_j(\mathbf{P}_j(\mathbf{Z}_j)) + \sum_t \mathbf{X}_{jt}(\mathbf{P}_j(\mathbf{Z}_j)). \tag{21}$$

Total differentiation yields:

$$d\mathbf{Z}_j = \left[\frac{\partial \mathbf{C}_j}{\partial \mathbf{P}_j} + \frac{\partial \mathbf{I}_j}{\partial \mathbf{P}_j} + \sum_t \frac{\partial \mathbf{X}_{jt}}{\partial \mathbf{P}_j} \right] \frac{\partial \mathbf{P}_j}{\partial \mathbf{Z}_j} d\mathbf{Z}_j,$$

where $\partial./\partial.$ are matrices of partial derivatives. Let $\hat{\mathbf{P}}_j$ be a diagonal matrix with the elements of $\mathbf{P}_j$ on the diagonal, and define $\hat{\mathbf{Z}}_j$, $\hat{\mathbf{C}}_j$, $\hat{\mathbf{I}}_j$, $\hat{\mathbf{X}}_{jt}$ in a similar way. It is then trivial to transform the previous system to exhibit elasticities:

$$d\mathbf{Z}_j = \left[\mathbf{E}(\mathbf{C}_j, \mathbf{P}_j)\hat{\mathbf{C}}_j\hat{\mathbf{Z}}_j^{-1} + \mathbf{E}(\mathbf{I}_j, \mathbf{P}_j)\hat{\mathbf{I}}_j\hat{\mathbf{Z}}_j^{-1} + \sum_t \mathbf{E}(\mathbf{X}_{jt}, \mathbf{P}_j)\hat{\mathbf{X}}_{jt}\hat{\mathbf{Z}}_j^{-1} \right]$$
$$\times \mathbf{E}(\mathbf{P}_j, \mathbf{Z}_j)d\mathbf{Z}_j, \tag{22}$$

where $\mathbf{E}(,.)$ are matrices of elasticities.[10] Non-cooperative behaviour implies that firm f solves this system with $dz_{ij}^f = 1$ and all other elements of $\mathbf{dZ}_j$ set to zero. This yields the value of the right-side term of (12) for firm f. Conceptually, the computation of an equilibrium requires solving one such system for each firm $f \in i$ in all markets j. The cost of such a calculation would be prohibitive without the assumption of symmetry between domestic firms.

To work a tractable formula, I introduce the following notation for cross-elasticities:

$$\varepsilon_{ij}^k = -\frac{\partial \log \left(c_{ij}^f + I_{ij}^f + \sum_t x_{ijt}^f \right)}{\partial \log p_{kj}^g}, \quad \Psi_{ij}^k = -\frac{\partial \log p_{ij}^f}{\partial \log z_{kj}^g}, \quad f \in i, \ g \in k, \ f \neq g,$$

and identify the corresponding own-elasticities by a tilde ($\sim$):

$$\tilde{\varepsilon}_{ij}^i = -\frac{\partial \log \left(c_{ij}^f + I_{ij}^f + \sum_t x_{ijt}^f \right)}{\partial \log p_{ij}^f}, \quad \tilde{\Psi}_{ij}^i = -\frac{\partial \log p_{ij}^f}{\partial \log z_{ij}^f}, \quad f \in i.$$

Observe that $\tilde{\varepsilon}_{ij}^i$ and $\tilde{\Psi}_{ji}^i$ are the variables on the right side of the pricing equation (12). There is a simple relationship between own- and cross-elasticities:

$$\tilde{\varepsilon}_{ij}^i = \varepsilon_{ij}^i - \sigma_{ij}^*, \qquad \tilde{\Psi}_{ij}^i = \Psi_{ij}^i - \frac{1}{\sigma_{ij}^{**}}, \tag{23}$$

where

$$\sigma_{ij}^* = \frac{\sigma^f [c_{ij} + I_{ij}] + \sigma^x \sum_t x_{ijt}}{c_{ij} + I_{ij} + \sum_t x_{ijt}} \quad \text{and} \quad \frac{1}{\sigma_{ij}^{**}} = \frac{1/\sigma^f [c_{ij} + I_{ij}] + 1/\sigma^x \sum_t x_{ijt}}{c_{ij} + I_{ij} + \sum_t x_{ijt}}.$$

This reduces by one the dimension of the system (22). From this and the symmetry assumption, it can then be shown (by standard though tedious algebra) that the system (22) takes the following form:

$$0 = \sum_{k \in W} (n_k - \delta_{ki}) \varepsilon_{hj}^k \Psi_{kj}^i - \sigma_{hj}^* \Psi_{hj}^i + \varepsilon_{hj}^i \left(\psi_{ij}^i - \frac{1}{\sigma_{ij}^{**}} \right), \quad h = 1, \ldots, W, \tag{24}$$

$$\text{where } \delta_{ki} = \begin{cases} 1 & \text{if } k = i, \\ 0 & \text{if } k \neq i. \end{cases}$$

An analytical expression for the cross-price elasticities ε_{hj}^k is easily derived from preferences (4), technologies (6), (9), and assumptions (11):

$$\varepsilon_{hj}^k = [\sigma^f - 1] \left[\theta_{hj}^c \frac{p_{kj} c_{kj}}{p_j p_{cj} C_j} + \theta_{hj}^I \frac{p_{kj} I_{kj}}{w_j p_{Ij} I_j} \right] + [\sigma^x - 1] \sum_t \left[\theta_{hjt}^x \frac{p_{kj} x_{kjt}}{\alpha_{jt} v_{jt} Q_{jt}} \right], \tag{25}$$

where the θs are shares:

$$\theta^c_{hj} = \frac{c_{hj}}{c_{hj} + I_{hj} + \sum_t x_{hjt}}, \quad \theta^I_{hj} = \frac{I_{hj}}{c_{hj} + I_{hj} + \sum_t x_{hjt}},$$

$$\theta^x_{hjt} = \frac{x_{hjt}}{c_{hj} + I_{hj} + \sum_t x_{hjt}}.$$

Solving (24) and (25) for $h = 1, \ldots, W$, and making use of (23), one obtains the value of the right side of (12). This calculation has to be performed $\forall i, j \in W$, in each non-competitive sector $s \in \bar{C}$.

3 The policy experiment and evaluation of welfare

3.1 The trade experiment: Europe's move to a single market

Following Smith and Venables (1988), the completion of the European Single Market is implemented by forcing firms to switch from their initial segmented-market pricing strategy (12) to an integrated-market strategy determined from their average EU-wide monopoly power. Formally, rewrite the pricing equation as:

$$\frac{p_{isj} - \nu_{is}}{p_{isj}} = -\lambda \frac{\partial \log p_{isj}}{\partial \log z_{isj}} - (1 - \lambda) \frac{\partial \log p_{isEU}}{\partial \log z_{isEU}}, \quad i \in W, \, j \in EU, \, s \in \bar{C},$$

(26)

with $\lambda = 1$ in the calibration. The experiment consists in setting $\lambda = 0$. (The elasticity on the right is evaluated using the EU-aggregated demand.[11])

This experiment may be rationalized as follows. Although tariffs within Europe are negligible, various forms of non-tariff barriers (NTBs) exist (such as norms, government procurement policies, and security regulations). These barriers confer to firms the power to price discriminate between national markets. The European integration program is expected to restore cross-border arbitraging by suppressing all forms of NTBs. Firms would then be forced to charge a unique price within the EU. Modelling this is difficult because NTBs are essentially unobservable. The modelling strategy adopted, therefore, consists of treating these NTBs as latent variables, which underlie the existence of price-discrimination opportunities for firms in the pre-integration equilibrium. Once this is recognized, it suffices to infer from the data set the price system consistent with the optimal price-discrimination strategies of oligopolistic firms and to interpret these as resulting from the implicit structure of NTBs. The experiment then consists in forcing individual firms to adopt single pricing within Europe, prices being determined from their average EU-wide monopoly power, and interpreting this behavioural change as the optimal strategic reaction to the disappearance of the never-explicitly modelled NTBs.[12]

What can be expected from the trade integration experiment in terms of welfare? Firms are thought to charge higher prices in their domestic market, in which they usually hold the largest share. A move to a single-price strategy within the community would, therefore, induce a reduction of prices charged on home-markets, together with increases in export prices. The conjecture is that consumer prices will decline relative to factor prices and that European consumers will be better off. In addition, in the long run, a rationalization effect *à la* Harris (1984) could result from adjustments in industry structure. Indeed, the new pricing rule could reduce industry profits,[13] induce exit *à la* Chamberlin, so that a smaller number of surviving firms would operate on a larger scale with lower average costs.[14] The positive outcome for the consumer of this structural adjustment could, however, be offset by two companion effects. Exit of firms from an industry means reduced product diversity. This has a direct welfare cost, since consumers are endowed with love-of-variety type of preferences (see Dixit and Stiglitz 1977). Furthermore, diversity in available intermediate goods affects production efficiency in all sectors: everything else equal, exit of firms in an industry increases variable unit costs in all other sectors, competitive and non-competitive (see Ethier 1982). My aim is to measure these effects and analyse how they combine to affect the level and pattern – intertemporal and international – of welfare, production, and employment.

3.2   The welfare criterion

Central to any normative analysis is the measure of welfare, which is now made precise. Let $\hat{C}(t)$ be the reference stream of consumption and $C(t)$ the corresponding time profile computed after implementation at $t = 0$ of a once-and-for-all previously unexpected (or surprise) trade policy change. The welfare gain is determined from the following utility indifference condition:

$$\int_0^\infty e^{-\rho t} \frac{\lfloor \hat{C}(t)(1 + \phi) \rfloor^{1-\gamma}}{1 - \gamma} \, dt = \int_0^\infty e^{-\rho t} \frac{C(t)^{1-\gamma}}{1 - \gamma} \, dt, \qquad (27)$$

that is, the welfare gain resulting from the policy change is equivalent from the perspective of the representative household to increasing the reference consumption profile by ϕ per cent. The measure ϕ accounts for both transitional and long-term effects of the policy on the household's well being, putting relatively low weight on the latter because of discounting. It is sometimes useful to restrict the welfare analysis to steady state effects, in particular when making comparisons with predictions from static models. To do this, let me define $\lim_{t \to \infty} \hat{C}(t) = \hat{C}_{ss}$, $\lim_{t \to \infty} C(t) = C_{ss}$ and plug these constant values in the utility indifference condition; rearranging yields

$$\hat{C}_{ss}(1 + \phi_{ss}) = C_{ss}, \qquad (28)$$

where ϕ_{ss} is the (equivalent variation) welfare measure most frequently used in static applied general equilibrium analysis.

4 Calibration and computational strategy

The database includes bilateral trade flows, separate input-output tables for domestic and imported inputs; final demands by type and by sectoral origin, production, and labour earnings figures. All are collected from standard international publications. When necessary, consistency among the sources is ensured by using an RAS procedure. The literature includes numerous sources of Armington elasticities, from which reasonable estimates may be inferred. The calibration of the competitive side of the model is by now quite standard, so I shall not dwell on this; see, for example, Shoven and Whalley (1992).

The number of symmetric firms in non-competitive sectors (n_{is}) is inferred from Herfindahl industry concentration indices. Since we neither have reliable estimates on product differentiation, nor on returns to scale, nor on price-cost margins in oligopolistic industries, I exogenously supply reasonable values for the differentiation elasticities $\sigma_s{}^f, \sigma_s{}^x$. I then jointly determine, as detailed below, the base-year price system and scale elasticities consistent with the data base and the optimal price-discriminating Cournot–Nash behaviour of noncompetitive firms.

4.1 The joint calibration of initial markups and scale elasticities

The elasticities on the right side of the pricing equation (12), say $\partial \log p_{isj}/\partial \log z_{isj}$, depend on the substitution elasticities $\sigma_s{}^f, \sigma_s{}^x$, on the number of national competitors n_{is}, and on the market shares (say, θ_{isj}) the exporting country has in the client market j. Denote by $\tilde{e}_{isj}$ the current-price trade flows as supplied by the database. The market shares θ_{isj} are ratios of $\tilde{e}_{isj}$ and expenditure terms $(\rho_{sj}p_{sj}C_j, \varpi_{sj}p_{fj}I_j, \alpha_{sjt}\nu_{jt}Q_{jt})$. These expenditures are exogenous to the firm; see assumptions (11). Furthermore, they are known from the data set so that the θ_{isj} may be treated as parameters in the calibration. For calibration purposes, the elasticities can therefore be written in a convenient compact form as

$$-\frac{\partial \log p_{isj}}{\partial \log z_{isj}} = \mathrm{E}_{\mathrm{isj}}\left(\tilde{e}_{isj}, \sigma_s^f, \sigma_s^x, n_{is}\right), \quad s \in \bar{C}, \tag{29}$$

where $\mathrm{E}_{isj}(.)$ denotes a function of which we know the form and the parameter values. Substituting (29) in the Lerner formula (12b) and rearranging yields

$$\frac{p_{isj}}{\nu_{is}} = \frac{1}{1 - \mathrm{E}_{\mathrm{isj}}\left(\tilde{e}_{isj}, \sigma_s^f, \sigma_s^x, n_{is}\right)}, \quad s \in \bar{C}, \tag{30}$$

so that for a given (as yet unknown) level of the variable unit cost ν_{is}, the prices charged by firms in each national market may be computed from the data, exogenously supplied values of the σ_s and n_s.

Define $\bar{p}_{is}$ as the average selling price of the firm operating in country i; then, by definition, $\bar{p}_{is}$ satisfies

$$\bar{p}_{is} \sum_j^W e_{isj} = \sum_j^W \tilde{e}_{isj},$$

where $e_{isj} = \tilde{e}_{isj}/p_{isj}$. This definition equality may be rearranged as

$$\frac{\bar{p}_{is}}{\nu_{is}} \sum_j^W \frac{\tilde{e}_{isj}}{[p_{isj}/\nu_{is}]} = \sum_j^W \tilde{e}_{isj}, \quad s \in \bar{C}. \tag{31}$$

With $\bar{p}_{is}$ fixed at unity by normalization, equations (30) and (31) jointly determine the variable unit costs ν_{is} and the segmented-market price system, consistent with the data set, with preferences and with the competitive game assumed to prevail in the base year. The assumption of zero pure profits determines average costs: $V_{is} = \bar{p}_{is}$. The fixed costs can then be computed from (10):

$$(w_i L_{is}^F + r_i K_{is}^F) = \nu_{is} Q_{is}\left[\frac{V_{is}}{\nu_{is}} - 1\right], \quad s \in \bar{C}.$$

Due to the lack of reliable data on the composition of fixed costs, I assume that fixed and total costs have the same share of capital and labour inputs.

4.2   Calibration of the dynamic equations

We first note that the budget constraint (3) can be equivalently written in the following differential form:

$$\dot{F}(t) = \rho F(t) + w(t)L(t)$$
$$+ r(t)K(t) + \sum_s \pi_s(t) + G(t) - [p_c(t)C(t) + p_I(t)I(t)], \tag{32}$$
$$F(0) \text{ given}, \ \lim_{t\to\infty} e^{-\rho t}F(t) = 0,$$

where again I neglect country subscripts for notational ease. I next make use of results by Mercenier and Michel (1994a) on dynamic aggregation and write the following finite horizon discrete time approximation to the individual household's intertemporal choice problem:

$$\text{Max} \sum_{n=0}^{N-1} \alpha_n \Delta_n \frac{C(t_n)^{1-\gamma}}{1-\gamma} + \beta_N \frac{1}{\rho}\frac{C(t_N)^{1-\gamma}}{1-\gamma}$$

subject to

$$F(t_{n+1}) - F(t_n) = \Delta_n\left[\rho F(t_n) + w(t_n)L(t_n) + r(t_n)K(t_n)\right. \tag{33}$$
$$\left. + \sum_s \pi_s(t_n) + G(t_n) - p_c(t_n)C(t_n) - p_I(t_n)I(t_n)\right],$$
$$K(t_{n+1}) - K(t_n) = \Delta_n[I(t_n) - \delta K(t_n)],$$
$$F(t_0), K(t_0) \text{ given},$$

where t_n ($n = 0, \ldots, N$) are possibly unequally spaced dates, $\Delta_n = t_{n+1} - t_n$, α_n and β_N are (unknown) discount factors. This dynamic aggregation satisfies the property of steady-state invariance (i.e. a stationary equilibrium of (1)–(3) is also a constant solution of the time-aggregated approximation: see Mercenier and Michel 1994a) if and only if the discount factors α_n and β_N satisfy

$$\alpha_{n+1} = \frac{\alpha_n}{(1 + \rho\Delta_{n+1})}, \quad 0 \le n \le N - 2,$$

$$\beta_N = \alpha_{N-1}.$$

If the world economy is assumed initially in steady state, these results make the calibration of the intertemporal equilibrium straightforward using the following first order conditions:

$$\left[\frac{C(t_{n-1})}{C(t_n)}\right]^{-\gamma} = \frac{p_c(t_{n-1})}{p_c(t_n)}, \quad 0 < n \le N,$$

$$p_I(t_{n-1}) = \frac{1}{1 + \rho\Delta_n}[\Delta_n r(t_n) + (1 - \delta\Delta_n)p_I(t_n)], \quad 0 < n \le N,$$

$$p_I(t_N) = \frac{1}{\rho}[r(t_N) - \delta p_I(t_N)].$$

In the time-aggregated framework, the welfare criterion becomes: determine ϕ such that

$$\sum_{n=0}^{N-1} \alpha_n \Delta_n \frac{[\hat{C}(t_n)(1 + \phi)]^{1-\gamma}}{1 - \gamma} + \beta_N \frac{1}{\rho} \frac{[\hat{C}(t_N)(1 + \phi)]^{1-\gamma}}{1 - \gamma}$$

$$= \sum_{n=0}^{N-1} \alpha_n \Delta_n \frac{C(t_n)^{1-\gamma}}{1 - \gamma} + \beta_N \frac{1}{\rho} \frac{C(t_N)^{1-\gamma}}{1 - \gamma}$$

where $\hat{C}(t_n)$, and $C(t_n)$, $n = 0, \ldots, N$, denote respectively, the benchmark and counterfactual equilibrium profiles of aggregate consumption. Note that the model could easily be extended to include endogenous growth (say, *à la* Lucas 1988) using results on time-aggregation provided by Mercenier and Michel (2001). Reduced as it is by dynamic aggregation, the dimensionality of this five-period model is still a numerical challenge. To overcome this problem, I build on Negishi's (1961) existence proof of an imperfectly competitive GE. I first exo-genise oligopolistic markups and solve for the intertemporal equilibrium alloca-tions, prices, and industry structures.[15] Using these newly computed prices and market shares, I upgrade the optimal markups. I then iterate the Gauss–Seidel way until convergence at a fixed point.

This numerical procedure proved quite reliable and no computational diffi-culty is worth reporting. Nevertheless, there is little control on the search path with such a strategy, and no serious exploration of the possible existence of more than one equilibrium is possible. This is particularly unpleasant in view of the recent results of Mercenier (1995b), which suggest that in this generation of applied GE models, multiple equilibria can exist. It should be emphasised, however, that even though the structure of the instantaneous GE equilibrium of the present model bears strong similarities with the one I previously used, the treatment of factor markets differs substantially: I do not assume here that factors and factor-owners move internationally. Though there is no reason to believe that the change eliminates the risk of non-uniqueness, numerical tests with my 1995b model suggest that the risk is reduced.

5   Results

5.1   *The temporal aggregation issue: how reliable are the results*

The model is solved on a horizon of 35 years using five unequally distant grid dates: $t_0 = 1$, $t_1 = 5$, $t_2 = 11$, $t_3 = 20$ and $t_N = t_4 = 35$. For the sampling, I use a rule-of-thumb formula that builds on a criterion suggested in Mercenier and Michel (1994b).[16] (The use of Manne's 1988 criterion yields an almost identical grid.) Though the time-aggregation bias is obviously unknown – to evaluate this would require solving the system on a dense time grid but this is not possible given the size of the model – results reported in Mercenier and Michel (1994a, b) indicate that such approximations are quite accurate.

In this section, I provide some indirect evidence on the reliability of the approximation due to temporal aggregation. For this, I perform the policy experiment using successively two, three, four and five grid points, and compare the solution time profiles.[17] Figure 5.1 displays the computed time paths of the capital stock of a representative country *GB*. The results clearly suggest that little

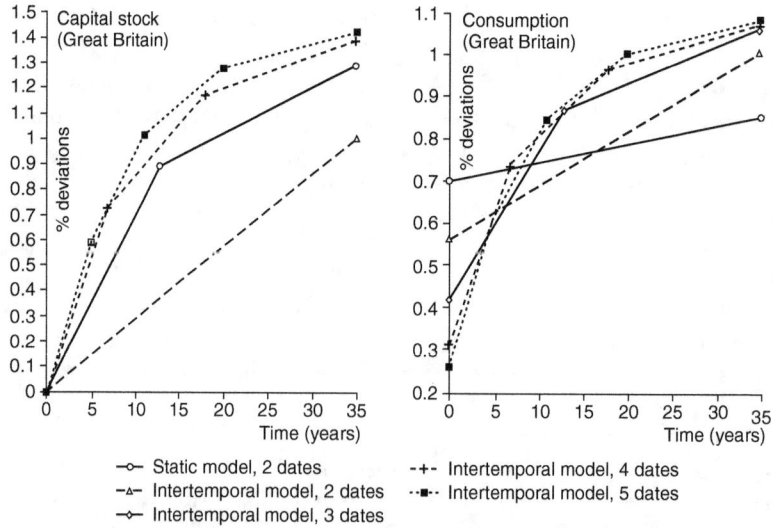

Figure 5.1 Sensitivity of computed paths of capital and consumption to alternative choices of time grid.

economic insight would be gained by using more than five dates. This conclusion is further confirmed by looking at the computed intertemporal pattern of aggregate consumption, as also shown in Figure 5.1. I have also represented in this graph the solution from the static version of the model.[18] The importance of intertemporal substitution is very apparent from this graph: it is optimal for consumers to trade present for future consumption. Clearly, a static model will miss important aspects of the structural adjustment effects of the trade policy.

5.2 *The basic mechanisms at work*

Though systematic sectoral patterns are not to be expected because of GE effects, one can trace the type of adjustments going on using selected sectoral variables and partial equilibrium arguments. For this purpose, I present in Table 5.1 some results for the British pharmaceutical industry. The first part of the table illustrates the importance of market segmentation in the calibrated equilibrium, and the effect this segmentation has on the firm's strategic pricing within Europe. British firms in this industry clearly price-discriminate taking advantage of their monopoly power on each national market. The monopoly power is an increasing function of market shares; it is therefore the largest on the domestic market on which the firm accordingly charges the largest price. The removal of all barriers to trade should force this firm to adopt a single price that, in partial equilibrium (i.e. holding everything else fixed) would be a weighted average of initial prices.

The second part of the table reports percentage deviations from initial segmented stationary equilibrium when European integration is implemented.[19]

Table 5.1 Selected results for the British pharmaceutical industry

	GB	1.011
Calibrated price spread:	Gr	0.941
	Fr	0.927
	It	0.954
	RE	0.952
	RoW	0.981
Impact & steady-state effects of integration (% deviations w.r. to base case)	First year	Last year (steady state)
Average selling price $\bar{p}$	1.72	1.32
Variable unit cost ν	2.04	1.53
Wage rate w	2.88	2.63
Rental price of capital r	2.86	0.90
Average unit cost V	3.19	1.31
Output scale z	− 3.91	1.33
Number of firms n	−	− 7.00
Efficiency gains	−	0.73

For clarity, I only report results for the first year following the policy implementation $(t_0 = 1)$ and for the new steady state $(t_4 = 35)$. Looking at the first year effects, we see that though the average price charged by the firms has increased *vis-à-vis* the numéraire, it has decreased compared to production costs: the variable unit cost has increased by 2.04 per cent, due to higher wages $(+2.88$ per cent) and capital rentals $(+2.86$ per cent) as well as higher prices of most material inputs (not reported). Fixed costs (that are incurred by the use of fixed capital and fixed labour) also increase by approximately 2.87 per cent. This means that, at the same level of output Q_0, the average unit cost has unambiguously increased, more so than the firms' average output price $\bar{p}$. Hence, the firm that had zero-profits initially would now experience losses at Q_0. The situation is actually worse: because of a combination of substitution and income effects, the firm's aggregate sales decline by some 3.9 per cent. The average scale in the British pharmaceutical industry is unambiguously too small for all existing firms to survive. Some producers will be forced out of the market, hence making it possible for survivors to operate on a larger scale so as to move down their average cost curve. The new long-term number of firms is 7 per cent lower in the post-integration equilibrium, each producing, on average, 1.3 per cent more than in the base year. The efficiency gains (i.e. the real cost savings due to increased scale on initial output) achieved in the sector because of this industry-rationalization mechanism amount to 0.75 per cent.

5.3   Welfare and employment effects

The first scenario assumes flexible wages with constant employment. Table 5.2 reports the welfare consequences of the trade experiment for member countries of the EU.[20] The static and dynamic versions of the model have been simulated so that the contribution of capital accumulation may be evaluated. As the comparisons between the first two columns indicate, accounting for growth increases the disparity of welfare gains across countries and confirms that the use of a static model for policy analysis could be misleading. As one expects, taking transitional costs into account mitigates these dynamic gains quite substantially, see columns 2 and 3 of the table. The broad conclusion that emerges from these numbers is quite clear, however: though positive, the gains to be expected from integration in Europe could be quite mild.

The previous results were generated with the assumptions of competitive labour markets and vertical labour-supply curves. This is an extreme and arguably unrealistic representation of European economies – obviously not the kind of world that policymakers considered when they launched the integration program. With little effort, one can imagine what they had in mind:

> the move to a single integrated market *should* result in a reduction of consumer prices with increased production efficiency and more intensive

competition for primary factors; in the short run, equilibrium in the labour market will be ensured by a combination of real wage increases and job creations; investment will also become more profitable, so that long-run production capacities will expand, presumably enough for the newly hired labour force to remain employed in the post-integration steady state.

In the previous scenario no job creation was allowed for, so that labour productivity gains were absorbed exclusively by real wage increases. I now explore the implications of the alternative extreme assumption: European wages are tied to consumer price indices during the first five years with employment determined by firms, labour supply being horizontal; the wages adjust in the long run so as to maintain the employed labour force at its $t_2 = 5$ years level.

The welfare results generated under these assumptions are reported in the second half of Table 5.2. We see that the welfare gains have, on average, approximately tripled when compared with the flexible-wage/fixed-labour supply case. All European countries unambiguously benefit from the trade integration. Employment rises between 0.75 and 2.5 per cent, depending on the country considered. This could represent more than 100,000 jobs created in Europe. The reason behind this is clear enough: by forcing down the average price charged by firms within the EU, the integration policy reduces cost-of-living indices of European consumers *vis-à-vis* the numéraire. Wage indexation, therefore, implies that European wages are reduced relative to the *ROW* labour costs without any loss in purchasing power for workers. The increase in the external competitiveness of the EU helps European producers gain market shares within as well as outside Europe, boost their output, and therefore move further down along their average-cost curves.

Table 5.2 Welfare gains from European trade integration

	Static model % Equivalent variation	Dynamic model % Equivalent variation at steady state	Dynamic model % Equivalent variation with transitional effects
Wages flexible			
GB	0.85	1.08	0.74
Gr	0.19	0.64	0.39
Fr	0.69	0.84	0.55
It	0.50	0.86	0.59
RE	0.19	0.02	0.20
Wages indexed (in the short term)			
GB		3.41	2.43
Gr		2.27	1.60
Fr		2.14	1.44
It		2.64	1.83
RE		0.86	0.70

Notes

1 In this paper, however, simulation results will be reported for the Cournot–Nash case only.
2 Namely, Great Britain (*GB*), the Federal Republic of Germany (*Gr*), France (*Fr*), Italy (*It*), the rest of the EU (*RE*), and the Rest of the World (*ROW*).
3 The four perfectly competitive sectors are: agriculture and primary products; food, beverage, and tobacco; other manufacturing industries (textile, wood, paper, metallurgy, minerals); transport and services. Imperfectly competitive sectors are: pharmaceutical products; chemistry other than pharmaceutical products; motor vehicles; office machinery, other machinery and transport materials. Note that though *C* also denotes aggregate consumption, no confusion can arise.
4 Thus, a subscript *isjt* indicates a flow originating in country *i* sector *s* with country *j* sector *t* as destination.
5 The symmetry assumption implies that imperfectly competitive domestic firms within a sector have the same cost structure and market shares, and consequently charge the same price even though the goods are imperfect substitutes.
6 This partial equilibrium compromise obviously simplifies the computations. It has also been advocated in the theoretical literature (Hart 1985, p.121) to avoid nonexistence problems highlighted by Roberts and Sonnenschein (1977) and Dierker and Grodal (1986). The implication of such an assumption, however, is that firms are modelled as making their strategic decisions with systematic errors.
7 The pricing equation (12) can be rearranged to yield:

$$p_{isj} = \left[1 + \frac{\partial \log p_{isj}}{\partial \log z_{isj}}\right]^{-1} \nu_{is}.$$

Hence, the optimal pricing strategy consists to mark-up prices over marginal costs.
8 The treatment of n_{is} as a real rather than an integer variable is widespread both in the theoretical trade literature and in the applied GE literature (for the latter, Mercenier and Schmitt (1996) is a notable exception). The reason for this is that it drastically simplifies both the analytics and the computations. (One would otherwise have to resort to mixed-integer programming techniques that are presently unable to handle large-scale nonlinear problems.) Though quite innocuous for many sectors where n_{is} is large, such an assumption may be thought to make little sense for highly concentrated industries. One has to consider, however, that the hypothesis is made jointly with that of symmetry, so that, in any case, firms are abstract objects. One should therefore regard n_{is} as an index of product variety rather than, strictly speaking, a number of real world firms.
9 It is well known that price normalization matters in the objective-Cournot–Nash–Walras GE model; see Gabszewicz and Vial (1972). This raises important questions concerning the theoretical consistency of the Cournot–Walras construction. Ginsburgh (1994) has recently called attention to the issue by producing a numerical example in which manipulating the numéraire may be more welfare improving than removing market imperfections such as consumer taxes. If we disregard theoretical consistency issues, a practical way out of this numéraire problem is to choose a normalization rule that involves only competitive prices.
10 For example, $\mathbf{E}(\mathbf{C}_j, \mathbf{P}_j) = (\partial \mathbf{C}_j / \partial \mathbf{P}_j) \hat{\mathbf{P}}_j \hat{\mathbf{C}}_j^{-1}$.
11 System (24) remains essentially unchanged (market *j* now represents the aggregate EU market), but the price elasticities are now weighted averages of those of

individual countries:

$$\varepsilon^k_{hEU} = \frac{\sum_{j\in EU} \varepsilon^k_{hj}\left[c_{hj} + I_{hj} + \sum_t x_{hjt}\right]}{\sum_{j\in EU}\left[c_{hj} + I_{hj} + \sum_t x_{hjt}\right]}.$$

The definitions of the σ^*_{hj} and σ^{**}_{hj} in (23) are accordingly amended:

$$\sigma^*_{hEU} = \frac{\sigma^f \sum_{j\in EU}\left[c_{hj} + I_{hj}\right] + \sigma^x \sum_{j\in EU}\sum_t x_{hjt}}{\sum_{j\in EU}\left[c_{hj} + I_{hj} + \sum_t x_{hjt}\right]} \text{ and}$$

$$\frac{1}{\sigma^{**}_{hEU}} = \frac{1/\sigma^f \sum_{j\in EU}\left[c_{hj} + I_{hj}\right] + 1/\sigma^x\sum_{j\in EU}\sum_t x_{hjt}}{\sum_{j\in EU}\left[c_{hj} + I_{hj} + \sum_t x_{hjt}\right]}.$$

12 It should be mentioned, however, that Ben-Zvi and Helpman (1992) have forcefully argued against the Cournot–Nash cum segmented market case. They construct a reasonable model of competition between oligopolies as a three-stage game, and show that the outcome is the Bertrand-integrated case.

13 Although from an individual firm's point of view, the switch to single pricing should reduce its profits if everything else is held fixed, it is far from obvious that this will be the case when all firms in the industry change their pricing strategy in a similar way.

14 Obviously, if only because of substitution effects, new firms could simultaneously enter the industry in some other countries.

15 All computations have been performed using GAMS/MINOS.

16 The formula used to generate the sample dates is:

$$t_n = \mathcal{N}\log\left(1 - \frac{n}{\mathcal{N}+1}\right)\bigg/ \log\left(\frac{1}{\mathcal{N}+1}\right).$$

17 All grids are generated using the same formula.

18 Investment is held fixed at its base year level equal to the steady state flow of capital depreciation. The stock of foreign assets initially held by each household is constrained to remain constant.

19 These results are for the flexible wage case.

20 The impact on the *ROW* is negligible and not worth reporting.

References

Armington, P. (1969) 'A theory of demand for products distinguished by place of production', International Monetary Fund *Staff Papers*, 16, 159–76.

Ben-Zvi, S. and Helpman, E. (1992) 'Oligopoly in segmented markets', in: Grossman, G. (ed.) *Imperfect Competition and International Trade*. Cambridge MA: MIT Press, 31–53.

Dierker, H. and Grodal, B. (1986) 'Nonexistence of Cournot-Walras equilibrium in a general equilibrium model with two oligopolists', in: Hildenbrand, W. and Mas-Colell, A. (eds) *Contributions to Mathematical Economics in Honor of Gerard Debreu*. Amsterdam: North-Holland, 167–85.

Dixit, A. K. and Stiglitz, J. E. (1977) 'Monopolistic competition and optimum product diversity', *American Economic Review*, 67, 297–308.

Ethier, W. J. (1982) 'National and international returns to scale in the modern theory of international trade', *American Economic Review*, 72, 389–405.

Gabszewicz, J. J. and Vial, J. P. (1972) 'Oligopoly "à la Cournot" in a general equilibrium analysis', *Journal of Economic Theory*, 4, 381–400.

Ginsburgh, V. (1994) 'In the Cournot-Walras general equilibrium model, there may be "more to gain" by changing the numéraire, than by eliminating imperfections: a two-good economy example', in Mercenier, J. and Srinivasan, T. N. (eds) *Applied General Equilibrium Analysis and Economic Development*, Ann Arbor: University of Michigan Press, 217–24.

Harris, R. (1984) 'Applied general equilibrium analysis of small open economies with scale economies and imperfect competition', *American Economic Review*, 74, 1016–32.

Hart, O. D. (1985) 'Imperfect competition in general equilibrium: an overview of recent work', in Arrow, K. J. and Honkapohja, S. (eds) *Frontiers of Economics*, Oxford: Blackwell, 100–49.

Lucas, R. E. (1988) 'On the mechanics of economic development', *Journal of Monetary Economics*, 22, 3–42.

Manne, A. S. (1988) 'Unequal time intervals in economic growth models', Stanford. (Revised June 1991), mimeo.

Mercenier, J. (1995a) 'Can "1992" reduce unemployment in Europe? On welfare and employment effects of Europe's move to a single market', *Journal of Policy Modelling*, 17(1), 1–37.

Mercenier, J. (1995b) 'Nonuniqueness of solutions in applied general equilibrium models with scale economies and imperfect competition', *Economic Theory*, 6, 161–77.

Mercenier, J. and Michel, P. (1994a) 'Discrete time finite horizon approximation of optimal growth with steady state invariance', *Econometrica*, 62, 635–56.

Mercenier, J. and Michel, P. (1994b) 'A criterion for time aggregation in intertemporal dynamic models', *Mathematical Programming*, 64, 179–97.

Mercenier, J. and Michel, P. (2001), 'Temporal aggregation in a multi-sector model of endogenous growth', *Journal of Economic Dynamics and Control*, 25, 1179–91.

Mercenier, J. and Schmitt, N. (1996) 'On sunk costs and trade liberalization in applied general equilibrium', *International Economic Review*, 37(3), 553–72.

Mercenier, J. and Yeldan, E. (1997) 'On Turkey's trade policy: is a customs union with Europe enough?', *European Economic Review*, 41(3–5), 871–80.

Mercenier, J. and Yeldan, E. (1999) 'A plea for greater attention to data in policy analysis', *Journal of Policy Modelling*, 21(7), 851–73.

Negishi, T. (1961) 'Monopolistic competition and general equilibrium', *Review of Economic Studies*, 28, 196–201.

Roberts, J. and Sonnenschein, H. (1977) 'On the foundations of the theory of monopolistic competition', *Econometrica*, 45, 101–13.

Shoven, J. and Whalley, J. (1992) *Applying General Equilibrium*. Cambridge: Cambridge University Press.

Smith, A. and Venables, A. J. (1988) 'Completing the internal market in the European Community: some industry simulations', *European Economic Review*, 32, 1501–25.

6 A conjectural variation computable general equilibrium model with free entry[*]

Roberto A. De Santis

1 Introduction

The CGE modelling literature has developed quite markedly in the last two decades. Initially, these models were constructed under the assumption of perfect competition and constant returns to scale. In the middle 1980s, under the wave of the 'new trade theory',[1] models with industrial organisation features were used to study the impact of trade policy actions when industries are characterised by endogenous market structure, and the economies to scale are exploited at firm level. These models, with imperfect competition and increasing returns to scale at firm level, usually employ the Lerner formula to set endogenously the price markup above the marginal cost. Examples of small open economy CGE models of this kind are those built by Harris (1984) and Devarajan and Rodrik (1989, 1991). Harris assumes that a firm of protected oligopolistic industries sets its price as a weighted average of the monopolistic Lerner price and the tariff-inclusive price of the importing competing goods. Devarajan and Rodrik define the inverse of the price cost margin in the domestic (export) market, as a product between the endogenous number of firms and the constant absolute value of the domestic (foreign) demand elasticity faced by the industry as a whole.[2] Examples of multi-country CGE models with industrial organisation features are those built by Gasiorek *et al.* (1992) and by Harrison, Rutherford and Tarr (henceforth, HRT) (1996, 1997b). In these studies, the price cost margin is defined as an inverse function of the endogenous price elasticity of demand perceived by the representative firm. Gasiorek *et al.* use a two-stage Dixit–Stiglitz utility function; whilst HRT employ a four-stage Dixit–Stiglitz utility function with an Armington specification at the second and third stages. The studies by HRT are based upon the assumption that firms compete in a quantity setting oligopoly with constant conjectures. The latter are endogenously calibrated. They express the optimal markup for each sector in each national market as a function of elasticities of substitution and firms' market share, but mistakenly assume that the price elasticities of

*I am indebted to Glenn Harrison, Thomas Rutherford, Frank Stähler and John Whalley for their valuable comments on an early stage of this paper. This paper has been written while the author was at the Kiel Institute of World Economics. The views expressed in this study are those of the author and do not necessary reflect those of the European Central Bank. All errors are author's responsibility.

demand perceived by a firm in the domestic and export markets are independent of conjectural variations parameters. In this chapter, I suggest a way to use the conjectural variation approach in CGE models, where the price elasticities of demand perceived by a firm in the domestic and export markets do depend upon strategic expectations among firms.[3]

The criticisms made by theoretical industrial economists to the conjectural variation approach are well known. It is argued that the notion of conjectural variation is *ad hoc* (Daughety 1985), or that strategic responses require a temporal setting (Makowski 1987). However, it is also understood that the conjectural variation approach is an approximation of the solution which emerges from the equilibrium of a dynamic oligopolistic game (Schmalensee 1989; Ferrel and Shapiro 1990).[4] Certainly, the conjectural variation models are used by empirical industrial economists because they can cover the entire range of market performance from competition to monopoly (Cowling 1976; Cowling and Waterson 1976; Slade 1987; Machin and Van Reenen 1993).

The conjectural variation approach is rarely used in CGE models for two main reasons: first, the demand tree of a typical CGE model is of a multi-stage type and the strategic behaviour of domestic and foreign firms can occur at different stages of the demand tree; second, the calibration of the key parameters of the markup equations can be tricky and is certainly demanding, causing problems associated with the convergence of the model.[5] In order to understand the problem, let me sketch a figure where the strategic interactions among domestic and foreign firms are clearly identifiable. Figure 6.1 depicts a typical three-stage demand tree for the imperfect competitive good employed in the CGE literature (see for example HRT 1996, 1997b). At the first stage, the final demand of the representative consumer and the intermediate demand of industries are satisfied by the supply of composite commodities. At the second stage, the aggregate demand for composite commodities is satisfied by the supply of domestic goods and imports, treated as imperfect substitutes. At the third stage, having decided the demand for domestic

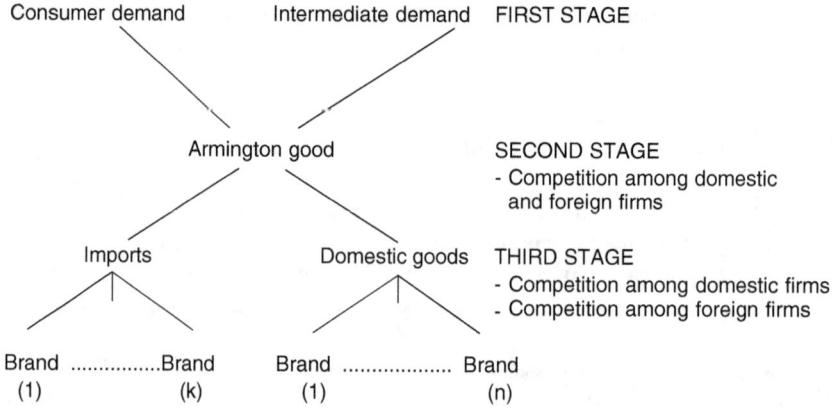

Figure 6.1 The demand system.

goods and for imports, consumers and industries purchase a variety of domestic goods and a variety of imports. Hence, domestic firms (as well as foreign firms) compete against each other at the third stage of the demand tree, whereas domestic firms and foreign firms compete against each other at the second stage of the demand tree. This implies that the expectation of a domestic (foreign) firm about the action of other domestic (foreign) firms to their own actions is formed at the third stage of the demand tree, whereas the expectation of domestic (foreign) firms about the action of the foreign (domestic) firms to their own actions is formed at the second stage of the demand tree.

In this chapter, I derive a general formulation for the price markup, where the price elasticity of demand is a function of the conjectured reactions of both the rival domestic and foreign firms. I show that the price cost margin formula used by HRT can be obtained as a special case when firms behave in a Cournot fashion. I also show how to calibrate the conjectural variation of the domestic (foreign) firm about the behaviour of the rival domestic (foreign) firms. In order to understand how welfare and output might be affected by the use of alternative conjectural variations, a single country open economy CGE model has been built for the Turkish economy, and the effects of a unilateral partial trade liberalisation policy are examined.

The remaining sections of this paper have been organised as follows: Section 2 describes the modelling framework; Section 3 derives the price markups of a representative firm in the domestic and foreign markets; Section 4 describes the CGE model for Turkey, the benchmark data set and the calibration procedure, and discusses the numerical results; Section 5 presents a summary.

2   The structure of the model

2.1   *The supply behaviour*

Assume that within an industry i a firm s faces fixed costs, f_i, and produces for the domestic market, $\tilde{d}_{is}$, as well as for the foreign market, $\tilde{e}_{is}$. Note that i denotes the sectors facing increasing returns to scale, whereas j denotes all economic sectors. The profit function of a representative domestic firm, π_i, takes the following form:

$$\pi_i = \tilde{p}_{is}^d \tilde{d}_{is} + \tilde{p}_{is}^e \tilde{e}_{is} - c_i(\tilde{d}_{is} + \tilde{e}_{is}) - f_i, \tag{1}$$

where $\tilde{p}_{is}^d$ and $\tilde{p}_{is}^e$ denote the brand prices of domestic output and exports, respectively; and c_i the marginal cost, which is assumed to be independent of output. The first order conditions yield the price cost margins in both the domestic and export markets

$$\frac{\tilde{p}_{is}^d - c_i}{\tilde{p}_{is}^d} = \frac{1}{|\tau_{is}|}, \quad \tau_{is} < -1, \tag{2}$$

$$\frac{\tilde{p}_{is}^e - c_i}{\tilde{p}_{is}^e} = \frac{1}{|\delta_{is}|}, \quad \delta_{is} < -1, \tag{3}$$

where τ_{is} and δ_{is} represent the price elasticities of domestic and export demands perceived by a domestic firm s, respectively. HRT (1997b) argue that

$$(\tilde{p}_{is}^d - c_i)/\tilde{p}_{is}^d = (1 + \Omega_i^d)/|\tau_{is}| \quad \text{and} \quad (\tilde{p}_{is}^e - c_i)/\tilde{p}_{is}^e = (1 + \Omega_i^e)/|\delta_{is}|,$$

where Ω_i^d and Ω_i^e denote the conjectural variations in the domestic and export markets, respectively (with $\Omega_i^d = \Omega_i^e = 0$ representing the Cournot case). However, they implicitly assume that τ_{is} and δ_{is} are independent of conjectural variations parameters. Conversely, as suggested by Smith and Venables (1988), τ_{is} and δ_{is} also depend on the perceived effect of the firm's action on industry aggregate supply. More precisely, I show in the next section that τ_{is} and δ_{is} are each a function of two conjectural variations parameters, since domestic firms also have conjectures about how foreign firms respond.

2.2   The demand behaviour

A typical CGE model with imperfect competition and increasing returns to scale is characterised by the three-stage demand system as depicted in Figure 6.1. At the first stage, the final demand of the representative consumer, C_i, and the intermediate demand of industries, X_i, are satisfied by the supply of composite commodities, Q_i:

$$C_i = \alpha_i I/p_i, \tag{4}$$

$$X_i = \sum_j a_{ij} Y_j, \tag{5}$$

$$Q_i = C_i + X_i = [\varphi_i D_i^{(\varepsilon_i - 1/\varepsilon_i)} + (1 - \varphi_i) M_i^{(\varepsilon_i - 1/\varepsilon_i)}]^{\varepsilon_i/(\varepsilon_i - 1)}, \tag{6}$$

where α_i denotes household budget shares, I household income, p_i the price of the Armington goods, Y_j sectoral output, a_{ij} the input requirements by sectors j which are supplied by the increasing returns to scale sectors, D_i domestic output, M_i imports, ε_i the elasticity of substitution between imports and domestic goods, and φ_i the share parameter of the Armington function. Equation (4) is derived by maximising the consumer's Cobb–Douglas utility function assumed at the first stage subject to his budget constraint, whereas the derivation of equation (5) is based upon the assumption that intermediate inputs are net complements (i.e. Leontief specification). Equation (6) gives the equilibrium in the goods market.

At the second stage, the aggregate demand for composite commodities is satisfied by the supply of domestic goods and imports, according to the Constant Elasticity of Substitution (CES) Armington specification. At the upper level, the solution of the Armington-dual problem yields the demand for domestic goods,

D_i, the demand for imports, M_i, and the Armington price, p_i:

$$D_i = \varphi_i^{\varepsilon_i} p_i^{d-\varepsilon_i} p_i^{\varepsilon_i} Q_i, \tag{7}$$

$$M_i = (1 - \varphi_i)^{\varepsilon_i} p_i^{m-\varepsilon_i} p_i^{\varepsilon_i} Q_i, \tag{8}$$

$$p_i = \left\{ \varphi_i^{\varepsilon_i} p^{d(1-\varepsilon_i)} + (1 - \varphi_i)^{\varepsilon_i} p_i^{m(1-\varepsilon_i)} \right\}^{1/(1-\varepsilon_i)}, \tag{9}$$

where p_i^d denotes the domestic price index and p_i^m the import price index.

At the third stage, having decided the demand for domestic goods and for imports, consumers and industries purchase a variety of domestic goods and a variety of imports, based again on CES functions:

$$D_i = \left[\sum_{s=1}^{n} \tilde{d}_{is}^{(\varsigma_i-1)/\varsigma_i} \right]^{\varsigma_i/(\varsigma_i-1)}, \quad \varsigma_i > 1, \tag{10}$$

$$M_i = \left[\sum_{r=1}^{k} \tilde{m}_{ir}^{(\xi_i-1)/\xi_i} \right]^{\xi_i/(\xi_i-1)}, \quad \xi_i > 1, \tag{11}$$

where ς_i and ξ_i represent the elasticities of substitution among n domestic varieties and k imported varieties, respectively; and $\tilde{m}_{ir}$ denotes output of each foreign brand r. Given (10) and (11), the solution of the dual problems yields

$$\tilde{d}_{is} = p_i^{d\varsigma_i} \tilde{p}_{is}^{d-\varsigma_i} D_i, \tag{12}$$

$$p_i^d = \left[\sum_{s=1}^{n} \tilde{p}_{is}^{d(1-\varsigma_i)} \right]^{1/(1-\varsigma_i)}, \tag{13}$$

$$\tilde{m}_{ir} = p_i^{m\xi_i} [\tilde{p}_{ir}^m (1 + t_i)]^{-\xi_i} M_i, \tag{14}$$

$$p_i^m = \left[\sum_{r=1}^{k} [\tilde{p}_{ir}^m (1 + t_i)]^{(1-\xi_i)} \right]^{1/(1-\xi_i)}, \tag{15}$$

where $\tilde{p}_{ir}^m$ denotes the price of the imported brand r, and t_i the *ad valorem* tariff rate.

3   The strategic interaction among firms

As suggested by Smith and Venables (1988), τ_{is} and δ_{is} also depend on the perceived effect of the firm's action on industry aggregate supply. In this section,

I will show that τ_{is} and δ_{is} are each a function of two conjectural variation parameters, since a domestic firm also has conjectures about how rival domestic and foreign firms respond. Thus, assume that domestic and foreign firms do respond to rivals' output choices with constant conjectures.

From (12), the inverse demand function can be log-linearised as

$$\ln \tilde{p}_{is}^d = 1/\varsigma_i \ln D_i - 1/\varsigma_i \ln \tilde{d}_{is} + \ln p_i^d. \tag{16}$$

By definition the derivative of (16) with respect to $\ln \tilde{d}_{is}$ yields the inverse of the price elasticity of domestic demand perceived by a firm:

$$\frac{1}{\tau_{is}} = \frac{1}{\varsigma_i} \frac{d \ln D_i}{d \ln \tilde{d}_{is}} - \frac{1}{\varsigma_i} + \frac{d \ln p_i^d}{d \ln \tilde{d}_{is}}. \tag{17}$$

The appendix shows that under symmetry among domestic firms and constant conjectures

$$\frac{1}{\tau_i} = -\frac{1}{\varsigma_i} - \frac{1}{n_i} \left\{ \frac{1}{\varepsilon_i} - \frac{1}{\varsigma_i} + \Psi_i \left(\frac{1}{\chi_i} - \frac{1}{\varepsilon_i} \right) \left[1 + \frac{1 - \varphi_i}{\varphi_i} \left(\frac{M_i}{D_i} \right)^{-1/\varepsilon_i} \mu_i \right] \right\}$$

$$\times \left[1 + \frac{\sum_{t \neq s} \left(\tilde{d}_{it}^{-1/\varsigma_i} \right)}{\tilde{d}_{is}^{-1/\varsigma_i}} \lambda_i \right], \tag{18}$$

where $\Psi_i = p_i^d D_i / [p_i^d D_i + p_i^m M_i]$ represents the domestic industry market share in the domestic market; χ_i is the absolute value of the price elasticity of aggregate demand; $\lambda_i = \partial \tilde{d}_{it} / \partial \tilde{d}_{is}$ denotes the conjectured reaction of rival domestic firms, $t = 1, \ldots, n - 1$; and $\mu_i = \partial M_i / \partial D_i$ can be interpreted as the conjectured reaction of foreign firms to the domestic firms' action in the domestic market. Regarding the price elasticity of aggregate demand, by using (4)–(6), it can be shown that $\chi_i = C_i / Q_i$ (see appendix). This implies that χ_i is endogenous and ranges between zero and one.

It is interesting to note that under Cournot $\lim_{n \to \infty} (1/\tau_i) = -1/\varsigma_i$. In other words, the price cost margin of a firm would be equal to the inverse of the elasticity of substitution among individual producers, as the number of brands converges to infinite. This result is in line with the monopolistic competitive literature (Dixit and Stiglitz 1977; Krugman 1979).

Similarly, one can determine the price elasticity of export demand perceived by a domestic firm and the inverse of the price elasticity of import demand perceived by a foreign firm. The former will be function of both the conjectured reaction of rival domestic firms and the conjectured reaction of foreign firms to the domestic firms' action in the foreign market; the latter will be function of both the conjectured reactions of rival foreign firms and the conjectured reactions of domestic firms to the foreign firms' action in the domestic market.

The absolute value of (18) corresponds to the price cost margin formula employed by HRT (1997b) if, and only if, Cournot is postulated. The formulas employed by HRT (1997b) are therefore a specific case of the general formulation presented in this study. Note also that (18) is consistent with the theory, which argues that a more collusive outcome is obtained for positive conjectural variations, if $\varsigma_i > \varepsilon_i > \chi_i$.

In order to get further insights regarding the expressions which define the price markups in the domestic and foreign markets, it is very useful to compute the total differential of (18), which is

$$
\begin{aligned}
\mathrm{d}(1/|\tau_i|) = & -\frac{G_i}{n_i^2} A_i \mathrm{d}n_i \\
& + \frac{1}{n_i} G_i \left\{ B_i \left[\left(\frac{1}{\chi_i} - \frac{1}{\varepsilon_i} \right) \mathrm{d}\Psi_i - \frac{\Psi_i}{\chi_i^2} \mathrm{d}\chi_i \right] + C_i \mathrm{d}\left(\frac{D_i}{M_i} \right) \right\},
\end{aligned}
\tag{19}
$$

where

$$G_i = (n_i - 1)\lambda_i + 1,$$

$$A_i = 1/\varepsilon_i - 1/\varsigma_i + \Psi_i(1/\chi_i - 1/\varepsilon_i)B_i,$$

$$B_i = 1 + (1 - \varphi_i)/\varphi_i(M_i/D_i)^{-1/\varepsilon_i}\mu_i,$$

$$C_i = \Psi_i(1/\chi_i - 1/\varepsilon_i)(1 - \varphi_i)/(\varepsilon_i\varphi_i)(M_i/D_i)^{\varepsilon_i/(1-\varepsilon_i)}\mu_i.$$

This exercise allows one to arrive at the following conclusions under the assumptions that $\varsigma_i > \varepsilon_i > \chi_i$:

- entry of new domestic firms leads to a fall in the domestic price markup;
- a larger aggregate price elasticity (in absolute value) in the domestic market implies a larger price elasticity of demand perceived by a domestic firm (in absolute value) in the domestic market if $B_i G_i > 0$;
- an increase in the market share of the domestic industry implies a rise in the price markup in the domestic market if $B_i G_i > 0$;
- a rise of domestic sales relative to the import volume implies a rise in the price markup in the domestic market if $C_i G_i > 0$.

All these conditions are fulfilled if $\mu_i \geq 0$ and $(1 - n_i)^{-1} < \lambda_i$. Hence, a check on the value of the conjectural variation parameters is very useful to understand and interpret the numerical results.

4 A CGE model for Turkey

The single country 3-sector CGE model presented in this section examines how robust the model is to alternative conjectural variation parameters. Given the fact that the model is working at an extremely aggregate level, one should interpret the results simply as numerical exercises to test the capacity of the model. Nevertheless, the outcome might result in a useful empirical application, because Turkey has markedly reduced its trade barriers on industrial goods in the 1990s. Hence, the construction of a CGE model with imperfect competition and scale economies, and the study of the elimination of Turkish tariffs on industrial goods can be empirically relevant.[6]

The CGE model contains two categories of industries: those where perfect competition and constant returns to scale are assumed to prevail (agriculture and services), and that which is characterised by increasing returns to scale (industry). The production function has a two stage nested CES structure. At the first stage, I assume a Leontief function among primary factors of production and intermediate inputs, which are in turn assumed to be net complements. At the second stage, the elasticity of substitution among the mobile labour and the mobile capital is assumed to be positive. The production possibility frontier of the industries facing perfect competition and constant returns to scale is a CET specification of domestic products and exports, treated as imperfect substitutes. On the demand side, the representative household demand, government spending, and the intermediate demand are satisfied by a composite of domestic and imported goods, as described in Section 2.2. Government spending is set exogenously, so it does not play any role. The household demand at the first stage is derived from a Cobb–Douglas utility function. The country is assumed to be the price taker for the commodities traded internationally, with the exception of exports produced by sectors facing increasing returns to scale, for which a downward sloping demand curve is supposed. The latter has been derived by assuming that an hypothetical foreign consumer purchases a variety of domestic goods and a variety of Turkish exports, treated as their substitutes. Foreign domestic production is set exogenously. The trade balance and the public budget balance are always in equilibrium. With regard to the remaining variables of the sectors facing imperfect competition and increasing returns to scale, (1), (2), (3), (7) and (10) endogenously determine n_i, $\tilde{p}_{is}^d$, $\tilde{p}_{is}^e$, D_i and $\tilde{d}_{is}$, whereas the zero profit condition and the price cost margin for the foreign firm, plus (8) and (11) determine k_i, $\tilde{p}_{ir}^m$, M_i and $\tilde{m}_{ir}$. I postulate that the Turkish trade liberalisation policy does not have any impact on foreign factor prices.

Regarding the numéraire of the model, the world price of constant returns to scale goods is normalised to unity. It is well known that the choice of the numéraire matters in general equilibrium models with imperfect competition (Gabszewicz and Vial 1972; Dierker and Grodal 1986; Ginsburgh 1994). However, as suggested by Ginsburgh (1994) and Ginsburgh and Keyzer (1997), in models where markets are competitive for some commodities, all agents take the prices on the competitive markets as given. Hence, a numéraire among the prices of these goods can be chosen. This choice does not solve the problem *per se*, but at least the behaviour of oligopolists would not be affected (Cripps and Myles 1988). The problem of choosing the numéraire does not arise in a single country open economy model, because an exogenous world price can be normalised to unity.

4.1 Benchmark and calibration

The theoretical model outlined above and applied to Turkey requires a bench-mark data set to calibrate unknown parameters, such that the observed value of endogenous variables constitutes an equilibrium of the numerical model.

The main bulk of the data comes from the official 1990 Input–Output table for Turkey (see Table 6.1). The activities and commodities are disaggregated into three different types: agriculture, industry and services.

In order to calibrate the variables of the sector facing increasing returns to scale, the algebraic structure of the model required further information on price-cost margin, fixed costs and the number of symmetric firms. I assume that labour and capital inputs used in fixed proportion are 60 per cent of the primary factor inputs employed in manufacturing. This allows me to calibrate the marginal cost and the cost disadvantage ratio, which is equal to 16.3 per cent. I also assume that the number of domestic and foreign firms is 50 each. The number of firms is large enough to avoid problems associated with integer values. The elasticity of substitution among domestic brands and among foreign brands is set equal to 7, such that $(1 - n_i^0)^{-1} < \hat{\lambda}_i$, $(1 - n_i^0)^{-1} < \hat{\lambda}_i^*$ and $(1 - k_i^0)^{-1} < \hat{\lambda}_i^m$, which yield $\hat{B}_i^v > 0$ and $\hat{C}_i^v \geq 0$ (v denotes the domestic market, the import market and the export market).[7] This permits the calibration of the firms' perceived price elasticities in each market.

The conjectural variation parameters Ω_i^v and λ_i^v are endogenously calib-rated. Under the HRT formula, the conjectural variation parameters in the

Table 6.1 The benchmark data set for Turkey

	Billion of 1990 TL	*Agriculture*	*Industry*	*Services*
Domestic sales	514,105	0.177	0.360	0.463
Exports	52,060	0.048	0.513	0.439
Imports	69,033	0.038	0.903	0.059
Import duties	13,396	0.035	0.965	0.000
Labour	96,257	0.316	0.134	0.551
Capital	178,661	0.180	0.250	0.570
Intermediate demand for:				
agricultural goods	40,060	0.373	0.554	0.074
industrial goods	158,654	0.053	0.588	0.358
services	92,533	0.083	0.420	0.498
Private consumption	262,204	0.204	0.368	0.427
Government spending	43,083	0.012	0.118	0.870
			Elasticities	
Labour/Capital		0.900	0.9	1.8
Domestic goods/Imports		2.000	2.0	2.0
Domestic goods/Exports		3.000	—	3.0
Domestic brands			7.0	
Foreign brands			7.0	

Source: SIS (1994) for the national account statistics.

domestic $(\hat{\Omega}_i)$, export market $(\hat{\Omega}_i^*)$ and import market $(\hat{\Omega}_i^m)$ are calibrated as follows: $\hat{\Omega}_i = \hat{\theta}_i|\hat{\tau}_i| - 1$, $\hat{\Omega}_i^* = \hat{\theta}_i|\hat{\delta}_i| - 1$, and $\hat{\Omega}_i^m = \hat{\theta}_i|\hat{\gamma}_i| - 1$, where $\hat{\theta}_i$ denotes the calibrated price cost margin, which is assumed equal to the cost disadvantage ratio for both domestic and foreign firms. Thus, $\hat{\theta}_i$ is equal to 0.163. Under the correct approach, the conjectural variation parameter in the domestic market $(\hat{\lambda}_i)$ is calibrated as follows:

$$\hat{\lambda}_i = \left\{ \frac{n_i^0(\hat{\theta}_i - 1/\varsigma_i)}{1/\varepsilon_i - 1/\varsigma_i + \hat{\Psi}_i(1/\hat{\chi}_i - 1/\varepsilon_i)\left[1 + (1 - \hat{\varphi}_i)/\hat{\varphi}_i(M_i^0/D_i^0)^{-1/\varepsilon_i}\mu_i^0\right]} - 1 \right\}$$
$$\times (n_i^0 - 1)^{-1}. \tag{20}$$

The conjectural variation parameter μ_i is set exogenously. It is important to note that (20) can be re-arranged as $\hat{G}_i = n_i^0(\hat{\theta}_i - 1/\varsigma_i)/\hat{A}_i$. If $\hat{\theta}_i > 1/\varsigma_i$, $\hat{G}_i$ has the same sign as $\hat{A}_i$. This result can be extended to the other markets.

Table 6.2 shows the calibrated quantity conjectures and the price elasticities perceived by domestic and foreign firms under the HRT approach and the correct approach. The conjectural variation parameters are very close to the Cournot case, though those under the HRT approach are slightly larger. The price elasticities are also very similar among the two approaches. Note that the approach proposed in this study permits one to set the absolute value of the price elasticity perceived by firms equal to the inverse of the price cost margin, and to calibrate the conjectured reactions of the rival domestic firms. The study considers three alternative scenarios: $\mu_i^0 = \mu_i^{0*} = \mu_i^{0m} = 0$ (i.e. CV1 scenario); $\mu_i^0 = \mu_i^{0*} = 15$ and $\mu_i^{0m} = 0$ (i.e. CV2 scenario); $\mu_i^0 = \mu_i^{0*} = 0$ and $\mu_i^{0m} = 15$ (i.e. CV3 scenario). Note that $(1 - n_i^0)^{-1} < \hat{\lambda}_i$, $(1 - n_i^0)^{-1} < \hat{\lambda}_i^*$ and $(1 - k_i^0)^{-1} < \hat{\lambda}_i^m$, $\mu_i^v \geq 0$, $\hat{\theta}_i > 1/\varsigma_i^v$, $\varsigma_i > \varepsilon_i > \hat{\chi}_i$, $\varsigma_i^* > \varepsilon_i^* > 1$ and $\xi_i > \varepsilon_i > \hat{\chi}_i$. As a result, the individual producer can charge a larger price cost margin in the three markets if: (i) the conjectural variations parameters are positive; (ii) its industry concentrates; (iii) the market

Table 6.2 Calibrated conjectures and firms' price elasticities

	Conjectural variation parameters			Price elasticities		
	Domestic market	Export market	Import market	Domestic market	Export market	Import market
HRT	0.036	0.085	0.065	−6.365	−6.664	−6.541
CV1	−0.010	0.306	0.000	−6.144	−6.144	−6.144
CV2	−0.020	0.127	0.000	−6.144	−6.144	−6.144
CV3	−0.010	0.036	−0.018	−6.144	−6.144	−6.144
CV4	−0.020	0.127	−0.018	−6.144	−6.144	−6.144

Note: HRT = Harrison–Rutherford–Tarr approach; CV1: Correct approach under the assumption that $\mu_i^0 = \mu_i^{0*} = \mu_i^{0m} = 0$; CV2: Correct approach under the assumption that $\mu_i^0 = \mu_i^{0*} = 15$ and $\mu_i^{0m} = 0$; CV3: Correct approach under the assumption that $\mu_i^0 = \mu_i^{0*} = 0$ and $\mu_i^{0m} = 15$.

share of its industry increases; (iv) the sales of its industry rise relative to the sales of the rivals; (v) the absolute value of the price elasticity of aggregate demand becomes smaller.

4.2 Scenarios: partial trade liberalisation in Turkey

The policy experiment consists of eliminating the tariff rate levied on Turkish industrial imported goods (i.e. the benchmark *ad valorem* tariff rate is 20.74 per cent), under the hypothesis that the firm's output choice on how to react to its rivals' output choices is given a priori and is independent of the trade policy impact. As public revenues decline with a tariff fall, endogenously determined net transfers to the representative consumer ensure that the government budget is in equilibrium. The CGE model assumes free entry/exit. Hence, the benchmark generates a long run reference equilibrium by setting pure profits to zero. This reference equilibrium is then the basis for comparison in counterfactual trade policy analysis. The results are shown in Table 6.3.

The approach suggested by HRT, which implicitly assumes Cournot competition among domestic and foreign firms, produces similar findings compared to those obtained with the conjectural variation approach, where Cournot competition is explicitly postulated (CV1). However, if domestic firms believe that foreign firms will increase their production as they grow (CV2), or if foreign firms believe that domestic firms will change production as they expand (CV3), then the results can change.

First, let me discuss the scenario HRT and CV1, as the results are very similar. A fall in tariff in industrial goods leads to an increase in industrial imports by 19.5–19.7 per cent and reduces the protection enjoyed by domestic firms. As a result, the equilibrium number of domestic firms declines by 5.2–5.4 per cent, while the number of foreign firms increases by 17.7–18.2 per cent. However, a fall in the protection rate does not imply a large output contraction, because of the scale effect due to the use of intermediate imported goods in the production process of industrial goods. The welfare gains, however, are small. Given the revealed comparative advantage in industry and services compared to agriculture, the trade balance equilibrium is achieved via a large increase in exports in these two sectors. Resources are therefore pulled out from both agriculture and industry, and shifted to services which expands by 1.9 per cent. The price cost margin in the domestic market increases, because the negative impact of the decrease in the number of firms dominates both the negative impact of the decline in the domestic industry market share and the positive impact of a larger aggregate price elasticity. With regard to the export market, since the number of firms declines and the market share increases, the price cost margin in the export market increases. In the import market, the market structure effect and the larger aggregate price elasticity seem to dominate the industry market share effect. As a result, the price cost margin of the foreign firms declines.

I have assumed that foreign and domestic firms play Cournot. How would the results be affected by relaxing this assumption? The scenario 'CV2' is based upon

Table 6.3 The economic impact of tariff liberalization and competition policies

Welfare	HRT 0.002			CV1 0.002			CV2 0.000			CV3 0.005		
	Agr	Ind	Ser	Agr	Ind	Ser	Agr	Ind	Ser	Agr	Ind	Ser
Output	−0.013	−0.010	0.019	−0.013	−0.010	0.019	−0.020	−0.043	0.018	−0.013	−0.003	0.017
Domestic sales	−0.018	−0.057	−0.002	−0.018	−0.058	−0.003	−0.026	−0.067	−0.007	−0.017	−0.058	−0.002
Export volume	0.154	0.318	0.233	0.152	0.322	0.231	−0.061	0.190	0.120	0.127	0.382	0.203
Import volume	−0.118	0.195	−0.134	−0.117	0.197	−0.133	−0.148	0.157	−0.160	−0.102	0.231	−0.119
Domestic industry market share		−0.088			−0.089			−0.083			−0.091	
Export industry market share		0.202			0.207			0.068			0.267	
Foreign industry market share		0.262			0.263			0.248			0.269	
Number of domestic firms		−0.054			−0.052			−0.017			−0.050	
Number of foreign firms		0.182			0.177			0.141			0.086	
Domestic firm's domestic output		−0.003			−0.006			−0.050			−0.009	
Domestic firm's exports		0.393			0.396			0.139			0.455	
Domestic firm's aggregate output		0.047			0.045			−0.026			0.050	
Foreign firm's output		0.010			0.017			0.015			0.133	
PCM in the domestic market		0.003			0.006			0.025			0.004	
PCM in the export market		0.003			0.002			0.268			0.003	
PCM in the import market		−0.009			−0.014			−0.012			−0.101	
Aggregate demand price elasticity		0.025			0.025			0.033			0.027	

Note: Agr: Agriculture; Ind: Industry; Ser: Services. PCM: Price cost margin. HRT: Harrison–Rutherford–Tarr approach; CV1: Correct approach under the assumption that $\mu_i^0 = \mu_i^{0*} = \mu_i^{0m} = 0$; CV2: Correct approach under the assumption that $\mu_i^0 = \mu_i^{0*} = 15$ and $\mu_i^{0m} = 0$; CV3: Correct approach under the assumption that $\mu_i^0 = \mu_i^{0*} = 0$ and $\mu_i^{0m} = 15$.

the hypothesis that domestic firms believe that foreign firms will expand their output if they grow. Since trade liberalisation generally implies a fall in domestic sales, imports rise by a smaller percentage. These expectations are also reflected in a higher price cost margin in the domestic market (2.5 per cent), and a lower degree of exit (-5.0 per cent). The consequent fall in domestic sales in the industrial sector by 6.7 per cent together with a smaller increase in imports are the main reason why welfare does not increase.

The scenario 'CV3' is based upon the assumption that foreign firms expect the rival domestic firms to expand their production, as imports increase due to a tariff fall. This conjecture limits entry of foreign firms, whose number rises by only 8.6 per cent and causes a large expansion in the size of existing firms, that is, 13.3 per cent. The fact that $\mu_i^m > 0$ implies that $\hat{B}_i^m > 1$ and $\hat{C}_i^m > 0$. Hence, the foreign industry market share effect and the effect of the import volume relative to domestic sales play a bigger role compared to the previous scenarios. This is the reason why the price cost margin of the foreign firms declines by 10.1 per cent. As a result of a fall in foreign prices, domestic demand is satisfied by a larger volume of industrial imports, which increases by 23.1 per cent. This leads to larger welfare gains equal to 0.5 per cent of consumer income.[8]

5   Summary

This study proposes a procedure to embody the conjectural variation approach in CGE models, which are characterised by scale economies and free entry in order to capture the strategic interactions among rival firms in international markets. The model is similar to that used by HRT (1997b) to examine the regional impact on output and welfare of the reforms of the Uruguay Round, when firms compete in a quantity setting oligopoly with calibrated constant conjectures. It assumes that the price cost margin faced by national firms is endogenous, and derives the price elasticities of demand perceived by a firm in a multistage demand system.

I show that the price elasticities of demand perceived by a firm in the domestic and export markets are a function of the conjectured reactions of the rival domestic and foreign firms. I show also that the formulas suggested by HRT can be obtained under the hypothesis of Cournot competition. I indicate an approach to calibrate the conjectural variation parameters, and I set up a CGE model for Turkey for an empirical analysis. The numerical simulations indicate that the HRT approach, which implicitly assumes Cournot competition among domestic and foreign firms, leads to the same outcome produced with the conjectural variation approach of this study, when Cournot competition is explicitly postulated. However, if firms have alternative expectations, then the results can change. One of the contributions of this study is that the conjectural variation of domestic and foreign firms can be modelled within large-scale applied general equilibrium models. This would allow modellers to assess better the effects of economic policies once the strategic interactions among domestic and foreign firms are known.

Appendix: Equations

Derivation of (18)

Given (10)

$$\frac{\partial D_i}{\partial \tilde{d}_{is}} = D_i^{1/\varsigma_i} \tilde{d}_{is}^{-1/\varsigma_i} \left[1 + \frac{\sum_{t \neq s} (\tilde{d}_{it}^{-1/\varsigma_i})}{\tilde{d}_{is}^{-1/\varsigma_i}} \lambda \right], \tag{A1}$$

Since from (12) $D_i^{1/\varsigma_i} \tilde{d}_{is}^{-1/\varsigma_i} = \tilde{p}_{is}^d / p_i^d$, then

$$\frac{d \ln D_i}{d \ln \tilde{d}_{is}} = \frac{\tilde{p}_{is}^d \tilde{d}_{is}}{p_i^d D_i} \left[1 + \frac{\sum_{t \neq s} (\tilde{d}_{it}^{-1/\varsigma_i})}{\tilde{d}_{is}^{-1/\varsigma_i}} \lambda \right]. \tag{A2}$$

Since, by using the chain rule, $\partial p_i^d / \partial \tilde{d}_{is} = (\partial p_i^d / \partial D_i)(\partial D_i \partial \tilde{d}_{is})$, then

$$\frac{d \ln p_i^d}{d \ln \tilde{d}_{is}} = \frac{\tilde{p}_{is}^d \tilde{d}_{is}}{p_i^d D_i} \frac{D_i}{p_i^d} \frac{\partial p_i^d}{\partial D_i} \left[1 + \frac{\sum_{t \neq s} (\tilde{d}_{it}^{-1/\varsigma_i})}{\tilde{d}_{is}^{-1/\varsigma_i}} \lambda \right]. \tag{A3}$$

Given the symmetry assumption, (A3) and (A2) into (17) yield

$$\frac{1}{\tau_i} = -\frac{1}{\varsigma_i} + \frac{1}{n_i} \left(\frac{1}{\varsigma_i} + \frac{D_i}{p_i^d} \frac{\partial p_i^d}{\partial D_i} \right) \left[1 + \frac{\sum_{t \neq s} (\tilde{d}_{it}^{-1/\varsigma_i})}{\tilde{d}_{is}^{-1/\varsigma_i}} \lambda \right]. \tag{A4}$$

By applying similar steps at the second stage of the demand tree, then

$$\frac{D_i}{p_i^d} \frac{\partial p_i^d}{\partial D_i} = -\frac{1}{\varepsilon_i} + \Psi_i \left(\frac{1}{\varepsilon_i} - \frac{1}{\chi_i} \right) \left[1 + \frac{1 - \varphi_i}{\varphi_i} \left(\frac{M_i}{D_i} \right)^{-1/\varepsilon_i} \mu \right], \tag{A5}$$

where $\chi_i = -(p_i/Q_i)(\partial Q_i/\partial p_i)$. Equation (A5) into (A4) yields expression (18).

Derivation of the price elasticity of aggregate demand

The price elasticity of aggregate demand can be derived by using (4)–(6), as follows:

$$\chi_i = -\frac{\partial Q_i}{\partial p_i} \frac{p_i}{Q_i} = -\frac{p_i}{Q_i} \left(\frac{\partial X_i}{\partial p_i} + \frac{\partial C_i}{\partial p_i} \right) = -\frac{p_i}{Q_i} \frac{\partial X_i}{\partial p_i} + \frac{C_i}{Q_i}.$$

Under a Leontief specification $\partial X_i / \partial p_i = 0$. To show this assume that production is undertaken by using intermediate inputs only, which are substitutes. Then, the intermediate demand can be written as $X = a^b p^{-b} q^b Y$, where $q = [a^b p^{1-b} + (1-a)^b \bar{p}^{-1-b}]^{1/(1-b)}$, p is the price of the intermediate good X, $\bar{p}$

the price of its substitute, a a share parameter, and b the elasticity of substitution among inputs. In this case, $\partial X/\partial p = -ba^b Y p^{-1-b} q^b [1 - a^b (p/q)^{1-b}]$, which means that $\lim_{b\to 0}(\partial X/\partial p) = 0$.

Since I assume a Leontief specification between value added and intermediate inputs, which are in turn assumed to be net complements, then $\partial X_i/\partial p_i = 0$. Given the Cobb–Douglas utility function, the price elasticity of aggregate demand reduces to $0 \leq \chi_i = C_i/Q_i \leq 1$.

Notes

1 The 'new trade theory' began with models facing imperfect competition and increasing returns to scale. Alongside the gains from trade due to the conventional comparative advantage, it is argued that, by enlarging markets, international trade raises competition and allows greater exploitation of economies of scale (Krugman 1979).

2 Devarajan and Rodrik (1991) calibrate the price elasticity of domestic demand as a positive function of the ratio between the price of imports and the price of domestic goods.

3 The number of CGE models with imperfect competition and scale economies available in the literature is rather large. Further examples are the models of Wigle (1988), Brown and Stern (1989), Markusen and Wigle (1989), Markusen *et al.* (1995), Mercenier (1995), Mercenier and Schmitt (1996), De Santis (2000a).

4 Note that, in linear oligopolies and for an open set of values of the discount factor, the conjectural variation solution is the reduced form of the equilibrium of a quantity-setting repeated game with minimax punishments during T periods (Cabral 1995). Similarly, Pfaffermayr (1999) shows that a conjectural variation model may represent a reduced form of a price-setting supergame in a differentiated product market, which allows a wide range of outcome from perfect competition to joint unconstrained monopoly.

5 By calibration procedure I mean the estimation of unknown parameters, such that the observed values of endogenous variables constitute an equilibrium of the CGE model.

6 CGE studies, which have examined the economic implications of Turkish trade policies in the 1990s, are those of HRT (1997a) Mercenier and Yeldan (1997) and De Santis (2000b, 2001b).

7 Variables and parameters with ^ mean that they are calibrated, whilst variables with 0 are observed in the base year.

8 In a twin paper, I show how to incorporate Iceberg trade costs and the same model is proposed for competition policy experiments against illegal collaboration among competitors. The results indicate that large welfare gains can be generated if trade costs fall or if competition policies are introduced to break the collusive behaviour among either domestic firms or foreign firms. However, if these policies are brought in to weaken the collusive behaviour among exporting firms, then a welfare loss might occur because of a large deterioration of terms of trade (De Santis, 2001a).

References

Brown, D. K. and Stern, R. M. (1989) 'U.S.–Canada bilateral tariff elimination: The role of product differentiation and market structure', in: Feenstra, R. C. (ed.), *Trade Policies for International Competitiveness*, Chicago: Chicago University Press.

Cabral, L. M. B. (1995) 'Conjectural variations as a reduced form', *Economic Letters*, 49, 397–402.

Cowling, K. (1976) 'On the theoretical specification of industrial structure-performance relationships', *European Economic Review*, 8, 1–14.

Cowling, K. and Waterson, M. (1976) 'Price-cost margin and market structure', *Economica*, 43, 267–74.

Cripps, M. W. and Myles, G. D. (1988) *General equilibrium and imperfect competition: profit feedback effects and price normalisation*, Department of Economics of Warwick University, Warwick Economic Research Papers, n. 295.

Daughety, A. F. (1985) 'Reconsidering Cournot: the Cournot equilibrium is consistent', *Rand Journal of Economic*, 16, 368–79.

Devarajan, S. and Rodrik, D. (1989) 'Trade liberalization in developing countries: Do imperfect competition and scale economies matter?', *American Economic Review, Papers and proceedings*, 79, 283–7.

Devarajan, S. and Rodrik, D. (1991) 'Pro-competitive effects of trade reform. Results from a CGE model of Cameroon', *European Economic Review*, 35, 1157–84.

De Santis, R. A. (2000a) 'Optimal export taxes, welfare, industry concentration and firm size: a general equilibrium analysis', *Review of International Economics*, 8, 319–35.

De Santis, R. A. (2000b) 'The impact of a customs union with the EU on Turkey's welfare, employment and income distribution: An AGE model with alternative labour market structures', Forthcoming in *Journal of Economic Integration*.

De Santis, R. A. (2001a) 'A computable general equilibrium model for open economies with imperfect competition and product differentiation'. *Journal of Economic Integration*, Forthcoming.

De Santis, R. A. (2001b) 'The 1990 trade liberalisation policy of Turkey: An applied general equilibrium assessment'. Forthcoming in the *International Economic Journal*.

Dierker, H. and Grodal, B. (1986) 'Nonexistence of Cournot–Walras equilibrium in a general equilibrium model with the oligopolists', in: Hildenbrand, W. and Mas Colell, A. (eds), *Contributions to Mathematical Economics in Honor of Gerard Debreu*, Amsterdam: North Holland.

Dixit, A. K. and Stiglitz, J. (1977) 'Monopolistic competition and optimum product diversity', *American Economic Review*, 67, 297–308.

Ferrel, J. and Shapiro, C. (1990) 'Horizontal mergers: An equilibrium analysis', *American Economic Review*, 80, 107–26.

Gabszewicz, J. J. and Vial, J. (1972) 'Oligopoly à la Cournot in general equilibrium analysis', *Journal of Economic Theory*, 4, 381–400.

Gasiorek, M., Smith, A. and Venables, A. (1992) '1992: Trade and welfare; a general equilibrium model', in Winters, L. A. (ed.), *Trade Flows and Trade Policy After '1992'*, Cambridge: Cambridge University Press.

Ginsburgh, V. (1994) 'In the Cournot–Walras general equilibrium model, there may be 'more to gain' by changing the numéraire than by eliminating imperfections: A two-good economy example', in: Mercenier, J. and Srinivasan, T. N. (eds), *Applied General Equilibrium and Economic Development. Present Achievements and Future Trends*, Ann Arbor: The University of Michigan Press.

Ginsburgh, V. and Keyzer, M. (1997) *The Structure of Applied General equilibrium Models*, Cambridge: The MIT Press.

Harris, R. (1984) 'Applied general equilibrium analysis of small open economies with scale economies and imperfect competition', *American Economic Review*, 74(5) 1016–32.

Harrison, G. W., Rutherford, T. F. and Tarr, D. G. (1996) 'Increased competition and completion of the market in the European Union: Static and steady state effects', *Journal of Economic Integration*, 11(3) 332–65.

Harrison, G. W., Rutherford, T. F. and Tarr, D. G. (1997a) 'Economic implications for Turkey of a customs union with the European Union', *European Economic Review*, 41, 861–70.

Harrison, G. W., Rutherford, T. F. and Tarr, D. G. (1997b) 'Quantifying the Uruguay Round', *Economic Journal*, 107, 1405–30.

Krugman, P. (1979) 'Increasing returns, monopolistic competition, and international trade', *Journal of International Economics*, 9, 469–79.

Machin, S. and Van Reenen, J. (1993) 'Profit margins and the business cycle: evidence from UK manufacturing firms', *Journal of Industrial Economics*, 41, 29–50.

Makowski, L. (1987) 'Are 'rational conjectures' rational?', *Journal of Industrial Economics*, 36, 35–47.

Markusen, J. R., Rutherford, T. F. and Hunter, L. (1995) 'Trade liberalization in a multinational-dominated industry', *Journal of International Economics*, 38, 95–117.

Markusen, J. R. and Wigle, R. (1989) 'Nash equilibrium tariffs for the United States and Canada: The roles of country size, scale economies, and capital mobility', *Journal of Political Economy*, 97, 368–86.

Mercenier, J. (1995), 'Can '1992' reduce unemployment in Europe? On welfare and employment effects of Europe's move to a single market', *Journal of Policy Modelling*, 17, 1–37.

Mercenier, J. and Schmitt, N. (1996) 'On sunk costs and trade liberalization in applied general equilibrium', *International Economic Review*, 37, 551–71.

Mercenier, J. and Yeldan, A. E. (1997) 'On Turkey's trade policy: Is a customs union with Europe enough?' *European Economic Review*, 41, 871–80.

Pfaffermayr, M. (1999) 'Conjectural-variation models and supergames with price competition in a differentiated product oligopoly', *Journal of Economics*, 70, 309–26.

Schmalensee, R. (1989), 'Industrial economics: An overview analysis', *Economic Journal*, 98, 643–81.

Slade, M. E. (1987) 'Interfirm rivalry in a repeated game: an empirical test of tacit collusion', *Journal of Industrial Economics*, 35, 499–516.

Smith, A. and Venables, A. J. (1988) 'Completing the internal market in the European Community. Some industry simulations', *European Economic Review*, 32, 1501–25.

State Institute of Statistics Prime Ministry Republic of Turkey (1994) *The Input–Output Structure of the Turkish Economy 1990*, Ankara.

Wigle, R. (1988) 'General equilibrium evaluation of Canada–U.S. trade liberalization in a global context', *Canadian Journal of Economics*, 21, 539–64.

7 Market power in a liberalized power market

The case of Italy

Giancarlo Pireddu and Christian M. Dufournaud

1 Introduction

The Italian electricity market is changing following implementation of the legislative decree no.79, dated 16 March 1999, 'implementation of directive 96/92/EC establishing common rules for the internal market in electricity'. Electricity generation and supply are liberalized activities, while transmission and distribution activities remain natural monopolies with the principle of regulated third party access (RTPA) to the grids. The legislative decree distinguishes between eligible and franchised customers. Eligible customers are allowed to buy power from unregulated generators in power exchange markets (PX) with unrestricted price formation. Franchised customers continue to buy electricity at regulated tariff rates, which are to be replaced gradually transforming all franchised consumers into eligible ones. One role of the PX, to be established by 1 January 2002, is to hold auctions determining hourly prices. Supply and demand bids determine the market-clearing price for electricity.

There are at least four benefits of liberalization and the PX. First, multiple and bilateral negotiations are no longer necessary. Second, centralization of trading brings sellers, buyers and providers of transmission, distribution and ancillary services together to arrive at a market-clearing price. A consequence of bringing agents together is that the auction provides a convenient mechanism to trade, buy and sell orders at any time of day. Third, the PX provides a neutral and independent clearing and settlement function. The PX minimizes the risk associated with the failure of bilateral contracts by handling credit clearances and managing credit risks according to a specific set of rules. Fourth, through the auction process, the PX allows even small generators and suppliers to access the market. Electricity economics traditionally focussed on engineering cost minimization and plant optimization. The PX transforms electricity generation and supply activities into a profit maximization process.

Electricity generation and supply liberalization determines a new structure for the Italian electricity supply industry. Price formation and market power are the most crucial issues if only a small number of firms compete in this newly liberalized market.

Market power is the ability of the larger firms to elevate the price of electricity above competitive levels over a sustained period of time. The market power issue is important for two reasons. First, if a producer acquires too large a share of the overall electricity supply industry capacity it could create conditions for market power abuse. Second, market power would give dominant firms an opportunity to charge market-based rates that are unreasonably high, well above a competitive market level.

There are two principal mechanisms by which firms may exercise market power: strategic bidding and capacity withholding. Strategic bidding involves firms bidding prices significantly above the production costs of their generating units, with the intent of forcing up the market-clearing price. Strategic bidding is facilitated by the fact that the bids submitted by generating firms typically apply to the next 12-hour period. Since electricity demand fluctuates over a 12-hour period firms must anticipate these changes in demand in their submission of the bidding schedule for this period to the market operator.

Capacity withholding, the second mechanism for exercising market power, involves firms withholding some of their capacity in the bidding process, in an effort to cause more expensive units higher up the system-wide supply curve to set the market-clearing price. Firms that attempt this strategy must ensure that the foregone revenues from not having some of their infra-marginal capacity dispatched in a given time interval are more than offset by the additional revenues paid for the capacity that is dispatched in that interval. Empirical studies have shown that such a strategy on electricity prices may be very significant.

There are two kinds of indicators typically used for measuring market power: implicit and explicit indicators. Implicit indicators do not attempt to directly measure the impact of market power, but rather measure factors which could reflect conditions and/or potential for the exercise of market power. A typical example is the Herfindahl–Hirschman index (HHI), which is an indicator of market power concentration. The HHI is defined as

$$\text{HHI} = \sum_i S_i^2 \quad \text{and} \quad \sum_i S_i = 100,$$

where S_i is the market share of the ith firm in the market. If the market share is expressed in percentage terms, the HHI lies between 0 (i.e. no market power) and 10,000 (i.e. monopoly). The minimum value of HHI occurs when the electricity supply industry comprises a very large number of firms with negligible market shares.[1] According to the Federal Energy Regulatory Commission's Order 888, a market is deemed to be 'not concentrated' if its HHI is less than 1,000; 'moderately concentrated' if its HHI lies between 1,000 and 1,800; and 'highly concentrated' if its HHI is greater than 1,800.

Explicit indicators of market power, on the other hand, are designed to directly reflect the ultimate impact of market power, such as a change in consumer prices. In order to quantify firms' ability to exercise market power in a PX market, it is possible to define the Price-Cost Margin Index (PCMI). The PCMI quantifies the degree to which the actual price deviates from its 'perfectly' competitive price. The 'perfectly' competitive price of electricity occurs when it is equal to the variable cost of the marginal unit, which is equal to the system-wide short-run marginal cost of generation. The PCMI is thus an explicit indicator of market power, defined as

$$\text{PCMI} = \frac{\text{Actual price} - \text{Perfectly competitive price}}{\text{Perfectly competitive price}}.$$

The PCMI has a minimum value of zero, for a perfectly competitive market, and has an unbounded maximum value.[2] If the PCMI is above 5 per cent, according to the US Department of Justice, the market cannot be characterized as fully competitive. The PCMI is similar to the well-known Lerner Index, in which the price margin is measured against the actual price as opposed to the 'perfectly' competitive price as in the PCMI case. These two indicators are connected in the following way:

$$\text{Lerner Index} = \frac{\text{PCMI}}{(1 + \text{PCMI})}.$$

The topic of market power in electricity markets has received a great deal of attention by explicitly modelling the strategic behaviour of firms. Research in this subject has used the 'supply function equilibrium' approach to oligopoly modelling, first developed by Kemplerer and Meyer (1989). Generation costs are represented by smooth, continuous cost curves. Step function of generation costs was introduced by Von der Fehr and Harbour (1993) to model the UK spot electricity market. Relevant contributions to the analysis of market power in electricity markets are, among others, in Green and Newbery (1992), Andersson and Bergman (1995), Green (1996), Biewald and White (1997), Borenstein and Bushnell (1997), Patrick and Wolack (1997), Weiss (1997), Rudkevich and Duckworth (1998) and Amundsen et al. (1999).

The purpose of this paper is to develop and apply a numerical model to determine the price level on the Italian electricity market after liberalization and to explicitly measure the market power of dominant firms in the liberalized power market and their ability to influence price formation through strategic behaviour. The paper is structured as follows: Section 2 includes the main assumptions and a brief description of the analytical model; Section 3 describes numerical results and outcomes.

2   Description of the model

2.1   *Introduction*

The introduction of individual firms as active agents is the key feature and chief innovation of the numerical model developed, among others, by Green and

Newbery (1992) and Anderson and Bergman (1995). What is new here is considering individual firms that actually own generating plants and thereby control their utilization level. In other words, individual firms in the numerical model own a portfolio of generating units and compete with each other in the electricity market. The strategic interaction among different players is important for the market outcome. Each individual firm possesses a specific set of technologies available to meet its market demand both in peak and off-peak periods. The inclusion of individual firms enables findings from oligopoly theory to be used in this numerical model of the Italian electricity market.

Using published data from Italy, a benchmark scenario reflecting the situation prior to liberalization is compared to gains and losses from competitive and strategic behaviours. The numerical model endogenously computes the equilibrium clearing price of electricity, market shares of firms and operating surplus. The numerical model is also used to simulate changes in market power following the break-up of the dominant firm into smaller units, and the full liberalization of electricity imports. The model does not take into account the dynamic effect of the actual and potential new entry of more efficient firms into the market. The threat of entry may reduce not only the degree of market power but also the competitive electricity price in the long run. The modelling approach depends on the specific institutional set-up of the liberalized electricity market. If all transactions on the market have to go via the pool, the modelling focus must be on the firms' behaviour when placing bids to the power pool (see Green and Newbery 1992, for the case of the England and Wales pool). If only a small share of total electricity generation is traded on the spot market and bilateral contracts are typical contracts that are actually traded, the modelling focus must be on the firms' behaviour when defining the contract price. As it is assumed the Italian electricity market is likely to allow a mixture of short-run spot market trade and longer-run bilateral contracts, the same numerical model developed by Anderson and Bergman (1995) for the case of Sweden is adopted.

Electricity consumers pay a final price composed of four different cost components: distribution, transmission, capacity (fixed generation costs) and energy (variable generation costs). The clearing electricity price in the model represents the last of the four components and the model computes the energy price component according to the marginal cost dispatching approach and the strategic interaction among the model players. The numerical model is solved by means of (General Algebraic Modeling System) GAMS (see Brooke *et al.* 1988).

2.2   *Demand*

In the model, a single representative buyer of electricity exists combining eligible and franchised consumer demand. The single buyer has no market power. The bulk energy market determines an equilibrium price for both eligible and franchised consumers. The total demand excludes quantities supplied by the domestic electricity industry at preferred administrative rates and quantities imported at fixed prices established by long-term contracts.

Demand D of the representative buyer is given by:

$$D = D_0 \left(\frac{P_e}{P_0}\right)^{\eta} \tag{1}$$

where D is the total demand, P_e is the equilibrium (clearing) price in the bulk energy market, D_0 is the total demand prior to liberalization (benchmark), P_0 is the benchmark price, η is the price elasticity of demand which is supposed to be constant and equal to -0.5. Total demand is equal to the sum of total domestic production, X, and spot imports, M, that is, $D = X + M$. The equilibrium price can be expressed as a function of total demand

$$P_e = P_0 \left(\frac{X + M}{D_0}\right)^{(1-\eta)/\eta} \tag{2}$$

The single representative buyer buys imported electricity only if the import spot price P_m is cheaper than the equilibrium price P_e, that is, $P_m \leq P_e$, and if there is enough physical import capacity, K_m, available for spot imports, that is, $M \leq K_m$. K_m is set equal to 3 TWh.

2.3   Supply

The electricity generation is represented by:

a   seven firms;
b   five technologies for base-load plants (hydro, combined cycle gas turbine, conventional oil-fired plants, coal-fired plants, geothermal plants);
c   three technologies for peak-load plants (hydro, open cycle gas turbine, other fossil-fired plants).

Each firm possesses a specific basket of technologies and installed capacities, which remain fixed in the simulations. In the benchmark, each firm is also characterized by a market share both in peak and off-peak periods.

2.4   Cost function

Production technologies have specific production costs. The seven technologies considered are available at equal costs to all firms, but each firm has specific total and marginal cost functions according to its installed capacity and market share. Firms minimize total cost, CT, constrained by their generation capacity, using base-load and peak-load plants according to the so-called 'merit order', that is, using plants with respect to an increasing order of their marginal costs.

Total cost is given by the sum of base-load and peak-load production costs, and each production cost is given by the sum of fixed costs, CF, and unit variable costs, c, times the specific quantity produced. Unit variable costs c are equal for all producers but differentiated by technologies.

The total output X_f of the fth firm is equal to the sum of the output X_i of the ith base-load plant and the output X_j of the jth peak-load plant. The firm solves the following constrained optimization program:

$$\min_{X_i, X_j} CT_f(X_f, K_{if}, K_{jf}) = \sum_{i=1}^{I} c_i X_i + CF_i + \sum_{j=1}^{J} c_j X_j + CF_j$$

subject to

$$\sum_{i=1}^{I} X_{if} + \sum_{j=1}^{J} X_{jf} \geq X_f \quad \mu_f \quad f = 1, 2, \dots, F$$

$$- X_{if} \geq -K_{if}; \quad \lambda_{if}; \quad i = 1, 2, \dots, I$$

$$- X_{jf} \geq -K_{jf}; \quad \lambda_{jf}; \quad j = 1, 2, \dots, J$$

(3)

where K_{if} and K_{jf} represent, respectively, installed capacity limits of the ith base-load plant and the jth peak-load plant.

The Kuhn–Tucker first order conditions are:

$$\frac{\partial L}{\partial X_{kf}} \geq 0 \quad \Rightarrow \quad c_{kf} + \lambda_{kf} - \mu_f \geq 0$$

$$X_{kf} \cdot \frac{\partial L}{\partial X_{kf}} = 0 \quad \Rightarrow \quad X_{kf}(c_k + \lambda_{kf} - \mu_f) = 0$$

$$X_{kf} \geq 0$$

(4)

where $k = i$ (base-load plants), j (peak-load plants).

The marginal cost of output produced by the kth plant is defined by

$$\frac{\partial CT_f}{\partial X_{kf}} = c_k + \lambda_{kf} = \mu_f$$

The Lagrangean multiplier μ represents the marginal cost of the fth firm and λ represents the 'scarcity rent' of each technology owned by the firm. The cost function is not differentiable at the points of switching technology: $X_f = K_{1f}$; $X_f = K_{2f}$; etc., and the marginal cost is a stepwise function.

2.5 Equilibrium price

Several possibilities are conceivable to determine the equilibrium (clearing) price according to how each firm conjectures that the outputs of its rivals change in response to its own changes in output. If a firm believes that increasing its output leaves total industry output unchanged, that is, its rivals reduce their output, the highest marginal cost of the technology allowed to supply the market determines the equilibrium price. An alternative conjecture yields a Cournot equilibrium.

In this case the firm knows the market demand and maximizes its profit, taking the output of its rivals as given in determining its own strategy.

The total output of each firm, X_f, can be modelled by the following profit maximization problem:

$$\max_{X_f} \pi_f = P_e(X_f, X_{-f}) \cdot X_f - CT_f(X_f, K_{if}, K_{if}) \tag{5}$$

where X_f is the output of the firm and X_{-f} is the sum of its rivals' total output. Total domestic production, X, is equal to $X_f + X_{-f}$.

The conjectural variation relevant to this maximization problem is

$$P_e + X_f \frac{\partial P_e}{\partial X_f} \left(1 + \frac{\partial X_{-f}}{\partial X_f}\right) = \frac{\partial CT_f}{\partial X_f} \tag{6}$$

where the conjectural variation is introduced via the term $\partial X_{-f}/\partial X_f$. If it is set equal to -1, the outcome is determined by competition in prices (pure competition or competition à la Bertrand). If it is set equal to zero, the outcome is determined by Cournot–Nash equilibrium. If it is set equal to zero only for the dominant firm and equal to -1 for all its rivals, the outcome is determined by Stackelberg equilibrium. For 'fringe' firms, as well as under Bertrand competition, the impact on the equilibrium price exerted by the output is assumed to be zero.

3   Numerical results

3.1   Benchmark

The benchmark scenario is replicated using published[3] Italian data for 1996. Active firms include the nationalized utility Enel (dominant firm), the largest municipal utility, the two largest private generators, aggregation of a small number of municipal utilities and of independent power producers, respectively, as individual firms. The remaining power producers are aggregated into one group, that is, fringe firms, that passively adapts its strategy to those of the active players. The domestic production and market share of the firms in the benchmark are shown in Table 7.1. Spot imports are set equal to the spot import capacity limits.

The equilibrium price in the benchmark is slightly higher than the highest marginal cost for the most expensive technology used to fill domestic demand, in order to recover a small proportion of inefficiency costs via a mark-up. In the benchmark scenario, the mark-up is assumed to be equal for all firms. The spot import price is lower than the equilibrium price.

3.2   Price formation and market power

The main rationale behind electricity market liberalization is to promote lower prices through competition. The benchmark equilibria represent a relevant basis of comparison.

Table 7.1 Domestic production, spot imports and market share in the benchmark

Players	Supply (TWh)	Market share %
Enel	184.171	80.2
Municipalities	13.270	5.8
IPP	28.009	12.2
Fringe firms	1.090	0.5
Domestic production	226.540	98.7
Spot imports	3.000	1.3
Total demand	229.540	100.0

Fierce competition à la Bertrand yields a substantial market demand increase (+11.6 TWh) and a lower equilibrium price (0.89 index) with respect to benchmark. The equilibrium price reduction is achieved by increasing efficiency, eliminating the need for firms to mark-up energy marginal costs.

The Cournot–Nash behaviour, given unchanged technology endowment and a fixed price elasticity of demand, shows a surprisingly high price level (3.72 index) and a significant reduction in total domestic output (− 112.9 TWh), primarily due to the high market share of the dominant firm and the price elasticity demand rigidity. Saturation of import transmission wires limits the feasibility of cheap spot imports to compete in the domestic market to 3 TWh. The Stackelberg equilibrium is driven by the decision of the dominant firm, as its rivals follow. Due to limited physical import capacity, the dominant firm's market share and the price elasticity demand rigidity, the equilibrium price and the domestic demand are close to the Cournot–Nash equilibrium.

The results are summarized in Table 7.2. The equilibria are also compared in terms of changes in welfare, that is, operating surplus. The operating surplus of the firm is computed as the total revenue minus the total variable (i.e. energy) cost. An index of the operating surplus is shown in Table 7.2 as a change from the benchmark index of 100.

When the strategic behaviour moves from the benchmark equilibria to the Cournot–Nash one, the result is a 50 per cent drop in the market share of the dominant firm accompanied by a tripling of its operating surplus. The other producers also realize welfare gains, all paid by consumers.

3.3 Price determination and market power after dominant firm break-up

In order to investigate the impact of increasing the number of players in the model and reducing the market share of the dominant firm, the various equilibria are recomputed, using the scheduled break-up strategy programme defined by the Italian government.[4] According to this programme, Enel must divest 15,000 MW of its power capacity.

Table 7.2 Scenario and simulation equilibria

Domestic production	Enel (TWh)	Municipalities (TWh)	IPPs (TWh)	Fringe firms (TWh)	Spot imports (fixed) (TWh)	Demand (TWh)
Benchmark	184.171	13.270	28.009	1.090	3.000	229.540
Competitive equilibrium	192.954	13.979	30.037	1.159	3.000	241.129
Cournot–Nash equilibrium	52.798	17.874	41.421	1.504	3.000	116.597

Market share (%)

	Enel	Municipalities	IPPs	Fringe firms	Spot imports	Total
Benchmark	80.2	5.8	12.2	0.5	1.3	100.0
Competitive equilibrium	80.0	5.8	12.5	0.5	1.2	100.0
Cournot–Nash equilibrium	45.3	15.3	35.5	1.3	2.6	100.0

Operating surplus index (benchmark = 100)

	Enel	Municipalities	IPPs	Fringe firms		Total
Benchmark	100.0	100.0	100.0	100.0		100.0
Competitive equilibrium	80.1	78.9	81.7	93.4		80.3
Cournot–Nash equilibrium	208.5	980.2	1,032.2	535.0		353.3

Price index

Benchmark	1.00
Competitive equilibrium	0.89
Cournot–Nash equilibrium	3.72

The model is used to simulate new equilibria after divestiture of the dominant firm into four independent firms in accordance with this programme. The market share of the new dominant firm is lower than 50 per cent, the maximum level each firm is allowed to produce and import according to the government's programme. The new firms are endowed with installed capacities of sufficient size, base- and peak-load capacity mixes, and technology plant mixes that can guarantee their ability to compete in the PX market. Repowering of divested plants yields energy efficiency increase and marginal cost reductions.

Under the new generation structure, the Cournot–Nash equilibrium changes considerably. The results summarized in Table 7.3 show that the size of the national utility is very important in determining total production, equilibrium price and welfare.

Table 7.3 Production, imports, equilibrium prices, market shares and operating surplus index variations after Enel break-up (new enel and new gencos)

Domestic production	'New Enel' (TWh)	'New Gencos' (TWh)	Municipalities (TWh)	IPPs (TWh)	Fringe firms (TWh)	Spot imports (fixed) (TWh)	Demand (TWh)
Competitive equilibrium	105.438	87.516	13.979	30.037	1.159	3.000	241.129
Cournot–Nash equilibrium	58.086	83.750	15.318	28.498	1.112	3.000	189.764

Market share (%)

	'New Enel'	'New Gencos'	Municipalities	IPPs	Fringe firms	Spot imports	Total
Competitive equilibrium	43.7	36.3	5.8	12.5	0.5	1.2	100.0
Cournot–Nash equilibrium	30.6	44.1	8.1	15.0	0.6	1.6	100.0

Operating surplus index variation

	'New Enel'	'New Gencos'	Municipalities	IPPs	Fringe firms	Total
Competitive equilibrium	−45.4	—	0.0	0.0	0.0	0.0
Cournot–Nash equilibrium	−66.5	—	−77.8	−81.2	−72.1	−53.0

Price index

	'New Enel'
Competitive equilibrium	0.89
Cournot–Nash equilibrium	1.44

Following the break-up, in the Cournot–Nash equilibrium the total domestic production increases to 186.8 TWh from 113.6 TWh, the equilibrium price drops to 1.44 from 3.72, and the total operating surplus decreases by 67 per cent. The new dominant firm after the break-up maintains 30.6 per cent of the market.

The Cournot–Nash equilibrium following the break-up resembles the competitive equilibrium also following the break-up. Total domestic production under the competitive equilibrium is equal to 238.1 TWh while the equilibrium price index remains equal to 0.89. The new dominant firm after break-up maintains 43.7 per cent of the market, below the maximum level of 50 per cent each firm is allowed to produce and import in the liberalized electricity market in Italy. Its operating surplus is lowered by 45 per cent due to the reduction in its domestic market share from 80 to 44 per cent. Because of the relative size of the divested dominant firm and the limited share of the liberalized electricity imports, the equilibrium price in the newly liberalized Italian electricity market can remain higher than prior to break-up. Given the size of the largest firm, the number of small firms does not determine the outcome. Liberalization and dominant firm break-up are only a necessary condition for the achievement of competition and they do not secure a competitive market.

3.4   Physical import capacity and price responsiveness

The European electricity directive aims to create a single electricity market in the European Union and not fifteen liberalized national electricity markets. Current physical import capacity limits among European countries are one of the most important constraints to the creation of a single market. As a consequence, cheap electricity imports cannot compete against inefficient domestic production. The combined effect of the dominant firm break-up and the relaxation of physical import capacity limits on Cournot–Nash and competitive equilibria are compared in Table 7.4.

The spot import quantity is free to float up to 90 per cent of the actual maximum level of import capacity (approx. 40 TWh per annum).

Table 7.4 Cournot–Nash and competitive equilibria after Enel break-up (new Enel and new Gencos) and spot imports liberalization

Domestic Production	'New Enel' (TWh)	'New Gencos' (TWh)	Municipalities (TWh)	IPPs (TWh)	Fringe firms (TWh)	Spot imports (free) (TWh)	Demand (TWh)
Competitive equilibrium	100.230	83.710	11.485	27.401	1.083	29.369	253.278
Cournot–Nash equilibrium	53.529	83.713	14.064	27.904	1.096	36.660	216.966

Market share (%)

	'New Enel'	'New Gencos'	Municipalities	IPPs	Fringe firms	Spot imports	Total
Competitive equilibrium	39.6	33.1	4.5	10.8	0.4	11.6	100.0
Cournot–Nash equilibrium	24.7	38.6	6.5	12.9	0.5	16.9	100.0

Operating surplus index variation

	'New Enel'	'New Gencos'	Municipalities	IPPs	Fringe firms		Total
Competitive equilibrium	−15.3	−15.7	−27.1	−27.0	−15.2		−17.5
Cournot–Nash equilibrium	−34.7	−34.9	−41.6	−37.6	−25.3		−35.6

Price index

	'New Enel'						
Competitive equilibrium	0.81						
Cournot–Nash equilibrium	1.10						

Numerical results confirm the expected solution, that cheap electricity imports have a crowding-out effect on domestic production and reduce the equilibrium price equal to the highest marginal cost of the plant in the merit order. Second, the size of the largest firm is less essential for this outcome since import competition collapses the Cournot–Nash equilibrium close to the competitive one. Under the new institutional framework, the Cournot–Nash equilibrium changes considerably. Demand increases from 189.8 to 217.0 TWh, spot imports increase from 3 to 36.7 TWh, the total domestic production drops to 180.3 from 186.8 TWh, the equilibrium price drops to 1.10 from 1.44, and the total operating surplus decreases by 53 per cent.

Under the competitive equilibrium, total demand increases to 253.3 from 241.1 TWh, domestic production decreases to 223.9 from 238.1 TWh because of cheap spot import, market share increases to 12 per cent from 1.2 per cent. The crowding-out effect pushes down competitive clearing price to 0.81 from 0.89.

The crowding-out effect pushes inefficient plants out of the market. The results suggest that international market integration can effectively reduce market power as long as there is a sufficient import/export transmission capacity. However, bottlenecks in the transmission lines tend to protect the market power of the dominant firm, as it may be able to exert it by creating congestion in the transmission lines.

4 Conclusions

Given the current Italian industry structure, characterized by a high degree of concentration, liberalization and deregulation are not sufficient conditions for a lower electricity price in the bulk generation market. The results show that the equilibrium price may be higher than was the case prior to liberalization. Under liberalization, if the dominant firm is left intact, and all firms act strategically, the equilibrium price is substantially higher than the benchmark one.

If the dominant firm is broken-up according to the pattern described above and all firms act strategically, the equilibrium price remains above the benchmark price, but substantially below the equilibrium price if the dominant firm is not broken-up. Perfect competition, regardless of whether or not the dominant firm is broken-up, always leads to an equilibrium price below the benchmark price.

The sensitivity of this conclusion to a change in the price elasticity of demand was tested. The results confirm the previous conclusion if the price elasticity of demand is lowered. If it is raised, the market must be open to cheap imports in order to meet the increasing demand that a fall in price generates.

Once imports are allowed to compete in the domestic generation market, regardless of the strategic behaviour adopted by domestic firms, the equilibrium price approaches the competitive one. Though this conclusion is not surprising, it does suggest that once the electricity generation market is open to European-wide competition, strategic behaviour of domestic firms is neutralized. A caveat to this conclusion is that dominant firms in the European-wide market could practice strategic behaviour to dominate in various national markets.

Mitigation measures available for market power control include demand side actions, contractual methods, price caps, increasing the number of owners of generation plants, the control of pumped storage hydro plants by an independent transmission system operator and the threat of entry of more efficient firms. It appears that national regulatory rules are necessary in order to prevent strategic behaviour by dominant firms in a national liberalized market if competitive import capacity is small with respect to the relevant market. Some rules may be necessary in the single European electricity market.

Notes

1 Ten thousand divided by HHI yields a number which can be regarded as the effective number of identically-sized firms in the market. For example, if there are ten identically-sized firms, the HHI is 1,000, while a market with five identically-sized firms has an HHI of 2,000.
2 The PCMI concept appears implicitly in the US Department of Justice guidelines for competition (Statement Accompanying Release of Revised Merger Guidelines, 2 April 1992).
3 Annuario *Dati statistici sull'energia elettrica in Italia 1996*, Enel 1997.
4 *Piano per le cessioni delle centrali Enel*, published in 'Staffetta Petrolifera', 7 August 1999, pp. 3–8.

References

Amundsen, E. S., Bergman, L. and Andersson, B. (1999) 'Trade and market power on the northern European market for electricity', in: *New Equilibria in the Energy Markets: the Role of New Regions and Areas, Conference Proceedings, 22nd IAEE Annual International Conference*, Rome 9–12 June 1999, vol. 2.

Andersson, B. and Bergman, L. (1995) 'Market structure and price of electricity: an ex ante analysis of the deregulated Swedish electricity market', *The Energy Journal*, 16 (2), 97–109.

Biewald, B. E. and White, D. E. (1997) 'Horizontal market power in New England electricity market: simulation results and a review of NEPOOL's analysis', Paper prepared for the New England Conference of Public Utility Commissioners.

Borenstein, S. and Bushnell, J. (1997) 'An empirical analysis of the potential for market power in California's electricity industry', University of California Energy Institute, Berkeley, draft.

Brooke, A., Kendrick, D. and Meeraus, A. (1988) *GAMS. A User's Guide*, Redwood City, California: Scientific Press.

Green, R. J. (1996) 'Increasing competition in the British electricity spot market', *Journal of Industrial Economics*, XLIV(2), 205–16.

Green, R. J. and Newbery, D. M. (1992) 'Competition in the British electricity spot market', *Journal of Political Economy*, 100(5), 929–53.

Klemperer, P. D. and Meyer, M. A. (1989) 'Supply function equilibria in Oligopoly under uncertainty', *Econometrica*, 57(6), 1243–77.

Patrick, R. H. and Wolak, F. A. (1997) 'Estimating the customer-level demand for electricity under real-time market prices', Stanford University, Preliminary draft.

Rudkevitch, A. and Duckworth, M. (1998) 'Strategic bidding in a deregulated generation industry: implications for electricity pricing, asset valuation, and regulatory response', *The Electricity Journal*, 11(1), 73–83.

Von der Fehr, N. and Harbour, D. (1993) 'Spot market competition in the UK electricity industry', *The Economic Journal*, 103, 531–46.

Weiss, J. (1997) 'Market power issues in the restructuring of the electricity industry: an experimental investigation', Harvard Business School, Draft.

Part III

Environment

8 The Kyoto Protocol

Implications of international capital
mobility on trade and regional welfare

Katrin Springer

1 Introduction

As the environmental conferences in Kyoto 1997, in Buenos Aires in December
1998, and in The Hague and Bonn 2000 and 2001 have shown, there exists a
broad consensus about the necessity of reducing greenhouse gas emissions in
order to protect world climate. The specific policy measures and instruments for
reducing emissions, however, are still under debate. The Kyoto Protocol (UN,
1997) contains quantified emission constraints for the industrialized (Annex-I)
countries. The acceptance of the Kyoto Protocol by national legislative bodies
and further commitments to emission reductions considerably depend to a large
extent on the economic costs related to the implementation of emissions control.
Appropriate policy measures have now to be imposed by the signatory countries
in order to match their emission reduction objectives. National policies will
induce allocational adjustments of production and consumption patterns in the
countries, and will, therefore, lead to a change in their international competitiveness. Through international spillovers national emission reduction policies will
also affect non-abating countries. It is less clear whether a specific country –
subject to emission control or not – will benefit or lose from the changes in
international prices.

Most multi-regional models analysing the impacts of climate change policies
on sectoral allocation, international trade, and welfare, while rich on sectoral
detail, neglect the explicit analysis of international mobility of physical capital.
However, it is very likely that the impacts of abatement policies will change if
international capital mobility is considered. When capital is internationally
mobile, a climate policy with differentiated emission targets for certain regions
can affect national welfare through impacts on the trade balance, on the
foreign ownership of domestic capital, and (via change in terms-of-trade) on the
international competitiveness of import-competing and export-oriented sectors.
Furthermore, international capital mobility creates an additional channel through
which domestic policy measures can impose spillover effects on other economies
(cf. Bovenberg and Goulder, 1993).

International cross-ownership of capital has become more extensive in the past
decades. While the globalization of international capital markets in the 1990s has

restored a degree of international capital mobility not seen since this century's beginning, the labour market remains mainly nationally segmented. Therefore, this chapter focuses on the incorporation of international mobility of physical capital into a multi-regional trade model where the factor labour is internationally immobile.

According to the theoretical literature, international capital mobility changes allocational and distributional outcomes of a domestic policy. Especially, in trade models with differences in production technologies between countries, trade barriers, or other market distortions on the production side, the consideration of international capital mobility may significantly change the policy results compared to the case where only trade in goods is taken into account.

This chapter analyses the influence of different degrees of international capital mobility on the outcomes of an international climate policy. Therefore, it assesses the allocational and distributional implications of the Kyoto Protocol for several regions by comparing the simulation results for the cases with perfect, restricted, and without international capital mobility. The amount of greenhouse gas leakage for all three cases is determined. The quantitative analysis is based on a recursive dynamic global, multi-regional, multi-sectoral Computable General Equilibrium (CGE) model where the regions are linked by bilateral trade and capital flows.

The policy scenario shows that the outcome of the Kyoto Protocol differs depending on the specification of capital mobility. However, only the incorporation of perfect capital mobility leads to qualitatively different messages while imperfect and no capital mobility give similar results.

The remainder of the chapter is as follows. Section 2 summarizes theoretical work which deals with the interrelation of trade in goods and international capital movements. Section 3 presents a short description of the DART model, its parameterization and calibration, and explains how three different types of international capital mobility are implemented in the model. Section 4 discusses the effects of the Kyoto Protocol in the presence of immobile capital and compares the results with the corresponding predictions with imperfect and perfect capital mobility. Section 5 provides a summary perspective.

2   International trade and capital mobility: theoretical implications

An examination of the linkages between international capital movements, domestic production and international trade gains importance today given the fast increase of international capital flows observed through the 1980s and 1990s. From 1980 to 2000, for example, the growth of direct investment for any region (industrialized countries as well as developing countries) was higher than that of foreign exports which in turn was higher than that of GDP (Siebert, 1999).

Most trade models examine the international exchange of commodities and ignore international movements of productive factors. Indeed, the classical trade theory and its modern descendants see international factor immobility as the basic cause of international trade. There, international differences in endowments of factors induce trade in goods. This was formalized in the Heckscher–Ohlin–Samuelson (HOS) model. Mundell (1957) was the first to formally analyse the implications of physical capital mobility for international trade in the HOS framework. In the HOS context with identical countries which differ only in factor endowments, perfect factor mobility across sectors within and over economies provides a tendency for commodity-price equalization, even in the absence of international trade in goods. Mundell considered a situation where a prohibitively high tariff on imports shuts off trade in goods and raises the return to capital in the country where it is the relatively scarce factor. This leads to a capital inflow in that country and, through the Rybczynski effect, an increase in the production of the capital-intensive good (i.e. the import good before the tariff was in place) until factor prices are equalized. This result complements the Stolper–Samuelson theorem, which demonstrates the tendency for factor-price equalization as a consequence of goods trade, even in the absence of international movements of factors. Thus, the HOS model predicts that trade in goods perfectly substitutes for direct movement of factors in two senses: first, either of them – trade in goods or international capital flows – reaches the same world equilibrium, and second, an increase in the volume of trade will reduce the volume of capital flows and vice versa. Therefore, gains from trade can be realized either through the movement of goods or of factors, the two being equivalent.

If trade in goods and international capital mobility are completely equivalent, this raises the question whether it is necessary to consider explicitly capital mobility in an international trade model. However, subsequent theoretical work has demonstrated that models which diverge from the standard HOS assumptions can result in complementarity, rather than substitutability, between factor movements and goods trade. Markusen (1983), Svensson (1984), Wong (1986) and Ethier (1996) have shown that the equivalence depends crucially on the basic production assumptions made in the model. With trade based not on differences in relative factor endowments, but on differences in production technologies across countries (Kemp 1966; Jones 1967; Purvis 1972; Markusen and Svensson 1985 and Neary 1995), distortions in production and factor markets, external economies of scale, or imperfect markets (Markusen 1983; Wong 1995), there is a presumption that factor movements and trade in goods are complements, that is, they tend to go together. In all these cases, the world equilibrium depends on whether only international trade in goods or international factor mobility, or both, are allowed.

The complementary relationship between international trade in goods and capital mobility can be shown in a simple example. Assume, for example, a two-country world in which countries have different technologies. Suppose each of two countries has the same labour productivity but one country enjoys higher capital productivity. The country with higher capital productivity exports the capital-intensive good. International mobile capital seeks the highest return and flows to the high capital-productivity country.

Through the Rybczynski effect, the capital inflow increases the production of the capital intensive good (the export good) and decreases the production of the labour-intensive good (the import good). Therefore, an increase in the volume of capital flows leads to an increase in the volume of the traded goods. However, the complementarity depends on whether the export good is initially capital- or labour-intensive, whether the country is a net capital exporter or importer, and whether the productivity advantage occurs in the labour- or in the capital-intensive sector (cf. Wong 1995; Springer 2000, 2002). Analytically, no univocal results can be derived. However, empirical studies seem to support a complementarity between international trade in goods and international capital movements (cf. Goldberg and Klein 1998; Pfaffermayr 1994; and partly Goldberg and Klein 1999).

Thus, understanding the relationship between trade in goods and factor movements is important for obtaining a complete picture of international linkages. The effect of a certain policy shock on production and trade can only be predicted by taking into account the non-trivial interactions between goods trade and factor mobility (Norman and Venables 1995). Furthermore, Norman and Venables have shown that for the results of a policy scenario, it is crucial whether capital earnings are repatriated to the home country or not. Hence, keeping track of capital ownership may lead to other allocational as well as distributional outcomes due to a policy shock then ignoring cross-capital ownership.

Lane and Milesi-Ferretti (1999) also find empirical evidence that results differ depending on whether net flows or accumulated gross flows of capital are considered in the analysis. They confirm the complementary relationship between goods trade and capital flows by the fact that greater trade openness is associated with larger gross stocks of foreign direct investment (FDI) and equity. Also, Willenbockel (1999) has found some evidence that the consideration of foreign asset cross-ownership patterns in applied general equilibrium trade policy studies may change the results relative to the studies where only the net foreign asset position is taken into account. However, for empirically relevant parameter constellations the quantitative 'error' incurred by ignoring the actual foreign asset cross-holding structure underlying a given net foreign asset position will remain moderate.

Concluding from these considerations, it is very likely that the incorporation of international capital mobility will change the allocational and distributional outcomes of a climate policy simulation. The incorporation of international capital mobility into a trade model seems essential if there are differences in production technologies, trade barriers or other distortions on the production side in order to derive valid welfare results from the policy analysis. Furthermore, aggregate regional welfare may be affected by the reallocation of capital across regions. Therefore, one has to keep track of capital ownership by extending the accounting framework of the model to accommodate foreign capital ownership, foreign investment and foreign income receipts and payments in order to get valid policy results.

3 The extended Dynamic Applied Regional Trade (DART) model with international capital mobility

3.1 The basic DART model

The influence of international capital movements on the results of a certain climate policy scenario is analysed with the DART model.[1] The DART model is a multi-region, multi-sector, recursive dynamic CGE model. The economic structure for each region covers production, consumption, investment and governmental activity. Markets are perfectly competitive. Prices are fully flexible. For each region, the model incorporates three types of agents: the producers, distinguished by production sectors, the representative private household and the government.

Producer behaviour

All industry sectors are assumed to operate at constant returns to scale. Output of each production sector is produced by the combination of energy, non-energy intermediate inputs, and the primary factors labour and capital (land in the agricultural sector). Figure 8.1 shows the nested production structure.

Composite investment is a Leontief aggregation of Armington inputs by each industry sector. Investment does not require direct primary factor inputs. Figure 8.2 shows the production structure of the investment activity. Producer

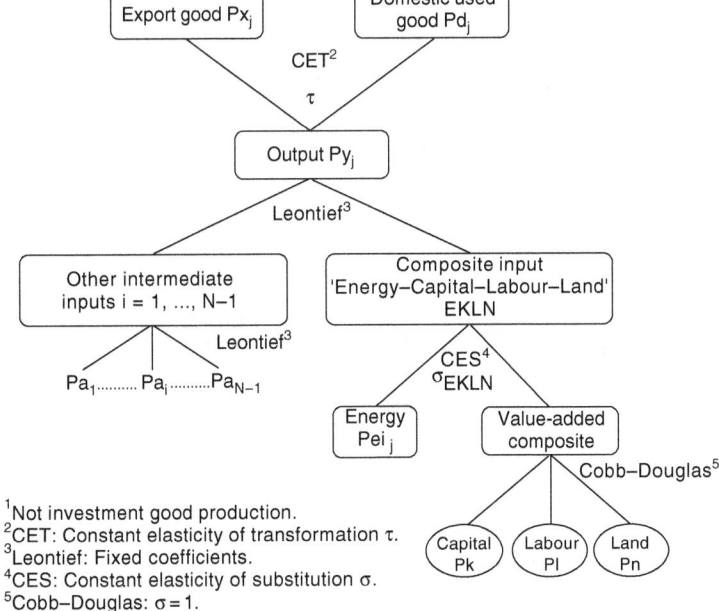

[1] Not investment good production.
[2] CET: Constant elasticity of transformation τ.
[3] Leontief: Fixed coefficients.
[4] CES: Constant elasticity of substitution σ.
[5] Cobb–Douglas: $\sigma = 1$.

Figure 8.1 Production structure of industry sector j in region r.[1]

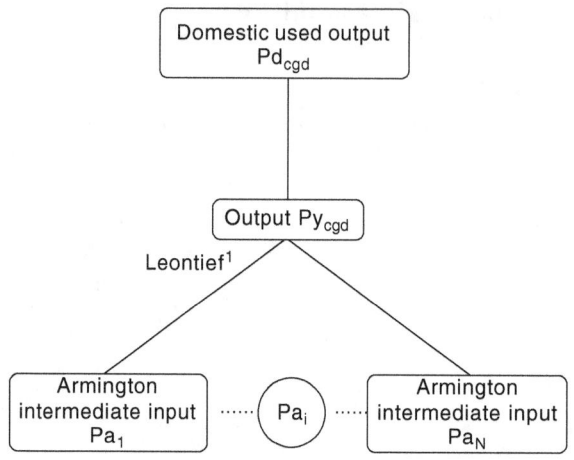

[1]Leontief: Fixed coefficients.

Figure 8.2 Production structure of the investment good sector cgd in region r.

goods are directly demanded by regional households, governments, the invest-ment sector, other industries, and the export sector.

Consumption, and government expenditure

The representative household receives all income generated by providing primary factors to the production process. Disposable income is used for maximizing utility by purchasing goods after taxes and savings are deducted. The consumer decides between different primary energy inputs and non-energy inputs depending on their relative prices in order to receive this consumption with the lowest expenditures. Figure 8.3 shows the structure of household and government behaviour. The consumer saves a fixed share of income in each time period which is invested in production.

The third agent, the government, provides a public good which is produced with commodities purchased at market prices. Public goods are produced with the same two-level nesting structure as the household 'production' function (see Figure 8.3). The public good is financed by tax revenues.

Foreign trade

The world is divided into economic regions, which are linked by bilateral trade flows. All goods are traded among regions, except for the investment good. Following the proposition of Armington (1969), domestic and foreign goods are imperfect substitutes, and distinguished by country of origin. The structure of import demand is shown in Figure 8.4. Transport costs, distinguished by

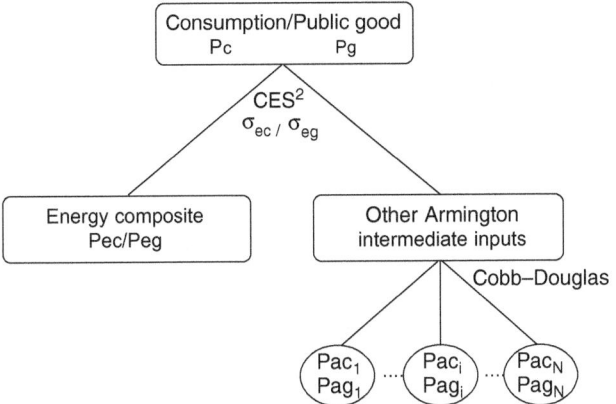

¹Lower case roman letter c stands for household and g for government.
²CES: Constant elasticity of substitution $\sigma_{ec} / \sigma_{eg}$.
³Cobb–Douglas: $\sigma = 1$.

Figure 8.3 Household/government production structure[1].

commodity and bilateral flow, apply to international trade but not to domestic sales.

On the export side, the Armington assumption applies to final output of the industry sectors destined for domestic and international markets. Here, produced commodities for the domestic and for the international market are non-perfect substitutes. Exports are not differentiated by country of destination.

Factor markets

Factor markets are perfectly competitive and full employment of all factors is assumed. Labour is assumed to be a homogeneous good, mobile across industries within regions but internationally immobile. In the basic version of the DART model capital is inter-sectorally but not internationally mobile. Capital stock is given at the beginning of each time period and results from the capital accumulation equation. In every time period the regional capital stock, Kst_r, earns a correspondent amount of income measured as physical units in terms of capital services, K_r. The primary factor 'land' is only used in agricultural sectors and exogenously given.

3.2 Dynamics of the DART model

The DART model is recursive-dynamic, meaning that it solves for a sequence of static one-period equilibria for future time periods connected through capital accumulation. The major driving exogenous factors of the model dynamics are population change, the rate of labour productivity growth, the

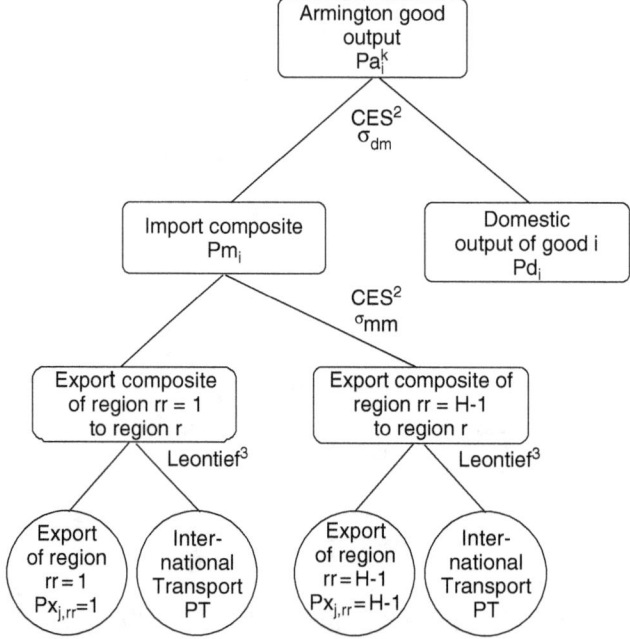

[1] Armington output is distinguished by agent with k = {Y, C, G}.
[2] CES: Constant elasticity of substitution.
[3] Leontief: Fixed coefficients.

Figure 8.4 Structure of foreign trade (Armington good production of good i in region r).

change in human capital, the savings rate, the gross rate of return on capital, and thus, the endogenous rate of capital accumulation. The savings behaviour of regional households is characterized by a constant savings rate over time.[2] This rather *ad hoc* assumption seems consistent with empirical observable, regional different, but nearly constant savings rates of economies, which adjust according to income developments over very long time periods (for savings rates cf. Schmidt-Hebbel and Servén 1997). Additionally, a wide range of empirical evidence in macroeconomic literature neglects the theoretically elegant permanent income hypothesis and shows that a huge fraction of the consumption decisions are based entirely on current after-tax income. Campbell and Mankiew (1990), for example, reexamined the consistency of the permanent income hypothesis with aggregate postwar US data. They estimated that the fraction of income which accrues to individuals who consume their current income rather than their permanent income is about 50 per cent. Labour supply considers human capital accumulation and is, therefore, measured in efficiency units, $L_{r,t}$. It evolves exogenously over time. Hence, labour supply $\bar{L}$ for each region r at the beginning of time period $t+1$ is given by:

$$\bar{L}_{r,t+1} = \bar{L}_{r,t} \cdot (1 + gp_{r,t} + ga_r + gh_r) \tag{1}$$

where the bar denotes exogenous variables. An increase of effective labour implies either growth of the human capital accumulated per physical unit of labour, gh_r, population growth, gp_r, or total factor productivity improvement, ga_r, or the sum of all.

The version of the DART model used here assumes constant, but regionally different labour productivity improvement rates, ga_r, constant but regionally different growth rates of human capital, gh_r, which stem from Hall and Jones (1999), and declining population growth rates over time, $gp_{r,t}$, according to the World Bank population growth projections (Bos et al. 1994). For the derivation of the growth rates of human capital, see Springer (2002) and the web site of the book. Because of the lack of data for the evolution of the labour participation rate in the future, the growth rate of population instead of the labour force is used implying that the labour participation rate is constant over time.

The supply of the sector-specific factor 'land' is held fixed to its benchmark level over time. The current period's investment augments the capital stock in the next period. The aggregated regional capital stock, Kst at period t is updated by an accumulation function equating the next-period capital stock, Kst_{t+1}, to the sum of the depreciated capital stock of the current period and the current period's physical quantity of investment, $Iq_{r,t}$, given by $Iq_{r,t} = Inv_{r,t}/Pi_{r,t}$ where $Inv_{r,t}$ is the value of investment in region r in period t and $Pi_{r,t}$ denotes the costs of constructing a unit of capital. The equation of motion for capital stock $Kst_{r,t+}$ in region r is given by:

$$Kst_{r,t+1} = (1 - \delta)Kst_{r,t} + Iq_{r,t} \quad \text{for } t \geq 1 \tag{2}$$

where δ denotes the exogenously given constant depreciation rate. The allocation of capital among sectors follows from the intra-period optimization of the firms.

3.3 Implementation of international capital mobility

For the analysis, three degrees of capital mobility are considered:

(1) international immobile capital (the basic version of the DART model),
(2) perfect capital mobility, and
(3) imperfect capital mobility.

First, *immobile capital* means there are no capital flows among regions. Each regional household saves a constant fraction of its income and reinvests it in the home region. The amount of regional savings and investments may differ according to a region's current account deficit or surplus which is held fixed at its benchmark share to regional GDP.

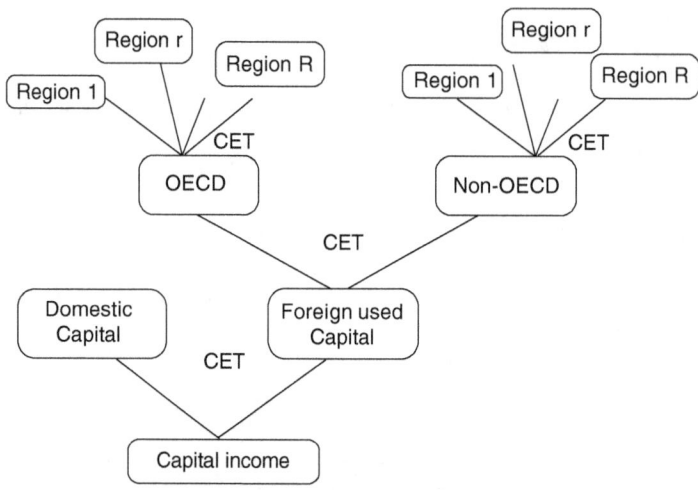

Figure 8.5 Household decision.

Second, the *perfect capital mobility* scenario assumes only one capital stock world wide which is allocated to the regions so that the return to capital is equalized among regions and sectors. In this scenario capital owners move with the capital. No cross-hauling of capital flows occurs.

In the third scenario with *imperfect capital mobility*, the model distinguishes between domestic and foreign capital services. These two types of capital are non-perfect substitutes which leads to a cross-hauling of capital flows. The imperfect substitutability of domestic and foreign capital prevents a complete equalization of regional rate of return on capital. Foreign capital earnings are repatriated to the home country. Therefore, capital accumulation and wealth accumulation by region are different. Imperfect capital mobility is implemented into the DART model in the following way: The regional household owns a certain amount of capital and decides if it wants to use the capital at home or abroad. This decision is driven by rate of return on capital differentials among regions. However, capital is not allowed to flow immediately to the region where it earns the highest return. The imperfectness is modelled by a constant elasticity of transformation (CET) function (Figure 8.5). Hence, domestic and foreign used capital are non-perfect substitutes. This specification is justified by the stylized fact that individual portfolios are concentrated on domestic securities.[3]

A global bank collects the foreign capital invested by regional households. This step is necessary because bilateral capital flows are unknown. The allocation of the global fund to the regions takes place within two steps. First, the global fund is allocated among the OECD and the non-OECD as sub-regions. This is due to the fact that around 90 per cent of all capital movements worldwide take place only among OECD regions; the rest goes to the non-industrialized regions (Wong 1995). In the second step, the OECD sub-fund is allocated among the

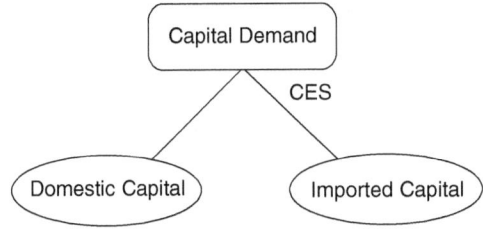

Figure 8.6 Capital demand in each region.

OECD regions with a fairly high elasticity of transformation implying a high substitutability of capital flows. The same specification applies to the non-OECD regions but with a smaller elasticity.

Capital demand in each region is a composite good of domestic and imported capital (Figure 8.6). The two types of capital are non-perfect substitutes in production. This assumption leads to a cross-hauling of capital flows in the model.

3.4 Parameterization and calibration[4]

All three capital mobility specifications are calibrated on the Global Trade Analysis Project (GTAP) database version 3 for 1992 (GTAP, 1997) which is adjusted for primary energy flow data by the International Energy Agency – the GTAPIEA database. The version of the DART model used for this chapter runs in a 11 regions by 10 sectors aggregation (see Table 8.1).

The fossil fuel (coal, crude oil and natural gas) supply is calibrated so that the carbon emissions resulting from the use of fossil fuels in the model match the projections of scenario B by IIASA and the World Energy Council (1999). The resulting price elasticities of fossil fuel supply are given in Table 8.2.

The growth path of the DART model is calibrated on exogenous assumptions concerning growth rates of population and technological change, change in human capital, savings rates, and capital to GDP ratios. These *ad hoc* specifications of growth rates and key parameters reflect plausible development paths of the economies. The GDP is then derived endogenously. A detailed discussion of the dynamic benchmarking of the DART model is given in Klepper and Springer (2000). The dynamic key parameters are represented in Table 8.3.

Restricted international capital mobility is modelled by implementing two types of physical capital – domestic and foreign capital – and by imperfect substitution between these two types of capital on the supply and on the demand side. These modelling assumptions may be interpreted as reflecting imperfections in the world capital market, increased risks inherent to foreign investment, legal restrictions on ownership of foreign property, and asymmetric information between domestic and foreign investors. The implementation is flexible for different interpretations depending on the chosen degree of substitutability. When the elasticity of substitution (transformation) equals zero, households (or firms)

Table 8.1 Regions and commodities in the 11 by 10 GTAP aggregation

---

Regions in the 11 by 10 GTAP aggregation

WEU	*Western Europe*: European Union 12, Austria, Finland and Sweden
NAM	*North America*: United States of America, Canada
PAO	Australia, New Zealand, Japan
FSU	Former Soviet Union
MEA	Middle East and North Africa
CPA	China, Hong Kong
PAS	Republic of Korea, Indonesia, Malaysia, Philippines, Singapore, Thailand, Taiwan
IDI	India
LAM	*Latin America*: Mexico, Argentina, Brazil, Chile, Rest of South America
AFR	Sub-Saharan Africa
ROW	Rest of South Asia, Central America and Caribbean, European Free Trade Area, Central European Associates, Rest of the World

Commodities in the 11 by 10 GTAP aggregation

COL	Coal
CRU	Crude oil
OIL	Petroleum and coal products (refined)
GAS	Natural gas
EGW	Electricity
Y	*Other manufactures and services*: Beverages and tobacco, other minerals, textiles, wearing apparel, leather goods, lumber and wood, machinery and equipment, other manufacturing products, Construction, other services (private), other services (public), dwellings
ISM	*Iron, steel and minerals*: Non-metallic mineral products, Primary ferrous metals, non-ferrous metals, fabricated metal products
CPP	*Chemicals, Plastics and paper*: Pulp and paper, chemicals, rubber and plastics
AGR	*Agriculture*: Paddy rice, wheat, grains, non-grain crops, wool, other livestock, processed rice, meat products, milk products, other food products, forestry, fishing
TRN	*Transport industries*: Transport industries, trade and transport
CGD	Capital goods demand

---

maintain the shares of domestic and foreign capital irrespective of differences in rates of return. As the elasticity approaches infinity, foreign and domestic capital are perfect substitutes where the slightest difference in returns leads households (firms) to hold (demand) only the type of capital offering the higher (lower) return. An elasticity of one would imply that the value share of foreign and domestic capital, and, therefore, the structure of capital flows remains constant. The elasticities used in the *ad hoc*, and thus far not empirically proved, specification in the model are shown in Table 8.4. This specification is a first shot at implementing imperfectness into a recursive dynamic CGE model.

As a first rough (gu)esstimate, the shares of regional capital inflows and outflows are derived from the inward and outward foreign direct investment flows as a percentage of gross fixed capital formation as reported in the UN World Investment Report 1998 – Annex B5 (UN, 1998). Table 8.5 gives the share of

Table 8.2 Key elasticities

Fossil fuel supply elasticities	
Coal	0.55
Gas	1.30
Crude oil	0.25
Armington elasticities	
Domestic vs. imports (all goods)	4.00
From different destinations (all goods)	8.00
Elasticity of transformation exports vs. Domestic sales	2.00

Table 8.3 Dynamic key parameters for the off-steady state scenario for the year 1993

	Growth rates for efficiency labour (in per cent)				Savings rate (in per cent)
	Exogenous technical progress	*Human capital growth (1993)*	*Growth rate of population (1993)[c]*	*Total*	
WEU	1.00	1.20	0.40	2.60	20.3
NAM	0.70	0.15	1.00	1.85	16.1
PAO	0.70	1.00	0.40	2.10	30.1[a]
FSU	2.50	0.55	0.20	3.25	18.9
MEA	1.00	2.50	2.40	5.90	19.6
CPA	3.50	1.90	1.10	6.50	31.7[b]
PAS	2.50	2.10	1.70	6.30	31.5[b]
IDI	1.50	2.70	1.80	6.00	21.6
LAM	1.50	2.30	1.70	5.50	19.0
AFR	1.50	3.20	2.50	7.20	15.8
ROW	1.00	2.30	1.60	4.90	20.9

Notes:
a Falls by 1 percentage point per year up to 2010.
b Falls by 0.5 percentage point per year up to 2010.
c Taken from Bos *et al.* (1994).

Table 8.4 Parameterization of imperfect capital mobility

Elasticity of transformation regional household decision	4
Elasticity of transformation between OECD and non-OECD	2
Elasticity of transformation between OECD regions	8
Elasticity of transformation between non-OECD regions	4
Elasticity of substitution between domestic and imported capital inputs	4

imported capital relative to total capital used in production of region *r* and the share of exported capital relative to total capital holdings of the household in region *r* in 1993. Figure 8.7 shows the resulting benchmark capital inflows and outflows for each region in 1993.

Table 8.5 Shares of capital in- and outflows relative to
total capital use (in per cent)

Region	Imported capital to total used capital	Exported capital to total capital holdings
WEU	4.0	5.8
NAM	3.0	4.1
PAO	3.9	2.7
FSU	0.9	0.2
MEA	4.4	0.6
CPA	6.0	1.0
PAS	4.0	2.0
IDI	0.4	0.0
LAM	3.9	0.5
AFR	5.2	3.1
ROW	2.9	0.8

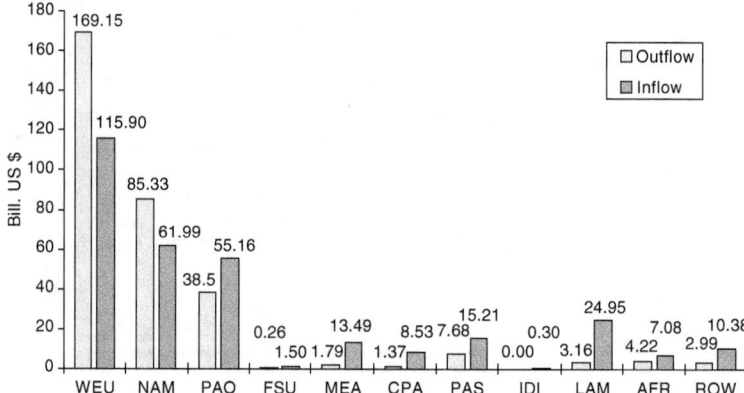

Figure 8.7 Benchmark capital in- and outflows in 1993.

4 Climate policy analysis

The increased integration of industrial and (to a far smaller extent) non-industrialized economies, especially in the capital market, opens beside international trade in goods a new channel through which domestic policies may affect other economies. When capital is internationally mobile, a climate policy which imposes differentiated emission targets for several regions can affect national welfare through impacts on the trade balance, on the foreign ownership of domestic capital, and (via changes in terms-of-trade) on the international competitiveness of import-competing and export-oriented sectors.

The Kyoto Protocol is used for testing the influence of different capital mobility specifications on the policy outcome and is implemented in the following way. The policy simulation imposes carbon emission reduction targets of 8 per cent for

WEU, 7 per cent for NAM, 3 per cent for PAO, and constant emissions for FSU by 2010 compared to the 1990 emission level. It is assumed that the reduction has started in 1990 and takes place at a constant rate until 2010. Thereafter, the emissions remain constant for the four Annex I regions. The non-Annex-I countries face no constraints. In this setting of differentiated emission targets, spillovers through trade in goods as well as international capital movements are likely to occur. Therefore, the welfare impacts of the Kyoto Protocol on the different world regions are estimated and compared for the three different capital mobility scenarios.

The welfare effect of the Kyoto Protocol is measured in percentage change of Hicksian equivalent variation relative to the base run in the year 2010. The results for the three capital mobility scenarios are shown in Figure 8.8. The welfare results are very similar for the case with internationally immobile capital and restricted capital mobility. They differ only slightly in magnitude. For these two cases, CPA, PAS, and IDI will benefit from the Kyoto Protocol while WEU, NAM, FSU, MEA, LAM, AFR, and ROW experience a welfare loss due to changes in international competitiveness.

PAO as an emission abating region takes an outstanding position. It benefits from the change in international prices and can improve its relative comparative advantage in the scenario with immobile capital. On one hand, this is due to the fact that the carbon constraint is less binding in PAO compared to the other Annex-I regions since PAO's production is relatively energy-efficient. On the other hand, PAO seems to experience positive spillovers from the good performance of its major trading partners PAS and CPA.

In contrast to this, keeping carbon emissions constant means the highest emission reduction relative to the base run for the FSU, since the industries in the FSU produce relatively carbon-intensive. This leads to a fast growth of carbon dioxide emissions at the base run path. Hence, cutting carbon emissions to the 1990 emission level forces the FSU to a considerable reallocation of resources and leads to a loss in output because of restricted substitution possibilities (cf. also Figure 8.9).[5] High adjustment costs and loss in welfare, respectively, are the consequences for the FSU.

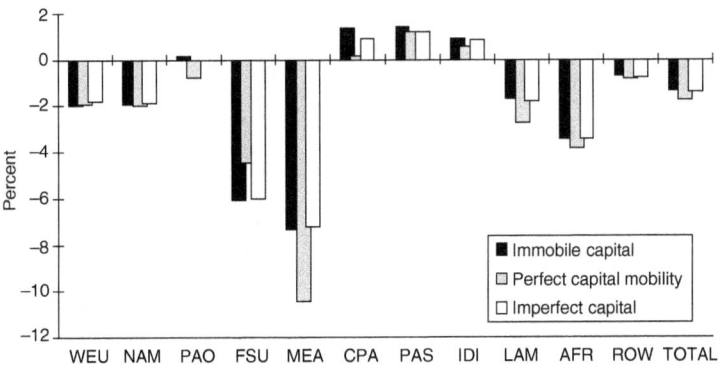

Figure 8.8 Welfare effects of the Kyoto Protocol relative to the benchmark in 2010.

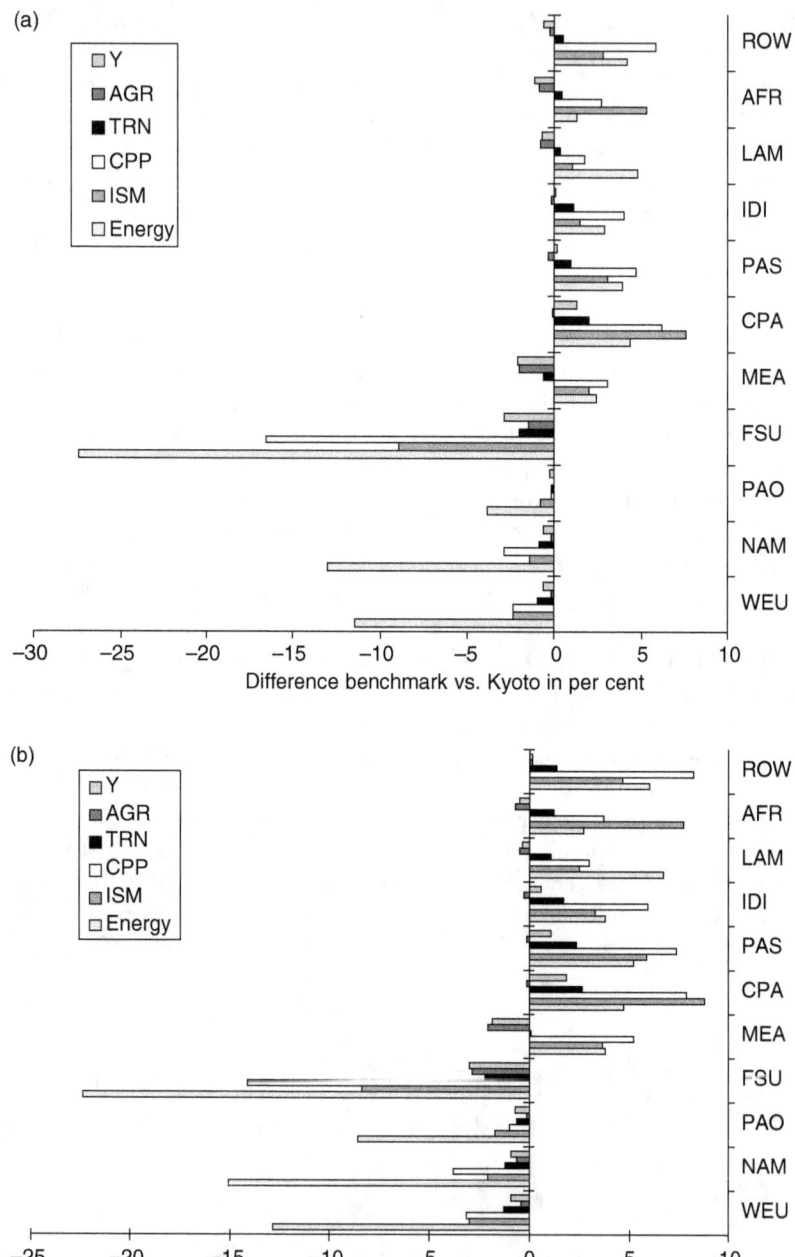

Figure 8.9 Change in sectoral output in 2010. (a) Imperfect capital mobility, (b) perfect capital mobility.

Three main causes for the welfare losses in non-abating regions such as MEA, LAM, AFR, and ROW can be identified. First, the reduction of world demand for their major export good, crude oil, decreases income and thus welfare. Second, through the change in international prices, the countries lose in those sectors where they normally have a comparative advantage, for example, labour-intensive sectors, and gain competitiveness where they initially have a comparative disadvantage as in the energy-intensive sectors. Third, the decline in income in the Annex-I countries has a dampening effect on the export opportunities of the developing countries.

Comparing the welfare results for different capital mobility specifications, an increase in capital mobility seems to amplify the welfare loss. While PAO increases its welfare with immobile capital, the welfare change is nearly zero with imperfect capital mobility (-0.01 per cent) and negative with perfect capital mobility. Other regions lose more or less with perfect capital mobility compared to no or imperfect capital mobility. Hence, perfect capital mobility leads to slightly different results in magnitude as well as in direction of the result compared to immobile or restricted mobile capital. With perfect capital mobility the economies are linked more intensively and negative spillovers can affect other regions more directly than in the case where economies are only linked by goods' trade flows.[6] Thus, the induced international capital flows support the adverse shift in comparative advantage, that is, away from labour-intensive production towards energy- and capital-intensive production.

The differentiated emission reduction objectives also lead, via the change in international prices, to a sectoral reallocation in all regions. Figure 8.9 depicts changes in sectoral output quantities for the Kyoto Protocol relative to the benchmark in 2010. It can be seen that the Kyoto Protocol causes a shift in production of fossil fuel intensive industries, like energy (which is the sum of coal, gas, oil, EGW in Figure 8.9), ISM and CPP, from the Annex-I to the non-Annex-I regions. By comparing the changes in sectoral output with imperfect (or immobile capital)[7] and perfect capital mobility (Figures 8.9a and b) differences in magnitude can be recognized, especially in the reallocation of energy-intensive industries. The ROW region also shows some difference in the direction of changes. ROW is able to increase output in all sectors with perfect capital mobility while it experiences a decrease in output of agriculture and other products with imperfect (no) capital mobility.

The reallocation of energy-intensive industries from abating to non-abating regions indicates that the emission reduction targets of the Annex-I regions may be offset by increased carbon dioxide emissions in the non-abating countries, resulting in a change of the effectiveness of the climate policy. The effectiveness of the Kyoto Protocol to enforce global reductions of greenhouse gas emissions can be measured by the leakage this policy setting causes. The leakage rate for the different capital mobility scenarios, that is, the increase of carbon emissions in non-Annex-I regions relative to the reduced emissions in Annex-I regions, is shown in Figure 8.10. In all scenarios, the leakage rate increases until 2010 and then decreases again. This behaviour is caused by the implementation of the

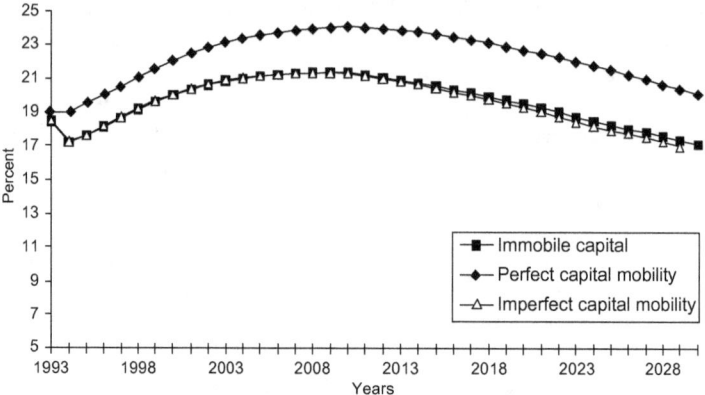

Figure 8.10 Leakage rate in per cent.

climate policy scenario in the model which assumes that reduction takes place up to 2010; after that the Annex-I regions have to keep their emissions constant. Again, only perfectly mobile capital may induce significantly different results. There, 24 per cent of the reduced carbon emissions are offset by increased emissions (relative to the base run) in the non-Annex-I regions in 2010, while in the other two scenarios it is around 21 per cent. Higher capital mobility, thus, supports the shift of energy-intensive industries to the developing countries.

The climate policy simulation allows the conclusion that the specification of international capital mobility quantitatively and (to some extent) qualitatively influences the outcome of a certain policy. However, the results from the restricted capital mobility case barely differ from the case with immobile capital. This outcome corresponds to Burniaux and Martins (1999) who also find almost no influence of international capital mobility on the size of leakage.

5   Conclusions

This chapter has analysed to what extent the prevailing modelling practice of ignoring international capital mobility and capital cross-ownership in applied general equilibrium models dealing with global climate change policies may give rise to distorted predictions. This was done by comparing distributional and allocational outcomes of the Kyoto Protocol with respect to different capital mobility specifications.

Theory suggests that in a HOS world the consideration of international capital movements in addition to trade in goods would not change the policy results because international trade in goods and factor movements are perfect substitutes leading to the same world equilibrium. However, the real world does not look like pure HOS. If the basis for trade is not a difference in factor endowments, but differences in production technologies, supply side distortions across regions, existing external economies of scale, or imperfect markets, then factor movements and trade in goods are complements. Hence, the world equilibrium depends on whether only international trade in goods or international capital mobility, or both simultaneously are considered. Furthermore, the extent of cross-ownership of capital may influence the policy outcomes.

The policy simulations have shown that international capital mobility alters the results of the Kyoto Protocol quantitatively and qualitatively. Here, the distinction between perfect capital mobility and internationally immobile capital seems more relevant than the distinction between imperfect capital mobility and immobile capital. Hence, the simulation results do not really confirm the predictions from the theoretical literature. The consideration of cross-capital ownership instead of net capital flows seems to play no role for the policy implications of the Kyoto Protocol since the results for imperfect capital mobility and immobile capital are nearly the same. Willenbockel (1999) derives the same result, in his analysis as long as for each region affected by a policy change the gross property income from and/or to the rest of the world remains low in relation to domestic product. This is indeed the case in the specification of capital flows in the simulation used here.

Furthermore, the similarity of results for the immobile capital and the imperfect capital mobility case may be caused by the way restricted international capital mobility is implemented into the model. Because of the recursive dynamic nature of the model, constant savings rates for each household are assumed, independent of changes in the rate of return on capital. Hence, in every time step the model is forced to an allocation of capital similar to the model version with immobile capital. Thus, this model specification allows little space for reallocation of capital. Furthermore, only physical capital is mobile and the model is calibrated to the capital in- and outflows as given in Table 8.5, which represent just a small fraction of total capital. Therefore, dramatic changes are not likely to occur compared to the case with immobile capital when the Kyoto Protocol is imposed, since with imperfect capital mobility not much capital is in fact mobile, especially between the Annex-I and the Non-Annex-I regions.

These shortcomings of the analysis suggest further research work in the following directions: the assumption of constant savings rates should be replaced by a more flexible and economically more reasonable specification of the savings behaviour of the household. Instead of mobile physical capital, one can implement capital assets for the household. Information about bilateral capital flows would be useful in order to avoid the modelling of a global bank.[8] Furthermore, more empirically sophisticated parameters and data about international capital flows are needed. And, of course, other treatments of imperfections in the capital market like a risk component of the regional rate of return to capital or transactions costs on capital flows can be tested.

Notes

1 For a detailed description of the DART model see Springer (1998, 2002), Klepper and Springer (2000), and the web site of the book.

2 The savings rate is allowed to adjust to income changes in regions with extraordinarily high benchmark savings rates.
3 There is a great variety of literature dealing with the home bias of capital investment. Gordon and Bovenberg (1996) give an excellent summary of this literature.
4 For further information about parameterization and calibration of the model see web page of the book.
5 Here, one drawback of the model occurs: the model does not explicitly model inefficiencies like 'hot air' for the FSU, but what is highly relevant for the actual international climate negotiations.
6 Trade is modelled via the Armington assumption, that is, domestic and imported goods are non-perfect substitutes. This implies that domestic markets are partly protected from the world market since changes in international prices do not lead to a one-to-one change in domestic prices.
7 Since the results are nearly the same for the case with immobile capital and imperfect capital mobility, only the results for restricted capital mobility are shown in this chapter.
8 For a capital mobility specification considering household's assets and bilateral capital flows see Springer (2002).

References

Armington, P. (1969) 'A theory of demand for products distinguished by place of production', *IMF Staff Papers*, 16: 159–78.

Bos, E., Vu, M. T., Massiah, E. and Bulatao, R. A. (1994) *World Population Projections: Estimates and Projections with Related Demographic Statistics*, World Bank. Baltimore: The Johns Hopkins University Press.

Bovenberg, A. L. and Goulder, L. H. (1993) 'Promoting investment under international capital mobility: an intertemporal equilibrium analysis', *Scandinavian Journal of economics*, 95: 133–56.

Burniaux, J.-M. and Martins, J. O. (1999) Carbon Emission Leakages: An Analytical General Equilibrium View, Paper presented at the 2nd Annual Conference on Global Economic Analysis.

Campbell, J. Y. and Mankiew, N. G. (1990) 'Permanent income, current income, and consumption', *Journal of Business and Economic Statistics*, 8(3): 265–78.

Ethier, W. J. (1996) 'Theories about trade liberalisation and migration: substitutes or complements?', in: Lloyd, P. J. D. and Williams, L. S. (eds) *International Trade and Migration in the APEC Region*. Melbourne: Oxford University Press.

Goldberg, L. S. and Klein, M. W. (1998) 'Foreign direct investment, trade and real exchange rate linkages in developing countries', in: Reuven G. (ed.) *Managing Capital Flows and Exchange Rates: Lessons from the Pacific Basin*. Cambridge University Press.

Goldberg, L. S. and Klein, M. W. (1999) *International trade and factor mobility: an empirical investigation*, NBER Working Paper No. 7196, Cambridge, MA.

Gordon, R. H. and Bovenberg, A. L. (1996) 'Why is capital so immobile internationally? Possible explanations and implications for capital income taxation', *American Economic Review*, 86: 1057–75.

Hall, R. E. and Jones, C. I. (1999) 'Why do some countries produce so much more output per worker than others?', *The Quarterly Journal of Economics*, 114(1): 83–116.

IIASA, World Energy Council (1999) 'Global energy perspectives: a joint IIASA–WEC study', *http://www.iiasa.ac.at/Research/ECS/docs/book_st/wecintro.html*.

Jones, R. W. (1967) 'International capital movements and the theory of tariffs and trade', *Quarterly Journal of Economics*, 81: 1–38.

Kemp, M. C. (1966) 'The gain from international trade and investment: a neo-Heckscher–Ohlin approach', *American Economic Review*, 61: 788–809.

Klepper, G. and Springer, K. (2000) *'Benchmarking the future – calibrating a long-run, multi-regional, multi-sectoral CGE model*, Kiel Working Paper 976, Kiel Institute of World Economics.

Lane, P. and Milesi-Ferretti, G. M. (1999) *The external wealth of nations: measures of foreign assets and liabilities for industrialized and developing countries*, Paper presented at the Annual Congress of the European Economic Association 1999.

Markusen, J. R. (1983) 'Factor movements and commodity trade as complements', *Journal of International Economics*, 14: 25–43.

Markusen, J. R. and Svensson, L. E. O. (1985) 'Trade in goods and factors with international differences in technology', *International Economic Review*, 26: 175–92.

McDougall, R. (ed.) (GTAP 1997) *Global Trade, Assistance, and Protection: The GTAP 3 Data Base*. Center for Global Trade Analysis, Purdue University.

Mundell, R. (1957) 'International trade and factor mobility', *American Economic Review*, 67: 321–35.

Neary, P. (1995) 'Factor mobility and international trade', *Canadian Journal of Economics*, 28: S4–S23.

Norman, V. D. and Venables, A. J. (1995) 'International trade, factor mobility, and trade costs', *Economic Journal*, 105: 1488–504.

Pfaffermayr, M. (1994) 'Foreign direct investment and exports: a time series approach', *Applied Economics*, 26: 337–51.

Purvis, D. D. (1972) 'Technology, trade and factor mobility', *Economic Journal*, 82: 979–99.

Schmidt-Hebel, K. and Serén, L. (1997) *Saving across the world: puzzles and policies*, World Bank Discussion Paper No. 354. Washington, D.C.

Siebert, H. (1999) *The World Economy*. London: Routledge.

Springer, K. (1998) *The DART general equilibrium model: a technical description*, Kiel Working Paper No. 883, September 1998. Kiel.

Springer, K. (2000) *Do we have to consider international capital mobility in trade models?*, Kiel Working Paper 964. Kiel Institute of World Economics, Kiel.

Springer, K. (2002) Climate policy in a globalizing world: A CGE model with trade and Captial Mobility. Berlin: Springer Verlag.

Svensson, L. E. O. (1984) 'Factor trade and goods trade', *Journal of International Economics*, 16: 365–78.

United Nations (UN) (1997) *Kyoto Protocol*. FCCC/CP/1997/L.7/Add.1. Bonn: United Nations.

United Nations (1998) *World investment report 1998: trends and determinants*. Annex Table B.5. New York and Geneva.

Willenbockel, D. (1999) 'Dynamic applied general equilibrium trade policy analysis in the presence of foreign asset cross-ownership', *Economic Modelling*, 16: 371–88.

Wong, K.-Y. (1986) 'Are international trade and factor mobility substitutes?', *Journal of International Economics*, 21: 341–56.

Wong, K.-Y. (1995) *International Trade in Goods and Factor Mobility*. Cambridge MA: MIT Press.

9 Carbon taxation and various pollutants in Europe

Combining general equilibrium and integrated system approaches

T. Huw Edwards and John P. Hutton

1 Introduction

At the Kyoto Conference in December 1997, the European Union agreed upon targets for reducing carbon dioxide (CO_2) emissions by 8 per cent of 1990 levels by 2010. Despite expected improvements in fuel use and efficiency, expected economic growth means a cut is needed relative to 'business as usual' forecasts for 2010 of about 11 per cent growth in emissions (Marshall 1998). There is, therefore, a role for a taxation or marketable permits to meet these goals. Such taxes/permits are bound to affect the terms of trade and real incomes, and since they affect patterns of fuel use they are also relevant to international pollution issues, such as the costs of acid rain pollution and its abatement.

This chapter summarises the adaptation of a large, static, multi-country computable general equilibrium model of the European Union (Fehr, Rosenberg and Wiegard 1995 – the FRW model) to analyse environmental taxation. Section 2 outlines changes to make the model more suitable for energy analysis, as well as development of a link to IIASA's integrated environmental assessment model RAINS (Regional Acidification Information and Simulation), which helps identify effects on other international pollutants. In the past, such modelling approaches have usually been treated separately – pollutant models like RAINS take energy consumption as exogenous, while general equilibrium models take as input more primitive variables such as technology, tastes and policy. The geographical scope (European rather than global) and reasons for interest in other pollutants distinguish this study from other integrated pollutant/general equilibrium model studies (e.g. the MIT Global Climate Change programme).[1] Section 3 then summarises some simulations on our models.

1.1 Reasons for a Common General Equilibrium (CGE) approach

Clarke *et al.* (1996) discuss a variety of approaches to assess the costs of carbon abatement. CGE models are popular because environmental tax reforms can have effects well beyond the energy sector. CGE models produce a useful summary of the net effect on economic activity (real GDP or GNP) and welfare (equivalent variation), and, compared to traditional macroeconomic models, may be more suited to assessing the long-term effects of action to combat global warming, since they allow for a greater degree of microeconomic adjustment.

Depending on their specification, CGE models can deal with a number of important aspects.

(i) *Interaction of a carbon tax with existing energy taxes and subsidies*   If a tax shifts demand away from subsidised industries, (e.g. Edwards' 1998 study of German coal), its overall cost is reduced, while if it is applied to fuels already bearing high taxes or profit mark-ups (see Clarke and Edwards 1998), the cost of the tax will be increased. While we do not use the same detail of cross-subsidisation as in the above articles, we allow for subsidies on fuel production and different specific and *ad valorem* taxes on different fuels to different users.

(ii) *Uses of recycled tax revenue*   There have been suggestions that by using carbon tax revenues to cut taxes on labour, European countries could actually gain a net economic benefit. However, CGE studies (sometimes even with non-clearing labour markets – for example, Conrad and Schmidt 1998) have generally dampened early optimism about this 'double dividend' (see Boehringer *et al.* 1998), since in a general equilibrium framework taxes on production or consumption ultimately raise the cost of consumer goods. This reduces the value of work time against leisure, and so has similar effects to an income tax in terms of deterring labour supply (Bovenberg and De Mooij 1994).

Where income taxes are progressive, transferring taxation from income to consumption tends to encourage labour supply at the expense of worsened income distribution (though only a few CGE studies, such as Pench, 1998, actually look at distribution). If existing taxes are not progressive, there is only a gain if the initial tax system is poorly designed. An equation listing is shown in Appendix I. For a detailed description of the FRW model see Ruocco (1996). Our treatment of labour markets is similar to the original FRW (unlike Duncan *et al.* (1998) and Hutton and Ruocco (1999)), since we prefer to allow for more detailed treatment of other aspects of the model rather than labour markets. Nevertheless, we employ a positive labour supply elasticity, so the nature of revenue recycling will have important effects on labour supply, output and welfare.

1.2   The international dimension of the problem in Europe

Since much environmental policy is now decided jointly by EU member states, simulations based on action by a single country are not realistic. In addition, members' environmental policies have substantial effects on their neighbours.

(i) *Carbon leakage*   Attempts by one country to reduce carbon emissions can be offset by shifts of carbon-intensive industries to other countries. In practice, as Boehringer *et al.* (1998b) find, leakages are only important in models (e.g. the Ricardo–Viner specification) where goods produced by a particular industry in different countries are perfect substitutes. Under the more common Armington approach, where goods from different countries are treated as qualitatively different, leakages are small. The Armington formulation is probably more plausible for our model, given that sectors are relatively aggregated (so exports from one sector in different countries may consist of quite different commodities, such as French wine and Irish beef), and also given that there is considerable two-way trade within sectors (something not consistent with the Heckscher–Ohlin/Ricardo–Viner assumptions).[2]

(ii) *Tax export* (Markusen 1975)   Effects on world fuel prices, or on real exchange rates may mean that some of the cost of a carbon tax is borne by countries other than those imposing the tax. Global or North–South models (e.g. Whalley and Wigle 1991), have looked at these effects in some detail. The terms of trade effect, where an energy-importing country imposing a carbon tax sees a reduction in its import bill and consequent rise in its exchange rate, has been large enough in some single-country studies – for example, Germany in Edwards (1998), or Italy in Pench (1998) – to outweigh other effects and actually cause a rise in real incomes in the country imposing the tax, at least for modest tax rates. Given that Germany and Italy both trade largely with their European neighbours, a multi-country model of Europe would seem appropriate for assessing these effects further.

Many CGE models have implicitly ruled out sizeable terms of trade effects: for example Boehringer *et al.*'s (1998a) model of Germany, while using an Armington specification, has fixed import and export prices.[3] In Conrad and Schmidt's 1998 European multi-country study, prices for Europe's trade with the rest of the world are fixed, ruling out tax export to the rest of the world. By contrast, in the FRW model, all countries produce differentiated products, and while the trade effects are largest between European neighbours, the rest of the world's import and export prices can also be affected by demand changes.

(iii) *International pollution*   Edwards (1998) finds sulphur dioxide (SO_2) emissions change by a very similar proportion to CO_2 in response to a carbon tax in both Japan and Germany (both pollutants being emitted in similar proportions from the main fossil fuels), while nitrogen oxides/ozone (NO_x) are less affected by a carbon tax, and particulates are affected a good deal in Japan but less in Germany. Valuations based on estimates of health and environmental gains from savings in this pollution can be quite substantial relative to the other costs and benefits involved (Clarke and Edwards 1997).

Much of the cost of pollution changes is borne abroad. The costs of CO_2 emissions are worldwide, while those of SO_2 and NO_x are spread across Europe. Particulates tend to be mostly more local. Alternatively, if the country imposing a carbon tax has agreed to limit its emissions of these other pollutants to fixed target levels, the consumption of less polluting fuels can reduce the need to install abatement technology, meaning the saving is internalised. Conrad and Schmidt look at this possibility for SO_2 and NO_x, with simplified abatement cost curves.

2   Structure of the model and database

This study runs a multi-country CGE model of the European Union, developed from the FRW model, in conjunction with the RAINS model of transboundary SO_2 and NO_x pollution and abatement costs.

For an environmental study it was necessary to alter the FRW model's disaggregation. In addition, there is an extra stage of the production function to allow for aggregation of energy and other goods. The indirect taxation structure is more sophisticated, but unlike the FRW original, government spending is not differentiated from household consumption. Aspects of the modelling that are altered from the original FRW model are marked with asterisks **.

The model has four regions: the UK, Germany, the rest of the (12 member 1992) EU and the rest of the world (ROW). There are 3 non-energy and 9 energy sectors. The latter are highly aggregated to allow for more disaggregation of energy. Output can be sold to other sectors or to consumers at home or abroad. Consumers are an aggregate of households, government and non-profit-making bodies. All sectors are perfectly competitive. Of the two factors of production, labour is mobile between sectors but not between countries, while capital can move freely around the world: consequently there is a single global cost of capital, while wages vary between countries.

2.1 Data sources

Starting from Fehr's (1996) data set for 1992, it was necessary to disaggregate energy from an energy and water sector. For this reason, for European energy sectors we have used data from the International Energy Agency's *Energy Statistics of OECD Countries* and *Energy Prices and Taxes*. Average prices for the rest of the EU were approximated by average French and Italian prices. Accuracy of data for the ROW is not so important for this study. Energy tables for ROW were based on Table A10 of the 1992 World Bank *World Development Report*, with prices and taxes assumed to be somewhat lower than in the EU. Trade volumes were derived from total import and export figures by area.

The non-energy sectors have been highly aggregated from the original FRW model, into an energy-intensive sector (chemicals, steel and paper, pulp and printing), an agriculture, services and transport sector (no separate transport data were available in the FRW database), and an other industry sector.

2.2 Production function

The model uses a nested CES production function, with goods in the same stage of nesting being closer substitutes for one another.

(1) Imports from different countries are combined to form a single composite imported input.
(2) The composite imported input is combined with home-produced inputs.
(3)** Inputs are aggregated to form composite inputs of energy, non-energy materials and value added.
(4)** Energy, materials and value added are combined to form total output.

2.3   Consumer sector and labour supply

For consumption, again nested CES functions are exploited. The stages are:

(1) Merge imports of each commodity from different countries as a CES aggregate.
(2) Combine the aggregate import with the home-produced version of the same good.
(3) Aggregate the various consumer goods, to form aggregate consumption.
(4) Disposable income is spent entirely on the aggregate consumer good. Household utility is a CES aggregate of consumption and leisure.

2.4   The government sector

Unlike the FRW model**, government spending is simply treated as a transfer to households. Taxes comprise the following. (1) On production: (a) A production tax/subsidy per unit of output and (b)** Specific taxes per unit volume on inputs of energy. (2) On trade, import tariffs between the EU and non-EU countries. (3) On consumption (a) Specific taxes** and (b) Value added taxes with variable rates across goods. (4) Income tax applies to both labour and capital income of a single representative household, with 'representative marginal income tax rates' derived from Hutton and Ruocco (1999).

2.5   International trade

Trade is modelled using the 'Armington specification', in which all countries produce differentiated goods. The household and government balances are fixed at zero, which implicitly fixes the balance of payments at zero too. All elasticity assumptions are given in the Table 9.1.

Table 9.1 Elasticity assumptions

Production function:
  (i) Between imported intermediates from different countries: $\sigma_4 = 2$
  (ii) Between imported and non-imported intermediates: $\sigma_3 = 2$
  (iii) Between capital and labour: $\sigma_2 = 0.8$
  (iv) Between fuels: $\sigma_{EN} = 2$ for UK or Germany. 1.25 for Other EU12 or ROW.
      Except in power generation $\sigma_{EN} = 4$ for UK/Germany and 2.5 for Other EU12/ROW.
      or in ag/comm (which includes transport) $\sigma_{EN} = 0.8$ for UK/Germany or 0.5 for Other EU12/ROW.
  (v) Between non-fossil fuels: $\sigma_{ONF} = 0.5$
  (vi) Top level between energy, non-energy and value added: $\sigma_{TOP} = 0.5$

Consumption function:
  (i) Between imports from different source countries: $\sigma_3 = 2$
  (ii) Between composite imports and home-produced goods: $\sigma_2 = 2$
  (iii) Between different consumption goods: $\sigma_1 = 0.5$

Labour supply:
Uncompensated labour supply elasticity: ELLSUP $= 0.15$

2.6 Modelling energy consumption and carbon emissions

The carbon calculations are derived from primary fossil fuel consumption, using the following carbon content figures (tonnes carbon per tonne of oil equivalent):

Hard coal	1.12 tC/toe
Soft coal	1.37 tC/toe
Crude oil	0.84 tC/toe
Natural gas	0.64 tC/toe

The carbon content of secondary fossil fuels is based upon the carbon from primary fossil fuels used in their calculation. Where the secondary fuel is an import, we use the total carbon content of primary fossil fuels used in the production of the secondary fuel. The Carbon Tax is in ECU per tonne carbon to all primary fuels according to their *initial (base case) carbon content*, and to all imported secondary fossil fuels from outside the EU. No tax is applied to imported electricity.

2.7 Link to the RAINS model of sulphur and nitrogen emissions and deposition

RAINS, developed by IIASA (see Alcamo *et al.* 1990; Bertok *et al.* 1993; Klaassen 1996), is the most widely used model of emissions, deposition and abatement of sulphur dioxide (SO_2) and nitrogen oxides (NO_x). The model has sulphur and nitrogen modules, each of which uses scenarios combining an energy pathway (a set of projected demands by fuel, country and sector, for 5-year intervals) with an abatement scenario (based only on technological measures). For our work, the output from the CGE model, showing the effects of a carbon tax on fuel use, is used as the basis for a revised energy pathway. We are interested in the consequential geographical distribution of SO_2 and NO_x.

Combining the models raises a number of complications. RAINS is a scenario model for a series of 5-year snapshots, while the CGE solves for the energy economy in a single base year for alternative tax policies. We have therefore concentrated on looking at one year only in the RAINS pathways, 1995, which is reasonably close to the 1992 base for the CGE model, and using that as the base case for simulations. In addition, RAINS uses a greater disaggregation of fuels and sectors than the CGE model, with categories not agreeing exactly, so we have had to make assumptions as to which fuels and sectors in the CGE correspond to which in RAINS.

RAINS is also more disaggregated in terms of countries. The CGE 'other EU 12' grouping is split down into 10 individual member states for RAINS. The non-EU countries of Europe are all covered separately in RAINS, but form just part of the 'ROW' grouping in the RAINS model.

The base case shares of different fuels within a sector vary greatly between different countries of other EU 12 and ROW. This can cause unrealistic effects (e.g. if oil is substituted for coal across the other EU 12 group as a whole, countries which are oil-intensive may see fuel use rise in response to a tax, while countries which are coal-intensive will see it fall). This effect is reduced by alternately rescaling energy use by country and by sector.

3   Some carbon tax simulations

Table 9.2 shows some key statistics of our database in 1992. The total EU accounts for 13.3 per cent of global carbon emissions. Of EU members, the UK

Table 9.2 Energy statistics from the database

A: Some key statistics of our database for the economies in the base year 1992

	GNP	Energy consumption final	MTOE Primary	Carbon dioxide MT Carbon
UK	0.91	144.5	192.4	160.0 (2.6%)
Germany	1.44	229.8	278.6	257.6 (4.1%)
Rest of EU 12	3.53	541.6	538.2	412.9 (6.6%)
Total EU	5.88	915.9	1,009.2	830.5 (13.3%)
Rest of the World	17.00	4,915.6	6,341.0	5,412.6 (86.7%)
Global total	22.88	5,831.5	7,350.2	6,243.1 (100%)

B: Energy price per unit carbon

	(a) Expenditure by final energy users ECU mn	(b) M Tonnes carbon emitted	(a)/(b) Final expenditure per tC
UK	72,204	160	451
Germany	123,579	258	479
Rest of EU	333,183	413	807
Total EU	528,966	831	637
Rest of the world	1,727,291	5412	319
Global total	2,256,257	6243	361

C: Net energy export/imports

	(a) Net exports MTOE	(b) Primary consumption MTOE	(a)/(b) Net exports share
UK	− 4.9	192.4	− 2.5%
Germany	− 186.7	278.6	− 67.0%
Rest of EU	− 486.1	538.2	− 90.3%
Total EU	− 677.7	1,009.2	− 67.2%
Rest of the World	677.7	6,741.0	+ 10.1%

and Germany, which are relatively more coal-dependent, produce 20 and 30 per cent respectively. The UK imports a very small fraction of its fuel. Germany imports about two-thirds of its primary energy needs, while the rest of the EU is almost totally dependent on imports. As a result, the terms of trade effect of a carbon tax is much more marked in the other EU 12 countries than in Germany or, particularly, the UK.

For simulation purposes, the chosen level of carbon tax is 30 ECU per tonne carbon (tC) (1992 prices). Table 9.2B calculates the average expenditure by all final users on energy, relative to the total carbon emissions of the country concerned. As can be seen, a 30 ECU/tC tax is modest compared to 450–800 ECU expenditure per tC across the EU. But prices of some fuels to some sectors (e.g. of coal to power generation) will rise much more sharply.

A final comment: long-term CGE models tend to produce lower cost estimates for environmental taxes than shorter-run macroeconomic studies, since they allow more microeconomic flexibility for the economy to adapt to the tax. For a carbon tax to produce a 'large' economic loss requires either a very high rate of tax, or that the tax compounds existing distortions in the economy.

3.1   Basic simulations of a carbon tax (Table 9.3)

This study considers four scenarios: where carbon taxes are imposed in the UK alone, in Germany alone, in the rest of the EU 12 and across the EU. It is assumed that the revenue is recycled as lower VAT, which would have less labour market effect than recycling as lower income tax, but should be more equitable in terms of income distribution (which we cannot analyse, but see Barker and Kohler 1998). This paper is not intended specifically to investigate a 'double-dividend' effect of reducing labour taxes, although labour market effects mean that the efficiency effects of changes in the incidence of indirect taxes are amplified.

Column A shows the effects of a 30 ECU carbon tax in the UK. Perhaps surprisingly, the carbon tax at 30 ECU/tC has no net cost to GNP. This reflects partly the fact that in our base year, domestic energy in the UK was exempt from VAT, so the carbon tax is actually serving up to a point to equalise tax rates across commodities. Also, the carbon tax reduces energy imports, which, given the Armington trade assumptions, allows a rise in the real exchange rate, improving Britain's terms of trade by 0.45 per cent. As a result, much of the cost of the tax is actually felt abroad (if 20 per cent of the UK's GNP is imported, the terms of trade gain to the UK would be 0.09 per cent of GNP). The effect on the rest of Europe and the world is a small reduction in real incomes.

Offsetting the terms of trade gain, real wages fall marginally, which deters labour, despite the cut in VAT. However, increased leisure means that welfare in the UK, including leisure, is fractionally raised by the tax change.

Interestingly, carbon emissions outside the UK also fall slightly, so there is no carbon 'leakage' problem in this model. This is partly because the tax slightly reduces incomes abroad. Also, secondary energy (refined oil and electricity) export prices from the UK are raised by a carbon tax, which raises energy prices

Table 9.3 European multi-country CGE model: simulations of the effects of a 30 ECU per tonne carbon tax compared to base

		30 ECU/tC tax applied in			
		A *UK only*	*B* *Germany only*	*C* *Other EU* 12	*D* *All EU*
UK	CO_2 emissions	−17.15%	0.07%	0.18%	−17.54%
	Primary energy cons	−15.52%	0.04%	0.37%	−15.55%
	Real wage	−0.02%	−0.01%	−0.06%	−0.07%
	Real GNP	0.00%	−0.01%	−0.04%	−0.04%
	Welfare (eq varn)	0.01%	−0.01%	−0.03%	−0.04%
	Terms of trade	100.45%	99.95%	99.82%	100.22%
Germany	CO_2 emissions	0.28%	−20.44%	−0.68%	−21.07%
	Primary energy cons	0.45%	−16.33%	0.62%	−15.99%
	Real wage	−0.01%	−0.17%	−0.04%	−0.22%
	Real GNP	0.00%	−0.06%	−0.05%	−0.12%
	Welfare (eq varn)	0.00%	−0.04%	−0.04%	−0.10%
	Terms of trade	99.99%	100.37%	99.79%	100.10%
Other EU	CO_2 emissions	−0.67%	−0.09%	−20.10%	−20.23%
	Primary energy cons	−0.23%	0.08%	−18.14%	−17.85%
	Real wage	−0.02%	−0.01%	0.10%	0.11%
	Real GNP	−0.01%	−0.02%	0.03%	0.02%
	Welfare (eq varn)	−0.01%	−0.01%	0.03%	0.01%
	Terms of trade	99.96%	99.90%	100.89%	100.74%
Rest of World	CO_2 emissions	−0.03%	0.00%	−0.17%	−0.20%
	Primary energy cons	−0.03%	0.00%	0.01%	0.00%
	Real wage	−0.09%	0.00%	−0.06%	−0.06%
	Real GNP	−0.05%	−0.01%	−0.03%	−0.04%
	Welfare (eq varn)	−0.04%	0.00%	−0.02%	−0.03%
	Terms of trade	99.90%	99.86%	99.32%	99.12%
Carbon emissions			Change MTC		
	UK	−27.44	0.11	0.28	−28.05
	Germany	0.72	−52.67	−1.76	−54.28
	Other EU	−2.75	−0.38	−82.98	−83.54
	Total EU	−29.47	−52.93	−84.46	−165.87
	Rest of World	−1.66	0.14	−9.11	−10.96
	Global	−31.14	−52.79	−93.58	−176.84
	Leakage (+)/extl savgs(−)	−3.70	−0.13	−10.59	−10.96

in the rest of Europe slightly. In column *B* the tax is introduced in Germany only. Since Germany, particularly the Eastern Laender, consumes much highly polluting soft coal in its power generation, there is more scope than in the UK for low-cost fuel switching. Consequently, a similar tax rate produces slightly larger proportionate reductions in carbon emissions: nearly 20.5 per cent. However, as this means the substitution of imported oil and gas for home-produced soft coal, the effect of the carbon tax on the terms of trade is actually slightly less than in the UK, with an improvement of 0.37 per cent. Also, since Germany already has substantial VAT on domestic fuel, the carbon tax does not offset an existing distortion there, so the cost effects on GNP and welfare are rather higher than in the UK. GNP is reduced by 0.06 per cent, though the net effect on welfare including leisure is rather less than this.

A tax of 30 ECU in Germany produces a slight increase in carbon emissions outside the EU, as production of energy-intensive industries shifts to the rest of the EU and to the ROW (presumably Central and Eastern Europe).

Column *C* shows the effect of a 30 ECU tax in the EU excluding Germany and the UK. Because this is a heterogeneous country grouping, and oil or nuclear fuel inputs in one may not easily substitute for coal in another, the fuel substitution elasticities for the 'other EU' countries have been reduced by 3/8 compared to the UK and Germany. The overall effect is for the 30 ECU/tC tax to reduce carbon emissions by 20 per cent: less than with a similar tax in Germany, but more than in the UK. The terms of trade effect, however, is greater (a rise of nearly 0.9 per cent), and this contributes to a rise in real wages, real GNP and welfare. The tax export effect means that incomes in the UK, Germany and the Rest of the World are reduced somewhat.

Column *D* shows the effects of a tax across the EU. The effect of the tax on emissions is marginally greater than when the countries introduce the tax individually. The tax still has more effect proportionally in Germany, and less in the UK, than in the rest of the EU. Since European countries trade with one another, the terms of trade gain to the countries introducing the tax is less than when they do so individually. Consequently, GNP in the UK and Germany falls slightly instead of rising, though that in the rest of the EU still rises a little. Real GDP in the ROW is reduced by 0.04 per cent.

3.2   Implications for other pollutants

Table 9.4 A and B show the implications of scenario 4 (the 30 ECU/tC tax across the EU 12) in 1995 for SO_2 and NO_x emissions respectively. These assume no change in the application of abatement technology, so that the reduced fuel use and switch to cleaner oil and gas away from coal reduce SO_2 and NO_x emissions. For SO_2 (Table 9.4A), German emissions are reduced by more than a third, due to the replacement of dirty brown coal in power generation. Spain, Ireland, Denmark and the Netherlands, which all rely on dirty coal-fired generation also see large improvements. The effects are much less in the UK, where the main coal-fired power stations already had abatement technology fitted, and improvement is about 10 per cent, or in Italy, where generation is largely oil-fired. The overall reduction in emissions in the EU 12 was 23 per cent, but half of European emissions in the base case come from outside the EU (particularly Poland and the Czech Republic) where the EU carbon tax has little effect on emissions. NO_x emissions (Table 9.4B) are more linked to oil consumption, especially in transport, and are less affected by a carbon tax. The reduction in the UK is just 4 per cent, while emissions in Germany are reduced by 7.86 per cent, and the other EU 12 (except Ireland and Luxembourg) see reductions in the range 4–10.5 per cent.

Table 9.5 A and B from the deposition module of the RAINS model show that the benefit in terms of lower excess sulfur deposition (above the critical threshold where acid starts to build up) are concentrated largely in Germany, with Sweden and Poland also benefiting substantially, but much of the EU seeing much smaller effects. The reduction in excess deposition of nitrogen in acid rain is more evenly spread, with France the largest beneficiary, followed by the Scandinavian countries, Germany and Belgium.

If, alternatively, countries spent less on abatement, keeping emissions constant, the benefit would be internal to the countries imposing the tax. In the case of the

Table 9.4 Change in (A) Sulphur emissions based on 1995 energy use and second sulphur protocol controls and (B) NO$_x$ emissions based on 1995 energy use and current controls, assuming that EU 12 impose 30 ECU/tC carbon tax

	Base kT	*Change kT*	*Change per cent*
(A) Sulphur emission			
Region 1: UK	2,395.40	−237.37	−9.91
Region 2: Germany	4,705.62	−1,580.10	−33.58
Region 3: Other EU 12	6,390.90	−1,330.17	−20.81
Italy	2,089.12	−235.88	−11.29
Spain	1,838.06	−643.38	−35.00
France	883.43	−122.17	−13.83
Greece	426.95	−96.85	−22.68
Belgium	344.56	−47.43	−13.77
Netherlands	232.33	−61.39	−26.42
Denmark	224.58	−66.22	−29.49
Portugal	218.86	−21.12	−9.65
Ireland	123.49	−35.73	−28.93
Luxembourg	9.52	0	0.00
Total EU 12	13,491.92	−3,147.64	−23.33
Region 4: Rest of Europe	14,054.93	17.5	0.12
Poland	2,572.35	6.51	0.25
Russia	2,341.69	−1.01	−0.04
Ukraine	1,711.35	−0.14	−0.01
Czech	1,428.67	3.26	0.23
Bulgaria	1,350.08	5.6	0.41
Romania	922.05	2.48	0.27
Hungary	804.52	0.94	0.12
Others	2,924.22	−0.14	0.00
SEAS	575.89	0	0.00
Total European emissions	28,122.74	−3,130.14	−11.13

Table 9.4 (Continued)

	Base kT	Change kT	Change per cent
(B) NO$_x$ emissions			
Region 1: UK	1,186.06	− 48.13	− 4.06
Region 2: Germany	1,107.40	− 87.09	− 7.86
Region 3: Other EU 12	3,752.27	− 240.02	− 6.40
Italy	1,225.84	− 58.46	− 4.77
Spain	768.75	− 66.06	− 8.59
France	706.34	− 28.37	− 4.02
Greece	65.72	− 15.47	− 5.82
Belgium	190.12	− 9.55	− 5.02
Netherlands	232.39	− 19.4	− 8.35
Denmark	139.06	− 14.52	− 10.44
Portugal	153.27	− 16.08	− 10.49
Ireland	61.20	− 12.05	− 19.69
Luxembourg	9.58		− 0.63
Total EU 12	6,045.73	− 375.24	− 6.21
Region 4: Rest of Europe	6,853.82	6.18	0.09
Poland	675.66	1.00	0.15
Russia	2,328.27	2.08	0.09
Ukraine	1,256.49	1.47	0.12
Czech	213.97	0.16	0.07
Bulgaria	221	0.13	0.06
Romania	422.86	0.5	0.12
Hungary	163.13	0.07	0.04
Others	1,572.44	0.77	0.05
SEAS	635.74	0.00	0.00
Total European Emissions	13,535.29	− 369.06	− 2.73

UK, the saving from lower costs of sulphur abatement (if the tax had been in place in 1995) would have been ECU 85 bn (1990 prices), or about 0.01 per cent of GDP. The UK saving on NO$_x$ abatement would have been just ECU 5 bn, though as the cost function for NO$_x$ abatement is highly nonlinear, in later years, when more abatement technology is expected to be applied, the marginal costs of abating NO$_x$ (and hence the value of reducing emissions by other means, such as a carbon tax) will be higher.

In Germany, the reduction in sulphur emissions in 1995, if the carbon tax had been imposed, is greater than the total effects of technological abatement in place at that date.

4   Summary and conclusions

This paper has shown how a static, multi-country CGE model can be used to analyse the economic effects of carbon abatement policy, taking account of

Table 9.5 RAINS model (A) Sulphur and (B) Nitrogen excess deposition (5% level) change from a 30 ECU carbon tax 1995

		Excess deposition			
	Ecosystem area	*No carbon tax*	*Carbon tax*	*Change*	*Change × area*
(A) Sulphur					
UK	7,890	645.5	633.9	− 11.6	91,524.0
Germany	8,693	1,687.9	1,341.2	− 346.7	3,013,863.1
Belgium	621	1,678.8	1,441.0	− 237.8	147,673.8
Denmark	974	312.0	197.1	− 114.9	111,912.6
France	14,483	118.4	88.9	− 29.5	427,248.5
Greece	2,455	0	0	0	0
Ireland	489	32.6	30.5	− 2.1	1,026.9
Italy	6,627	381.7	339.7	− 42	278,334.0
Luxembourg	88	1,231.1	1,053.9	− 177.2	15,593.6
Netherlands	320	1,999.1	1,699.4	− 299.7	95,904.0
Portugal	2,829	0	0	0	0
Spain	8,523	42.5	22.6	− 19.9	169,607.7
Austria	4,872	1,207.5	1,081.6	− 125.9	613,384.8
Finland	32,208	81.3	71.2	− 10.1	325,300.8
Sweden	43,650	204.9	172.5	− 32.4	1,414,260.0
Norway	32,065	153.2	135.8	− 17.4	557,931.0
Switzerland	1,189	810.4	701.8	− 108.6	129,125.4
Czech	2,656	1,966.8	1,654.8	− 312	828,672.0
Estonia	1,891	55.5	44.7	− 10.8	20,422.8
Hungary	1,670	226.3	212.5	− 13.8	23,046.0
Poland	6,372	1,641.7	1,392.1	− 249.6	1,590,451.2
Slovenia	906	905	874.3	− 30.7	27,814.2
(B) Nitrogen					
UK	7,890	440.1	433.3	− 6.8	53,652.0
Germany	8,693	819.3	801.5	− 17.8	154,735.4
Belgium	621	1,082.1	1,055.8	− 26.3	16,332.3
Denmark	974	315.5	196.4	− 119.1	116,003.4
France	14,483	93.1	71.7	− 21.4	309,936.2
Greece	2,455	0	0	0	0
Ireland	489	22.6	22.2	− 0.4	195.6
Italy	6,627	268.0	262.6	− 5.4	35,785.8
Luxembourg	88	750.0	732.5	− 17.5	1,540.0
Netherlands	320	1,837.2	1,813.8	− 23.4	7,488.0
Portugal	0	0	0	0	
Spain	8,523	0.2	0.1	− 0.1	852.3
Austria	4,872	739.3	727.4	− 11.9	57,976.8
Finland	32,208	67.5	60.5	− 7.0	225,456.0
Sweden	43,650	171.0	165.3	− 5.7	248,805.0
Norway	32,065	146.5	141.4	− 5.1	163,531.5
Switzerland	1,189	806.9	783.0	− 23.9	28,417.1
Czech	2,656	585.0	572.8	− 12.2	32,403.2

Table 9.5 (Continued)

	Ecosystem area	No carbon tax	Excess deposition Carbon tax	Change	Change × area
Estonia	1,891	51.0	46.6	− 4.4	8,320.4
Hungary	1,670	65.5	64.4	− 1.1	1,837.0
Poland	6,372	689.0	676.7	− 12.3	78,375.6
Slovenia	906	436.9	428.3	− 8.6	7,791.6

international effects. It has also established a link with the RAINS model of acid rain depletion, which shows that there is a strong connection between carbon and sulphur emissions, and a weaker one with nitrogen emissions.

Had a 30 ECU/tC carbon tax been applied across the 12 EU members in our base year (1992), our model indicates that carbon emissions would have been around 20 per cent lower: this is rather larger than the EU would need to achieve (compared with business as usual) in 2010, but such a saving might well be required in future commitments. Tax export effects mean the cost of the tax when applied across the EU is 0.12 per cent of GNP in Germany and 0.04 per cent in the UK, with a small gain in GNP in other EU countries, where the terms of trade benefit is greater. When the UK or Germany undertake a carbon tax on their own, they experience a terms of trade benefit greater than when EU members act in concert, and their GNP is barely affected by a 30 ECU/tC tax.

Sulphur abatement provides a further benefit of a carbon tax, as fuel saving and switching towards cleaner fuels means either lower emissions or less need to spend on cleaning up technology. If sulphur emissions fall, the main beneficiary would probably be Germany. In the event of countries choosing instead to keep emissions constant, but spending less on abatement, benefits would be more widespread. The UK would gain about an extra 0.01 per cent of GDP.

The reduction in NO_x emissions is smaller. The benefits are more widespread across the EU, but the reduction, at least in the early years, could be achieved at low cost by other means.

Appendix I: Equation listing for CGE model

LDEQUAZ: Labour demand in value added for industry n in country i

$$L_{i,n} = \delta 2_{i,n} \cdot VA_{i,n} \cdot (PVA_{i,n}/W_i)^{\sigma 2_{in}}$$

KDEQUAZ: Capital demand in value added

$$K_{i,n} = (1 - \delta 2_{i,n}) \cdot VA_{i,n} \cdot (PVA_{i,n}/R)^{\sigma 2_{in}}$$

PVAEQUAZ: Unit cost of value added

$$PVA_{i,n} = (L_{i,n} \cdot W_i + K_{i,n} \cdot R)/VA_{i,n}$$

VAEQUAZ: Demand for value added

$$VA_{i,n} = \alpha_{i,n} \cdot YQ_{i,n} \cdot (PG_{i,n}/PVA_{i,n})^{\sigma top_{i,n}}$$

CENEQUAZ: Demand for energy products by an industry

$$CIT_{i,n,en} = \delta en_{i,n,en} \cdot VEN_{i,n} \cdot (PEN_{i,n}/PCIT_{i,n,en})^{\sigma en_{in}}$$

PENEQUAZ: Average price of energy inputs to industry n in country i, calculated as average cost.

$$PEN_{i,n} = \left(\sum_{en} CIT_{i,n,en} \cdot PCIT_{i,n,en} \right) / VEN_{i,n}$$

VENEQUAZ: Total energy input into industry n in country i,

$$VEN_{i,n} = \alpha en_{i,n} \cdot YQ_{i,n} \cdot \left(PG_{i,n}/PEN_{i,n}\right)^{\sigma top_{i,n}}$$

CMAEQUAZ: Shares of each non-energy material in aggregate input of non-energy materials into industry n in country i

$$CIT_{i,n,ma} = \delta ma_{i,n,ma} \cdot VMA_{i,n} \cdot \left(PMA_{i,n}/PCIT_{i,n,ma}\right)^{\sigma ma_{i,n}}$$

PMAEQUAZ: Price or average cost of non-energy material inputs into industry n in country i.

$$PMA_{i,n} = \left(\sum_{ma} CIT_{i,n,ma} \cdot PCIT_{i,n,ma} \right) / VMA_{i,n}$$

MAEQUAZ: Demand by industry n in country i for aggregate non-energy materials

$$VMA_{i,n} = \alpha ma_{i,n} \cdot YQ_{i,n}(PG_{i,n}/PMA_{i,n})^{\sigma top_{i,n}}$$

PGEQUAZ: Average unit production cost of n in country i, calculated by average cost of inputs per unit output, less the URBT rebate (only for scenarios where carbon tax expenditure is rebated to the industry) and grossed up/down by the production tax/subsidy

$$PG_{i,n} = (VA_{i,n} \cdot PVA_{i,n} + VEN_{i,n} \cdot PEN_{i,n} + VMA_{i,n} \cdot PMA_{i,n}$$
$$- VEN_{i,n} \cdot URBT_{i,n}) \cdot (1 + TP_{i,n})/YQ_{i,n}$$

CIX1EQUAZ: Demand in country i for home-produced inputs of n by industry

$$CIX1_{i,n,nn} \cdot \mu H_{i,n,nn} = \alpha CIX_{i,n,nn,i} \cdot CIT_{i,n,nn}$$
$$(PCIT_{i,n,nn} \cdot \mu H_{i,n,nn}/(PG_{i,nn} + SPTAX_{i,nn,i,n}))^{\sigma 3_{i,n,nn}}$$

CIX1BEQUAZ: Demand for composite imports of nn into industry n in country i

$$CIX1B_{i,n,\text{nn}} \cdot \mu M_{i,n,\text{nn}} = (1 - \alpha CIX_{i,n,\text{nn},i}) \cdot CIT_{i,n,\text{nn}}$$
$$\cdot (PCIT_{i,n,\text{nn}}/PCIX1B_{i,n,\text{nn}})^{\sigma 3_{i,n,\text{nn}}}$$

PCITEQUAZ: Price for composite imported inputs of nn into industry n in country i.

$$PCIT_{i,n,\text{nn}} = \left(\begin{array}{c} CIX1_{i,n,\text{nn}} \cdot (PG_{i,\text{nn}} + SPTAX_{i,\text{nn},i,n}) \\ + CIX1B_{i,n,\text{nn}} \cdot PCIX1B_{i,n,\text{nn}} \cdot \mu M_{i,n,\text{nn}} \end{array} \right) \Big/ CIT_{i,n,\text{nn}}$$

CIX2EQUAZ: Demand for imported intermediate inputs of nn from country ii into industry n in country i.

$$CIX2_{i,n,\text{nn},\text{ii}} \cdot \mu_{\text{ii},\text{nn},i,n} = \alpha CIX2_{i,n,\text{nn},\text{ii}} \cdot CIX1B_{i,n,\text{nn}} \cdot \mu M_{i,n,\text{nn}}$$
$$\times \left(PCIX1B_{i,n,\text{nn}} \cdot \mu_{\text{ii},\text{nn},i,n} \Big/ \left(\begin{array}{c} PG_{\text{ii},\text{nn}} \cdot (1 + TTARPB_{\text{ii},\text{nn},i,n}) \\ + SPTAX_{\text{ii},\text{nn},i,n} \end{array} \right) \right)^{\sigma 4_{i,n,\text{nn}}}$$

PCIX1EQUAZ: Price of the composite input of nn into industry n in country i

$$IPCIX1B_{i,n,\text{nn}} = \left(\sum_{\text{ii} \neq i} CIX2_{i,n,\text{nn},\text{ii}} \cdot \left(\begin{array}{c} PG_{i,\text{nn}} \cdot (1 + TTARPB_{\text{ii},\text{nn},i,n}) \\ + SPTAX_{\text{ii},\text{nn},i,n} \end{array} \right) \right) \Big/$$
$$\left(\begin{array}{c} CIX1B_{i,n,\text{nn}} \\ \times \mu M_{i,n,\text{nn}} \end{array} \right)$$

Consumer side

MDEF: Full disposable income including net-of-tax income from capital owned and valuation of the full endowment of labour plus leisure, plus various transfers.

$$INC_i = (R \cdot KSB_i + W_i \cdot EB_i) \cdot (1 - INCTAXR_i)$$
$$+ ALLOW_i \cdot INCTAXR_i + TRANSFER_i \cdot PUT2_i + \sum_{\text{ii}} GRANTRAN_{\text{ii},i}$$

LLEQUAZ: Demand for leisure time

$$LEIS_i = \gamma L_i (INC_i / PUT1_i) \cdot \langle PUT1_i | (W_i (1 - INCTAXR_i)) \rangle^{\delta_i}$$

UT2EQUAZ: Utility from consumption in i.

$$UT2_i = (INC_i - LEIS_i W_i (1 - INCTAXR_i)) / PUT2_i$$

PUT1EQUAZ: Cost of utility function including utility from leisure.

$$PUT1_i = ((\gamma L_i \cdot W_i \cdot (1 - INCTAXR_i))^{(1-\delta_i)}$$
$$+ \gamma C_i \cdot PUT2_i^{(1-\delta_i)})^{(1/(1-\delta_i))}$$

XD1EQUAZ: Final consumer commodity demand for good nn in country i.

$$XD1_{i,\text{nn}} = \gamma 1_{i,\text{nn}} \cdot UT2_i \cdot (PUT2_i/PXD1_{i,\text{nn}})^{\sigma 1_i}$$

PUT2EQUAZ: Price of aggregate consumer bundle.

$$PUT2_i = \sum_{\text{nn}} XD1_{i,\text{nn}} \cdot PXD1_{i,\text{nn}}/UT2_i;$$

XD2EQUAZ: Final consumer demand for home-produced good nn in country i.

$$XD2_{i,\text{nn}} = \gamma 2_{i,\text{nn},i} \cdot XD1_{i,\text{nn}}$$
$$\cdot \left\langle PXD1_{i,\text{nn}} \middle| \left(\frac{SPCTAX_{i,i,\text{nn}}}{+PG_{i,\text{nn}} \cdot (1 + TT_{i,\text{nn}} \cdot TT1_i)} \right) \right\rangle^{\sigma 2_{i,\text{nn}}}$$

XD2BEQUAZ: Final consumer demand in country i for aggregate imported commodity nn.

$$XD2B_{i,\text{nn}} = \gamma 2B_{i,\text{nn},i} \cdot XD1_{i,\text{nn}} \cdot (PXD1_{i,\text{nn}}/PXD2B_{i,\text{nn}})^{\sigma 2_{i,\text{nn}}}$$

PXD1EQUAZ: Price index for final consumer demand for nn in I.

$$PXD1_{i,\text{nn}} = \left(\begin{array}{c} XD2_{i,\text{nn}} \cdot (SPCTAX_{i,i,\text{nn}} \\ +PG_{i,\text{nn}} \cdot (1 + TT_{i,\text{nn}} \cdot TT1_i)) \\ +XD2B_{i,\text{nn}} \cdot PXD2B_{i,\text{nn}} \end{array} \right) \Big/ XD1_{i,\text{nn}}$$

XD3EQUAZ: Final consumer demand for imports of nn from country ii into country i.

$$XD3_{i,\text{nn},\text{ii}} = \gamma 3_{i,\text{nn},\text{ii}} \cdot XD2B_{i,\text{nn}} \left\langle PXD2B_{i,\text{nn}} \middle/ \left(\begin{array}{c} SPCTAX_{i,\text{ii},\text{nn}} + PG_{\text{ii},\text{nn}} \cdot \\ x(1 + TT_{i,\text{nn}} \cdot TT1_i) \cdot (1 + TAR_{i,\text{ii},\text{nn}}) \end{array} \right) \right\rangle^{\sigma 3i.\text{nn}}$$

PXD2BEQUAZ: Price index for the final consumption of the aggregate import bundle.

$$PXD2B_{i,\text{nn}} = \left(\sum_{\text{ii} \neq i} \left(\frac{XD3_{i,\text{nn},\text{ii}} \cdot SPCTAX_{i,\text{ii},\text{nn}}}{+nPG_{\text{ii},\text{nn}} \cdot (1 + TT_{i,\text{nn}} \cdot TT1_i) \cdot (1 + TAR_{i,\text{ii},\text{nn}})} \right) \right) \Big/$$
$$2B_{i,\text{nn}}$$

Market clearing equations

EXMKTG: Market clearing in the goods market for good nn in country i.

$$XD2_{i,nn} + \sum_{ii \neq i}(XD3_{ii,nn,i}) + \sum_n \sum_{ii \neq i} \left(CIX2_{ii,n,nn,i} + \sum_{nn} CIX1_{i,nn,nnn} \right)$$
$$- YQ_{i,nn} = 0$$

GOVBUDGET: Equation balancing the government budget. Income tax plus import tariff revenue on consumer goods, plus VAT on imported consumer goods, plus VAT on home-produced consumer goods, plus specific taxes on imported inputs, plus specific taxes on home-produced inputs, plus tariffs on imported inputs, plus production taxes, minus various transfers equals zero (there is no direct government spending).

$$INCTAXR_i \cdot (R \cdot KSB_i + W_i \cdot (EB_i - LEIS_i) - ALLOW_i)$$
$$+ \sum_{nn} \sum_{ii \neq i}(XD3_{i,nn,ii} \cdot PG_{ii,nn} \cdot TAR_{i,ii,nn})$$
$$+ \sum_{nn} \sum_{ii \neq i}(XD3_{i,nn,ii} \cdot PG_{ii,nn} \cdot (1 + TAR_{i,ii,nn}) \cdot TT_{i,nn} \cdot TT1_i)$$
$$+ \sum_{nn} XD2_{i,nn} \cdot PG_{i,nn} \cdot TT_{i,nn} \cdot TT1_i$$
$$+ \sum_{nn} \left(XD2_{i,nn} \cdot SPCTAX_{i,i,nn} + \sum_{ii \neq i} XD3_{i,nn,ii} \cdot SPCTAX_{i,ii,nn} \right)$$
$$+ \sum_n \sum_{ii \neq i} CIX2_{i,n,nn,ii} \cdot SPTAXii, nn, i, n$$
$$+ \sum_n \sum_{nn} CIX1_{i,n,nn} \cdot SPTAX_{i,nn,i,n}$$
$$+ \sum_n \sum_{nn} \sum_{ii \neq i} CIX2_{i,n,nn,ii} \cdot PG_{ii,nn} \cdot TTARPB_{ii,nn,i,n}$$
$$+ \sum_n (YQ_{i,n} \cdot PG_{i,n} \cdot TP_{i,n}/(1 + TP_{i,n}))$$
$$- TRANSFER_i \cdot PUT2_i - \sum_{ii} GRANTRAN_{i,ii} - \sum_n URBT_{i,n} \cdot VEN_{i,n} = 0$$

EXMKTL: Total labour employed equals labour endowment less leisure.

$$\sum_n (LD_{i,n}) - (EB_i - LEIS_i) = 0$$

Appendix II: Listing of variables in the model

Production side:

$YQ_{i,n}$	Gross output of industry n in country i.

Inputs

$CIT_{i,n,en}$	Energy type en into industry n in country i.
$CIT_{i,n,ma}$	Non-energy material type ma into industry n in country i.
$CIX1_{i,n,nn}$	Home-produced nn into industry n in country i.
$CIX1B_{i,n,nn}$	Composite imports of nn into n in country i.
$CIX2_{i,n,nn,ii}$	Input of nn from country ii into n in country i.
$K_{i,n}$	Capital employed in industry n in country i.
$L_{i,n}$	Labour employed in industry n in country i.
$VA_{i,n}$	Value added of industry n in country i.
$VEN_{i,n}$	Aggregate energy input into industry n in country i.
$VMA_{i,n}$	Aggregate input of non-energy materials into industry n in country i.

Input prices

$PCIT_{i,n,en}$	Energy type en into industry n in country i.
$PCIT_{i,n,ma}$	Non-energy material type ma into n in country i.
$PCIX1B_{i,n,nn}$	Composite import of nn into n in country i.
$PEN_{i,n}$	Aggregate energy input into industry n in country i.
$PG_{i,n}$	Unit cost of output of industry n in country i.
$PMA_{i,n}$	Aggregate non-energy materials input into industry n in i.
$PVA_{i,n}$	Unit cost of value added of industry n in country i.
R	Unit cost of capital worldwide.
W_i	Wage in country i.

Consumer side.

Incomes, transfers and taxes

INC_i	Full disposable income in country i.
$INCTAXR_i$	Income tax rate in country I (fixed for most scenarios).
$LEIS_i$	Time devoted to leisure rather than labour.
$TRANSFER_i$	Lump-sum transfer from government to consumers in country I (fixed for most scenarios).
$TT1_i$	Scalar to adjust all VAT rates in country i to give desired revenue.
$UT2_i$	Utility from consumption (excluding leisure) in country i.

Consumer price indices

$PUT1_i$	For utility (including leisure) in country i.
$PUT2_i$	For aggregate consumption in country i.
$PXD1_{i,nn}$	For consumption of nn in i.
$PXD2B_{i,nn}$	For aggregate import bundle of nn for final consumers in i.

Final consumer demand

$XD1_{i,nn}$	Good nn in country i.

$XD2_{i,nn}$	Home-produced good nn in country i.
$XD2B_{i,nn}$	Aggregate bundle of imports of nn for final consumers in i.
$XD3_{i,nn,ii}$	For nn from ii in i.

Listing of parameters
Production side:
Tax rates

$SPTAX_{ii,nn,i,n}$	Specific tax on inputs of nn from ii into production of n in i.
$TP_{i,n}$	Production tax on production of n in i.
$TTARPB_{ii,nn,i,n}$	Import tariff on inputs of nn from ii into n in i.
$URBT_{i,n}$	Rebate of carbon tax expenditure by industry n in I (for permit allocation study[4] only).

Share parameters

$\alpha_{i,n}$	Value added in total output.
$\alpha CIX_{i,n,nn,i}$	Home-produced n in total inputs into n in i.
$\alpha CIX2_{i,n,nn,ii}$	Imports of n from ii in total imported inputs into n in i.
$\alpha en_{i,n}$	Energy in total inputs into n in i.
αma_n	Energy materials in total inputs into n in i.
$\delta2_{i,n}$	Parameter for labour in value added
$\delta en_{i,n,en}$	Share of fuel en in total energy use in industry n in i.
$\mu_{ii,n,nn,i}$	Initial ratio of price of nn from ii used by n in I including tax to pre-tax price.
$\mu H_{i,n,nn}$	Initial ratio of price of home-produced nn used by n in I including tax to pre-tax price.
$\mu M_{i,n,nn}$	Initial ratio of price of composite import of nn used by n in I including tax to pre-tax price.

Elasticities of substitution – see Table 9.1.

Consumer side.
Taxes, transfers and allowances

$ALLOW_i$	Income tax allowance.
EB_i	Labour endowment in country i.
$GRANTRAN_{i,ii}$	Lump-sum transfers of windfall profits to shareholders in ii due to grandfathering of permits in country i.
$SPCTAX_{i,ii,nn}$	Specific tax on consumption of nn from ii in country i.
$TAR_{i,ii,nn}$	Tariff on imports of nn from ii for final consumption in i.
$TT_{i,nn}$	Basic VAT rate (before adjustment to make government balance) on nn in i.

Share parameters

γC_i	For labour in labour endowment in country i.
γL_i	For leisure in labour endowment in country i.
$\gamma1_{i,nn}$	For good nn in final consumption in country i.
$\gamma2_{i,nn,i}$	For home-produced good nn in final consumption in country i.

$\gamma 2B_{i,nn,i}$ For aggregate imported good nn in final consumption in country i.

$\gamma 3_{i,nn,i}$ For imports of good nn from ii in aggregate imports of nn in country i.

Substitution elasticities – see Table 9.1.

δ_i Between labour and leisure in country i.

Notes

1. See http://web.mit.edu/global change/www/reports.html for papers. The MIT group integrate the output of the OECD Green model with various climatological and pollutant models, but the scale is global and their interest is in climate, rather than in abatement costs and damage of more local pollutants.
2. For more detailed discussion see Vocke (1997). The Armington assumption, where different countries' shares in demand for a particular good depend only on relative prices, is perhaps best seen as an approximation to deal with the many reasons why goods from different countries are imperfect substitutes.
3. In Boehringer *et al.*'s model, imports, whose price is fixed, are an imperfect substitute for German produce, while, for German producers, exporting (at a fixed world price) is an imperfect substitute for sales to the home market. Hence imports and exports will change as a tax is introduced, but Germany's terms of trade are unaffected.
4. Edwards and Hutton (2001). The paper, which looks at the cost of different methods of allocating carbon permits in the UK, is an application of the model outlined in this paper.

References

Alcamo, J., Shaw, R.W. and Hordijk, L. (1990) *The RAINS model of Acidification, Science and Strategies in Europe*, IIASA reference BK-90-903. Doordrecht: Kluwer.

Barker, T. and Kohler, J. (1998) 'Equity and ecotax reform in the EU: achieving a 10 per cent reduction in CO_2 emissions using excise duties', *Fiscal Studies*, 19, 4: 375–402.

Bertok, I., Cofala, J., Klimont, Z., Schoepp, W. and Amann, M. (1993) '*Structure of the RAINS 7.0 Energy and Emissions database*', IIASA working paper WP-93-67. Laxenburg, Austria.

Boehringer, C. (1998) 'Unilateral taxation of international environmental externalities and sectoral exemptions', in: Fossati, A. and Hutton, J. P. (eds) *Policy Simulations in the European Union*. London: Routledge.

Boehringer, C., Pahlke, A. and Rutherford, T. (1998a) 'Environmental tax reforms and the prospects for a double dividend: an intertemporal general equilibrium analysis for Germany'. University of Colorado, Boulder, mimeo.

Boehringer, C., Rutherford, T. and Voss, A. (1998b) 'Global CO2 emissions and unilateral action: policy implications of induced trade effects', *International Journal of Global Energy Issues*, 11(1–4): 18–22.

Bovenberg, A. L. and De Mooji, R. A. (1994) 'Environmental levies and distortionary taxes', *The American Economic Review*, 84(4): 1085–9.

Clarke, R., Boero, G. and Winters, L. A. (1996) 'Controlling greenhouse gases: a survey of global macroeconomic studies', *Bulletin of Economic Research*, 48(4): 269–308.

Clarke, R. and Edwards, T. H. (1997) *The welfare effects of removing the West German hard coal subsidy*, Discussion Paper, 97–23. Dept of Economics, University of Birmingham.

Clarke, R. and Edwards, T. H. (1998) 'Deregulation of the Japanese oil products market', *Energy Policy*, 26, 2: 129–41.

Conrad, K. and Schmidt, T. F. N. (1998) *Double dividend of climate protection and the role of international policy coordination in the EU - an applied general equilibrium analysis with the GEM-E3 model*, Discussion Paper Nos 97–26. Mannheim: ZEW Centre for European Economic research.

Duncan, A., Hutton, J. P., Laroui, F. and Ruocco, A. (1998) 'The labour market effects of VAT harmonisation in a multicountry AGE model', in: Fossati, A. and Hutton, J. P. (eds) *Policy Simulations in the European Union*. London: Routledge.

Edwards, T. H. (1998) 'Modelling the effects of energy market distortions on the costs of carbon abatement: computable general equilibrium and partial equilibrium assessment', in: Fossati, A. and Hutton, J. P. (eds) *Policy Simulations in the European Union*. London: Routledge.

Edwards, T. H. and Hutton, J. P. (2001) 'Allocation of carbon permits within a country: a general equilibrium analysis of the United Kingdom', *Energy Economics*. Vol 23, issue 4, July 2001, pp. 351–376. Amsterdam: Elsevier.

Fehr, H. (1996) 'Construction of a microconsistent data set for the EU 1992', University of Tubingen, Germany, mimeo.

Fehr, H., Rosenberg, C. and Wiegard, W. (1995) *Welfare Effects of Value-Added Tax Harmonisation in Europe*. Berlin: Springer.

Hutton, J. P. and Ruocco, A. (1999) 'Tax reform and employment in Europe', *International Tax and Public Finance*, 6(3), pp. 263–287, August 1999, Kluwer.

International Energy Agency (1993) *Energy Statistics of OECD Countries*. Paris: OECD/IEA.

International Energy Agency (1998 q 3) *Energy Prices and Taxes*. Paris: OECD IEA.

Klaassen, G. (1996) *Acid Rain and Environmental Degradation. The Economics of Emissions Trading*, IIASA reference BK-96-002. Cheltenham, UK: Edward Elgar.

Markusen, J. R. (1975) 'International externalities and optimal tax structures', *Journal of International Economics*, 5: 15–29.

Marshall, Lord C. (1998) *Economic instruments and the business use of energy*. Report to Chancellor, HM Treasury, London.

Pench, A. (1998) 'Ecotaxes in a CGE model for Italy', in: Fossati, A. and Hutton, J. P. (eds) *Policy Simulations in the European Union*. London: Routledge.

Ruocco, A. (1996) *A multi-country general equilibrium model for the European Union: the basic features and coding structure*, Discussion Paper 83. University of Tubingen: Wirtschaftswissenschaftlichte Facultat.

Vocke, R. (1997) *A critical note on the use of the Armington conjecture in applied general equilibrium analysis*, working paper n.8/97. Genoa: Istituto di Finanza.

Whalley, J. and Wigle, R. (1991) 'The international incidence of carbon taxes', in: Dornbusch, R. and Poterba, J. M. (eds) *Global Warming: Economic Policy Responses*. London: MIT Press.

10 The efficiency costs of voluntary agreements in environmental policy*

Christoph Böhringer and Thomas F. Rutherford

1 Introduction

With respect to environmental protection, governments in many OECD countries are increasingly reluctant to impose fiscal or regulatory measures on firms because they fear adverse effects on production and employment. As an alternative strategy of improving environmental quality, voluntary agreements (VA) between industries and government are becoming more common. Past and current examples of VA in OECD countries include commitments for energy efficiency improvements in industrial sectors or cooperative agreements to increase fuel efficiency of motor vehicles (IEA 1997).[1] In the context of global warming, VA campaigns meanwhile have led to the suspension of CO_2 tax initiatives and other regulatory measures in several OECD countries. The embracement of VA by environmental policy makers has two major reasons. First, VA constitute a cooperative solution and appear more acceptable to industry as compared to administrative measures. Second, VA are perceived as cost-efficient, achieving energy or emission reduction 'at lower costs than regulatory and economic instruments' (IEA 1997: 11).

Economic efficiency is just one but rather important criterion for evaluating alternative instruments in environmental policy making (IPCC 1995). There are only a few scientific studies which qualitatively assess the efficiency implications of voluntary agreements. The study 'Voluntary Actions for Energy-Related CO_2 Abatement' by the International Energy Agency (IEA) concludes that 'voluntary agreements . . . could be part of a cost-effective flexible response to global climate change' (IEA 1997: 11; Kohlhaas and Praetorius 1995) stating that VA could be as cost-efficient as environmental taxes or permits when coordinated industrial abatement plans assure equalisation of marginal abatement costs.

None of these existing studies provides an analytical framework which makes it possible to assess the efficiency implications of VA. This paper suggests that VA can be formalised as a system of tradable grandfathered permits. We show that

*Helpful comments were received from Glenn Harrison and Don Fullerton. The views expressed here are those of the authors, who remain solely responsible for errors and omissions. None of the views expressed here should be attributed to any of our employers or research sponsors.

VA operated as grandfathered permits can induce significant efficiency losses as compared to uniform pollution taxes or auctioned permits. The reason is that VA programs create scarcity rents (i.e. revenues from tradable permits) which work as production subsidies to firms, hereby offsetting in general the optimality conditions for economic efficiency. In a competitive economy these subsidies distort the zero-profit condition of firms on the output side. In economies with oligopolistic competition and increasing returns to scale due to fixed costs, the excess costs of VA are magnified as scarcity rents retained by firms induce losses in economies of scale.

The remainder of the paper is as follows. Section 2 introduces the concept of VA in environmental policy making and describes our basic economic intuition on the efficiency implications of VA. Section 3 lays out the analytical representation of VA in a competitive small open economy model and extends this model to account for scale economies and imperfect competition. Section 4 reports numerical results. Section 5 concludes.

2 Voluntary agreements: practice and economic intuition

2.1 Practice

Voluntary agreements usually refer to contracts between the government and industries which involve negotiated targets with commitments and time schedules. They range from informal voluntary actions by individual firms to binding agreements between public agencies and industry representatives. Typically, VA involve a bargaining process between government and the private sector where industries agree to some kind of 'voluntary' behaviour, and in return the government abstains from legislating the desired behaviour. Rennings *et al.* (1996: 401) compare this process to medieval torture where the authorities show their instruments (punitive legislation) in order to achieve 'voluntary' concessions.

Voluntary agreements programs are increasingly popular with government policy makers who fear negative impacts of wide-ranging environmental regulation on economic performance, and who believe that VA have the potential to be less costly than traditional taxes, standards or permits. In embracing proposals for VA they stress the 'principle of cooperation in environmental policy'. Cooperation between government and industry underlies environmental legislation in various countries (e.g. Germany: Wicke 1989). The majority of environmental VA programs in the past have been related to the phase-out of specific harmful materials (e.g. chloroflurocarbons), waste management and energy-efficiency improvements as well as energy conservation in the industrial and commercial sectors (see e.g.: IEA 1997; UBA 1996; DSD 1996; VDA 1995). Recently, VA took over a major role in global warming policy as they have led to the suspension of CO_2 tax initiatives and other regulatory measures in OECD member countries (IEA 1997). In Germany, for example, the Federal

Government has refrained from imposing carbon taxes in return for the willingness of industries to reduce carbon emissions significantly till 2005 (Bundesregierung 1996).

2.2 *Basic economic intuition*

Contrary to the assertions of public and industrial policy makers, economic theory casts doubt on the notion of costly voluntary action by competitive firms. Within a competitive economy, the incentive for voluntary reduction of environmental pollution fails because any firm which undertakes additional costs is eventually forced out of business. In a competitive system 'voluntary' actions will only be undertaken if they make economic sense (i.e. save costs through no regret measures) or because of fear that without such action 'something worse' (i.e. more costly) such as regulatory legislation or taxation will be imposed.

The challenge from an analytical point of view is to develop a framework which captures the potential competitive effects of VA programs. Typically, VA programs simply include a set of environmental targets but leave it to the industries as to which mechanism or instrument to choose in order to meet the negotiated targets. The stated goal of industries within VA programs which apply to the industrial sector is that they meet environmental targets in a cost-efficient way. In economic terms this implies that industries not only equalise marginal abatement costs across firms for a given branch but also across all industries. The intuitive idea of how to operate VA programs then is to establish an industrial permit pool which allocates the amount of feasible emission rights across industries based on a negotiated distribution scheme and ensures tradability of emission rights. Effectively, this amounts to a system of tradable grandfathered permits. A 'voluntary' reduction of industrial pollution corresponds to a cutback in total pollution rights assigned to the industrial pool. Ownership of permits by industries ensures that there are no payments to the government, as would be the case with taxes or government-auctioned permits on polluting activities.

Having clarified how VA can be operated in a market economy, the next question is whether VA in terms of grandfathered permits induce excess costs as compared to alternative policy instruments such as uniform emission taxes or government-auctioned permits.

Advocates of VA programs argue that through offsets or swaps, equalised marginal abatement costs can ensure cost efficiency (Koutstaal *et al.* 1994: 1). However, this argument overlooks potentially important distortions on the output side of the economy. The intuition can be provided in a simple economy with a representative agent abstracting from initial tax distortions and adjustment costs. Compared to uniform emission taxes or auctioned permits where revenues accrue lump-sum to the representative agent, VA in terms of grandfathered permits produce revenues (scarcity rents) to the production sectors which work as disproportionate production subsidies. Hence VA programs offset a key optimality condition for efficient resource allocation: the identity of the marginal rate of transformation with the marginal rate of substitution across goods.

Figure 10.1 illustrates this point for a two-sector economy where good x is emission-intensive and the curve TT' characterises the production frontier subject to an overall emission constraint. Point A reflects an efficient resource allocation. The production frontier TT' and the social indifference curve U are tangent to the producer price ratio p and the consumer price ratio q after a lump-sum rebate of emission tax payments or emission permit revenues. VA programs violate efficiency conditions since the producer price ratio departs from the consumer price ratio. The producer price ratio p_{VA} is tangent to the production frontier TT', while the consumer price ratio q_{VA} is tangent to the indifference curve through B. Welfare is lower at B (utility level U_{VA}) than at the undistorted competitive equilibrium at A (utility level U). The movement on the production frontier towards the new distorted equilibrium B depends on the initial distribution and subsequent (mandated) reduction of emission rights across the production sectors. In Figure 10.1 we assume that the VA system works in favour of the emission-intensive industry x (Figures 10.3 and 10.4 present a numerical illustration of sector-specific gains and losses from VA as compared to uniform taxes).

In a general equilibrium framework, where all market decisions are linked through relative prices, the output distortions of VA programs spill over to the input side of the economy. Suppose that the distribution scheme of grandfathered permits subsidises emission-intensive sectors relative to the rest of the industry. This leads to relatively lower prices and higher demands for emission-intensive goods, which in turn creates higher demands for emission permits and drives up the permit price. The distribution scheme not only determines the differences in subsidy payments across sectors, but also alters the opportunity costs (prices) of input substitutes for production, that is, the shape and location of emission abatement cost curves across sectors. This induces additional efficiency losses because the private marginal cost of abatement across sectors does not correspond to the social marginal cost of abatement.

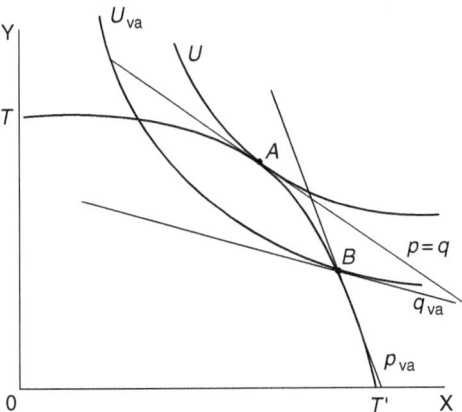

Figure 10.1 Output distortions of VA programs.

One could argue that VA programs operated as a system of tradable grand-fathered permits do not affect profitability of firms when permit revenues accrue lump-sum to the stockholders of the firms: in this case the recycling of the scarcity rent would not affect marginal revenue and therefore be non-distortionary.[2] Our proposition is that scarcity rents created by grandfathered permits are directly used to subsidise production. This assumption reflects the claim of industrial managers in emission-intensive industries that VAs (grandfathered permits) will reduce the adverse effects of environmental constraints on production and employment.

3   Analytical framework

3.1   Competitive economy

The distortionary effects of VA programs operated as a system of tradable grandfathered permits can be analysed using a general equilibrium model of a small open economy with constant returns to scale (CRTS) production. On the production side firms maximise profits using labour, capital, energy and resource inputs subject to technological constraints. There are two final (non-energy) goods and intermediate energy. The latter can be either produced domestically or imported at a given international price. On the demand side a representative agent with homothetic preferences allocates his income from fixed factor endowments to maximise utility of consumption from the final (non-energy) goods. All agents behave to the competitive paradigm, that is, they take market prices as given. Energy use is restricted by pollution rights assuming that pollution is linked in fixed proportions to the use of energy. Revenues from auctioned permits accrue to the representative agent.

Algebraically the economy can be represented by three classes of equilibrium conditions: (i) income balance for the representative agent, (ii) exhaustion of product (zero-profit) for CRTS producers, and (iii) market clearance for all goods and factors.[3] Without loss of generality we may scale prices so that the equilibrium income level is unity:

$$r\bar{K} + w\bar{L} + q\bar{R} + \tau\bar{E} = 1, \tag{1}$$

where

$\bar{L}, \bar{K}, \bar{R}, \bar{E}$ are initial endowments of labour, capital, energy-specific resources and pollution rights,

r, w, q are the prices of capital, labour and energy resources, and

τ is the equilibrium permit price for emissions.[4]

The zero-profit conditions for production of (non-energy) goods and intermediate energy are given by

$$p_x = c_x(r, w, p_E), \tag{2}$$

$$p_y = c_y(r, w, p_E), \tag{3}$$

$$p_E \leq \bar{p}_E p_y + \tau, \tag{4}$$

$$p_E \leq c_E(r, w, q) + \tau, \tag{5}$$

$$w, r, p_E, \tau, q \geq 0, \tag{}$$

where

p_x, p_y, p_E are prices of non-energy goods and intermediate energy,

$\bar{p}_E$ is the (exogenously fixed) international price of energy, and

c_i is the unit cost function for good i which in our numerical example below has the form:

$$c_i = \begin{cases} (\alpha_i(r^{\beta_i} w^{1-\beta_i})^{1-\sigma_i} + (1-\alpha_i)p_E^{1-\sigma_i})^{1/(1-\sigma_1)} & i \in x, y, \\ (\gamma_i r^{1-\sigma_i} + \delta_i w^{1-\sigma_i} + (1-\gamma_i-\delta_i)q^{1-\sigma_i})^{1/(1-\sigma_i)} & i \in E, \end{cases}$$

with

α_i denoting the value share of value added in total costs of supplying one unit of output $(i = x, y)$,

β_i denoting the value share of labour inputs in value added $(i = x, y)$,

γ_i denoting the value share of capital in total costs of domestically supplying one unit of energy $(i = E)$,

δ_i denoting the value share of capital in total costs of domestically supplying one unit of energy $(i = E)$, and

σ_i representing the elasticity of substitution between different inputs in production $(i = x, y, E)$

Equations (2) and (3) simply indicate that in a competitive equilibrium the market price for goods x and y is the same as marginal ($=$ average) cost. Equations (4) and (5) indicate that in equilibrium the market price of energy can be no higher than the lesser of the international and the domestic marginal costs.

In the exposition of the market clearance conditions we exploit Roy's identity and Shephard's Lemma to provide a compact representation of demand functions.

$$x = \frac{e(p_x, p_y)^{\sigma-1}}{p_x^{\sigma}}, \tag{6}$$

$$y = \frac{e(p_x, p_y)^{\sigma-1}}{p_y^{\sigma}}, \tag{7}$$

$$x\frac{\partial c_x}{\partial r} + y\frac{\partial c_y}{\partial r} + E\frac{\partial c_E}{\partial r} = \bar{K}, \tag{8}$$

$$x\frac{\partial c_x}{\partial w} + y\frac{\partial c_y}{\partial w} + E\frac{\partial c_E}{\partial w} = \bar{L}, \tag{9}$$

$$E\frac{\partial c_E}{\partial \rho} = \bar{R}, \tag{10}$$

$$E \leq \bar{E}, \tag{11}$$

where

x, y are levels of production (and consumption) for final goods,

$e(p_x, p_y)$ is the unit expenditure function which in our numerical example has the form:

$$e(p_x, p_y) \equiv \min p_x x + p_y y \quad \text{s.t.} \ U(x,y) = 1$$
$$= (\alpha_u p_x^{1-\sigma_u} + (1-\alpha_u)p_y^{1-\sigma_u})^{1/(1-\sigma_u)}$$

with

α_u denoting value shares of inputs in total costs of supplying one unit of utility, and

σ_u representing the elasticity of substitution between different inputs in utility formation.

The effect of VA represented as a system of grandfathered permits is to eliminate emission permit revenue from income of the representative agent and include instead subsidy payments to production in sectors x and y which are proportional to their shares $\bar{E}_x$ and $\bar{E}_y$ in total supply (endowment) of permits.

Recall our understanding that scarcity rents from permit sales are directly linked to output subsidies which affects the marginal revenue of industries. The equilibrium with VA then consists of the system of equations (1), (4)–(11) together with modified versions of the zero-profit conditions, equations (2′) and (3′):

$$p_x(1 - s_x)x = c_x(r, w, p_E)x \tag{2′}$$

$$p_y(1 - s_y)y = c_y(r, w, p_E)y \tag{3′}$$

where s_x, s_y are the effective subsidy rates which are determined by

$$s_x \equiv \frac{\tau \bar{E}_x}{p_x x}; \quad s_y \equiv \frac{\tau \bar{E}_y}{p_y y}.$$

Comparing equations (2)–(3) with (2′)–(3′) it is obvious that VA will typically induce an efficiency loss as compared to auctioned permits or a uniform tax because they drive wedges between relative producer prices and relative consumer prices. Only in the case that effective subsidy rates are the same across sectors, will VA policies to limit emissions just match a uniform tax or auction permit scheme in efficiency terms. In our simple numerical CRTS example below, the magnitude of the welfare loss induced by VA depends on a number of factors, including the way in which pollution rights are divided between the two sectors, subsequent reduction schemes, the relative importance of imported energy in total demand, and the elasticities of substitution in production and final demand.

3.2 Scale economies and imperfect competition

The excess costs of VA can be significantly magnified in a model with economies of scale and imperfect competition. When an imperfectly competitive industry operates with free entry driving profits to zero, the VA induces otherwise unprofitable firms to enter. This effect is predicated on the assumption that VA vouchers (permits) are allocated equally across (new and incumbent) firms within a given industry.[5]

In order to formally incorporate scale economies in the model, we need to alter our representation of sector X. We define an aggregate cost function at the firm level in the X sector as:

$$\xi(x_s) = p_F F + c x_s$$

where p_F is the price index for fixed costs, F are fixed costs (in physical units), c denotes marginal costs, and x_s is output of firm s with $\sum_s x_s = x$.

Increasing returns is inconsistent with perfectly competitive firm behaviour. If firms were to price output at marginal cost, they would have insufficient revenue to cover average cost. A common approach to these issues is to assume that firms in sector X cover fixed costs by charging a markup over marginal cost. The most common modelling framework in the computable general equilibrium literature is Cournot competition among identical firms (e.g. Lopez, Markusen and Rutherford 1994). The firm solves:

$$\max p_x(x)x_s - \xi(x_s)$$

and charges a profit-maximising markup on marginal cost,

$$p_x(1 - m) = c$$

in which p_x is the price gross of the markup m.

In this model the number of firms is determined endogenously. If we presume free entry, the number of firms is determined by

$$p_F F N = m p_x x$$

where N is the number of firms. Accounting for VA programs which are operated as a system of grandfathered permits, total profits of a firm include rents from permit rights. We can then determine the number of firms by

$$p_F FN = mp_x x + \tau \bar{E}_x.$$

We see from this last equation that the allocation of quota rights to firms produces an economic incentive to entry for otherwise unprofitable firms.

4 Numerical results

In this section we present numerical calculations based on our analytical model which illustrate various determinants of the welfare cost induced by VA. Table 10.1 gives an overview of the economic structure for the stylised economy in the benchmark year. The data presented in Table 10.1A. are in the form of a rectangular social accounting matrix in which we have one row for every market, and one column for each production sector and consumer. In the present model, there are four sectors $(X, Y, E$ and $ME)$ and one consumer (column RA).

This data table contains both positive and negative entries. A positive entry signifies a receipt (sale) in a particular market. A negative entry signifies an expenditure (purchase) in a particular market. Reading down a production column, we then observe a complete list of the transactions associated with that activity. For example, we can see that sector X sells 100 of output with costs of production represented by energy (20), labour (20) and capital (60). The column sums for each of the production sectors are zero, indicating a balance between the

Table 10.1 Benchmark data and key elasticities

	X	Y	E	ME	RA
A. Social accounting matrix (transactions in monetary units)					
X	100				− 100
Y		100		− 25* (1-dshr)	− 100 + 25 (1-dshr)
E	− 20	− 5	25* dshr	25* (1-dshr)	
L	− 20	− 75	− 5* dshr		95 + 5* dshr
K	− 60	− 20	− 5* dshr		80 + 5* dshr
R			− 15* dshr		15* dshr

B. *Key elasticities*

Elasticity of substitution in final demand: $F_u = 1$

Elasticity of substitution between energy and value added aggregate in production of non-energy goods: $F_i = 0.3$ $(i = x, y)$

Elasticity of substitution between capital, labour and energy-specific resource in production of energy $F_i = 1.5$ $(i = E)$

Key: X, Y final consumption goods (sectors); E: energy good (sector); L: labour; K: capital; ME: energy imports; RA: representative agent; dshr: share of domestic energy production in overall energy supply (benchmark value = 1, implying a closed economy).

costs of production and the value of output. In the counterfactual experiments emissions, or likewise energy demand,[6] are reduced by 20 per cent as compared to the benchmark. We consider two different instruments for emission abatement. First, a uniform emission (energy) tax is levied where tax revenues are recycled lump-sum to the representative consumer.[7]

Second, industries voluntarily commit to reduce emissions by 20 per cent using an inter-industrial grandfathering permit system where initial emission rights are proportionally cut back to achieve the given overall reduction target.[8] Efficiency costs of abatement are reported as Hicksian equivalent variations (EV) in benchmark income. The choice of a representative agent allows abstraction from equity issues and interpretation of EV in benchmark income as changes in social welfare.

4.1   The competitive, constant returns to scale economy

The first set of scenarios studies the effects of VA programs in a competitive economy with CRTS production. Figure 10.2 illustrates the efficiency implications. Depending upon the initial allocation of emission rights across sectors X and Y, VA programs imply disproportionate lump-sum production subsidies.

The distortion on the output side feeds back to the input side of the economy where the price for pollution does not reflect the true social marginal costs, but includes a premium which corresponds to the disproportionate subsidy payments to sectors X and Y. For a distribution scheme where emission rights are allocated in proportion to benchmark emissions, the welfare costs of emission abatement increase from 1.36 per cent (uniform tax) to 1.56 per cent (VA program) due to the implicit subsidisation of the pollution-intensive sector X.[9] We see that VA programs can at best break even with uniform taxes cum lump-sum rebate or

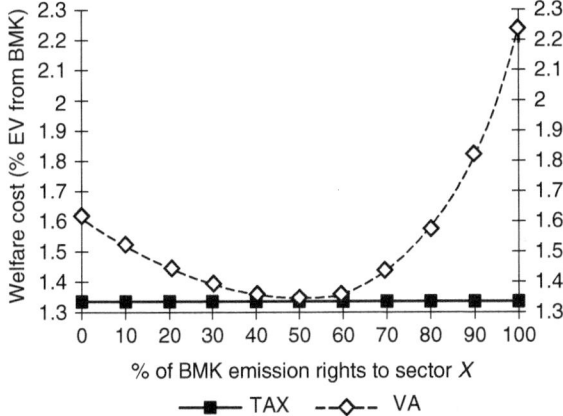

Figure 10.2 Welfare effects – competitive economy (20 per cent emission reduction).

auctioned permits. This case occurs when the emission rights are allocated in proportion to benchmark output, which implies that the effective subsidy rates for sector X and Y are the same and no distortion on the output side occurs. For all other allocations, however, VA programs induce excess costs as compared to uniform taxes.

Figures 10.3 and 10.4 investigate the impact of VA for production and employment. In most VA schemes initial pollution rights are issued in proportion to benchmark emissions. Compared to the uniform tax, the VA program lowers the adverse effects on employment and production in sector X (see X_TAX versus X_VA in Figures 10.3 and 10.4). But the benefits for sector X are at the expense of sector Y and society as a whole.

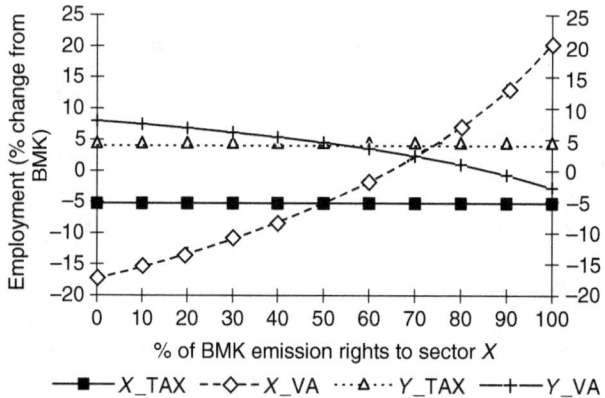

Figure 10.3 Employment effects – competitive economy (20 per cent emission reduction).

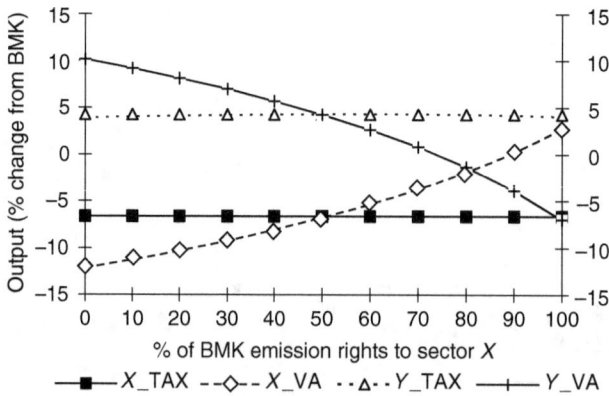

Figure 10.4 Output effects – competitive economy (20 per cent emission reduction).

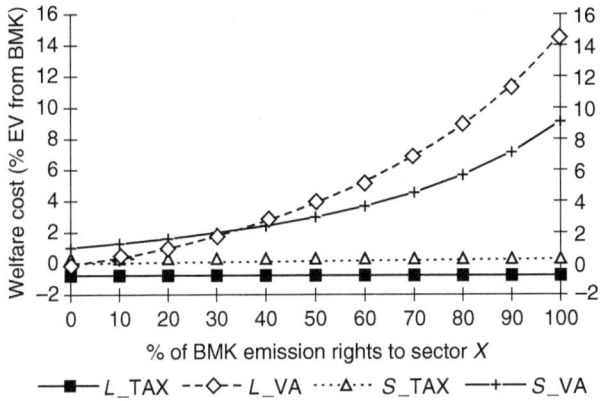

Figure 10.5 Welfare effects – imperfect competition (20 per cent emission reduction).

4.2 Increasing returns to scale with free entry

The second set of scenarios analyses the effects of VA in an economy where good X is produced subject to increasing returns to scale (IRTS) under oligopolistic competition.[10] Figure 10.5 illustrates the welfare costs of VA programs for the large group assumption, that is, the markup on marginal costs is fixed because any firm has only a small market share.[11] The excess costs of VA programs versus uniform taxes are significantly magnified in the IRTS model (see L_TAX and L_VA in Figure 10.5) as compared with the CRTS model (see TAX and VA in Figure 10.1). Larger quota payments to the X sector associated with the initial allocation of quota rights leads to a larger number of firms in sector X and increased efficiency losses due to reduced economies of scale. With emission rights allocated proportionally to benchmark emission (and a subsequent 20 per cent uniform cutback of rights across industries) the excess burden of the VA program amounts to 9.6 per cent of benchmark expenditure, an enormous figure considering the relatively modest share of energy in aggregate activity. Figure 10.6 which picks up the change in economies of scale with respect to the benchmark illustrates the source of magnified efficiency losses towards increasing shares of benchmark emission rights to the X sector. The application of a uniform emission tax and quota allocation schemes with small shares for the X sector produces a second-best effect: the costs of emission reduction due to reduced factor productivity are overcompensated by gains in economies of scale in X production where the output per firm ('consuming' fixed costs) increases.

4.3 Sensitivity analysis

In our basic calculations we analysed the excess costs of VA with respect to different assumptions on scale economies (CRTS versus IRTS) and the

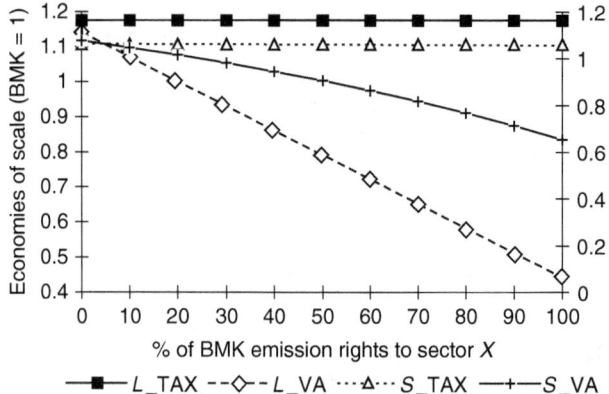

Figure 10.6 Output per firm – imperfect competition (20 per cent emission reduction).

inter-industrial allocation scheme of emission rights. To better understand the influence of the parametric framework we have undertaken a number of sensitivity calculations. We find that our conclusions are robust with respect to changes in the underlying elasticities and benchmark data.

Import share of total energy demand and energy supply elasticity

We have repeated our basic calculations for different import shares of the domestic energy market. The more elastic the domestic energy supply (imposed by the elasticity of substitution in energy production) the less costly are infra-marginal units of domestic supply as compared to imports purchased at fixed world market prices. For an elastic domestic energy supply, the welfare costs of abatement and the excess costs of VA programs increase with the amount of domestic production which must be curtailed. For a given allocation scheme of emission rights, a larger import share implies a smaller abatement cost.

Elasticities of substitution in production and final demand

As suggested by economic intuition, the higher the elasticities of substitution in production and final demand the lower the welfare costs of meeting an exogenous emission reduction target. The excess costs of VA programs compared to uniform taxes increase with lower substitution possibilities.

Level of emission abatement

The efficiency premium associated with VA programs for a given allocation scheme rises with the level of the targeted emission reduction. The higher the reduction target is the higher are the quota rents associated with the emission constraint and the higher the distortionary effects from VA.

5 Concluding remarks

We provide an analytical framework and numerical examples exploring the welfare implications of voluntary agreements in environmental policy. Using a general equilibrium approach we observe that VA programs can be interpreted as a system of grandfathered permits. We then develop an analytical framework to clarify the nature of potential inefficiencies associated with VA. We see that VA work as subsidies on the output side of an economy which can induce significant excess costs for meeting environmental quality as compared to uniform environmental taxes or auctioned permits. The magnitude of efficiency losses depends to a large extent on market structure. The excess cost of voluntary agreements, which can already be substantial in competitive markets, may be substantially increased in a monopolistic market, where the number of firms and the fixed cost of production is determined endogenously. Other determining factors include the distribution of tradable emission rights across industries, the share of imported energy in total demand, elasticities of substitution in production and final demand and the target level of emission reduction.[12]

In the present chapter, we abstract from initial tax distortions to avoid potential confusion on the sources of inefficiencies across alternative environmental policy instruments. Independent of existing tax distortions the efficiency properties of environmental policy instruments depend on the creation and ownership of scarcity rents associated with the specific policy instruments (see also Fullerton and Metcalf 1997). Whether the primary inefficiencies of VA programs in terms of grandfathered permits could help to mitigate or rather worsen pre-existing distortions is another issue. We leave the empirical assessment of potential trade-offs between output distortions induced by VA and existing tax distortions for future work.

Our analysis focuses on cost effectiveness of VA programs as compared to alternative policy instruments such as uniform taxes or auctioned permits. Admittedly, cost effectiveness is only one criterion for environmental policy making. There are features of VA programs – such as higher acceptance on the part of industries – which might overcompensate the efficiency losses from a public choice point of view. For rational policy making it is nevertheless important to realise that the VA approach has its own efficiency costs.

Appendix: Primal and dual mathematical programs of the analytical model

The distortionary effects of VA can be formalised using the Negishi representation where the competitive equilibrium is equivalent to decisions of a representative consumer who maximises overall social welfare subject to technological constraints and initial endowments. In this setting initial endowments may include environmental goods such as carbon emission rights, the quantity of which reflects the preferences of the society as to the level of environmental use.

With respect to our generic model of Section 4, the social planner's problem is as follows:[13]

Model NLP-P

$$\max U(x,y)$$

s.t.

$$x = f_x(K_x, L_x, E_x) \tag{A1}$$

$$y = f_y(K_y, L_y, E_y) - M_E \bar{p}_E \tag{A2}$$

$$E = f_E(K_E, L_E, \bar{R}) + M_E \tag{A3}$$

$$K_x + K_y + K_E = \bar{K} \tag{A4}$$

$$L_x + L_y + L_E = \bar{L} \tag{A5}$$

$$E_x + E_y = E \tag{A6}$$

$$E \leq \bar{E} \tag{A7}$$

where
U is a social welfare function. For our numerical calculations, we assume a specific linearly homogeneous function:

$$U(x,y) = (\alpha_u x^{1-1/\sigma_u} + (1 - \alpha_u) y^{1-1/\sigma_u})^{1/(1-1/\sigma_u)}$$

L_i, K_i, E_i are inputs of labour, capital and energy for sector $i = x, y$ or E,
f_i is the CRTS production function for commodity $i = x, y$ or E.
   In our numerical example we will adopt the functional forms:[14]

$$f_i \begin{cases} \varphi_i(\alpha_i(K_i^{\beta_i} L_i^{1-\beta_i})^{1-1/\sigma_i} + (1 - \alpha_i)E_i^{1-1/\sigma_i})^{1/(1-1/\sigma_i)} & i \in x, y \\ \varphi_i(\alpha_i K_i^{1-1/\sigma_i} + \beta_i L_i^{1-1/\sigma_i} + (1 - \alpha_i - \beta_i)\bar{R}^{1-1/\sigma_i})^{1/(1-1)(\sigma_i)} & i \in E \end{cases}$$

M_E is the level of energy imports,
φ_i is the efficiency parameter $(i = x, y, E)$
In the model *NLP-P* pollution permits are allocated efficiently and permit prices (pollution taxes) are paid by the different industries in proportion to energy use. In the absence of public goods and other taxes, the solution of *NLP-P* represents the first-best equilibrium. To obtain this solution, the standard approach would be to derive the first order optimality conditions (Karush–Kuhn–Tucker conditions) for the representative agent problem, where the equilibrium prices correspond to the

optimal Lagrange multipliers on the system of constraints. For the sake of a readily interpretable mathematical exposition we will present the corresponding dual Negishi problem *NLP-D* using the unit expenditure function. In the case of homothetic preferences the unit expenditure function conveys all of the information concerning the underlying preferences of the economic system.

Model NLP-D

$$\min r\bar{K} + w\bar{L} + q\bar{R} + \tau\bar{E} - \ln(e(p_x, p_y))$$
$$\text{s.t.} \quad (1) - (5)$$

The fact that voluntary agreements destroy efficiency is evident if we observe that system of equilibrium conditions (1), (2'), (3'), (4)–(11) corresponds to either of the following nonlinear programs.

Model NLP-D'

$$\max U(x, y) + \tilde{s}_x x + \tilde{s}_y y$$
$$\text{s.t.} \quad (A1) - (A7)$$

or

Model NLP-D"

$$\min r\bar{K} + w\bar{L} + q\bar{R} + \tau\bar{E} - \ln(e(p_x, p_y)) - \tilde{s}_x p_x - \tilde{s}_y p_y$$
$$\text{s.t.} \quad (2'), (3'), (4), (5)$$

in which the distortions operate through the subsidy effects in the objective functions. When we let $\tilde{s}_x = \tau^* \bar{E}_x / x$ with an analogous expression for $\tilde{s}_y$ we obtain solutions of the nonlinear programs *NLP-P** and *NLP-D** which correspond to the equilibrium solution imposed by equations (1), (2'), (3'), (4)–(11) of Section 4 (the asterisk above indicates the economic equilibrium values).[15]

Notes

1 The IEA study provides an analysis of more than 350 voluntary programs in 22 states – most of them with industry concerning energy efficiency improvements.
2 In fact, grandfathered permits would then be equivalent to emission taxes or auctioned permits.
3 The appendix provides equivalent representations of the competitive equilibrium formulated as a primal or dual mathematical program.
4 Note that the permit price is equivalent to the uniform tax rate which is necessary to achieve the emission reduction imposed by the emission constraint.
5 Another source of excess costs (not analysed in this chapter) are marketing arrangements of existing firms with respect to the distribution of pollution rights to restrict entry for

new firms. See Rennings *et al.*, 1996, who identify market concentration and vertical integration as important sources of inefficiencies in German waste recycling management.

6 Without loss of generality we assume that emissions are strictly proportional to energy use (see equation (11)).

7 As noted before the uniform tax instrument cum lump-sum rebate is equivalent to permits auctioned by the representative consumer.

8 Throughout these simulations we assume 'efficient' VA programs in the sense that these inter-industrial arrangements are free of transaction costs.

9 Lower relative prices for pollution intensive goods (as compared to the uniform tax case) lead to higher demands for these products. With higher demands for dirty (pollution intensive) goods, there are higher demands for permits and thus a higher permit price.

10 In the benchmark (see Table 10.1) we assume a markup of 20 per cent and adjust table entries (E, X) to (-10) and (K, X) to (-50).

11 Figure 10.5 also shows the welfare implications for the small group assumption (see S_TAX versus S_VA). In this case the markup of firms is determined endogenously as a small number of firms holds a relatively large market share.

12 Another source of inefficiency could be the quota allocation process within an industry which we have not attempted to model. If there are rent-seeking opportunities for firms, the cost of the VA programs could be even higher.

13 For lacking denotations see Section 4.

14 Note that f_x and f_y exhibit CRTS in L, K and E, while f_E exhibits constant returns in L, K and R. For this reason, a competitive equilibrium implies exhaustion of product due to free entry.

15 It is notable that the inefficient equilibrium cannot be computed by solving a single optimization problem because the adjustments to the objective function which account for the inefficiency must incorporate the equilibrium prices which arise from solving the nonlinear program. It is typically possible to compute the equilibrium using Jacobi iterations on the objective function adjustments, although it is much easier to compute the equilibrium directly as a complementarity problem.

References

Bundesregierung (1996) 'Erklärung der deutschen Wirtschaft zur Klimavorsorge', Presse- und Informationsamt der Bundesregierung, Pressemitteilung Nr. 118/96, Bonn.

DSD (1996), Duales System Deutschland: Kuratoriumsbericht 1995, Köln.

Fullerton, D. and Metcalf, G. (1997) *Environmental Controls, Scarcity Rents, and Pre-existing Distortions*, NBER working paper series no 6091, Cambridge, USA.

IEA International Energy Agency (1997) 'Voluntary actions for energy-related CO_2-abatement', *Energy and Environment – Policy Analysis Series*, Paris, France.

IPCC Inter-Governmental Panel on Climate Change (1997) *Climate Change 1995*, New York: Cambridge University Press, p. 401.

Kohlhaas, M. and Praetorius, B. (1995) 'Selbstverpflichtung der Wirtschaft zur CO_2 Reduktion: Kein Ersatz für aktive Klimapolitik.', DIW-Wochenbericht, 62. Jg., H. 14, pp. 277–83.

Koutstaal, P., Vollebergh, H. and de Vries, J. (1994) *Hybrid carbon inventive mechanisms for the European community*, research memorandum 9406, Research Center for Economic Policy (OCFEB), Erasmus University, Rotterdam, p. 1.

Lopez-de-Silanes, F., Markusen, J. R. and Rutherford, T. F. (1994) 'The auto industry and the North American free-trade agreement', in: Shields, C. and Francois, J. (eds),

Modeling Trade Policy: AGE Assessments of North American Free Trade, Cambridge: Cambridge University Press.

Rennings, K., Brockmann, K. L., Koschel, H., Bergmann, H. and Kühn, I. *et al.* (1996) *Nachhaltigkeit, Ordnungspolitik und freiwillige Selbstverpflichtungen*, Heidelberg: Physica-Verlag, Springer.

UBA (1996) 'Verzicht aus Verantwortung: Maßnahmen zur Rettung der Ozonschicht', Berlin: Umweltbundesamt, pp. 204–5.

VDA (1995) Freiwillige Zusage zur Kraftstoffverbrauchsminderung. Frankfurt/Main: Verband der Automobilindustrie, press release 22.3.1995.

Wicke, L. (1989), *Umweltökonomie*, München: Vahlen, pp. 144–6.

Part IV

Pension reform

11 The ageing of the population and justice between generations

A CGE and generational accounting approach for Belgium

Philippe Liégeois

1 Introduction

The reduction of the public debt and some spending financed by the collectivity in favour of specific age groups (retirement benefits, health care, education) induce transfers between generations. In most developed countries, the age distribution of the population is presently shifting towards the elderly. As a result, future (therefore presently young) generations could be progressively deprived.

This phenomenon is much debated, through tools like the Auerbach *et al.* (1991, 1994) and Kotlikoff's (1992) generational accounting. These aim to estimate, for a given year *t*, the expected present value of all the taxes and public transfers each individual alive in *t* will still suffer or benefit from, up to his death. This expected net payment is indexed on the age of the individuals alive in *t*. It is called the 'generational' account, as it refers to a representative member of a specific 'generation', from now on *the set of individuals born at the same time*. Then, Auerbach and Kotlikoff simply compare the generational account of the newborns in period *t* with the average burden left to the future generations, those in charge of the public intertemporal budget constraint. Stijns (1997) has shown for Belgium that this average burden could be 60 per cent higher than that supported by the 1995 newborns. Fortunately, more recent estimations seem to be less pessimistic.

We would like to go further and derive generational accounts for each future generation. Why would it be useful?

First, if an imbalance between the present and future generations occurred, due to the forthcoming ageing of the population, we would like to know if some future generations will suffer more than the others from this and, if so, which ones. We then need to estimate the distribution of the burden left to the future generations between those generations.

Second, if the distribution of the burden were known, we could assess whether it is equitable. Auerbach and Kotlikoff suggest that the distribution would be equitable if the generational accounts, relative to the lifecycle income of the individuals, were identical for all the generations. If our distribution is not 'A&K-equitable', we could implement a public policy able to restore it, at least partially.

The usual implementation of generational accounting does not allow computation of generational accounts specific to each future generation. It is based on a mechanical methodology of projection. The macroeconomic parameters and variables (interest rate, economic growth rate, tax rates, and so on) are supposed to be invariant in the long term. The microeconomic variables (labour supply, consumption and savings, transfers) stay invariant as well. Altogether, these assumptions make the computing of generational accounts for each future generation useless. These last accounts would be identical to those computed for the presently alive individuals, as the economic context is unchanged. This is the reason why Auerbach and Kotlikoff, thereafter 'A&K', only compute an *average* burden for the future generations.

To go further, we then need to endogenise some aspects of the future economic environment. For example, the ageing of the population will have an effect on the aggregate levels of public transfers. Then, the government will have to levy new taxes or sell new bonds. The stock of capital will change, the productivity of labour will be affected and some feedback effects on individual decisions will take place.

A general equilibrium framework seems well suited to deal with such interactions. It takes into account all the markets (goods, labour and bonds) on which three kinds of agents operate: individuals, firms and the government. The markets clear and prices (the interest rate, wages) are endogenous. It gives microfoundations to individuals' behaviour and is then appropriate to estimate the feedback effects resulting from the ageing of the population on relative prices and taxes. Moreover, it gives us a measure of individual well-being (the lifecycle utility) as a base for intergenerational comparisons. We build a computable general equilibrium model closely related to the Auerbach and Kotlikoff (1987) one. It synthesises as accurately as possible the Belgian economy, with particular attention given to the calibration of the age-structure of the population.

The chapter is organised as follows. Section 2 recalls the principles of A&K's generational accounting. Section 3 describes our computable general equilibrium model, its calibration and the method of simulation. Section 4 shows the distribution of the burden left to the future generations for Belgium. In Section 5, a public policy partially restoring 'equity' between the generations is implemented. Section 6 concludes. A complete description of the contents of Sections 2 to 4 can be found in Docquier, Liégeois and Stijns (1999) and Docquier and Liégeois (2001).

2   Generational accounting

A generation will be said to be 'alive' if *one of its members is still alive*. Given a reference period t – the 'present' period – and a generation still alive in t, the generational account for that generation in t is the amount of money that a representative member of the generation is expected to give to the government, that is the present value of the difference between the taxes he will pay and the public transfers he will receive, from now up to the end of his life. Public transfers are those for which the distribution between the age groups can be estimated (social transfers, education, child-care institutions).

We can split up the A&K methodology into 3 steps: (i) the estimation of the generational accounts for all the presently alive generations, (ii) the computation of the total burden left to the future generations, and (iii) the comparison of the average burden left to the future generations and the generational account of the newborns in *t*.

(i) The generational account $n_{t,k}$ of a presently alive generation whose members are born in *k* is:

$$n_{t,k} = \sum_{s=t}^{k+D} \frac{T_{s,k} p_{s,t,k}}{(1+\rho)^{s-t}}, \tag{1}$$

where $T_{s,k}$ is the average net payment to the government for the year *s*. The variable $P_{s,t,k}$ is the probability to be still alive in *s* if you are born in *k* and still alive in *t*, *r* is the actualisation factor (the real interest rate), and *D* is the maximum lifetime. The following hypotheses prevail for the anticipations:

- The individual taxes and transfers grow at the same rate as technical progress *g*

$$T_{s,k} \equiv T_{t,k-(s-t)} \times (1+g)^{s-t} T_{s,k}. \tag{2}$$

  For the transfers, this assumption is usually called vested rights and means that the individuals alive in *t* will benefit during their whole life from the transfers available in *t*.
- The actualisation factor and the rate of technical progress are constant through time.
- The probabilities to survive are those estimated in *t*.

From $n_{t,k}$, we derive $N_{t,k}$, the net future contribution of all the members of the generation *k* in *t*, by multiplying $n_{t,k}$ by the size of this generation in *t*, $P_{t,k}$. Therefore

$$N_{t,k} = P_{t,k} n_{t,k}. \tag{3}$$

(ii) The net contribution of all the future generations is derived from the public intertemporal budget constraint:

$$\sum_{k=t}^{t-D} N_{t,k} + \sum_{k=t+1}^{\infty} N_{t,k} = B_t + \sum_{i=1}^{\infty} \frac{G_{t+i}}{(1+\rho)^i}, \tag{4}$$

where B_t is the level of public debt in *t* and G_s is the public consumption in *s*. The budget constraint balances the revenues of the government (the net contributions of the presently alive and the future generations) and its spending (consumption and the repayment of the initial debt). In this expression, G_s is supposed to grow at the same rate as the technical progress. Therefore, the only unknown factor is the net contribution of the future generations $NCFG = \sum_{k=t+1}^{\infty} N_{t,k}$.

(iii) For the reasons explained in the introduction, the distribution of the net contribution of the future generations between those generations cannot be estimated. We then simply derive from $NCFG$ an average payment $\bar{n}$ for the members of the future generations. $\bar{n}$ is supposed to grow at the same rate as technical progress. Therefore:

$$CLGF = \bar{n} \sum_{i=1}^{\infty} \frac{P_{t+i,t+i}(1+g)^i}{(1+\rho)^i}. \tag{5}$$

Finally, $\bar{n}$ is compared to the generational account of the representative member of the newborns in t, $n_{t,t}$. If $n_{t,t} < \bar{n}$, then the future generations are disadvantaged.

3   The model

To go beyond the usual implementation of A&K's methodology and derive generational accounts specific to each future generation, we need to endogenise some aspects of the economic anticipations. We do it through a general equilibrium framework.

We first briefly describe the model, then we discuss the calibration and the methodology of simulation.

3.1   A brief description of the model

Given the nature of the problem, we use an overlapping generations (OLG) framework. This model describes an economy where, given any year, 105 generations of individuals differently aged overlap. Death probabilities are considered for individuals older than 40. An individual becomes an adult as soon as he is 20 years old and he maximises his expected utility on his whole adulthood. This utility depends on the consumption and leisure levels yearly chosen:

$$E(U_t) = \frac{1}{1 - 1/\gamma} \sum_{j=21}^{105} \frac{p_j}{(1+\delta)^{j-21}}$$
$$\times \left[c_{j,t+j-21}^{1-1/\rho} + v_j (Q_{t+j-21} \ell_{j,t+j-21})^{1-1/\rho} \right]^{(1-1/\gamma)/(1-1/\rho)}, \tag{6}$$

where $c_{j,t+j-21}$ is the consumption of the individual when he is $(j-1)$ years old (during the year $t+j-21$), $\ell_{j,t+j-21}$ his choice of leisure Q_{t+j-21}, the level of human capital growing, thanks to the exogenous technical progress, at a constant rate $(1+g)$, ν_j a parameter relating to the preference for leisure, γ the intertemporal elasticity of substitution, ρ the intratemporal elasticity of substitution and δ is the preference for the present period. Retirement is compulsory at 65 years old.

The expected utility is maximised taking into account the intertemporal budget constraint of the individual. This constraint stems from the fact that lifetime spending cannot exceed lifetime income. Individuals pay taxes and receive transfers from the government and from their parents through accidental bequests.

The government organises transfers to the individuals, receives taxes and consumes. Three kinds of taxes are levied: a tax on consumption, a tax on capital income and a tax on wages. To finance its transfers and its public consumption, the government can also sell bonds. Either the tax rates are fixed (exogenous) and the public debt yearly balances the public budget, or one of the taxes, the transfers or the public consumption fits the public budget constraint.

We make here a crucial assumption: the tax on wages will yearly balance the public budget, given the exogenous public debt/GDP ratio.

The local firms transform capital and the effective labour force into output through a constant return to scale technology (a CES production function). They optimise in a perfect competition world.

3.2   The calibration

We calibrate the model in order to replicate as closely as possible the Belgian economy, particularly its demographic structure.

Obviously, this last characteristic is essential in our context. So, we replicate as closely as possible the baby boom – baby bust shock observed in most developed countries from the 1940s up to the 1980s, and we take into account the demographic forecasts made for Belgium up to the year 2050. In order to get an exact structure for the population in 1985, the birth rates are defined from the year 1900 (1985 – 85 years of adulthood). These hypotheses generate a dependency rate evolving as shown in Figure 11.1. Clearly, a demographic shock appears around the year 2020.

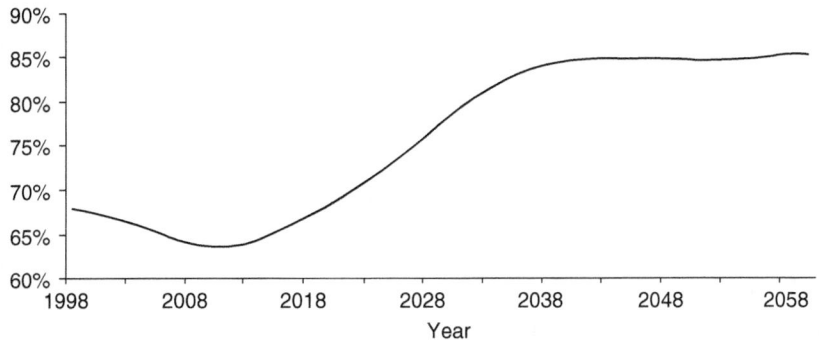

Figure 11.1 The dependency rate. $[20\text{–}64]/[[0\text{–}19]+[65\text{–}104]]$

Table 11.1 Calibration of the model

Parameters	Calibration
Labour intensity parameter in production	0.65
Capital intensity parameter in production	0.35
Rate of depreciation of capital	0.09
Elasticity of substitution between capital and labour in production	0.80
Intertemporal elasticity of substitution in utility	0.50
Intratemporal elasticity of substitution in utility	0.80
Rate of time preference in utility (gross value)	0.96
Exogenous variables	*Value*
Rate of technical progress	0.018
Tax rate for the consumption	0.15
Tax rate for the capital income	0.15
Tax rate for the labour income	(endogenous)

The calibration of the parameters and the choices made for the constant exogenous variables are shown in Table 11.1.

3.3   *The method of simulation*

Belgium is a small open economy and should consider the price of capital as given. But considering the interest rate constant, and therefore totally independent of the evolution of the demographic structure of the populations in the main developed countries, would be too strong a hypothesis. We should therefore endogenise the price of capital in some way to take into account the demographic variable and, perhaps, work in a closed economy framework. Nevertheless, this would imply that the political economy we will imagine for Belgium is supposed to be applied everywhere in its closed world. Such a constraint is not satisfactory, knowing that economic policy is a variable still partially autonomous. Moreover, some aspects of the Belgian economy are very specific. A clear example is the level of public debt in this country, greater than 110 per cent of GDP!

We then choose to perform the simulations in two steps. In the first one, a closed economy is calibrated on the basis of an 'average' European debt/GDP ratio. This gives us an international interest rate, sensitive to the demographic shock. In the second step, an open economy is simulated, calibrated for Belgium and considering as exogenous the interest rate derived from the first step. This simulation in two steps is equivalent to a unique one performed on a two-country model, one of these countries being a very small economy.

The public budget is balanced yearly, given an exogenous debt/GDP ratio (compulsory), by changing the tax on wages. Up to the year 1998, the level of the debt is that observed for Belgium. From 1998 on, the debt/GDP ratio is decreased as announced by the Belgian Bureau du Plan. The ratio will reach the threshold of 60 per cent in 2020, that is an average decrease of 2.6 per cent

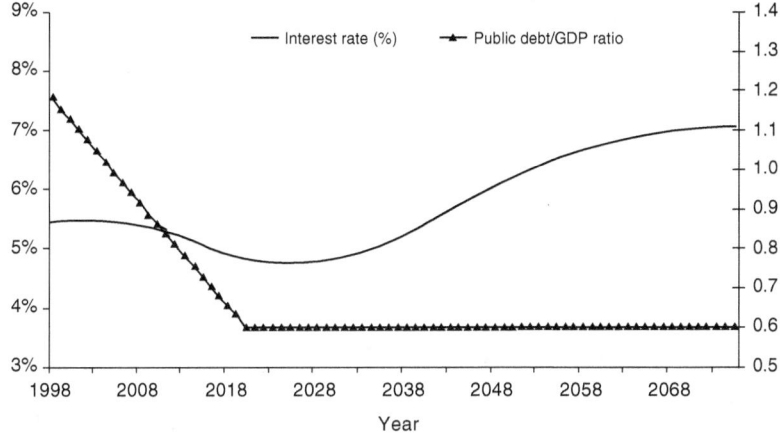

Figure 11.2 The 'International' interest rate and the public debt/GDP ratio.

per year. Finally, public consumption will grow at the same rate as technical progress, that is 1.8 per cent per year.

Figure 11.2 shows the trajectories for the international interest rate and for the Belgian public debt/GDP ratio.

The method used for solving the model is described in Docquier and Liégeois (2001). Let us just say that we move away the terminal conditions[1] in simulating the model up to the year 2285.[2]

4 The tax on wages and the distribution of the burden left to the future generations

Three contexts are formalised:

- in the context of 'constant transfers', public transfers grow at the same rate as technical progress;
- in the context of 'increasing transfers' (resp. 'decreasing transfers'), public transfers grow at a rate 0.05 per cent/year higher (resp. 'lower') than technical progress.

The tax on wages is estimated through the general equilibrium framework. Figure 11.3 shows its evolution under the three scenarios. After a small decline due to the temporary downturn in the dependency rate, the tax increases again from 2008, suddenly drops around the year 2020 (due to the end of the reduction in the public debt) and grows again up to a maximum in 2057, putting on 8 per cent in the scenario of constant transfers. Between the years 1998 and 2038, the gain will be 3 per cent lower if the 'decreasing transfers' scenario is applied.

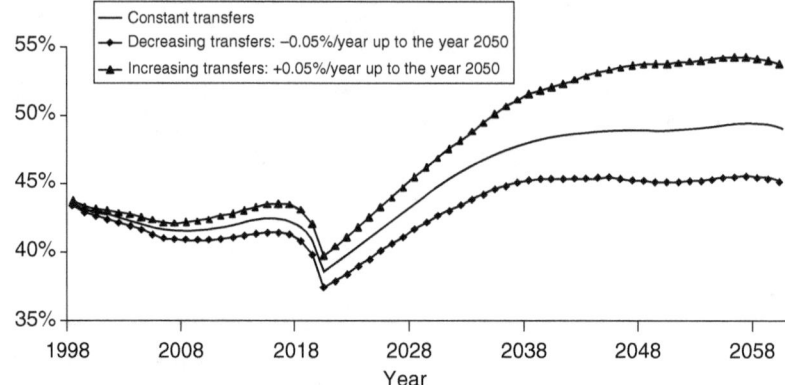

Figure 11.3 The rate of tax on wages.

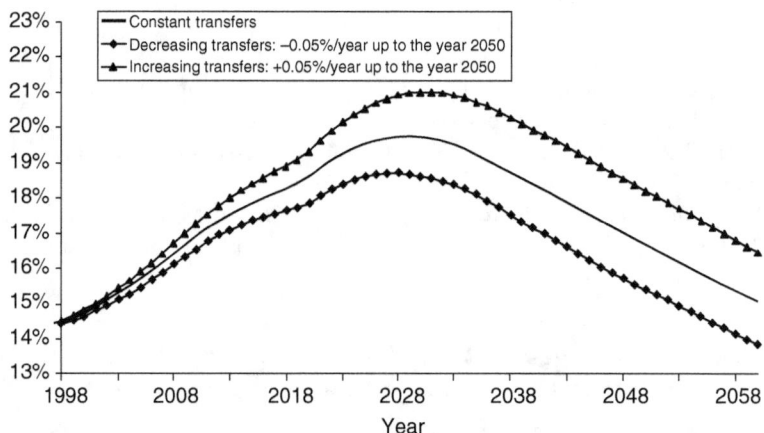

Figure 11.4 The generational accounts relative to the lifecycle revenue of a 20-year-old-individual in 1995, taking into account the productivity growth.

In Belgium, the evolution of the tax on wages mainly depends on the dependency rate and on the variation of the interest rate, which modifies the capital/labour ratio and the productivity of labour. The impact of ageing on the tax is double: direct, due to higher aggregate public transfers, and indirect, through the reduction of the tax bases (gross wages, consumption, labour supply and savings). If these bases were constant, the effect of ageing on the tax on wages would be cut by half.[3]

4.1   *The distribution of the burden left to future generations*

Figure 11.4 shows the generational accounts for the successive generations, relative to their gross lifecycle income.[4] We will call these ratios the 'relative generational accounts'. Obviously, the choice of such an indicator is not neutral. This is the A&K view. It states that the net contribution of an individual should be divided, for comparison reasons, by the lifecycle income. In Figure 11.4, the abscissa relates to the date individuals enter their 21st year of life.

Between 1998 and 2037, the relative generational account will grow from 14.5 per cent up to a maximum of 21.8 per cent. This means that the newborns of the year 2017 will suffer most from the forthcoming ageing of the population. If the feedback effects of higher taxes were ignored, we can show that the maximum gap would be strongly reduced. The relative generational account is still high in the long term, due to a progressive decrease in lifecycle income.

5   Looking for equity between the generations

A&K suggest considering as equitable a distribution of the remaining burden that would equalise the generational account/gross lifecycle income ratio, the relative generational account, for all the members of the successive generations.

It is clear from Figure 11.4 that the distribution of the left burden between the generations will not be A&K-equitable, as far as the results stemming from our simulations are considered to be relevant to such an analysis.

We discuss here the principles of a public policy able to partially restore the intergenerational equity, that is, generating through some complementary transfers a relative generational account identical for all the generations.

We partly deviate from the A&K criteria in the sense that we intend to equalise the generational accounts themselves, corrected to take into account the evolution of technical progress (close to, but not identical to the evolution of the lifecycle income). Here are the main characteristics of the correcting policy:

- If the distribution of the burden due to ageing is not equitable, it must be modified. We choose to do this through complementary transfers between the generations, more precisely through an adaptation of the public debt.
- The reform takes place at the beginning of the year t.
- For each given year $s \geq t$, we implement a complementary public transfer, possibly positive (a payment, for the individual), identical for all the individuals alive in s.
- These complementary transfers are aggregated and will reduce (or increase) the level of public debt at the end of the year s.
- The complementary transfers must be chosen so as to equalise the generational accounts (modified to take technical progress into account) of all the generations.
- As it could be impossible to impose the (possibly negative) transfers on the oldest generations alive in the initial year t, the reform will affect only some of the generations alive in t, but all the future generations.

We are now ready to shape the correcting policy, in 3 steps: (i) if the ex post generational account must be the same for all the generations, taking technical progress into account, what will be the value of this common contribution $\tilde{n}$; (ii) which yearly complementary transfers do we need to equalise the generational accounts and reach the average level $\tilde{n}$; (iii) as soon as the transfers have been determined, we will aggregate them to get their impact on the evolution of the public debt; an 'optimal' evolution of the public debt will then be derived and compared to the anticipations of the Belgian Bureau du Plan.

5.1   Looking for a common generational account $\tilde{n}$

The government decides to impose complementary transfers able to restore 'equity' between the generations. The reform will take place suddenly from the year t on. It will affect all the future generations and, amongst the individuals already alive in t, only those who are at most Q years old. It could be impossible to impose complementary, possibly positive, transfers on too old individuals in t. For simplicity, we will suppose that $Q \leq 40$.

The average contribution $\tilde{n}$ can be computed as follows:

$$\sum_{s=0}^{\infty} \left(N_{t,t-Q+20+s} \middle/ \prod_{j=1}^{s}(1 + \rho_{t-Q+20+j}) \right)$$

$$= \sum_{s=0}^{\infty} \left(\tilde{n}(1+g)^s P_{t-Q+20+s,t-Q+20+s} \middle/ \prod_{j=1}^{s}(1 + \rho_{t-Q+20+j}) \right).$$

5.2   Deriving the yearly complementary public transfers

The government will impose complementary public transfers, one per year $k \geq t$, and identical for all the individuals alive in k. We note these transfers $-AT_k$. They must be calibrated in order to fit the following conditions.

For all the individuals born before the year t (in $t - Q + 21 + s$, where $s = 0, 1, \ldots, 19$), we must get

$$n_{t-Q+20+s,t-Q+20+s} + \sum_{j=0}^{105-Q-s} \left(p_{t+j,t,t-Q+20+s}AT_{t+j} \middle/ \prod_{l=1}^{j} 1 + \rho_{t-Q+20+s+l} \right)$$

$$= \tilde{n}(1+g)^s.$$

For an individual born in t or later ($t+s$ where $s = 0, 1, \ldots$), we must get

$$n_{t+s,t+s} + \sum_{j=0}^{105-1} \left(p_{t+s+j,t+s,t+s}AT_{t+s+j} \middle/ \prod_{l=1}^{j} 1 + \rho_{t+s+1} \right) = \tilde{n}(1+g)^{Q-21+s}.$$

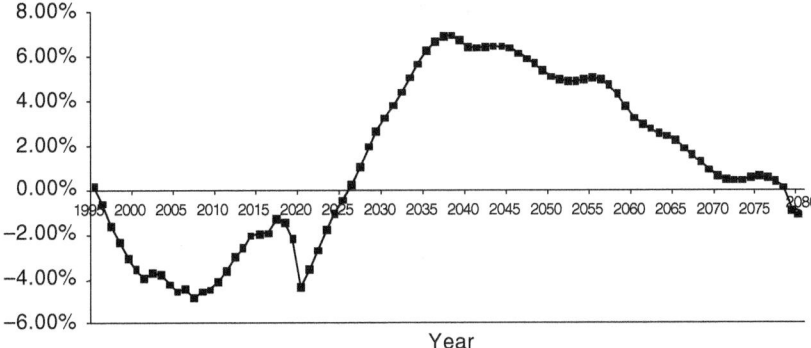

Figure 11.5 Complementary individual public transfers relative to GDP per head.

Figure 11.5 shows the evolution of the transfers AT_k when $t = 1995$ and $Q = 40$ (slightly lower than the median age of the population in the year 1995). The complementary transfers are given relative to GDP per head. They have been derived from a slightly modified scenario (due to the high collinearity of the previously described system of equations).

During the first periods following the year 1995, the transfers will be negative, letting the generational account of the generations alive in 1995 or to be born in the next years increase to reach the average level $\tilde{n}$. Later, the complementary transfers will become positive in order to compensate the future generations for contributing ex ante more than the average to the balancing of the public intertemporal budget.

5.3   The impact on the public debt

If the government organises the system of complementary public transfers, it will yearly get an aggregate contribution from the population. Suppose that this contribution is used to modify the level of public debt. During the first three decades, the aggregate contribution will be positive for the government, leading to a relative reduction in public debt. From 2026 on, the government will compensate individuals, letting public debt grow again, on a relative basis, up to the year 2078.

Figure 11.6 shows what the public debt/GDP ratio would be if complementary transfers were implemented. This level is to be compared with the one observed (up to the present year 1998) or anticipated for Belgium. Between 1995 and 1998, the observed and 'equitable' levels of public debt coincide! Later, they will diverge if the anticipated curve is not too pessimistic. Clearly, an equitable intergenerational distribution of the burden due to the ageing of the population would lead to a threshold of 60 per cent as early as the year 2010! It must be noticed that these results are derived from a static estimation of complementary public transfers, and do not take into account the feedback effects that would be induced by such a public policy.

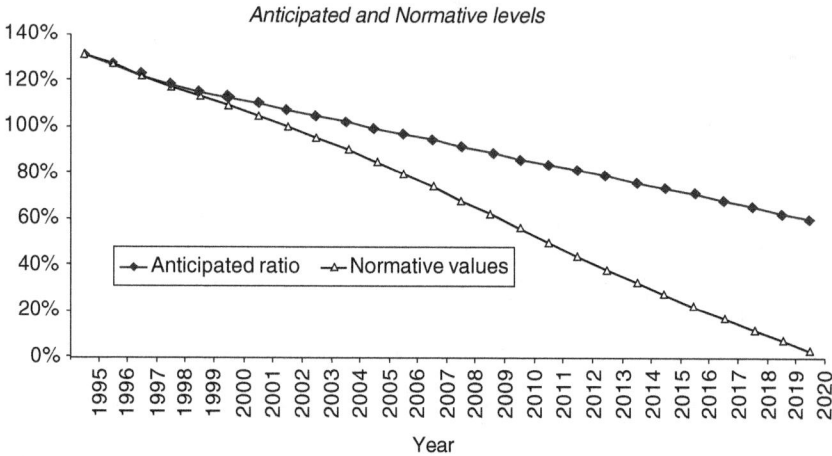

Figure 11.6 Debt/GDP ratio.

6   Conclusions

In this chapter, we analyse some contributions of the general equilibrium framework – including microeconomic foundations for individuals' choices – to the generational accounting methodology, developed by Auerbach and Kotlikoff, in order to evaluate the consequences of the ageing of the population.

We develop a *computable general equilibrium* model with overlapping generations in which lifetime is uncertain and the labour supply is endogenous. The model has been calibrated to fit the Belgian data and we have particularly focused on the demographic structure. Its takes into account the impact of ageing on the relative prices of factors as well as on the levels of consumption, savings and leisure chosen by the individuals. Social transfers from the government towards each individual grow at the same rate as productivity and the public debt/GDP ratio is constrained to follow the anticipations available for Belgium (leading to a threshold of 60 per cent in 2020 and constant later). A crucial hypothesis is that the yearly public budget will be balanced through an alteration of the tax on wages.

We show that the forthcoming ageing of the population in Belgium could induce an increase of 8 per cent on the tax rate on wages between 2020 and 2057. Consequently, the individuals to be born at the very beginning of the next century will have to contribute more than the others to the financing of the burden due to ageing. The government might wish to restore 'equity' between the generations. Equitable contribution is defined by Auerbach and Kotlikoff as that which would equalise across the generations the level of generational accounts, taking into account the individual lifecycle income.

This constant relative participation could be reached through complementary yearly lump-sum public transfers.

We have estimated the average contribution as well as the complementary transfers leading to such an equitable financing of ageing. Fiscal reform was supposed to have been implemented by 1995. If it had been, the government would have asked for a complementary effort up to the year 2026. Later, it would have compensated the future generations through a reduction in taxes. If those corrections were aggregated and used to modify the level of the debt, the public policy would lead to a threshold of 60 per cent as early as 2010 for the public debt/GDP ratio. Finally and surprisingly, the level of 'optimal' debt would have been that observed between the years 1995 and 1998!

Notes

1 Nevertheless, Liégeois (1994) shows that the choice of the terminal year does not significantly influence the results of the simulations, as far as the transition between an initial state and a final stationary state is concerned.
2 The model is made up of 200,000 simultaneous equations (500 equations per year over 400 years). To perform the simulation, we use the 'stacked-time algorithm' developed in the software TROLL.
3 This is the hypothesis set in the so-called 'mechanical' models. See Beine *et al.* (1998).
4 The gross lifecycle income is the expected present value of future wage income.

References

Auerbach, A. J., Gokhale, J. and Kotlikoff, L. J. (1991) 'Generational accounts: a meaningful alternative to deficit accounting', in: Bradford, D. (ed.) *Tax Policy and the Economy*, Cambridge: MIT Press, 55–110.

Auerbach, A. J., Gokhale, J. and Kotlikoff, L. J. (1994) 'Generational accounts: a meaningful way to evaluate generational policy', *The Journal of Economic Perspectives*, 8(1), 73–94.

Auerbach, A. J. and Kotlikoff, L. J. (1987) *Dynamic Fiscal Policy*, Cambridge: Cambridge University Press.

Beine, M., Cattoir, Ph. and Docquier, F. (1998) 'Réformes institutionnelles, solidarité interrégionale et intergénérationnelle', in: Cifop (ed.), *Rapport préparatoire du Congrès des Economistes belges de Langue Française*, Charleroi (Belgium).

Docquier, F. and Liégeois, Ph. (2001) 'Simulating computable overlapping generations models with Troll', *Computational Economics*, forthcoming.

Docquier, F., Liégeois, Ph. and Stijns, J. P. (1999) 'Comptabilité générationnelle et vieillissement démographique: les enseignements d'un modèle d'équilibre général calculable calibré pour la Belgique', *Actualité Economique*, 75, 333–356.

Kotlikoff, L. J. (1992) *Generational Accounting*, New York: The Free Press.

Liégeois, Ph. (1994) 'Computational experience with an OLG model with two sectors and various numbers of generations', Université Libre de Bruxelles, CEME/ECARE, mimeo.

Stijns, J.-Ph. (1997) 'Generational Accounts for Belgium', in: Auerbach, A. J. and Kotlikoff, L. J. (eds) *Generational Accounting around the World*, Chicago: University of Chicago Press.

12 Ageing population and pension reform in Italy

Barbara Cavalletti and Eckhard Lübke

1 Introduction

The ageing process of the population put considerable pressure on the pension system operating in Italy as well as in almost all the western countries. In the presence of negative trends in demography and growth, along with the monetary crisis, the pension system was widely reformed in 1992 (Amato reform) and 1995 (Dini reform).

Nevertheless, since the reformed regime does not affect retirees and workers on the verge of retirement, the burden of the reforms is not evenly distributed among generations and remains on the shoulders of young workers. Furthermore, the high level of the current contribution rate reinforces the negative redistribution effects on young and future generations within a system which penalizes savings and growth and appears on the whole inefficient (Castellino and Fornero 1997). On this premise there are grounds for investigating alternative reform proposals in favour of a larger role for a funded component.

A pension reform in the context of ageing population is not a question of a Pareto improving policy.[1] It is a question of a policy that distributes the demographic burden over the generations. Generational Accounting[2] and intuition tells us that the pay-as-you-go (PAYG) scheme leads to a redistribution from future to current generations when the population is ageing whereas in a fully funded (FF) pension scheme the present value of contribution is by definition equal to the present value of benefits. An FF system therefore leads to a pure intertemporal redistribution. If a pension reform is to correct intergenerational redistribution one can perform a transition to at least a partially funded (PF) or an FF system. The advantages of the FF pension scheme are doubtless since the rate of return of the PAYG is lower than the rate of return of the FF pension system. The crucial point is how to carry out a transition from a PAYG to a FF pension scheme in view of the transition costs.

The aim of this paper is three-fold:

1   To analyse the Italian pension scheme and its reforms from a microeconomic perspective; in accordance with the literature, we will argue that much progress has been achieved through the reforms. Notwithstanding this progress, the problems imposed by adverse demographics still remain.

2 We will first study the effects of the recent reforms through analysis of a simulation exercise, which represents the current system and includes the major changes operated by the Amato and Dini reforms. This first simulation is not a projection or a forecast, but represents a broad outline of the trends in the Italian economy under the influence of demography and of the pension reforms.

3 As an alternative scenario, we simulate a proposal for a transition from the current PAYG, as reformed by Amato and Dini, to a PF pension scheme. To this purpose, we exploit the savings generated by the decline in the contribution rate as a consequence of the rise in the pension age according to the reforms to collect a capital stock. This capital stock is then used to finance part of the demographic burden and transition to the PF pension scheme. Starting from the year 2002 workers are required to pay a sum to a social fund in addition to the current contribution rate, which at the rate of return of 7.2 per cent in the initial steady state will accumulate enough by the year 2019 to allow for a reduction in the total contribution rate. In this way, during the transition phase workers are asked to finance the benefits of current retirees and fund part of their own future benefits. The transition therefore implies that at a certain moment, once the first who contributes to the fund retires, he will receive a status quo annuity. Part of this annuity is paid out from the PAYG and part from the fund (i.e. according to what he has paid, the part of the annuity that he receives from the fund is equal to the present value of his contribution to the fund).

In performing the simulations we use a general equilibrium framework, with a dynamic model of the Auerbach and Kotlikoff type (AK model) which includes population trends on the basis of a cohort-component projection method using mortality and fertility tables. To this end the basic model has been extended in order to capture the features of the Italian pension system and the modifications introduced by the two reforms.

The paper is organized as follows: Section 2 describes the pension system in Italy and the Amato and Dini reforms; Section 3 presents the model and modifications to the model to represent the situation in Italy[3] and the details of the partial transition from PAYG to FF; Section 4 discusses the results of our simulations. Finally, conclusions and comments are given in Section 5.

2 The pension insurance scheme in Italy

A first noteworthy reform of the pension system was undertaken in 1992, with the aim of:

1 harmonizing the regimes of different occupational groups by gradually abolishing the preferential treatment of civil servants;
2 stabilizing the expenditure trend to GDP.

To this purpose, the principal measures concern:

- the age of retirement for the old-age pension,[4] which goes from 60 to 65 for men and from 55 to 60 for women;
- the reference income now determined on the basis of the last 10 years – instead of the last five – of the working life;
- the indexation of pension benefits to wages is abandoned; pensions will be indexed to prices only. No indexation is carried out in 1992, while for the year 1993 it is limited to 3.5 per cent of the total indexation;
- the introduction of a supplementary funded insurance regulated by law.

The 1995 reform substantially modifies the mechanism for computing retirement benefits in that it replaces an income-based system with a contribution-based system, operating on a PAYG basis. The main changes introduced in the area of retirement are:

- benefits are linked to lifetime contribution;
- old age and seniority pensions are merged into a single scheme, which penalizes early retirement. The years of contributions required for seniority pensions are increased from 35 to 40 and, in any case, a minimum amount of contributions is necessary; in short, criteria are: at least 57 years of age with a minimum of 5 years of contributions, or at least 40 years of contributions.

Due to the introduction of a formal link between benefits and contribution, the main differences between the Amato and Dini reforms concern the computation of pensions: under the Amato regime, the pension benefits of an individual retiring in year T with N years of contribution were computed as a fixed percentage (2 per cent) of the reference income (RI), adjusted by the years of contribution (at least 35), that is:

$$P_T = 0.02\,N\,RI$$

where the pensionable income is computed as the average income over the whole contribution period, with real wages (W_t) revalued at the rate of 1 per cent annually

$$RI = \frac{1}{N} \sum_{t=T-N}^{T-1} W_t(1.01)^{(T-t)}$$

The pension formula of the Dini regime is such that, the present value – at the time of retirement – of pension benefits to be paid during the probable remaining lifetime should be equal to the present value of the lifetime contributions, so that

$$P_T = \beta^e \tau \sum_{t=T-N}^{T-1} W_t \gamma_t$$

where β^e is transformation coefficient, stipulated by law, denoting the yield per year of contribution, depending on age of retirement (e); τ is the contribution rate and γ is the accrual rate. Retirement is allowed in a range between 57 and 65 years of age; the contribution rate is fixed at 33 per cent for employees and 20 per cent for self-employed;[5] the accrual rate corresponds to a moving average of rates of GDP growth,[6] with the hypothesis of 1.5 per cent annually.

As for pension benefits, the present value is calculated on the basis of constant annual pension payments, discounted at a rate of 1.5 per cent, so that the total number of annuities, as well as the relative amount, depends on the age of retirement. Unlike the Amato regime, the yield per year of contribution, given by the transformation coefficients, is related to the age of retirement as a function (inversely proportional) of the life expectancy at that time.

Given the hypothesis of the reform and a 2 per cent real-wage growth rate, the yields per year of contribution are lower, under the Dini system, for employees retiring before the age of 62, with 37 years of contribution; that is, the new system tends to be less generous than the Amato system. This implies a relatively lower replacement rate (measured as a proportion of the last wage) and should be able to generate some saving in pension outlays, since, in the long run, the equilibrium contribution rate is calculated, irrespective of the effective age of retirement, as if each pensioner would retire at the age of 62 with 37 years of contributions.[7] Antichi (1995: 106) shows that in the long run (around 2050), the equilibrium rate would tend to the statutory 33 per cent for employees, five percentage points below that generated by the old system.

3 The model

3.1 The AGE model

The model used in this paper is an extended version of the AK model. The AK model consists of a life cycle model, a social security system, a state sector and an AGE model including an enterprise sector. In addition to this, our model includes a detailed population model based on the cohort-component projection method with family relationships and an inheritance model. The model is described in detail in Lübke (1997) and Lübke (1998); in what follows, we simply give an overview of the main components of the model.

To depict the behaviour of the individuals in the model we use a life-cycle approach.[8] The individuals maximize their expected lifetime utility subject to the lifetime budget constraint. Accordingly, we take account of probable life expectancy for particular age cohorts.[9] Consumption, labour supply and saving decisions in each period of an individual's lifetime are determined endogenously. The beginning and end of the working phase of the individuals are fixed exogenously. The individuals in the model keep a given percentage of their wealth in private pension insurance and the rest as personal assets in the capital market, according to an exogenous portfolio quota.

The population model simulates the demographic development of the model population. It is based on the cohort-component projection method and computes the evolution of the model population through time in terms of its fertility and mortality. The fertility tables are reproduced by means of the normal distribution function. The level of fertility is determined by setting the net reproduction rate (NRR) for each year of the simulation period. This parameter has a lasting effect on the demographic process. Life tables are represented by means of a logistic function. This function can be adjusted to reproduce mortality trends such as an increase in life expectancy. Finally, the cohort-component projection method is applied in order to simulate the evolution of the Italian population through time.

This population model is expanded to take account of first-degree family relationships. The inheritance model transfers inheritances on the basis of family relationships. If an individual in the model population dies, his assets are divided evenly among his children.

The implementation of the Italian social security system into the model is described in detail in Section 3.2. The state has a quite simple structure in this model. It levies capital income taxes, value-added taxes and inheritance taxes. Public expenditures are a percentage of gross national product while annual public debt stands in a fixed relation to gross national product. The state has to pay interest on its public debt. In order to balance the budget, the wage-tax rate is determined endogenously.

The corporate sector is represented by a linear homogeneous Cobb–Douglas production function. It produces a homogeneous good with the factors labour and capital. The production function is subject to labour-augmenting technical progress.

The AGE model completes the whole model by providing a macroeconomic framework. The AGE model can be set up to represent a closed economy with endogenous interest rates or a small open economy with fixed interest rates. In the latter case, transactions with other countries are recorded in external accounts.

3.2   The pension scheme in Italy

The current system

This section explores the features of the reforms that have been portrayed in the model. Figure 12.1 gives an overview on a typical definition of a PAYG pension system. After a person has reached retirement age, the premium pension is calculated on the basis of the pension formula. In the following years this premium pension is adapted for instance to inflation or wage growth. Finally, the contribution rate of the PAYG scheme for a given year is calculated to cover all pension payments in this year minus subsidies from the state.

The Italian pension scheme has changed through time, especially the formula for calculating the premium pension and indexation, while computation of the

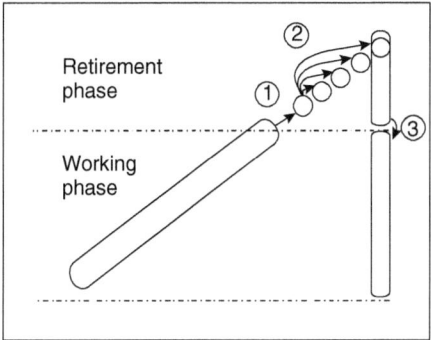

Figure 12.1 Definitions of a PAYG pension scheme.

Notes:
1 Premium pension: fixed percentage of lifetime average earnings.
2 Pension adaptation: adaptation to inflation etc.
3 Contribution calculated on a PAYG basis.

equilibrium contribution rate has remained unchanged. In modelling the pension scheme we abstract from many of the details in the real system and take only the most important elements into consideration. The pension scheme in the model is represented as follows:

1 PREMIUM PENSION

Computation of the premium pension in the model is represented by three different formulas, namely P_1, P_2, P_3, which capture the features prevailing in three main phases, according to the legislation: by the end of the 1960s; in the period 1968–95; from 1996 on.

(a) Until 1967 we calculate the premium pension on the basis of a simplified pension formula. The premium pension is set to a value of 50 per cent of gross labour income. The actual conditions are quite well represented since the last person to retire in 1967 has almost no effect on the future financing problems of the Italian pension scheme. $P_{1T} = 0,5 \cdot \text{wage}_{T-1} \cdot \text{total labour demand}_{T-1}/\text{population}_{T-1}$.

(b) In the period 1968–95, the premium pension of a worker retiring in year T with N_T years of contribution (maximum 40) is defined as:

$$P_{2T} = \frac{N_T}{40} \alpha RI_T$$

where

$$\alpha = \begin{cases} 0.65 & \text{in 1968} \\ 0.74 & \text{in 1969–76} \\ 0.80 & \text{thereafter} \end{cases}$$

and the reference income

$$
RI_T = \begin{cases}
\frac{1}{5} \displaystyle\sum_{t=T-5}^{T-1} Y_t^L, & T < 1993 \\[2ex]
\frac{1}{10} \displaystyle\sum_{t=T-10}^{T-1} Y_t^L(1.01)^{T-t}, & T \geq 1993 \ and \ N_{1993} \geq 15 \\[2ex]
1/\mathrm{Min}(5 + (T - 1993), N) \displaystyle\sum_{t=T-\mathrm{Min}(5+(T-1993),N)}^{T-1} Y_t^L(1.01)^{T-t}, \\[1ex]
\qquad\qquad T \geq 1993 \ and \ N_{1993} < 15
\end{cases}
$$

where Y_t^L is the labour income.

(c) With the Dini reform in 1995, the premium pension formula is greatly modified by the introduction of a contribution-based system for computing retirement benefits. The new system, however, has no effect whatsoever on workers with 18 years of contribution on 31 December 1995. Moreover, due to long phasing-in of the reform, a variable part of the total benefits still corresponds to those generated by the old system, even for workers with fewer than 18 years of contribution on 31 December 1995. Therefore, for pensions paid from 1996 on, the premium pension is computed as follows:

$$
P_{3T} = \begin{cases}
\beta_T \displaystyle\sum_{t=T-N_T}^{T-1} Y_t^L \gamma_t, & T > 1995 + N_T + 1 \\[2ex]
\dfrac{N_T - (T - 1994)}{N_T} P_{2T} + \dfrac{T - 1994}{N_T} \beta_T \displaystyle\sum_{t=T-N_r}^{T-1} Y_t^L \gamma_t, \\[1ex]
\qquad 1995 - 18 + N_T + 1 < T \leq 1995 + N_T + 1 \\[2ex]
P_{2T}, & T \leq 1995 - 18 + N_T + 1
\end{cases}
$$

where τ is the contributive rate, set at 33 per cent for dependent workers (both in the public and private sector) and 20 per cent for self-employed; β is the transformation coefficient stipulated by law, whose values (varying with the age of retirement) are taken from annex A to the reform law (L.335/95) and

$$
\gamma_t = \prod_{j=t}^{T}(1 + \pi_j)
$$

π_j being the 5-year moving average (ending in t) of annual GDP growth rates. As a final remark to this section, we should point out that our method for modelling premium pensions according to the legislation does not reflect all the transitional arrangements and exceptions, which are numerous.

2 INDEXATION

Before the year 1984 we do not consider any indexation mechanism in the model. In the period 1984–92 the mechanism for indexation takes wages into account.

Finally, with the 1992 reform, the mechanism is revised again and pensions are indexed only to prices.

3 EQUILIBRIUM CONTRIBUTION RATE

Finally, the equilibrium contribution rate is calculated so that all outlays of the pension scheme are financed by state subsidy and contributions.

Reform proposal

Figure 12.2 shows the functioning of the reform. The pensions calculated in the PAYG system after the Amato and Dini reforms are not changed. In addition to the contribution rate calculated in the current system, we introduce a demographic and transitional component.

The reform consists of three parts:

1   The same ratio pension/average labour income as in the current system is maintained;
2   Contributions are set corresponding to an error correction model;
3   Individual surplus of contribution over benefits in the PAYG system is used to finance part of the demographic burden and transition to a PF system.

The contribution rate is changed according to the following error correction rule:

$$\Delta c = e \cdot \left(1 - \frac{W_{ss}}{e \cdot 10 \cdot Y} \right)$$

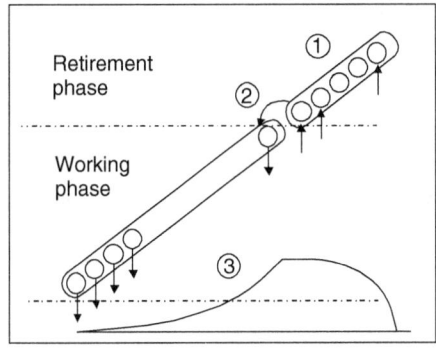

Figure 12.2 Alternative reform proposal: a partial transition to the FF pension scheme.

Notes:
1   Same ratio pension/average labour income as in the current system.
2   Contribution are set corresponding to the error correction rule.
3   Individual surplus of contribution over benefits (PAYG) to finance demographic burden and transition to a partial funded system.

where W_{ss} are social security reserves; e is the parameter determining the maximum rise in the contribution rate and the equilibrium level of social security reserves; Y is the GDP and Δc is the change in contribution rate.

In short, this error correction rule says: if, for example, $e = 0.05$ then collect an additional contribution of five percentage points, as a maximum, until the reserves of the social security system are lower than a certain percentage of GDP in each year. Once these reserves have been built up, the system gains from the interest rate, which is higher than the growth rate of GDP. The change in contribution thus becomes negative.

To be more precise, the reform proposal consists of:

1   A calculation of the premium pension and the contribution rate, in line with the Amato and Dini reform.
2   An increase in the resulting contribution rate to collect a capital stock. This capital stock is used, (a) to finance part of the demographic burden, and (b) to perform a partial transition to a PF pension scheme.
3   Use of the error correction rule to raise the contribution rate. In the first year of the reform, social security reserves (W_{ss}) are zero.

The rule results in an increase in the contribution rate of, for example, five percentage points. Subsequently, social security reserves grow and, according to the rule, Δc shrinks. It will eventually become negative since social security reserves gain a rate of return that is higher than the growth rate of GDP. Once again, we look at the rule. If social security reserves grow at a higher rate than GDP, the difference can be used to pay part of the contributions.

This rule is only one example of how to change the contribution rate to collect a capital stock. Other rules might be even more successful. We would simply like to demonstrate that transition to a PF pension scheme is possible using a rule that levels out the evolution of the contribution rate.

Parameter values and demographic trends

1   AGE OF RETIREMENT

The first point to be examined is the age of retirement. Old-age pensions in Italy require a minimum number of years of contribution (15 before 1992, then 20). In alternative to old age, seniority pensions require a minimum number of years of contribution, independently of age.

Until the Amato reform, in 1992, the requirement for old age was 55 years for women and 60 years for men, well below the average in the other OECD countries, as is shown in Table 12.1.

The requirement for seniority pensions was set at 35 years of contributions for employees and self-employed workers, while civil servants benefited from a favourable regime, which fixed the number of years of contribution at 20 for men and 15 for women. Therefore, for this latter category of workers, the pensionable

Table 12.1 Normal retirement age in 1991

Economy	Female	Male
Austria	60	65
Denmark	67	67
France	60	60
Germany	65	65
Italy	55	60

Source: Worldbank 1994: 367 f.

age was quite variable and on the whole not relevant, since they mainly retired at a relatively younger age. This makes the benefit schedules implied relatively onerous for the system. To have an idea of the magnitude, one should remember that in the year preceding the Amato reform in 1992, total expenditure on pensions amounted to about 12.6 per cent of GDP, while pensions paid by the public sector represented approx. 18 per cent of the total number of pensions and about 27 per cent of the total expenditure.[10]

The Amato reform gradually raises the age of retirement to 60 for women and 65 for men. For seniority pensions, the required 35 years of contribution is gradually extended to all categories of workers. The new rules have immediate application for those workers with no more than 8 years of contribution.

Finally, with the Dini reform in 1995, old age and seniority pensions are merged into a single scheme, which requires a minimum age of 57 for men and women and a minimum of 5 years of contributions paid, or, alternatively, a minimum of 40 years of contribution, independent of age. It must be noted, however, that the new requirements affect in full only new workers, those whose pensions will be paid from 2036 onwards. For the others, the requirements are: 35 years of contributions and 57 years of age; 40 years of contribution, independent of age, or, in the transitional phase 1996–98, as in Table 12.2.

As it was impossible to represent in the model all the details for age requirements contained in the new legislation, it was important to illustrate the burden posed on the system by the relatively early age of retirement that prevails in Italy compared to other OECD countries. Figures[11] on labour force statistics in OECD countries over the period 1973–94 show that the rate of labour force participation for male workers aged 55 to 64 is exceptionally low in Italy, lying between 30 and 40 per cent. That means that around 70 per cent of male workers aged 55 to 64 do not work. This is due to a number of reasons, in particular to unemployment, whose rate in Italy was about 11 per cent in 1994, 3 percentage points above the average of OECD countries and slightly below the average in European countries.[12] However, early retirements also contribute to determining such a low figure. One can note in fact that in Germany, over the same period, the labour force participation rate declines from more than 70 to above 50 per cent, in the US it varies from about 80 to 65 per cent, while in Japan it remains almost stable at approx. 85 per cent.

Table 12.2 Retirement age in detail

Year	Dependent workers (Private and public)		Self-employed 35 years and a minimum age of
	35 years of contribution and minimum age of	Any age and a minimum years of contribution of	
1996	52	36	56
1997	52	36	56
1998	53		57
1999	53	37	57
2000	54	37	
2001	54		
2002	55		
2003	55		
2004	56	38	
2005	56	38	
2006	57	39	
2007	57	39	
2008 on		40	

Table 12.3 Age of retirement and average working period in the simulation

From year	To year	Age of retirement	Average working period
1850	1993	57	37
1994	1995	58	38
1996	1997	59	39
1998	1999	60	40
2000	2001	61	41
2002	2351	62	42

In view of the simulation to be performed, we have chosen to implement retirement age in the model as follows: the average age is 57 for both men and women, in the period preceding the reforms; starting from the year 1994, the average age grows to 62 in 10 years; the average working life is 37 years in the time preceding the reform, then going up to 42 (Table 12.3).

2   ECONOMIC PARAMETER

The values of the economic parameter are set according to Table 12.4. These values are not changed over time. Some of them are calculated using OECD data. For the other values we have made plausible assumptions.

3   DEMOGRAPHIC PARAMETER

The demographic parameters are set to represent the ageing process in Italy. The net reproductive rate first rises and then declines (Table 12.5). We assume that

Table 12.4 Economic parameter values in the simulations

Parameter	Value	Source
Government expenditure as a share of GDP	0.17	OECD (1997: 155, Tab. F)
Debt ratio	1.20	OECD (1997: 67, Tab. 20)
Indirect tax as a percentage of consumption	0.17	Calculated[1]
Inheritance tax rate	0.03	Assumption
Capital gains tax rate	0.25	Assumption
State subsidy to pension scheme	0.00	Assumption
Output elasticity of capital	0.25	Assumption
Rate of technical progress	0.015	Assumption
Portfolio quota	1/3	Assumption

Note:
1 On the basis of OECD (1997: 152, Tab. C) and OECD (1997: 155, Tab. F).

Table 12.5 Demographic parameter values in the simulations

	From year	To year	Starting value	Ending value
Net reproductive rate				
	1850	1945	1.00	1.00
	1946	1951	1.00	1.05
	1952	1957	1.05	1.05
	1958	1965	1.05	1.21
	1965	1988	1.21	0.63
	1989	1999	0.63	0.63
	2000	2050	0.63	1.00
	2051	2351	1.00	1.00
Life expectancy				
	1850	1950	67.0	67.0
	1951	2050	67.0	79.0
	2051	2351	79.0	79.0
Child mortality				
	1850	1950	0.10	0.10
	1951	1980	0.10	0.01
	1981	2351	0.01	0.01

this parameter will rise again in the near future (2000–50) up to the reproductive value of one. Life expectancy is assumed to go from 67 years in 1950 to a value of 79 years in 2050. The child mortality parameter is shrinking from a value of 10 per cent up to 1950 to a value of 1 per cent in 1980. Thereafter this value is assumed to be constant.

4   Simulation results

In this section we will compare the results of two simulations performed. The first one represents the current system and takes into account the pension system as modified by the Amato and Dini reforms. The second simulation performs a proposal for a transition to a PF pension scheme. By performing this simulation we vary the parameter *e* of the transition rule. Thereby we can show that the extent to which a funded pension scheme is installed can be varied. The details of both the simulations are described in Section 3.2 above, and the main results are summarized in Figures 12.3 and 12.4 below.

In interpreting the comparative effects of the simulations performed it should be remembered that they do not represent a forecast of the future economic evolution of the Italian economy, rather they aim to highlight the distribution of the transition costs implied by the two scenarios, which are proxied by the difference of the equilibrium contribution rate in the current system and in our reform proposal.

Bearing this in mind, our results seem quite reasonable. The return on capital in the initial steady state is 7.2 per cent. Although this value is in line with actual trends observed in selected OECD countries (Worldbank 1994: 301), it might be considered too high for Italy.[13] However, the interest rate trend in Italy is not

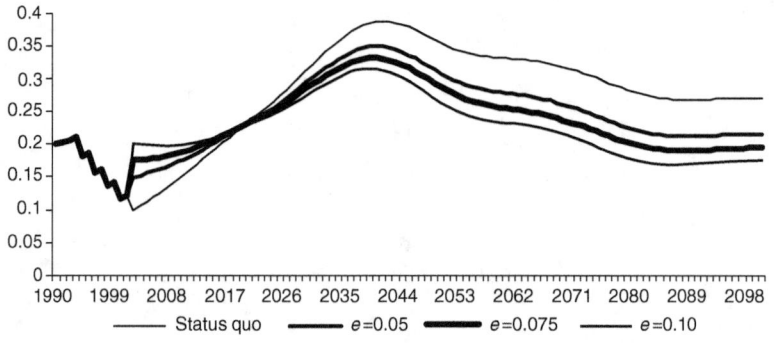

Figure 12.3 Simulation results – contribution rate.

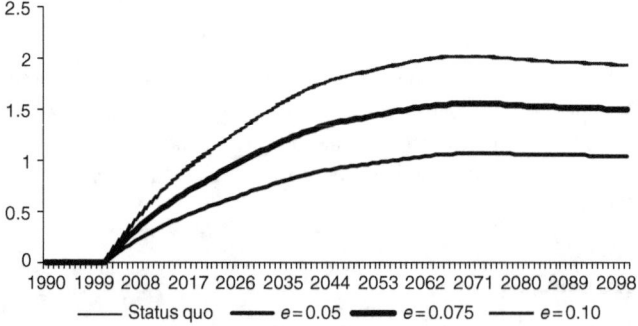

Figure 12.4 Simulation results – social security reserves (in per cent of GDP).

reliable in the long run because of high inflation, while equity premia are quite variable due to the limited development of the stock market (Castellino and Fornero 1997: 22). The contribution rate is 21 per cent, in 1993. Considering a rough average of the current contribution rates for dependent and self-employed workers, this value is about 2.5 points below the current level in 1993.

Figure 12.3 compares the evolution of the contribution rates of the simulations. As one can note, the current system leads to a sharp decline in the contribution rate until 2002. This is due to the rise in retirement age, seen in Table 12.3 above. As a consequence, the total number of workers rises while the total number of pensioners falls compared to the situation before the reforms. However, it must be pointed out that the rising retirement age has a second, opposite effect on the contribution rate: as the average working period rises (Table 12.3), the premium pension rises as well, based on the pension formulas. This counteracts the future decline in the contribution rate. In fact, from 2002 onwards there is a sharp increase in the contribution rate.

In our reform proposal simulation we exploit the savings generated by the decline in the contribution rate that follows the rising retirement age. These savings are conveyed to the accumulation of a capital stock by means of a surcharge on the contribution rate. In this way the savings deriving from the higher retirement age are postponed to future periods. Comparing the new trend of the contribution rate to the one generated by the current system, one can see that the peak in the contribution rate in 2040 is considerably lower. Secondly, the transition to a PF pension scheme results in lower contribution rates in each year of the remaining simulation period. With an initial increase of 5, 7.5 or 10 per cent points in the first year of the transition, the level of the contribution rate remains above the one that would have prevailed in the current system, until around the year 2020. At this point, the accumulated reserves allow a decrease in the contribution rate. Starting from the year 2040, the equilibrium rate is steadily below that generated by the current system of around 5, 7 or 9 per cent points. Finally, the evolution of the contribution rate is smoothed out.

The pension reserves in our reform proposal rise to a level of around 100, 150 or 200 per cent of GDP (Figure 12.4).

5   Conclusions

The present chapter discusses the effects of the Amato and Dini pension reforms on the sustainability of the PAYG pension scheme in Italy. Given the hypothesis of the reform, the new regime should be able to produce a lower ratio of pension to GDP, due to the combined effect of the tightening of eligibility criteria and of the incentive to postpone retirement, which is implicit in the new system for computing the premium pension. The results of simulations, however, highlight the problems posed by adverse demographic trends in combination with the PAYG pension scheme. In fact, while the new system will be phased-in only from 2036 onwards, the pensions computed under the new rules will not reach an important share of total pensions before the second half of the next century.

Hence, the decrease in pension outlays will not be able to overcome the negative effects deriving from the expected increase in the dependency ratio in the first part of the next century. Moreover, since the new system is still based on the PAYG scheme, the burden of the adverse demographic transition will mostly be borne by generations working from 2015 onwards, as the system's equilibrium rate increases over the next decades to reach a peak around 2040.

The problems posed by adverse demography within a PAYG scheme then require some adjustments to the system, so that a certain part of the negative effects of the surge in retirements expected around the year 2040 is borne by current generations. This would require running a surplus over the next decades.

In order to achieve this result, we propose the implementation of a rule to vary the contribution rate, which is the base for the creation of a capital stock in order to perform a transition to a PF system and spread the demographic burden more evenly among generations.

This reform proposal has several consequences:

1   Until we perform the transition in a Pareto improving manner, at least one generation will have to bear transition costs.
2   Transition costs are borne by the generations that would otherwise gain from the demographic process.
3   The reform proposal not only leads to a partial transition to an FF system, but also lowers the burden of demographic trends.

Notes

1   See for instance Breyer (1989), Verbon (1989) and Homburg (1990) for a discussion on a Pareto-improving transition from PAYG to FF.
2   Generational Accounting was pioneered by Auerbach et al. (1991).
3   Also considering the choice of the reference value to obtain the parameters of the model and demographic trends and the specific features of the pension system.
4   The reform also revises the criteria for seniority pensions, starting from 1994. This will produce relevant effects on civil servants in particular. In the regime preceding the reform, in fact, the age of retirement for this category was quite variable and, on the whole, of little relevance, due to the fact that they easily met the requirement of a minimum number of years of contribution (20 for men and 15 for women) for seniority pensions. With the 1992 reform, the minimum number of years of contribution for seniority pensions rises to 35 for both men and women and for all categories.
5   These 'notional' rates are higher than the effective contributive rate, in particular for self-employed, implying that the remaining gap should be financed by general taxation.
6   IMF Italy Background Economic Issues, 1996.
7   Antichi (1995: 103).
8   Cf. Brumberg and Modigliani (1979) and Ando and Modigliani (1963).
9   Cf. Yaari (1965).
10 Data are taken and elaborated from INPS (1993) and ISTAT (1992).
11 Cf. OECD (1996).
12 Ministero per il bilancio e la programmazione economica (1995: I-11).
13 A range between 3 and 5 per cent could be considered cautious (Castellino and Fornero 1997: 22).

References

Ando, A. and Modigliani, F. (1963) 'The "life cycle" hypothesis of saving: aggregate implications and tests', *American Economic Review*, 53, 55–84.

Auerbach, A. J., Gokhale, J. and Kotlikoff, L. J. (1991) 'Generational accounts: a meaningful alternative to deficit accounting', in: Bradford, D. (ed.) *Tax Policy and the Economy*, vol. 5, Cambridge: MIT Press, 55–110.

Antichi, M. (1995) 'Considerazioni sulla sostenibilitá della riforma del sistema pensionistico', *Quaderni di Economia e Finanza*, n. 4, 83–113.

Breyer, F. (1989) 'On the intergenerational Pareto efficiency of pay-as-you-go financed pension systems', *Journal of Institutional and Theoretical Economics*, 145, 643–58.

Brumberg, R. and Modigliani, F. (1979) 'Utility analysis and aggregate consumption function: an attempt at integration', in: Abel, A. (ed.) *Collected Papers of Franco Modigliani*, vol. 2, Cambridge, Cambridge University Press.

Castellino, O. and Fornero, E. (1997) 'From PAYG to funding in Italy: a feasible transition?', Mimeo.

Homburg, S. (1990) 'The efficiency of unfunded pension schemes', *Journal of Institutional and Theoretical Economics*, 146, 640–47.

IMF (1996) *Italy – Background Economic Issues*, Report N.96/35.

INPS (1993) *Le Pensioni Domani*, Bologna: Il Mulino.

ISTAT (1992) *Statistiche sui trattamenti pensionistici al 31 dicembre 1990*, Collana d'informazione n.22, Roma.

Lübke, E. (1997) *Ersparnis und wirtschaftliche Entwicklung bei alternder Bevölkerung – Entwicklung und Anwendung eines dynamischen Allgemeinen Gleichgewichtsmodells*, Heidelberg: Physica-Verlag.

Lübke, E. (1998) 'Development and application of an AGE-model with a variable population', in: Fossati, A. and Hutton, J. (eds) *Policy Simulations in the European Union*, London: Routledge.

Modigliani, F. Ceprini, M. L. and Muralidhar, A. S. (1999) *An MIT Solution to the Social Security Crisis*, Sloan Working Paper: SWP 4051, March.

OECD (1996) *Ageing in OECD Countries – A Critical Policy Challenge*, Social Policy Studies no. 20, Paris.

OECD (1997) *Economic Survey of Italy*, Paris: OECD.

Ministero per il bilancio e la programmazione economica (1995) *Relazione Generale sulla situazione economica del Paese 1994*, Roma.

Verbon, H. A. (1989) 'Conversion policies for public pension plans in a small open economy', in: Gustafsson, B. A. and Klevmarken, N. A. (eds), *The Political Economy of Social Security*, Amsterdam: North Holland, 83–95.

Worldbank (1994) *Averting the Old Age Crisis* – A World Bank policy research report.

Yaari, M. E. (1965) 'Uncertain lifetime, life insurance, and the theory of the consumer', *Review of Economic Studies*, 32, 137–50.

13 Pension funding reforms in a small open welfare state*

Hans Fehr and Erling Steigum

1 Introduction

Due to rapid demographic transitions caused by rising life expectancy and declining fertility, many countries around the world are seeking ways to reform their unfunded pay-as-you-go (PAYG) systems of old age social security. Various proposals for reforms have been suggested, the most radical one being to privatize, that is, to replace the PAYG scheme by a funded system in which workers make contributions to private pension funds. In most industrialized countries, however, particularly in Europe, all citizens are entitled to a minimum pension from the government. The question of funding will therefore only pertain to the earnings related part of the PAYG pension scheme.

We focus on a particular country (Norway) and simulate the welfare, distribution, and macroeconomic growth effects of a transition from a PAYG system to a partially funded system using a calibrated overlapping-generations model. Norway is a typical North-European welfare state with a large public sector including a generous social security system financed on a PAYG basis, as well as a progressive income tax system. A special feature of Norway, however, is the considerable wealth of the government, both in terms of net financial assets and ownership and taxation rights in Norway's large oil industry. Our estimate of the value of net public wealth is well above one year's GDP. The existence of these assets could facilitate privatization of the earnings-related part of the present system.

We use a calibrated Auerbach–Kotlikoff model of a small open economy, extended by five intragenerational income groups to simulate the distributional and efficiency consequences of alternative pension and tax reforms. Three novel features of the model are worth emphasizing. First, similar to Fehr (2000) we introduce a realistic demographic transition, that is, we do not start from an initial steady state situation in regard to population and labour supply. This permits us to account for the expected ageing of the Norwegian population. Second, the model captures the Norwegian piecewise linear income tax and

*Thanks are due to Carl E. Gjersem, Hans Husum and Tarmo Valkonen for useful discussion. Hans Fehr also acknowledges financial support from the Ruhrgas AG.

pension benefit schedules, involving jumps in the marginal tax rates. Third, we isolate an efficiency effect from the welfare effects in order to get a picture of which generations enjoy the fruits of the reductions in the deadweight loss generated by the fiscal reforms.

A number of recent papers analyze pension reforms by means of quantitative overlapping generations models with several income groups within each generation, see for example, Kotlikoff *et al.* (1998) and Fehr (1999). These studies do not capture a demographic transition, however, but assume a constant population growth rate. Other papers, for example Auerbach *et al.* (1989), Broer and Westerhout (1997), Chaveau and Loufir (1997), Miles (1999) and Steigum (1993) simulate a demographic transition, but do not account for intragenerational heterogeneity.[1] Our model combines these two strands of literature and offers two additional extensions: first, it is able to deal with jumps in marginal tax rates, and second, it distinguishes income and efficiency effects of different fiscal reforms.

The simulation experiments are done as follows. We first compute a baseline equilibrium calibrated to the growth path presented in the recent long-term program of the government. In the baseline, we let the government run a surplus (in per cent of GDP) of 5 per cent per year for 15 years, reducing it linearly to zero during the following 20 years. In all simulations of pension reforms, a time profile of the government's budget surplus is specified in advance. The consumption tax rate is adjusted over time to fulfil the budget target. Given this baseline path of the economy we simulate four alternative scenarios for phasing-in the elimination of the earnings related part of the pension scheme.

In addition to the effects of employment, growth, consumption, investment and foreign assets, we also calculate an index of efficiency gains due to lower taxes as well as welfare indices for each age and income group. The results highlight the trade-off between efficiency and distribution.

The rest of the chapter is organized as follows. In the next section we present the model and explain the calibration. In Section 3 we present and discuss the simulation results. Section 4 concludes.

2   A simulation model of the Norwegian economy

This section describes the simulation model that is used to evaluate alternative pension reform plans. In section 13.2.1 we sketch its general structure and explain the main differences compared to other simulation models in the Auerbach–Kotlikoff tradition. Then we discuss how the model represents the Norwegian tax and transfer system. Finally, we describe how the model is calibrated and report some important characteristics of the baseline simulation.

2.1   General structure

The framework of the Auerbach–Kotlikoff (1987) overlapping-generations model is by now a fairly standard tool in quantitative analysis of public finance issues dealing with intergenerational redistribution. The economy is disaggregated into households, firms and the government.

As for household behaviour, consumption, savings and labour supply decisions are derived from a 55 period life-cycle model. Each generation enters the labour market at age 20 and expects to die 55 years later. There is no uncertainty. Labour supply is endogenous; each household chooses how many hours to work and when to retire. The latter decision is based on a comparison between the reservation wage and the market wage. We take into account that the productivity first rises during the life cycle and then falls later on. In each year, a new generation is born. In order to capture the essentials of the Norwegian demographic structure, the population growth rates differ across periods, permitting the model to mimic the initial structure as well as the ageing of the population in the long run. As in Fehr (2000), we distinguish between five different types of households within each generation, which differ with respect to labour productivity and therefore belong to different lifetime income quintiles. Each household maximizes (in a time-consistent way) a time-separable CES-utility function defined over consumption and leisure, subject to a lifetime budget constraint. Agents are only concerned with their own welfare (and the welfare of their children before age 20), that is, there is no bequest motive. Parameter values and functional forms are assumed to be the same for each household. This reflects the belief that poor households would behave in the same way as rich households, provided they had the same high lifetime income and other assets.

The producer side of the economy is simply represented by an aggregate Cobb–Douglas production function using labour and capital as inputs. There is no technical progress. Investment decisions follow the modern Q-theory of investment, according to which firms invest whenever the stock market value of their assets exceeds the cost of replacement. This is consistent with maximizing the market value of firms when capital formation is subject to strictly convex installation costs. Note, however, that there are no installation costs in steady state.

The government sector supplies public goods exogenously. The latter enter the utility functions additively. The other items on the expenditure side are various transfer programs and old-age pensions. Government spending is financed by direct and indirect (consumption) taxes and wealth income.

2.2   *The Norwegian fiscal system*

Compared to other European countries, the financial position of the Norwegian government is very strong. The huge petroleum wealth in terms of the expected income stream from the oil industry is well above one year's GDP.[2] In addition, the government has a positive net financial asset position. It is a large shareholder in Norwegian non-oil industry and banking. Since the mid-1990s, large government surpluses have been transformed into foreign assets in a Petroleum Fund administered by the Central Bank. There is no separate social security budget as for example in Germany. We write the consolidated government budget (central and local government, including the Central Bank and the social security system) as

$$B_{t+1} - B_t = rB_t + T_t - G_t - P_t - TR_t$$

Here B_t is net government wealth (including an estimate of its petroleum wealth) at the beginning of year t. G_t is government spending on goods and services (excluding government investment in the oil industry). T_t is indirect and direct taxes (excluding taxes paid by the oil industry), P_t is old-age pensions, and TR_t is other transfers (net of subsidies to firms). The latter include disability pensions, unemployment and sickness benefits and family allowances. The present old-age pension system was introduced in 1967 and is still maturing. In order to receive maximum benefits, people have to participate in the labour market for 40 years. The first generation of pensioners receiving full benefits will therefore retire in 2007. The mandatory retirement age is 67, but in recent years, generous options for early retirement have been introduced as a result of negotiation between the central government and labour market organizations. Granting of disability pensions to old workers is also widespread, reducing the effective average retirement age to about 60 years. In the model we assume that all households receive old-age pensions starting at age 61. To capture the maturing of the system, we also assume that pensioners who enter the labour market after 1967 receive lower pensions proportional to the ratio of the years passed since 1967 to 40. The pension formula calculates the average of the best twenty working years. This average income is then converted into pension benefits according to the function illustrated in Figure 13.1.[3] If the average annual wage income is below NOK 137,000, the worker is entitled to a tax free minimum pension of NOK 82,000 (slightly above DM 4,000). Then the pension benefit increases linearly up to an average income of NOK 255,000, corresponding to a before tax pension of NOK 131,750. The slope of the schedule is further reduced in the third bracket. For average incomes above NOK 510,000, the pension is constant

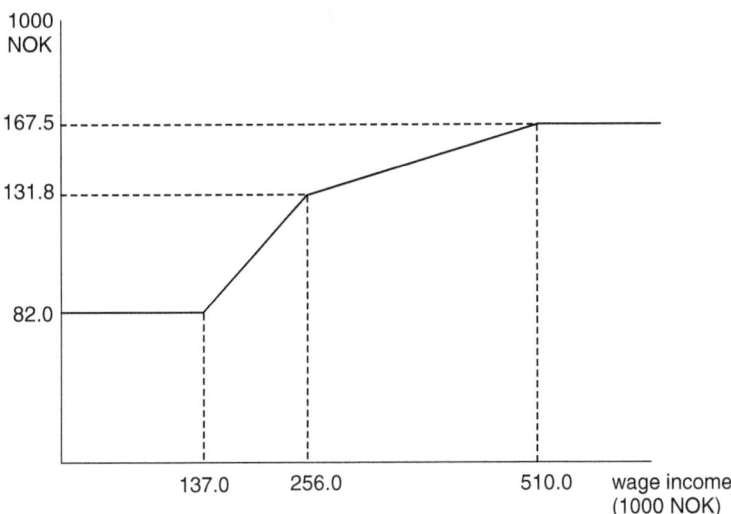

Figure 13.1 The pension function.

and equal to NOK 167,450. Due to the progressivity of the benefit schedule, workers have small incentives to stay in the work force after the 20 expected best years have passed, since further participation will not change the final pension.[4]

In regard to government spending on goods and services (G), we assume that public consumption per household is constant for each age group. Hence the changes in the size and structure of the population over time trigger changes in G over time. On the revenue side of the government's budget, we distinguish between taxes on income, wealth and consumption. Norway operates a dual income tax system, in which wage income and pensions are taxed according to a progressive tax schedule and (nominal) capital income is taxed according to a flat rate of 28 per cent. The model captures the essentials of the progressive (and piecewise linear) wage income tax code (see Figure 13.2). The figure does not include the so-called 'social security contribution', which is an additional (proportional) wage income tax, see below.

Below an annual taxable wage income of NOK 24,100, income tax is exempted. In the second tax bracket, which ends at NOK 186,000, the marginal tax rate is 22.9 per cent. After that the marginal tax rate is 29 per cent up to an income of NOK 267,000, above which the marginal tax rate is 42.2 per cent. Apart from the general allowance of NOK 24,100, we assume a special allowance of NOK 10,000 for the two lowest income classes.

In addition to the progressive wage income tax, workers and firms pay 'social security contributions'. There is, however, no connection between these tax revenues and social security spending or future benefits to retired workers. This

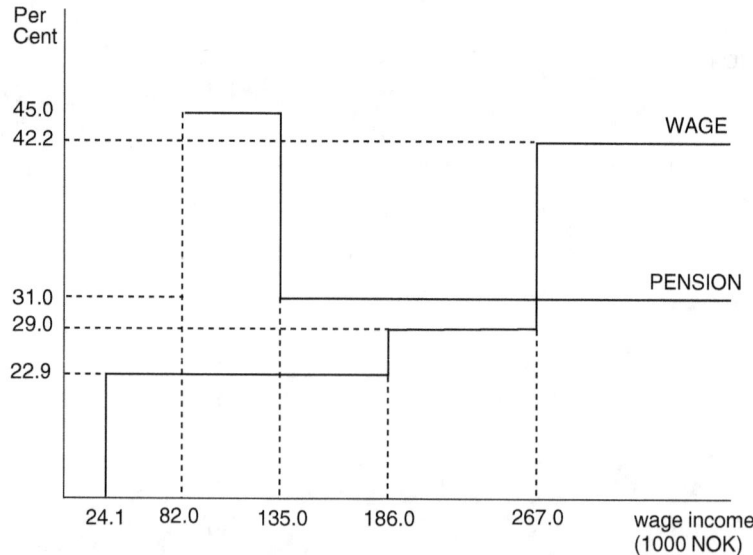

Figure 13.2 Marginal tax rate schedule for wage and pension income.

tax amounts to 7.8 per cent of wage income above NOK 24,100. Employers' contributions (the payroll tax rate) vary across regions in Norway, being lowest in the northern part of the country. The maximum rate is 14 per cent. To simplify, we assume an aggregate contribution rate of 16 per cent levied on all wage income.

Pensions are tax exempted up to the minimum pension of NOK 82,000. Then the marginal tax rate increases to 45 per cent up to NOK 135,000 and falls again to 31 per cent for additional pension income.

The proportional taxation of capital income involves an exemption level for low capital income. In the model, the capital income tax rate is 20 per cent.[5] The Norwegian government also taxes wealth progressively. However, private housing is valued far below market values for wealth tax purposes. Below NOK 120,000, wealth tax is exempt. Above that, the wealth tax is 1.1 per cent up to NOK 235,000. Then the marginal tax rate increases to 1.3 per cent up to NOK 530,000, after which the marginal wealth tax is 1.5 per cent. In the model, we simply assume that the first NOK 200,000 of wealth are tax exempted. Above that level, the wealth tax rate is 1.1 per cent. Norwegian firms have to pay a corporate income tax after deducting dividends from the tax base, that is, a full imputation system. In the model, we only allow 70 per cent subtraction of dividends in order to get a realistic corporate tax revenue in our calibration. We also assume that the firms finance 30 per cent of their investment by corporate debt and the rest by retained earnings (i.e. no share issues).

The last item on the revenue side is consumption taxes. In the model, we specify the path of surpluses $(B_{t+1} - B_t)$ exogenously and adjust the consumption tax rate in each period accordingly. In the baseline simulation, the surplus is 5 per cent of GDP until 2010 and then decreases linearly to zero by 2030.

2.3 Calibration

For a given set of endowments and parameters that describe preferences, technology, population structure and the fiscal system, the model can be solved numerically. In the original Auerbach–Kotlikoff model, the initial equilibrium is a steady state due to the time-invariant population growth rate. Due to the time-variant population growth rate, the baseline path of the present model is not a steady state growth path. In order to compute this baseline path, Auerbach *et al.* (1989) start in a steady state with a stable population and then change the population growth rate each year until they arrive at a demographic structure which approximates that of the base year. Consequently, they need a 75-year-long transition before they arrive at a realistic demographic structure. In the present model, we adopt a different and more efficient method.

First, we compute in a separate simulation an artificial steady state where we apply the parameters and fiscal rules of the base year. Then we endow each household of our base year with the assets and pension rights from this simulation. This allows us to compute immediately the base year equilibrium and the baseline path of the economy for a given realistic demographic structure.

Since we assume a stable population structure in the long run, the model converges to a steady state.

Our specific preference and technology parameters are available upon request. They are mainly in line with the values chosen by Auerbach and Kotlikoff (1987: 50). In order to distinguish the five different lifetime income classes, we have to specify the parameters of the respective human capital profiles. Due to lack of data, we simply assume the same shape of these profiles as in Auerbach and Kotlikoff (1987: 52). Furthermore, we normalise the level of the lowest class to unity and assume that the levels of the following quintiles are 1.3, 2.0, 2.5 and 3.3 respectively. Hence, the endowment of the top quintile is 230 per cent higher than the endowment of the lowest income group. We next turn to the calibration of the population. As explained above, each household lives exactly 75 years and the annual exogenous population growth rates are chosen to capture the demographic structure of the following years of the transition, starting from the demographic structure in 1995. Table 13.1 compares the model projection with the official population projection of the recent Long Term Program of the government.

In the model we assume that the population growth rate approaches zero during the course of the next 15 years and remains zero after 2010. Since the model individuals do not die before age 75, the total population size is slightly above the official projections during the transition, but approaches the official forecast in the long run. On the other hand, the dependency ratios of the model fit the official ones very well (see Table 13.1). Nevertheless, one should keep in mind that the model is not able to account for people older than 75 years. Moreover, the model does not capture increased longevity in the future.

Table 13.2 describes the initial equilibrium and compares it with the corresponding numbers from official statistics. Comparing the two columns of Table 13.2, it is obvious that domestic real investment is too low in our calibration while private consumption is too high. This is due to the fact that we do not include technical progress. Therefore, in steady state (and zero population and labour-input growth), investment is only replacement investment which amounts to 7 per cent of the capital stock. Assuming a capital-output ratio of 1.8, investment amounts to about 12 per cent of GDP.

Table 13.1 Population projections

	1995	2005	2015	2025	2035	2050
Population (mill.)						
Official*	4.37	4.58	4.74	4.92	5.04	5.07
Model	4.37	4.64	4.91	5.10	5.12	5.12
Dependency ratio						
Official*	0.243	0.240	0.318	0.352	0.380	0.337
Model	0.248	0.247	0.315	0.387	0.402	0.375

*Source: Ministry of Finance, Norway.

Note: Dependency ratio is defined as the ratio of those aged 60–75 to those aged 21–59.

Table 13.2 Macroeconomic structure in the base year 1995 (per cent of output)

	Calibration	Norway (Mainland)
Expenditures on GPD (in % of GPD)		
Private consumption	65.7	58.0
Government consumption	25.8	24.6
Gross fixed investment	12.3	21.2
Net export	−3.8	−3.8
General government indicators (in % of GDP)		
Net government assets	164.6	164.6
Income from capital and wealth	10.7	10.7
Tax revenues		
Labour income tax	14.8	8.8
Indirect taxes	11.4	22.5
Social security contributions	11.2	10.1
Capital and corporate income tax	2.6	3.9
Wealth and pension tax	1.7	1.6
Pension outlays	6.8	5.3
Other transfers	14.8	7.5
Surplus	5.0	5.0
Net foreign assets	185.8	185.8
Interest rate (in %)	6.5	—

Neither does the fiscal structure in the benchmark match exactly the 1995 base year statistics. One of the deviations between the two columns in Table 13.2 pertains to the labour income tax revenues that are higher in the model than in the base year. The main reason for this deliberate deviation is that we tried to replicate a realistic distribution of taxable income in the model, while at the same time all individuals between age 20 and age 61 are working. Although more than 30 per cent of households pay no taxes since their income is below the exemption level of NOK 28,100, the model's aggregate average wage tax rate is fairly high (23.2 per cent), while the aggregate marginal tax rate is 34.4 per cent. Another factor contributing to high tax revenues in the model is deductions for interest payments, which are underestimated in the model.[6]

We now turn to the baseline (before reform) growth path of the economy during the transition to steady state, see Table 13.3. The last column in Table 13.3 is the consumption tax rate, which adjusts over time to satisfy the exogenous government asset growth path. We assume that in the baseline simulation, the annual surplus of the government is 5 per cent of GDP until 2010 and then decreases linearly to zero by 2030. This is broadly consistent with an economic policy which aims at avoiding increased tax burdens on future generations. According to Table 13.3 such a policy warrants a considerable accumulation of foreign assets (column 5). Looking more closely at the transition, we see that labour supply increases from 1995 to 2000 and then decreases again when the baby boom generations start to retire. The domestic capital stock increases by

Table 13.3 Baseline growth path (percentage deviation from base year)

Year	Labour	Capital	GDP	Private consump.	Foreign assets	Gov. assets	Consump. tax rate
1995	0.0	0.0	0.0	0.0	0.0	0.0	17.3
2000	7.0	5.8	6.7	10.2	14.6	11.9	16.8
2010	6.5	11.0	7.9	15.9	41.4	36.7	18.0
2020	0.9	10.5	3.8	19.5	65.7	58.9	19.6
2030	−2.0	8.7	1.2	20.7	70.7	66.7	18.5
2050	−0.5	8.5	2.1	19.5	62.6	60.6	14.5
2100	1.5	11.0	4.4	24.5	68.3	57.1	17.4
∞	1.6	11.2	4.5	24.3	67.2	56.9	17.4

more than labour because the net real rate of return from domestic capital in the base year was assumed to be slightly above the world real rate of interest. Private consumption increases considerably during the transition. This is mainly due to the ageing of the population.

3   Simulation experiments

We assume that all pension reforms are announced at the beginning of year 1996 without affecting the base year equilibrium. In all experiments, the consumption tax rate is used to satisfy the flow budget constraint of the government, given the exogenous path of government surpluses as a percentage of GDP. In the first experiment we assume that the government announces a new pension formula for all persons retiring in year 2000 and afterwards. The pensions of the latter are a weighted average of a flat minimum pension of NOK 82,000 and the pension they would have received under the old system. Since the phase-in period is 40 years, the first generation to receive only the minimum pension is the cohort retiring in 2040. The generation retiring in 2020, for example, becomes entitled to pensions, which are exactly half of the sum of the minimum pension and the pensions they would receive in the old earnings-related system. We shall refer to this experiment as the 'base case' because no other changes in fiscal instruments take place, except the endogenous consumption tax rate.

In the second experiment, we retain the same pension reform as in the base case, but reduce the payroll tax rate permanently from 16 to 14 per cent in year 2000. Since the growth path of government assets is not changed, the consumption tax rate increases. The third experiment adds a slowdown in the growth of government assets to experiment 2. Specifically, we assume that the government surplus is reduced linearly from 2005 to 2025. In other words, the process of elimination of the surplus starts and ends five years earlier than in the base case.

Finally, the fourth experiment (Accelerated privatization) builds on the third, but accelerates the phase-in of the new system from 40 to 20 years. Therefore, a person who retires in 2010 already receives half of the pension from the new flat scheme and half from the old. The generation retiring in 2020 (born 1959) is now the first to receive the minimum pension only.

3.1 Macroeconomic effects

Table 13.4 reports the macroeconomic consequences of the four simulation experiments. In the base case experiment (column 1), labour supply, the capital stock and GDP all increase only slightly but permanently compared to the baseline growth path. Lower public spending on pensions permits a lower consumption tax rate. The pension reform increases the incentives for future workers to save more. This generates higher capital income and wealth tax revenues that permit a further reduction in the steady state consumption tax rate. Increased saving leads to a build-up of foreign assets in the long run. Therefore, aggregate consumption increases significantly more than GDP in the long run.

In the second experiment (column 2), the payroll tax cut (combined with an increase in consumption taxes) stimulates labour supply more than in the base case simulation, both in the short and long run. This also boosts investment in fixed capital, increasing aggregate output and private consumption compared to the base case. Increased investment and consumption in the short and medium run generate a reduction in foreign assets. In the long run we see that both private consumption and foreign assets are larger than in the base case.

In the third simulation experiment (column 3), the growth of government assets is reduced on top of the pension reform. Compared to the previous experiment, the consumption tax rates can be reduced in the first phase of the transition. Lower consumption taxes increase private consumption and labour supply. Later on, the consumption tax rate rises above the previous level since revenues from government wealth are much lower now. This negative wealth effect reduces leisure and consumption demand. The increase in labour supply generates a higher capital stock and aggregate output in the steady state.

Finally, in the fourth experiment (column 4), the pension reform is accelerated. Otherwise the fiscal experiment is identical to the previous one. Consequently, the long run equilibrium is very similar to the one from the third experiment. During the transition, the faster decline in pension-spending permits lower consumption taxes than in the third experiment. While the former stimulates labour supply, the latter dampens labour supply. In the early transition the pension reduction dominates and consequently labour supply and output increase. Later on, the faster reduction in consumption taxes dominates and therefore labour supply is reduced compared to the third experiment.

3.2 Intergenerational welfare and distribution

Next we turn to the welfare consequences for different households of the four simulation experiments. Table 13.5 reports the welfare and efficiency effects for a selection of generations, aggregated over the five income groups. All numbers in the tables are in terms of percentage change in remaining lifetime income.

Table 13.4 Macroeconomic effects of pension reforms (in per cent)

	(1)	(2)	(3)	(4)
Labour input				
2000	0.0	0.2	0.0	0.5
2010	0.0	1.4	1.9	2.5
2030	0.6	1.4	1.2	1.5
2050	0.9	1.6	1.8	1.4
∞	0.3	1.0	1.4	1.4
Capital				
2000	0.0	0.3	0.3	0.4
2010	0.1	1.1	1.2	1.5
2030	0.4	1.4	1.4	1.7
2050	0.8	1.5	1.7	1.5
∞	0.3	1.1	1.4	1.4
GDP				
2000	0.0	0.2	0.1	0.4
2010	0.1	1.3	1.7	2.2
2030	0.5	1.4	1.2	1.6
2050	0.8	1.6	1.8	1.4
∞	0.3	1.0	1.4	1.4
Private consumption				
2000	0.0	0.3	0.4	0.5
2010	0.0	0.8	1.7	1.9
2030	0.2	1.6	0.5	2.0
2050	1.6	3.2	1.8	2.5
∞	2.6	4.4	2.8	2.8
Foreign assets	−0.2	−4.4	−5.1	−4.6
2010	−0.7	−0.6	−4.9	−1.0
2030	3.4	11.6	−5.0	8.2
2050	15.9	26.5	4.0	12.2
∞	27.6	39.1	14.8	15.2
Government assets				
2000	0.0	−0.1	−0.1	−0.1
2010	0.1	0.5	−3.3	−3.0
2030	0.2	1.2	−24.2	−23.9
2050	0.2	1.2	−23.3	−22.9
∞	0.1	1.1	−22.8	−22.5
Consumpt. tax rate[7]				
2000	0.0	0.9	0.9	0.6
2010	0.0	1.2	−0.6	−1.1
2030	−0.6	0.3	2.5	−0.6
2050	−3.2	−2.3	−0.2	−0.8
∞	−4.0	−3.2	−1.1	−1.2

A precise explanation of how welfare and efficiency is defined and measured when the change in policy is not marginal is found in Fehr (1999: 75). Basically, the efficiency effects are derived from an artificial transition path where each generation is compensated (by virtual lump sum transfers or taxes) for the income

Table 13.5 Intergenerational welfare changes (in per cent)

Year of birth	(1) Base case		(2) Payroll tax reduction		(3) Payroll tax/ surplus reduction		(4) Accelerated privatization	
	Welfare	Effic.	Welfare	Effic.	Welfare	Effic.	Welfare	Effic.
1935	0.00	0.00	−0.29	0.02	−0.17	0.03	−0.02	0.03
1955	0.03	0.00	0.07	0.16	0.19	0.20	0.42	0.22
1965	0.05	0.00	0.27	0.22	0.32	0.23	0.12	0.29
1976	0.10	0.01	0.44	0.25	0.43	0.25	0.42	0.31
1980	−0.20	0.02	0.26	0.35	0.23	0.34	0.59	0.41
1990	−0.06	0.05	0.48	0.41	0.31	0.35	0.79	0.46
2020	0.70	0.24	1.27	0.60	0.58	0.39	0.83	0.46
∞	0.97	0.33	1.57	0.69	0.90	0.49	0.91	0.49

effects of the considered fiscal reform. To simplify the presentation and to focus on the most important effects, we present only the results for eight generations. The oldest generation (1935) is born before the Second World War. We consider two baby boom generations (born 1955 and 1965 respectively) and three younger ones who are either 20 years old when the reform is announced (born 1976), or enter the labour market when the reform is about to be implemented or already working (born 1980 and 1990). Finally, two future generations born in 2020 and the final steady state (∞) represent those who enter the labour market after the reform is phased-in.

We see from column 1 (the base case) that the 1935 generation is not affected by the reform. This is also the case for those born before 1935. Also future generations benefit from the pension reform for familiar reasons. It is remarkable that even the 1976 generation gains from the reform. It definitely loses in terms of the present value of future pensions, but this is more than compensated by lower consumption taxes during its entire lifetime. Among the generations in between, the older benefit (the 1955, 1965 and 1977 generations) and the younger lose, that is, those born from 1980 onwards. The latter lose more from the expected decline in future pensions than from lower consumption taxes.

The second column of Table 13.5 reports the efficiency gains. They are mainly due to the long run reduction of the consumption tax rate. Therefore, the efficiency gain is zero for the oldest generations and strongest for future generations. For the others, the efficiency gain is very small.

Turning to the payroll tax cut simulation (Table 13.5, column 3 and 4), we see that the 1935 generation loses from the fiscal reform (which, of course, includes the pension reform from the base case). This is due to the increase in consumption taxes, which starts in 1996. In fact, all generations born before 1935 and up to 1945 lose. The other generations gain, future generations more than the presently alive (and born from 1955 and later). The welfare gains for future generations are considerably larger than in the base case. This is due to intergenerational redistribution but also due to efficiency gains. As column 4 reveals, the latter increase strongly compared to the base case since the switch from wage to consumption taxation generates efficiency gains for almost all generations.

In the third simulation experiment (Table 13.5, columns 5 and 6), some of the huge welfare gains for future generations are transferred back to the present cohorts. Also the oldest generations gain more than in the former experiment because the younger overlapping generations consume and save more than previously. They therefore pay more capital income and consumption taxes to the government, permitting a lower consumption tax rate than in the second experiment. Those born in 1935 and before still lose compared to the base case. Again we see that the induced consumption tax rate changes redistribute welfare from younger to older generations which overlap in time.

Finally, in the case of accelerated privatization (Table 13.5, columns 7 and 8), the welfare of those born around 1965 is reduced compared to the third experiment. The welfare of the 1976 generation is about the same. The baby boomers are most affected by the accelerated pension reform. The younger and future generations represented in the table benefit due to the induced consumption tax rate effects.

3.3 Welfare and distribution across generations and income groups

In Table 13.6 we turn to the distribution effects within each generation for each of the eight generations considered in Table 13.5. To facilitate the discussion of the main effects, it suffices to look at the first, third and fifth quintiles.

Turning first to the base case, we recall that those born in 1980 and 1990 lose from the pension reform. Table 13.6 shows that the losers are in the high-income group (quintile 5). In the latter income group, those born between 1980 and 2005 lose from the reform. In addition to the fifth quintile, the members of the fourth quintile of the 1980 and 1990 generations also lose (not shown in the Table). On the other hand, the three lowest income groups increase their welfare even though some of them lose in terms of lower present values of future pensions. This is due to the fact that the minimum pension represents a larger percentage of their pensions. Therefore, for the low- and middle-income groups the benefits from lower consumption taxes outweigh the welfare effect of reduced future pensions. Future generations of low- and middle-income earners also benefit relatively more than the high-income groups. Since their respective efficiency gains are lower, this must be mainly due to intragenerational redistribution.

The payroll tax cut simulation increases aggregate welfare for all generations born after 1935. As Table 13.6 (columns 3 and 4) shows, this is true for all income groups. The table also shows that the lowest income group of the two baby boom generations loses. This is also the case for the second income quintile (not shown). Therefore, the isolated effect of the payroll tax cut (and the endogenous increase in consumption taxes) is to tilt the intragenerational welfare distribution from low-income to high-income groups for young workers in the

Table 13.6 Household welfare changes (in per cent)

Year of birth	(1) Base case		(2) Payroll tax reduction		(3) Payroll tax/ surplus reduction		(4) Accelerated privatization	
	Welfare	Effic.	Welfare	Effic.	Welfare	Effic.	Welfare	Effic.
1. quintile								
1935	0.00	0.00	−0.32	0.01	−0.19	0.02	−0.05	1.02
1955	0.04	0.00	−0.23	0.05	−0.18	0.07	0.18	0.08
1965	0.06	0.00	−0.12	0.07	−0.06	0.07	0.28	0.10
1976	0.11	0.01	−0.01	0.08	0.00	0.06	0.36	0.10
1980	0.15	0.01	0.05	0.10	0.05	0.07	0.46	0.12
1990	0.31	0.03	0.29	0.13	0.13	0.08	0.68	0.14
2020	1.19	0.12	1.20	0.21	0.40	0.07	0.71	0.11
∞	1.53	0.18	1.57	0.28	0.79	0.13	0.80	0.13
3. quintile								
1935	0.00	0.00	−0.32	0.02	−0.18	0.03	−0.03	0.03
1955	0.04	0.00	0.00	0.14	0.14	0.16	0.39	0.19
1965	0.06	0.00	0.18	0.17	0.23	0.16	0.55	0.21
1976	0.11	0.01	0.34	0.21	0.34	0.19	0.68	0.25
1980	0.15	0.02	0.48	0.26	0.45	0.23	0.85	0.30
1990	0.30	0.04	0.72	0.32	0.55	0.24	1.06	0.35
2020	1.11	0.23	1.56	0.50	0.82	0.27	1.09	0.34
∞	1.41	0.33	1.89	0.60	1.17	0.38	1.18	0.38
5. quintile								
1935	0.00	0.00	−0.26	0.02	−0.15	0.03	0.00	0.03
1955	0.03	0.00	0.19	0.23	0.29	0.27	0.48	0.30
1965	0.05	0.00	0.43	0.30	0.47	0.34	−0.14	0.40
1976	0.09	0.01	0.62	0.38	0.60	0.40	0.30	0.47
1980	−0.47	0.02	0.20	0.52	0.16	0.53	0.49	0.62
1990	−0.34	0.06	0.40	0.60	0.24	0.55	0.66	0.69
2020	0.30	0.29	1.07	0.83	0.48	0.59	0.69	0.68
∞	0.52	0.40	1.32	0.95	0.75	0.72	0.75	0.72

early phase of the transition. This result demonstrates that low-wage groups consume relatively less leisure out of their total income than the high-wage groups. At a later stage the welfare effect is positive even for low-wage workers, however, because in the long run, higher tax revenues from capital income and wealth taxation permit a faster decline in the consumption tax rate than in the base case. In fact, in steady state, all income-groups are better off than in the base case. The efficiency gains are also largest for the high-wage groups. This is natural since the tax wedge in the labour market is much higher for the latter.

Next, we turn to the expansionary fiscal policy simulation (Table 13.6, columns 5 and 6), retaining the payroll tax cut of the second experiment. We see that this policy does not change the income distribution in each generation to any significant extent.

Finally, we look at the fourth experiment in which the pension reform is accelerated by halving the phasing-out time of the earnings-related pension (Table 13.6, columns 7 and 8). This permits a faster decline in the consumption tax rate during the transition, see Table 13.4. It therefore benefits the oldest generations compared to the previous experiment. As we have noted already, this reform hurts young high-wage groups more than low-wage groups because the former are entitled to relatively more earnings-related pensions than the latter.

Table 13.6 shows that the highest wage group of the 1965 generation loses compared to the base case. All the other households benefit both compared to the base case and compared to experiment 3 (except some households in the fourth quintile who are slightly worse off compared to experiment 3). Accelerated privatization is, therefore, clearly beneficial to low- and medium-wage groups of all generations. Even households that lose from the faster pension reform taken in isolation, gain when we take the endogenous reduction in the consumption tax rate into account.

4   Conclusions

A pension reform involving a shift from a PAYG system of old age social security to a funded system is a very complicated process, which could easily hurt the generations that are going to lose entitlements in the old system. Besides the potentially harmful changes in the welfare distribution between different generations, pension reforms could also change the income distribution within each generation in politically or ethically undesirable ways. This is particularly important for welfare states like Norway, where the governments give high priority to income redistribution and social insurance. In most OECD countries, however, the question of private pension funds only pertains to the earnings-related part of the pension, not the minimum pension. In many countries – welfare states in particular – a decent universal minimum pension is supported by a large majority of voters. A pension reform that involves only the earnings-related part of old age pensions is not likely to have dramatic effects if it is phased-in gradually. Our results confirm the intuition that a gradual phase-out of the old system does not have considerable welfare effects even if no generations are compensated for the loss of entitlements in the old earnings-related system (the base case). The most important reason is that all generations benefit from the permanent fall in the consumption tax rate. Consumption taxes decrease both because of the gradual reduction in government spending on pensions and because the extra saving and labour supply generates more government revenues that permit further cuts in the consumption tax rate. Still, if the government reduces its surpluses (or run deficits), it is possible to compensate the generations that are most hurt by the reform itself. A natural policy is to cut payroll taxes (or wage income taxes) for this purpose (experiment 3). This will however hurt the oldest generations that do not benefit from the tax cut, because the consumption tax rate increases. To avoid this effect, pension income taxation could be cut as well.

Finally, if the phase-out of the old system is accelerated while retaining the payroll tax cut, a better distribution of welfare between old and young generations could be obtained because the consumption tax rate does not have to increase.

The simulation results indicate, however, that an acceleration of the pension reform does not affect the income groups symmetrically. In fact, the upper income groups lose relatively more from the reform than the lower income groups because the share of earnings-related pensions in total pensions is much lower for the latter income groups.

Notes

1 A paper by Raffelhüschen and Risa (1995) analyses pension reforms using a calibrated overlapping generations model of the Norwegian economy, but neither focuses on the ageing problem nor on different income groups.
2 Future government revenues from the oil industry are however uncertain and petroleum wealth estimates are sensitive to the discount rate. The estimate of the government's petroleum wealth is also crucial for Norway's fiscal balance in the generational accounting sense, see Steigum and Gjersem (1999).
3 Workers in the public sector (both central and local government) receive somewhat more generous pension benefits than the schedule illustrated in Figure 13.1. For simplicity, we do not distinguish between pensions to employees in the public and private sector, however.
4 In the model we assume for simplicity that after 61, the marginal tax rate on labour income is 60 per cent. This represents in a crude way the disincentives to work when old.
5 For technical reasons the tax rate is somewhat lower than 28 per cent. The exemption level is NOK 20,000.
6 Home ownership is widespread in Norway. Households hardly pay any taxes on the implicit capital income from home ownership, but can deduct all interest payments (at the flat rate of 28) from their taxable income.
7 Percentage points.

References

Auerbach, A. J. and Kotlikoff, L. J. (1987) *Dynamic Fiscal Policy*, Cambridge: Cambridge University Press.

Auerbach, A. J., Kotlikoff, L. J., Hageman, R. P. and Nicoletti, G. (1989) 'The economic dynamics of an ageing population: The case of four OECD countries', *OECD Economic Studies*, 12, 97–130.

Broer, D. P. and Westerhout, E. M. W. T. (1997) 'Pension policies and lifetime uncertainty in an applied general equilibrium model', in: Broer, D. P. and Lassila, J. (eds), *Pension Policies and Public Debt in Dynamic CGE Models*, Heidelberg: Physica Verlag, 110–38.

Chaveau, T. and Loufir, R. (1997) 'The future of public pensions in seven major economies', in: Broer, D. P. and Lassila, J. (eds), *Pension Policies and Public Debt in Dynamic CGE Models*, Heidelberg: Physica Verlag, 16–73.

Fehr, H. (1999) *Welfare Effects of Dynamic Tax Reforms*, Tuebingen: Mohr Siebeck.

Fehr, H. (2000) 'Pension reform during the demographic transition', *Scandinavian Journal of Economics*, 102(3), 419–43.

Kotlikoff, L. J., Smetters, K. and Walliser, J. (1998) 'Social security, privatization and progressivity', *American Economic Review, Papers and Proceedings*, 88, 137–41.

Miles, D. (1999) 'Modelling the impact of demographic change upon the economy', *Economic Journal*, 109, 1–36.

Raffelhüschen, B. and Risa, A. E. (1995) 'Reforming social security in a small open economy', *European Journal of Political Economy*, 11, 469–85.

Steigum, E. (1993) 'Accounting for long-run effects of fiscal policy by means of computable overlapping generations models', in: Honkapohja, S. and Ingberg, M. (eds), *Macroeconomic Modelling and Policy Implications*, Amsterdam: North-Holland, 45–67.

Steigum, E. and Gjersem, C. E. (1999) 'Generational Accounting and depletable natural resources: The case of Norway', in: Auerbach, A. J., Kotlikoff, L. J. and Leibfritz, F. (eds), *Generational Accounting Around the World*, Chicago: University of Chicago Press, 369–95.

14 Social security in an ageing society

An applied general equilibrium analysis

D. Peter Broer

1 Introduction

Population ageing is a major topic in the policy debate. Projections by the United Nations show that for the OECD area as a whole the share of the elderly (people at age 65 or above) will increase from 15 per cent in 1990 to 22 per cent in 2040. At the same time, the old-age dependency ratio (the ratio of the elderly to the working-age population) is expected to rise from 20 per cent to 37 per cent. For developing countries, a similar change is expected at a later stage (United Nations 1994). Rising dependency ratios imply a decline in the size of the tax base. At the same time, the rising share of the elderly increases the outlays for health care and social security. In OECD countries, social security is largely on a pay-as-you-go (PAYG) basis, that is, the currently active population pays for the pensions of the retired population. Without a substantial cut in public expenditure programmes and transfers, the ageing process will cause a substantial increase in the net tax burden for younger generations.

The budgetary consequences of ageing have received widespread attention. However, next to generating a different tax burden for old and young generations, the ageing process will also affect the relative scarcity of production factors. On the transition path, the decline in the labour force will cause a reduction in labour supply that will depress investment and the demand for capital. On the other hand, life-cycle saving will, during the first stage of the transition, be at a maximum. Therefore, OECD countries may expect a relative scarcity of labour during the transition. To the extent that ageing is synchronized over countries, international capital flows will not be able to equalize capital returns over time, which will lead to a movement along the factor price frontier, boosting wages and depressing interest rates (Auerbach and Kotlikoff 1987; Börsch-Supan 1996; Chauveau and Loufir 1997; Miles 1999).

The intergenerational distribution is affected in several ways by a movement in factor prices. On the one hand, rising wages should lead to a partial restoration of the intergenerational balance. On the other hand, rising production costs of health care and wage indexation of pensions may lead to further increases in contribution rates for health care and social security. The net effect of factor price movements on the distribution is therefore difficult to ascertain a priori.

The distributional impact of the existing system of social security in the presence of population ageing has led to a reconsideration of its merits. As pointed out by Aaron (1966), the rate of return on PAYG social security is the population growth rate plus the real growth of wages. This rate of return must be compared with that of a funded system, the rate of interest. In the 1960s and 1970s, the rate of return on PAYG systems easily exceeded that on a funded system. In the 1980s and 1990s, the ranking was reversed. In the next century, a lower population growth rate lowers the return on a PAYG system, making a funded system more attractive. Many proposals to switch to funding have been made in recent years, for example, Feldstein (1995, 1996), Börsch-Supan (1998).

A transition to a funded system requires that some generations pay both the PAYG contribution rate for the pensions of the currently retired, as well as the contribution to the new funded system. Therefore a difference between the rates of return on a PAYG versus a funded system in itself is not an indication of a possible efficiency gain. What it does is primarily to affect the size of the redistribution between generations. To enable a Pareto-improving transition, the funded system must be financed in such a way that a distortion can be removed simultaneously.

The issue of a Pareto-improving conversion from a PAYG system to a funded system has been investigated by Raffelhüschen (1993), Breyer and Straub (1993), Broer *et al.* (1994) and Kotlikoff (1996). From these analyses, it appears that such a transition is feasible if it reduces the distortion of the labour supply decision sufficiently to enable current and future generations to pay off the burden of the PAYG system from the reduced deadweight loss. A limitation of these models is that they assume that households differ only by age. Intragenerational heterogeneity is introduced by Kotlikoff *et al.* (1998) and by Fehr (1999). From these studies it appears that a Pareto-improving transition is more difficult to achieve if intragenerational heterogeneity is also taken into account. Different income groups are affected differently by alternative financing modes of the reform, and have different tax-benefit linkages.

In this chapter, I investigate the issue of a transition to a funded system for the Netherlands in relation to the ageing of the population. In Broer *et al.* (1994), we showed that such a transition would be Pareto-improving. In this chapter I take up the same issue, but with intragenerational heterogeneity included. In comparison with both our previous work and the study by Kotlikoff *et al.* (1998), I use a calibration of the model to a baseline solution that includes the projected ageing of the population, that is, outside of the steady state. As pointed out above, the demographic transition produces its own redistribution of welfare across generations. The current system of taxation and social security in the Netherlands implies a substantial burden on future generations, with rising contribution rates for social security and health care. To judge the fairness of a social security reform, this burden should properly be looked at in conjunction with the redistributive effects of the social security reform. This means that a reform that in itself would harm certain generations may nevertheless be considered equitable if considered together with the distributive effects of the demographic shock.

Whether such a reform is also politically sustainable depends on the voting behaviour of the electorate. I investigate the feasibility of the reforms under simple majority rule.

This chapter investigates to what extent a transition towards a funded system improves the intergenerational balance by considering two reforms: first, a reduction in PAYG benefits, and second the creation of a buffer fund to smooth PAYG contribution rates. The first option comes close to the international privatization literature, whereby PAYG saving is replaced by private life-cycle saving, but it incorporates an idiosyncrasy of the Dutch pension system, that provides for a built-in compensation of existing elderly. This occurs through the supplementary occupational pension schemes that apply for most households participating in the labour market. The second option takes up the funding issue. On the transition path, PAYG contribution rates rise, which creates both an intertemporal labour supply distortion and a redistribution over generations. A transition to a funded system aims at rectifying both. The question is whether the efficiency gain outweighs the distributional burden for current generations. As a partial answer to this question, the percentage of voters that benefit from the reform is calculated.

The rest of the chapter is organized as follows: Section 2 presents an overview of the model, Section 3 reviews the calibration procedure, and Section 4 discusses the effects of population ageing for the Dutch economy. Section 5 discusses some policy options to combat the adverse effects of population ageing, and Section 6 offers some conclusions.

2   The model

The model is of the same type as the familiar Auerbach–Kotlikoff (1987) overlapping generations model, adapted for a small open economy. It is an extension of Broer *et al.* (1994) and Broer and Westerhout (1997). It consists of the following sectors: households, a private enterprise sector producing tradables, private health insurance firms, public health insurance (subdivided in two categories), health care, a pension sector (with both a basic and a supplementary pension scheme), a government sector, and a foreign sector. Four markets are distinguished, the labour market, the tradable goods market, the health care market, and the capital market. All markets clear, prices for tradables and capital are determined on world markets through arbitrage; the wage rate and the prices for health care are determined on the domestic markets. A summary description of the main characteristics of the model is given below.

A description of the calibration procedure and a full listing of the equations of the model can be found on the web site for this volume.

Households choose their consumption of goods, health care, and leisure by maximizing expected lifetime utility subject to a lifetime budget constraint and a time constraint per period. Lifetime is uncertain, and the death hazard increases with age. Households insure against this hazard by buying annuities. Preference for the consumption of leisure and health care is age-dependent. Households are free to retire when they choose, but they are eligible for old-age pensions from their sixty-fifth birthday, irrespective of their actual retirement date. Households differ both by age and by productivity (human capital). Productivity is exogenous to the individual household, but it varies by age. The wage level of a household determines whether it contributes to the supplementary pension scheme, and whether it is insured with the public health insurance system or with the private health insurance system. Both transitions define a discontinuity in the marginal tax rate facing the household, the first one upward, and the second one downward. The pension sector consists of two different pension schemes that represent actual pension institutions in the Netherlands. They differ with respect to their financing structure, the formulas that define the benefit levels and their contribution bases. The PAYG scheme provides a flat minimum benefit to residents who are 65 years and older. The contributions to this scheme are levied on the labour and capital income of those below 65 years of age. Residents of age 65 or older are exempt from PAYG contributions. The PAYG contribution rate is fixed and deficits of the PAYG scheme are part of the general government deficit.

The other pension scheme provides benefits that supplement those from the PAYG scheme for retired workers that used to earn wages above the social minimum. This scheme involves capital funding and a partial linkage between contributions and benefits. It is therefore called the funded collective (FC) scheme. Benefits are based on final pay (i.e. the wage prevailing in the year before the household becomes eligible for pension benefits) and are positive only so far as this pay exceeds a threshold linked to the PAYG benefit. The rights to FC benefits depend on the number of hours worked when younger than 65 years. FC contributions are levied on labour income above a certain threshold (the franchise). Contributions to the FC scheme are deductible for both the income tax and PAYG contributions but FC benefits are subject to income taxation. By adjusting its contribution rate, the FC scheme tries to match its assets and its projected benefit obligations to households that are currently participating in the fund. The tradable goods sector uses capital, labour and raw materials to produce goods and services that are freely traded on domestic and international markets at internationally determined prices. Investment in physical capital is subject to internal adjustment costs, which makes it internationally immobile in the short run. Firms issue debt in fixed proportion to the value of their capital, so that the marginal source of finance for investment is retained earnings. The labour input of different productivity types is perfectly substitutable.

The health sector uses only labour to produce health care services. Different productivity types are complementary in production, so that the skill distribution in the health sector is fixed. The form of health care insurance depends on the wage level of the household. Low-productivity households are publicly insured. The public health insurance firm levies both a proportional tax on labour income and a small, nominally fixed, contribution. It reimburses (nearly) all health care expenditures of its clients. The private health insurance sector levies a lump-sum contribution on households. In the model, it reimburses a fixed proportion of the health care expenditures of its clients. Both insurance firms close their budget annually by adjusting their contribution rate.

3   The effects of ageing on economic growth

Figure 14.1 shows the most recent projection of demographics by the Central Statistical Office (CSO) (see de Beer 1999).[1] The population is expected to grow till about 2040 (left *y*-axis). Extrapolating the fertility and mortality rates used by the CSO, the projection implies a small decline in the population thereafter. Shortly afterwards, the share of elderly reaches a maximum of 23 per cent (right *y*-axis). This share then falls off slightly again, but it remains at almost double its present size. The CSO projections also entail assumptions about immigration rates. In the model, these have been balanced with the mortality rates to obtain mortality rates that are slightly *negative* for young households.[2] Hence, immigration is assumed to continue at the rates projected for 2050. The baseline solution assumes that world interest rates are constant and that domestic exogenous variables are either constant, or grow at constant rates, except for the population, which follows the expected demographic path shown in Figure 14.1. In a sense, this baseline solution can therefore be interpreted as the response of the economy to the expected demographic shock. The baseline path has been computed using the income tax rate as a closure variable for the government budget constraint and assuming that government debt as a fraction of GDP at factor costs is kept constant at the calibrated value of 80 per cent. The income tax rate is displayed in Figure 14.2, using the left *y*-axis as a scale.

In the long run, the growth rate of the economy is determined by the rate of technical progress (2 per cent) and the growth rate of the population (−0.15 per cent). On the transition path, the growth rate deviates from this benchmark value

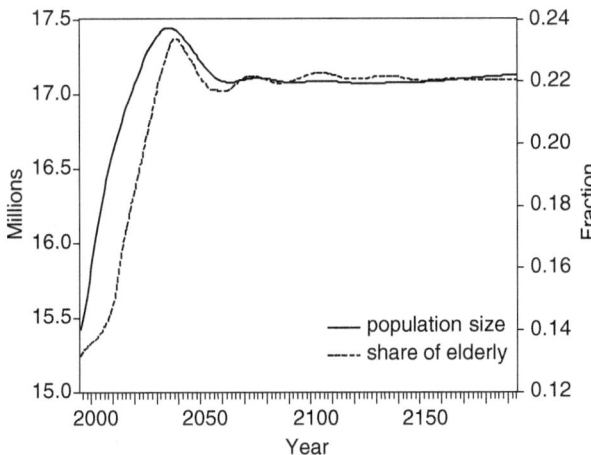

Figure 14.1 Population growth in the Netherlands, 1995–2194.

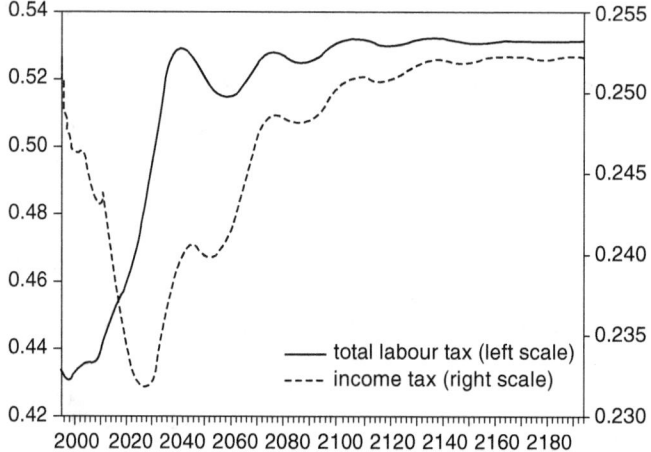

Figure 14.2 Income tax and marginal burden on labour.

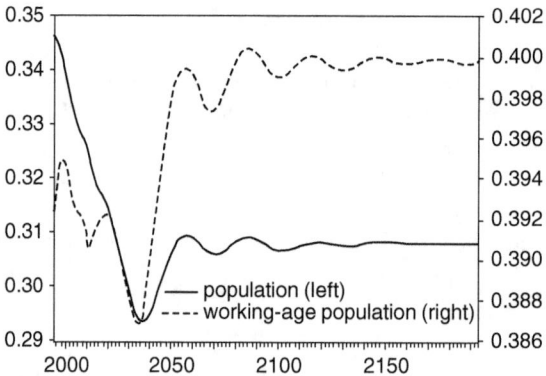

Figure 14.3 Participation rates.

as a result of demographic fluctuations. Figure 14.3 shows the change in the labour market participation rate of the population (values on the left *y*-axis). Overall participation rates fall until about 2035, to recover only partially thereafter. The end result is a fall in participation rates by about 4 per cent points. Obviously, this decline represents the increasing dependency ratio as a result of the ageing of the population. The endogenous part of this shift is largely captured by the participation rate of the working-age population. It appears from Figure 14.3 that after an initial decline, this participation rate is expected to increase somewhat in the second half of the next century. Figure 14.4 shows the consequences of these participation rate shifts for aggregate labour supply and labour supply employed in the tradable goods sector. Initially, labour supply in efficiency

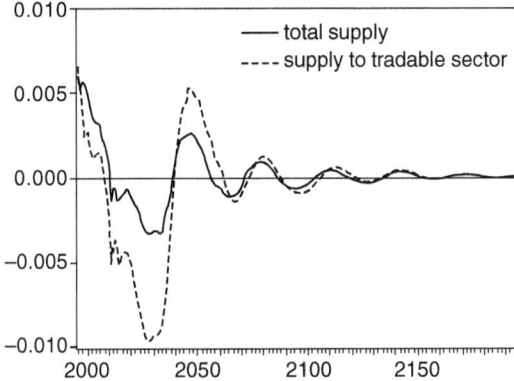

Figure 14.4 Growth of labour supply.

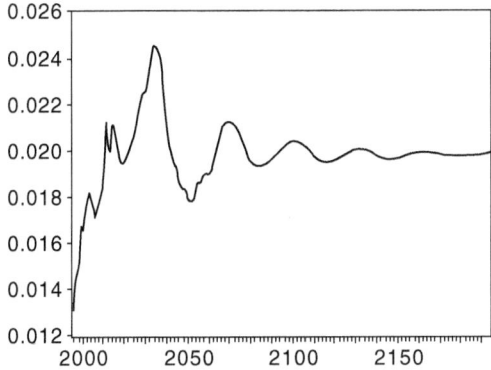

Figure 14.5 Market wage growth.

units grows, because the working-age population grows older, and therefore, more productive. From about 2010 on, these older cohorts retire, and labour supply stagnates. This effect is reinforced by the temporary decline in the participation of the working-age population. The resulting fall in employment in the tradable goods sector is particularly severe. This discrepancy reflects the weight of both government labour demand and labour demand by the health care sector. Government employment is constant as a percentage of the population, and health sector employment actually increases as a result of the ageing process. The result is a shortage of labour in the first half of the next century, which is at its maximum around 2030. This scarcity is also reflected in a sharp peak in wage growth at that time (Figure 14.5).

To explain the changes in labour market participation of the working-age population, we have to consider the development of the tax burden. Initially, total tax receipts grow because of the increase in consumption, that boosts indirect taxes. In addition, the slowdown of wage growth during the first decade is favourable for government expenditures, that are largely indexed on wages. To maintain a constant debt-GDP ratio, income tax rates fall, as shown in Figure 14.2.[3] The total tax burden as a percentage of GDP rises, however (Figure 14.6), which reflects both the decline in the labour income tax base and an increase in age-related government expenditures, namely, disability insurance and health care subsidies.

The decline in labour supply reduces the tax base for the social security contributions just when social security payments increase as a consequence of the ageing of the population. Figure 14.7 shows that the basic PAYG contribution rate increases substantially, by almost 8 per cent points.[4] This rise in the tax burden is reinforced by the increase in the health care contribution rates, shown

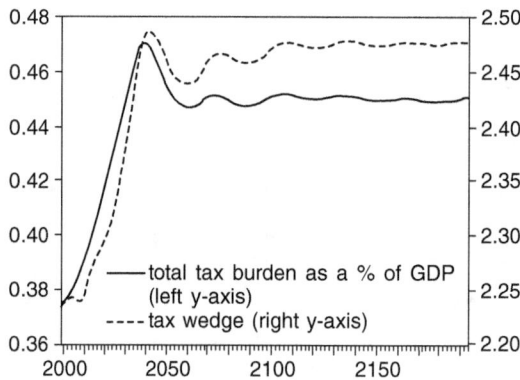

Figure 14.6 Total tax burden as a fraction of GDP.

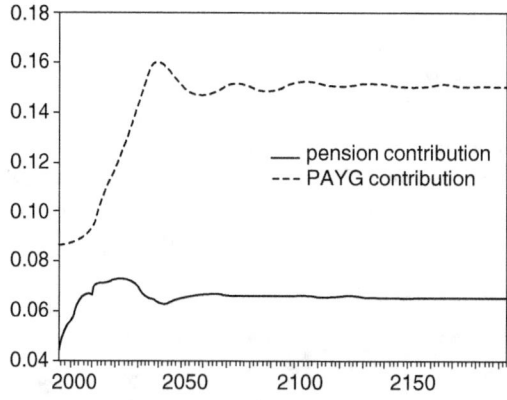

Figure 14.7 Social security contribution rates.

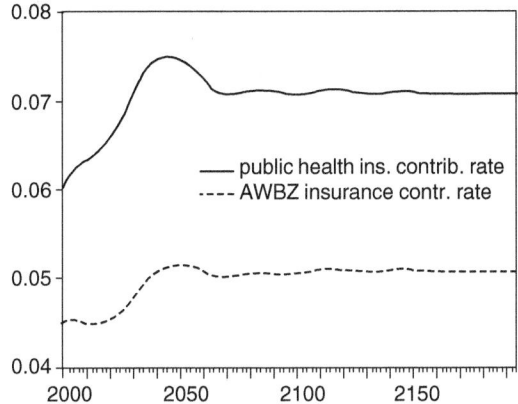

Figure 14.8 Health insurance contribution rates.

in Figure 14.8. The basic causal link for the rise in these rates is the same as for the PAYG premium, an increase in expenditures as a result of population ageing and a decline in the tax base due to the decline in labour supply (note however that the tax base also consists of capital income). The sharp increase in the PAYG contribution rate for the basic pension stands in marked contrast to the insignificant increase in the contribution rate for the (funded) supplementary pension fund. This relative constancy arises from the substantial assets owned by the pension fund in the base period. By legal obligation, these assets are sufficient to cover the accumulated pension rights by households that are currently participating in the fund. A rise in contribution rates must therefore reflect a rise in projected benefit obligations that exceeds the current accumulation rate of the fund. This may occur because of a future acceleration in wage growth, or as a result of a fall in future interest rates (that increase the present value of the obligations). Both possibilities in effect lead to intergenerational redistribution as a consequence of the lack of actuarial fairness of the pension fund. Figure 14.7 shows that a future change in wages leads to an increase in premiums of about 1.5 per cent points.

The propensity to consume reaches a maximum a few years after the peak in the share of elderly, demonstrating the aggregate effect of the life-cycle behaviour of individual households (Figure 14.9). Subsequently the consumption ratio for health care declines less than the consumption ratio of other goods and services, as a result of the extreme age-dependence of health care expenses. The boost of the propensity to consume is preceded by a more short-lived boost in the savings rate, as shown in Figure 14.10. The current account reaches an all-time high of 13 per cent of GDP around 2010, at a time when a large proportion of households are net savers, to fall back to a minimum value of 1 per cent around 2050 because of the retirement of these large cohorts of savers. The current account remains positive however as a result of a substantial surplus on the primary factor account. The trade balance of course shows a substantial deficit in later years. The shortage

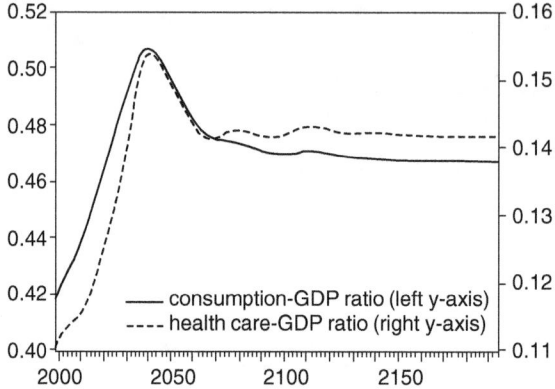

Figure 14.9 Consumption ratios.

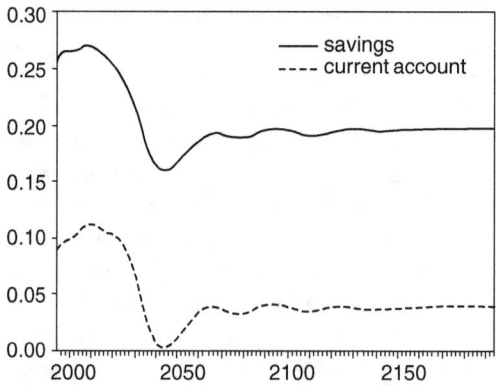

Figure 14.10 Current account surplus and savings as a fraction of GDP.

of labour, which is projected to occur in the first few decades of the next century, has an adverse effect on capital accumulation and output growth. Output growth falls by half a percent compared with the steady-state rate when the ageing process reaches its maximum. Then, as labour supply recovers because of both the demographic swing and the increase in the participation rate of the working-age population, output growth is boosted for over a decade.

The intergenerational distribution that corresponds with this baseline scenario is given in Figure 14.11. The distribution is defined in terms of the compensating variations required to bestow the same lifetime utility on all generations as the 1976 generation (that enters the labour market in 1994), *corrected for technological progress*. This correction is required because successive generations will experience a higher lifetime consumption and utility. To measure the extent of inter-generational redistribution, we must compare the actual utility levels with those on

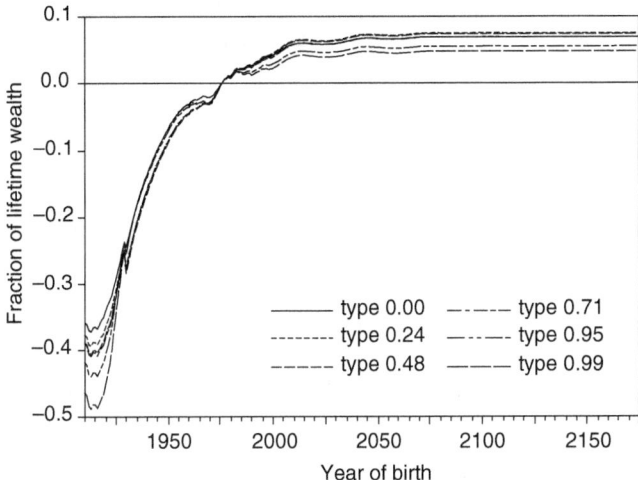

Figure 14.11 Compensating variations per generation, relative to the 1976 generation.

a steady-state growth path. On a steady-state growth path the correction would result in compensating variations equal to zero. Using this correction, the compensating variations in Figure 14.11 show that future generations do considerably worse than the current young generations. Regarding the intragenerational distribution, low-productive households do almost twice as badly as highly productive households. The intergenerational balance quickly worsens until about 2035 (generation 2016), when the ageing shock is maximal. This coincides with the peak in the labour tax burden (see Figure 14.2), and the minimum labour participation ratio (Figure 14.3). Afterwards, the distribution remains fairly stable.

Generations born before 1976 do considerably better. In Figure 14.11, the comparison with the 1976 generation is made in terms of *remaining* lifetime utility, again corrected for technical progress. Generations born around 1930 are on the brink of retirement, so they largely escape the coming rise in social security contribution rates. In comparison with the 1976 generation, this implies a 16 per cent higher net wage over their time in the labour force (corrected for technical progress). The remaining part of the compensating variation is largely due to a different saving profile over the life cycle. Future generations save less, because of a lower net interest rate, and so have comparatively fewer assets and lower remaining lifetime utility than current generations at the same stage of their life. The lower lifetime interest rate of future generations therefore generates an additional source of inequality.[5]

4   Social security reform

The analysis of the effects of the demographic shock identifies several problems. In the baseline projection the main problem is the sharp rise in the tax burden, which causes a pronounced generational imbalance, that can be read from Figure 14.11. Figures 14.2, 14.7 and 14.8 identify the source of this problem in terms of the rise in PAYG social security contributions and health care contributions. Of course, the increasing tax burden produces not only a distribution effect but also an efficiency loss. It is therefore attractive to try to correct both problems at once by a suitable reform of social security. Judging from the baseline projection, the obvious candidate for reform seems to be the PAYG social security system, as it contributes most to the increase in the tax burden.

To investigate these issues in this model, I have computed the effects of two reform measures, namely,

- a reduction in PAYG benefits, partially compensated for by an increase in supplementary pensions,
- a policy of PAYG premium smoothing, that keeps PAYG premiums constant by running an initial surplus.

4.1   A reduction in PAYG benefits

A reduction in PAYG benefits aims at a decrease in the distortionary impact of the PAYG contributions on labour and capital income. Existing generations in the Netherlands are to some extent sheltered from the income effects of a reduction in PAYG benefits, if they have a supplementary pension. The pension fund supplements PAYG benefits to a maximum of 70 per cent of the final wage before retirement, provided that a household has contributed to the fund during its entire working life. Households with a wage higher than the franchise threshold implied by this arrangement therefore receive a higher supplementary pension.

Table 14.1 presents a summary of the macroeconomic effects of this policy measure. The welfare effects for generations and productivity types are given in Figure 14.12.

Table 14.1 Effects of a decrease of 10 per cent in PAYG benefits[6]

	Year	1	10	20	30	40	50	200
L	%	0.13	0.25	0.30	0.30	0.30	0.10	−0.13
K	%	0	0.28	0.44	0.44	0.28	−0.35	−0.95
c	%	−0.55	−0.37	−0.09	0.28	0.65	0.98	1.99
S/Y	D%	0.27	0.48	0.66	0.77	0.92	0.89	0.54
I/Y	D%	0.08	0.03	−0.02	−0.05	−0.15	−0.27	−0.33
TB/Y	D%	0.16	0.27	0.26	0.13	0.11	−0.13	−0.94
A_e	%	0	−1.32	−2.69	−3.94	−5.44	−8.27	−15.6
t_y	D%	0.33	0.25	0.20	0.15	0.06	−0.00	−0.14
w	D%	1.06	0.32	−0.03	−0.17	−0.17	−0.07	−0.10
B_l	D%	−0.73	−0.79	−0.95	−1.13	−1.36	−1.41	−1.35
p_l	%	−0.23	−0.13	−0.06	−0.05	−0.18	−0.40	−0.51

Legenda: L labour, K capital, c consumption, S/Y saving ratio, I/Y investment ratio, TB/Y trade balance ratio, A_e foreign assets, t_y income tax rate, w contribution rate of supplementary pension scheme, B_l PAYG contribution rate levied on labour income of young households, p_l wage rate.

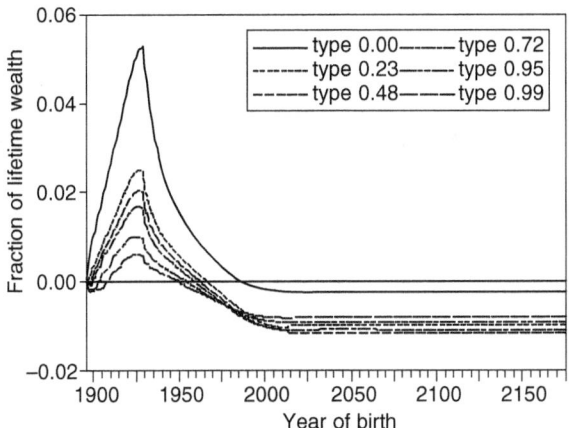

Figure 14.12 Compensating variations for a 10 per cent reduction in PAYG benefits.

Equity and efficiency

Overall, the reform is clearly efficiency-improving. The present value of the aggregate of compensating variations is $-f45$ milliards, 7 per cent of GDP. The efficiency gain results from the decrease in distortionary PAYG contributions and an implicit lump-sum tax on the elderly. Table 14.1 shows that the PAYG contribution rate initially falls by 0.7 per cent points, relative to the baseline solution. In later years it decreases further, to -1.35 per cent points. The PAYG contribution is to some extent replaced by a higher contribution rate from the funded supplementary pension system, at least in the first decade after the reform. However, this contribution is less distortionary, since pension benefits are linked to hours worked. Efficiency also increases due to the lump-sum component in the reform. Low productivity households are not included in the supplementary pension scheme, since their wage is not sufficiently above the PAYG benefit. Following the cut in PAYG benefits, they therefore receive no compensation from the supplementary pension fund, so that for them the reform operates as a lump-sum tax. Figure 14.12 shows that old generations of low-productivity households are indeed much worse off than households of the same age, but higher productivity. Nevertheless, most retired households lose from the reform. Supplementary pensions are indexed on the wage rate, which falls as a result of the increase in labour supply of working-age generations. Also, the income tax rises to compensate for the loss in tax revenues due to the decrease in consumption. In contrast to younger generations, retired generations do not profit from the simultaneous decrease in the PAYG contribution rate.

Macroeconomic effects

Labour supply increases because of the lower burden. Initially, the labour supply response is dampened by the increase in the pension contribution rate (w), that rises because the pension fund has to compensate most retired households for the fall in PAYG benefits. However, this contribution rate is less distortionary, as pension benefits are linked to hours worked. Over time, this rate declines again as the pension fund succeeds in regaining its desired coverage of future obligations. The increase in labour supply boosts investment as well, which gradually restores labour productivity and wages. The reform also stimulates savings, as the PAYG contribution also bears on capital income. This implies that consumption of young households falls initially. Consumption of retired households also falls, as a result of lower lifetime income. Since part of the increase in saving is invested abroad, this implies an initial decrease in the domestic tax base, and a compensating increase in the income tax rate.

The results of this analysis lead to the conclusion that a reform of old-age social security through a reduction in the basic PAYG pension benefits must hurt poor households. They cannot profit from the shelter offered by the funded pension scheme, because their income is already near the minimum level defined by the current PAYG scheme. This problem is unavoidable since the social security system must provide a basic income to all old households, independent of past contributions. Still, even for poor households the welfare losses associated with the reform are considerably less than the redistribution caused by the ageing itself. A comparison of Figures 14.11 and 14.12 shows that the combined effect of ageing and the reform is still beneficial for virtually all current generations.

Only a small fraction of poor households, born around 1976, would be worse off than in the absence of ageing. From an equity point of view, it may be argued that the effects of the shock, ageing, and the policy reform that addresses the shock should be evaluated together. Politically, the reference point is more plausibly the status quo, which includes ageing. This implies that current generations will compare their utility in the benchmark case with that under a proposed policy reform to determine how to vote. Table 14.3 gives the percentage of voters that benefit from the proposal to reduce PAYG benefits, subdivided by productivity type. Not surprisingly, a majority of the high-productivity households gains from the reform. All low-productivity households lose, however. It appears that only 36 per cent of households benefits from the reform, so that it is politically unsustainable.

4.2 Smoothing PAYG contributions

The policy of PAYG contribution rate smoothing has in fact been adopted recently by the Dutch government, by the creation of a buffer fund to save for the expected future increase in premiums. A buffer fund is similar to a policy of government debt reduction but it is not equivalent, due to a difference in the tax base of PAYG contributions and income taxes. PAYG contributions are not paid by retired households. As a result, the creation of a buffer fund implies a larger degree of tax smoothing and a lower distortion on labour, compared with an equal reduction in government debt. This section evaluates the effects of this reform by comparing it with the pre-existing situation of PAYG budgeting, which

Table 14.2 Effects of a transition to contribution rate smoothing for the PAYG
contribution rate

	Year	1	10	20	30	40	50	200
L	%	−1.19	−0.92	0.42	1.17	1.74	0.10	−1.42
K	%	0	0.67	3.34	4.55	4.12	−0.98	−4.48
c	%	−1.66	−1.84	−1.50	−0.94	0.11	1.17	6.77
S/Υ	D%	0.11	1.50	4.16	6.51	8.89	8.75	6.75
I/Υ	D%	0.12	0.41	0.46	0.37	−0.34	−1.11	−1.30
TB/Υ	D%	−0.07	−0.22	0.91	1.42	2.44	1.00	−3.76
A_e	%	0	0.36	0.50	−4.12	−11.8	−25.3	−52.9
t_y	D%	0.42	0.72	0.72	0.72	0.19	−0.06	−0.79
w	D%	1.16	0.26	−0.48	−0.66	−0.47	0.24	0.07
B_l	D%	3.13	2.87	1.26	−0.85	−3.42	−3.94	−3.29
p_l	%	1.59	1.83	2.32	2.22	0.79	−1.05	−1.31

Legenda: See Table 14.1.

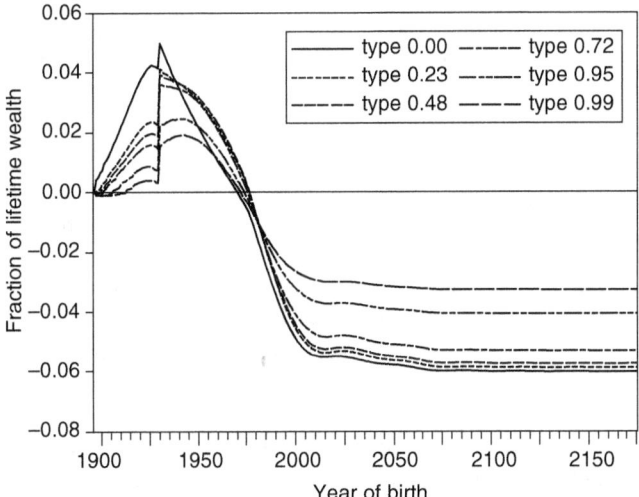

Figure 14.13 Compensating variations for a transition to premium smoothing for the
PAYG fund.

is still taken as the benchmark. Table 14.2 and Figure 14.13 present the effects of
a transition to a constant PAYG contribution rate. To maintain a constant
contribution rate, the PAYG fund must initially run a surplus in view of the
expected future increase in PAYG benefits.

Equity and efficiency

The reform is again efficiency-improving, if measured in terms of the present value
of aggregated compensating variations. The efficiency gain is approximately

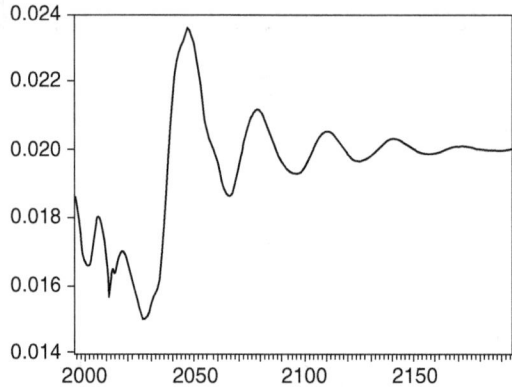

Figure 14.14 Growth rate of GDP per capita.

3 per cent of GDP. Despite the efficiency gain, all generations born before 1970 lose. They have to pay for the creation of the buffer fund through higher PAYG contributions, and they do not live long enough to experience a net benefit. Table 14.2 shows that it takes 30 years for the PAYG contribution rate to fall below the value on the baseline path. Retired households do relatively better than older working-age households, because they escape the higher PAYG contribution rates.

The intragenerational distribution shows a reversal in welfare effects. Poor households that are already retired at the moment of the reform fare comparatively badly, because they depend primarily on income indexed to net wages of working-age households, that is, transfer income and PAYG benefits. Rich households fare better, because the return on capital income falls less, notably because retired households do not pay PAYG contributions on their interest receipts. For future generations, this pattern is reversed. Now poor households do better, because the large decrease in the PAYG contribution rate boosts the net wage. Because of indexation, this increases the value of both PAYG benefits and transfers. Supplementary pension benefits are indexed on the gross wage rate, however. Households with a comparatively large interest in the supplementary pension scheme therefore profit less from the reduction in contribution rates.

A comparison of the distributional consequences of a transition to funding to those of population ageing shows that the net effect of ageing *and* social security reform is still beneficial to existing generations. While the total efficiency gain of funding PAYG security is less than that of the previous reform, privatization, the adverse effects for poor households are also less, and the gains for future generations are larger. The result of a comparison between both reforms therefore depends very much on one's point of reference.

Table 14.3 Percentage of current generations that benefit from a pension reform

Reform measure	Productivity type						
	0	0.24	0.48	0.71	0.95	0.99	All
A cut in PAYG contributions	0%	32%	41%	45%	50%	54%	36%
Smoothing of PAYG contributions	10%	2%	2%	3%	7%	10%	4%

Macroeconomic effects

To create the buffer fund the PAYG fund needs to run a surplus by raising its contribution rate. Long-term sustainability is achieved at a rate of 11.8 per cent, an initial increase of 3.1 per cent. On the intratemporal substitution margin, this leads to a reduction of labour supply and a fall in consumption. Because the funding leads to a stable contribution rate, future tax burdens are lower than current ones. On the intertemporal margin, this leads to a further reduction in labour supply. The effect on saving is ambiguous, however: the initial high PAYG contribution rate discourages saving, but the expected future decline in this rate encourages saving. The net result is a savings rate that is initially slightly larger. Table 14.2 shows that during the first decade after the reform the effect of the increase in funding on economic activity is negative, with lower employment and investment, and higher tax rates. It takes 30 years for the PAYG contribution rate to fall below its level in the baseline. After that, the economy quickly moves to a higher growth path, and 40 years from the start of the buffer fund employment is 1.7 per cent higher than it would have been without the reform.

This analysis shows that a switch to funding of the PAYG fund is efficiency-improving, but it takes a long time before the full benefits of the reform can be reaped, because the transition itself temporarily slows down the economy. In view of this required adjustment time, speedy implementation of the reform is important, to be able to realize the expansionary effects before the period of maximal ageing closes in.

As it takes a long time before the benefits of this reform can be reaped, most members of current generations suffer a welfare loss upon implementation of the reform. Table 14.3 shows that only 4 per cent of the current electorate benefits from the reform, all young households. In view of this result, it is difficult to explain why the reform has actually been implemented, if not for altruistic motives towards future generations.[7]

5 Conclusions

This chapter has studied the effects of the imminent ageing of the population on the system of social security and health care in the Netherlands, using a dynamic overlapping generation model, calibrated on a projected demographic path. The paper measures the distributional impact of the social security system on future generations in terms of a comparison of their lifetime utility. It concludes that future generations suffer the equivalent of some 5–8 per cent loss in lifetime wealth because of the redistributive effects generated by the impact of ageing on the social security and health care systems. Low- and mid-income groups are hit in particular.

The chapter identifies the PAYG social security system as the largest single distortionary influence on economic growth. PAYG contribution rates may rise by some 7 per cent points. This gives rise to large potential efficiency gains from a reform of social security. A cut in PAYG social security of 10 per cent leads to an aggregate welfare gain of 8 per cent of one year's GDP, and a redistribution of welfare towards future generations. Losses of most current generations are fairly small, as they are sheltered to some extent from the PAYG cut by the existing supplementary occupational pension schemes. Low-income groups are hit particularly hard, however, as they face not only the full size of the cut, but also an initial fall in wages, to which their social security benefits are indexed.

A transition to a funded system of social security, by means of a buffer fund to smooth contribution rates, results in an aggregate efficiency gain of 3.5 per cent of GDP. It appears that for current generations this gain is nullified by the long transition period that is required. This reform therefore also redistributes welfare to future generations. Welfare losses to current generations are larger than with a cut in social security, but welfare gains to future generations are also larger. Again, current low-income households suffer most, however, future low-income households profit more than others because this reform results in a higher after-tax wage.

A comparison of the combined distribution effects of ageing and social security reform put together shows that there is a clear case for a reduction in PAYG benefits, provided that existing low-income generations are offered shelter against the reduction in their income. For retired households this should be possible, since the required transfers are obviously non-distortionary. The design of a transition that minimizes the distortion for working low-income households sufficiently to make the reform equitable for them as well is the subject for a following paper.

Notes

1 The projections have been extended beyond 2050 by extrapolating the fertility and mortality rates for 2050 to later years.
2 This procedure implies that these cohorts receive a negative annuity from the life insurance fund, that compensates for their increase in numbers, and effectively provides immigrants with the same assets as the resident population. Otherwise, immigrants would have to be treated separately both by year of immigration and year of birth.
3 Note however that the initial debt-GDP ratio of 71 per cent is substantially above the ceiling agreed upon in the Maastricht treaty. Also, this projection assumes that the government will not increase its subsidies to the PAYG fund, allowing contribution rates to rise. Actually, the Dutch government has recently created a buffer fund to smooth PAYG contribution rates.

4 The increase in the PAYG premium is lower as a percentage of GDP, at about 5 per cent points.
5 It is not correct, however, to conclude from Figure 14.2 that the elderly are up to 40 per cent better off if evaluated over their entire life. A comparison in terms of remaining lifetime utility does not take into account past events, that may have adversely affected the utility of these generations. Calvo and Obstfeld (1988) show that a time-consistent treatment by a social planner requires discounting back to the birth dates of the generations involved.
6 All variables are given either as percentage deviations from the baseline solution (per cent), or as absolute deviations (D per cent).
7 The discussion at the time of the implementation centred around the expected lack of financial sustainability of the PAYG scheme, and the efficiency gain to be expected from tax smoothing.

References

Aaron, H. J. (1966) 'The social insurance paradox', *Canadian Journal of Economic and Political Science*, 32, 371–4.

Auerbach, A. J. and Kotlikoff, L. J. (1987) *Dynamic Fiscal Policy*, Cambridge: Cambridge University Press.

Beer, J. de (1999) 'Bevolkingsprognose 1998–2050', *CBS Maandstatistiek Bevolking*, January 1999, 8–19 (in Dutch: Population Forecasts 1998–2050).

Börsch-Supan, A. (1996) 'The impact of population ageing on savings, investment and growth in the OECD area', in: OECD, *Future Global Capital Shortages: Real Threat or Pure Fiction?*. Paris: OECD.

Börsch-Supan, A. (1998) 'Germany: a social security system on the verge of collapse', in: Siebert, H. (ed.) *Redesigning Social Security*, Tuebingen: Mohr Siebeck.

Breyer, F. and Straub, M. (1993) 'Welfare effects of unfunded pension systems when labor supply is endogenous', *Journal of Public Economics*, 50, 77–91.

Broer, D. P., Westerhout, E. W. M. T. and Bovenberg, A. L. (1994) 'Taxation, pensions, and saving in a small open economy', *Scandinavian Journal of Economics*, 96, 403–24.

Broer, D. P. and Westerhout, E. W. M. T. (1997) 'Pension policies and lifetime uncertainty in an applied general equilibrium model', in: Broer, D. P. and. Lassila, J. (eds), *Pension Policies and Public Debt in Dynamic CGE Models*, Heidelberg: Physica Verlag.

Calvo, G. A. and Obstfeld, M. (1988) 'Optimal time-consistent fiscal policy with finite lifetimes', *Econometrica*, 56, 411–32.

Chauveau, T. and Loufir, R. (1997) 'The future of public pensions in the seven major economies', in: Broer, D. P. and Lassila, J. (eds), *Pension Policies and Public Debt in Dynamic CGE Models*, Heidelberg: Physica Verlag.

Fehr, H. (1999) *Welfare Effects of Dynamic Tax Reforms*, Tuebingen: Mohr Siebeck.

Feldstein, M. (1995) *Would Privatizing Social Security Raise Economic Welfare*, NBER Working Paper 5281.

Feldstein, M. (1996) 'The missing piece in policy analysis: social security reform', *The American Economic Review, Papers and Proceedings*, 86, 1–14.

Kotlikoff, L. J. (1996) *Simulating the Privatization of Social Security in General Equilibrium*, NBER Working Paper 5776.

Kotlikoff, L. J., Smetters, K. A. and Walliser, J. (1998) 'The economic impact of privatizing social security', in Siebert, H. (ed.) *Redesigning Social Security*, Tuebingen: Mohr Siebeck.

Miles, D. (1999) 'Modelling the impact of demographic change upon the economy', *The Economic Journal*, 109, 1–36

Raffelhüschen, B. (1993) 'Funding social security through Pareto-optimal conversion policies', *Journal of Economics*, 7, 105–31.

United Nations (1994) *The Sex and Age Distribution of the World Populations*, United Nations.

Part V
Miscellaneous

15 Can tax progression raise employment?*

A study of four European economies

John P. Hutton and Anna Ruocco

1 Introduction

A principal objection to progressive income taxation is that it discourages the supply of effort and labour, and so reduces economic efficiency. Blum and Kalven (1953) set out the traditional arguments for and against progression, including those relating to equity, the benefit principle and macro-economic stabilisation; and for a more recent review see Myles (1995, Chapter 5). The effect of the efficiency loss typically shows up in the form of reduced output, employment and welfare indicators. In the general equilibrium analysis of tax policy it will, therefore, tend to be eliminated in favour of fairly uniform indirect taxes unless the analyst's model permits distributional criteria or, crucially, allows for pre-existing distortions. When we introduce non-clearing labour markets, however, the role of progression is much less obvious. Whether unemployment is a by-product of trade union activity (bargaining models) or missing markets (efficiency wage models) or uncertainty (search models), progression tends to reduce pre-tax wages, and hence stimulate the demand for labour. See for example Hoel (1990), Lockwood and Manning (1993), Goerke (1999) and Sorensen (1999), who also provide a review of the empirical evidence. The net outcome, with reduction in supply but increase in demand for labour, is, therefore, not clear *a priori*.

An increase in progression at a point in the wage distribution can be achieved either by increasing the marginal rate, or reducing the average rate at that point. In practice, we often wish to refer to some overall measure, and consider the rates experienced by some representative worker. If more progression increases employment, average rate and marginal rate increases have, respectively, negative and positive effects: the first proposition is not contentious, but the second is.

In a wide-ranging review of the possibilities of increasing employment through tax reform, OECD (1995) emphasised the negative employment effects of increasing average rates of labour income taxation, but recommended measures to reduce the burden of taxation on low-income families even at the cost of

*Acknowledgements: we have particularly benefited from discussion with Wolfgang Wiegard and Peter Lambert. All errors are our responsibility.

increasing the burden further up the scale. The damaging effects of marginal rates on human capital formation, tax compliance and entrepreneurship are noted, indicating that there are strict limits on what is possible. The idea of reducing rates of tax on low earners was to encourage participation, rather than that the increased progression would reduce wage rates. Nevertheless, there was some cautious endorsement of the idea that more progression may be recommended. And in a recent AGE study of the Netherlands, Graafland and de Mooij (1999) find that the best policies for reducing unemployment work by reducing the average rate and the level benefit, that is the replacement rate (of wages by unemployment benefit), even though this means raised marginal rates for most workers. In this chapter, however, we focus solely on the effects of progression on employment via wage rates.

It is clear that the presence of unemployment can sometimes reverse normal policy conclusions. For example, in the different context of international policy coordination, Fuest and Huber (1999) have recently shown that coordination in setting direct taxes can be welfare-reducing if the labour market is less than perfectly competitive. These results are derived from a theoretical model where unemployment can arise through wage-bargaining, and in which government can choose single capital and labour income tax rates. The question of progression does not arise, but their results provide another example of how the presence of unemployment can reverse results obtained in a competitive setting.[1]

Thus, it has recently become clear that in more realistic models, one can sometimes make second-best arguments in favour of progression and other forms of distortionary taxation. In the next section we develop a simple efficiency wage model in the style of Phelps (1994) to explore this issue. This model introduces training costs (representing also a range of related costs) incurred by employers depending on labour turnover. We will show that progression can indeed raise employment, but that when labour is not in fixed supply and when the benefit system is less generous, the effect can be reversed. In subsequent sections we pursue the same issues for fully calibrated general equilibrium models of several European economies. In Section 3 we describe the main features of our simulation model, putting particular emphasis on the labour market structure, while also briefly discussing the parameterisation of the model. We also show how we calculate alternative equivalent variations in order to measure the welfare effects of the policies at issue. Section 4 describes the policies analysed and presents the results obtained in simulation and their economic interpretation. Section 5 concludes with some further discussion and a summary of the main findings.

2   An efficiency wage model of the effect of tax progression on the labour market

We first consider a model of a single input, single output competitive firm, designed to be parameterised to explore subsequent full model properties. The firm employs only labour, but new workers are less productive and require training. Existing trained workers are liable to be tempted away by the prospect of higher wages in competing firms, especially when the labour market is tight and the prospect of re-employment is good. This provides our firm with an incentive to raise wages to deter quits and thus reduce its training and other labour turnover costs. Initially we assume that all workers participate in the labour market, so labour supply is fixed. Workers have fixed hours and pay income tax on their wages, and in the model the structure of the income tax affects the ability of the employer to use wages to reduce labour turnover. This efficiency wage model is based on that in Phelps (1994) and Campbell and Orszag (1998). For a review of efficiency wage, bargaining and search models with similar predictions see Sorensen (1997) and Sorensen (1999).

The firm maximises the present value of profits at time t_0, with output price normalised to unity,

$$V_{t0} = \int_{t0}^{\infty} e^{-\rho(t-t0)} [f(L_t) - w_t L_t - T_g(h_t)L_t] \, dt$$

subject to the dynamic constraint

$$\frac{\dot{L}}{L} = h - q(w^*, \tilde{w}_A^*),$$

where L is employment, $\dot{L}$ the rate of change of L, h the hiring rate, $f(L)$ a value added production function, T_g training costs (narrowly, the cost of using existing workers to train new workers, but representing all turnover costs), q is the quit rate which depends on w^*, the firm's wage rate net of direct taxes and on $\tilde{w}_A^*$, the expected alternative net-of-tax wage defined as $\tilde{w}_A^* = w_A^*(1-u) + bw_A^* u = w_A(1 - u(1-b))$ where w_A^* is the economy-wide wage rate net of average direct tax rate, u is the unemployment rate[2] (interpreted as the probability of remaining unemployed), and bw_A^* is the benefit level or unemployment income.

To be more specific about the tax rate definition, first define $g(w)$ as the tax function and then $t^A = g(w)/w$ is the average tax rate, while $t = \partial g(w)/\partial w$ is the marginal tax rate so that $w^* = w(1 - t^A)$.

We assume that hours are fixed, so L corresponds to the number of employees as well as the total input of labour, and the tax is therefore levied on labour income rather than just on the wage rate.

Firms behave in a Nash manner, treating economy-wide averages as given, but in equilibrium wages and employment are equated across firms. To solve the firm's problem, set up the current value Hamiltonian:

$$H_t = f(L_t) - w_t L_t - T_g(h_t)L_t + \lambda_t[h_t - q(w_A^*, \tilde{w}_{A,t}^*)]L_t$$

The first-order conditions are:

$$\frac{\partial T_g(h_t)}{\partial h_t} = \lambda_t \tag{1}$$

$$-\lambda_t \frac{\partial q}{\partial w_t} = 1,$$

that is,

$$- \lambda_t \frac{\partial q}{\partial w_t^*} \frac{\partial w_t^*}{\partial w_t} = 1$$

$$- \lambda_t \frac{\partial q}{\partial w_t^*} (1 - t) = 1 \tag{2}$$

$$\dot{\lambda}_t = \rho \lambda_t - \frac{\partial H_t}{\partial L_t}$$

that is,

$$\dot{\lambda}_t = \rho \lambda_t - \left[\frac{\partial f(L_t)}{\partial L_t} - w_t - T_g(h_t) \right]. \tag{3}$$

Equation (1) equates marginal training costs with the shadow value of an additional worker. Equation (2) sets the wage to balance the effect of the wage on replacement costs with the effect of a change in the wage on the total wage bill. Imposing the necessary transversality condition, integrating Equation (3) expresses the shadow value of an additional worker in terms of the present discounted value of future cash flows from hiring an additional worker:

$$\lambda_t = \int_t^\infty e^{-\rho(n-t)} \left[\frac{\partial f(L_n)}{\partial L_n} - w_n - T_g(h_n) \right] dn. \tag{4}$$

2.1   The wage curve

The next stage is to derive the wage curve, assuming that $q(\cdot)$ and $T_g(\cdot)$ are, respectively, constant elasticity and quadratic functions. As we have already specified the potential quitter compares his actual net-of-tax wage w^* with the expected alternative net-of-tax wage $\tilde{w}_A^*$ then, assuming a constant elasticity function we have

$$q(w^*, \tilde{w}_A^*) = B \left[\frac{w^*}{w_A^*(1 - u(1 - b))} \right]^{-\eta} \tag{5}$$

Assume that training costs increase with the hiring rate (following Campbell and Orszag (1998)), so that

$$T_g(h) = \frac{A}{2} h^2 \tag{6}$$

The first-order conditions (1) and (2) now become

$$A h_t = \lambda_t \tag{7}$$

and

$$- \lambda_t \frac{\partial q_t}{\partial w_t^*}(1 - t) = 1$$

that is,

$$\lambda_t B\eta(w_t^*)^{-\eta-1}(w_{A,t}^*)(1 - u_t(1 - b))^{\eta}(1 - t) = 1. \tag{8}$$

In equilibrium, $w = w_A$ and $w^* = w_A^* = w(1 - t^A)$, so Equation (8) becomes

$$\frac{\lambda B\eta(1 - u_t(1 - b))^{\eta}(1 - t)}{w(1 - t^A)} = 1,$$

$$w = \frac{1 - t}{1 - t^A} \lambda B\eta(1 - u(1 - b))^{\eta}. \tag{9}$$

Substituting equations (5) and (7) into equation (9), and imposing the steady-state condition that $h = q$, yields

$$w = \left(\frac{1 - t}{1 - t^A}\right) AB^2 \eta(1 - u(1 - b))^{2\eta}. \tag{10}$$

This is the wage curve. Taking logarithms as is conventional,

$$\log(w) = \log\left(\frac{1 - t}{1 - t^A}\right) + \log(AB^2\eta) + 2\eta \log(1 - u(1 - b)). \tag{11}$$

Note that increasing progression (i.e. decreasing $(1 - t)/(1 - t^A)$) will shift the wage curve down, and that increasing the value of benefits through the replacement rate b will flatten the wage-curve. Blanchflower and Oswald (1994) review the theory and evidence concerning this type of relationship, and suggest that an elasticity of w with respect to u of -0.1 is a robust empirical finding.

Preliminary comments on the wage curve

The term $(1 - t)/(1 - t^A)$ is the well-known index of residual progression, the elasticity of after-tax income to pre-tax income: see Lambert (1993) on the redistributive implications of a change on this index.[3] Similar functional forms for the wage curve, complete with the residual progression index, can be derived from the various models set out in Lockwood and Manning (1993) and Sorensen (1999). It therefore appears that the index of progression should be included as a matter of course in empirical wage curve studies, since this form of equation is consistent with the leading theories of equilibrium unemployment.

The intuition of the result is that a rise in the marginal tax rate reduces the benefit to a worker of working for an employer who pays above the market rate to reduce the quit rate; the worker will, therefore, be more likely to quit. The employer therefore lowers the wage and accepts a higher quit rate. This mechanism is independent of the level of unemployment, so the wage curve shifts down.

The other notable feature of this wage curve is that the effect of a higher benefit rate, b, is to reduce the slope of (i.e. flatten) the wage curve. This is because generous benefits reduce the costs of unsuccessful job search, damping the effects of unemployment on quit-and-search activity. In the limit, if benefits equal wages, the latter are set by the former and wages are exogenous.

This analysis suffers from some obvious defects. First, labour supply is fixed. Second, the progression index is assumed independent of the wage rate. We attempt to remedy both defects in the next section, by specifying both the household utility function and the form of the income tax schedule. A third defect, the partial nature of the analysis, is addressed later in the country simulations.

2.2   Variable labour supply

To allow a variable labour supply, but with workers having fixed hours so that the tax liability still depends on the wage rate, we will assume that supply varies with the proportion of members of an aggregate household deciding to participate.[4] Assuming a household Cobb–Douglas utility function[5] of consumption and lei- sure, $U = c^{\theta_1} \ell^{\theta_2}$, and budget constraint $c = w(1-t)(E-\ell) + t\mathcal{Z}$, we derive labour supply $L^S = E - \ell$. Thus

$$L^S = \theta E - \frac{(1-\theta)t\mathcal{Z}}{(1-t)w} \qquad (12)$$

where $\theta = \theta_1/(\theta_1 - \theta_2)$, E is time endowment and $\mathcal{Z}$ the level of tax-free allowance in a linear-progressive tax with constant marginal rate t. The average tax rate is now $t^A = (twL - t\mathcal{Z})/wL = t - (t\mathcal{Z}/wL)$. So the index of residual progression now depends on the wage rate, and is

$$\frac{1-t}{1-t^A} = \frac{1-t}{1-(t-t\mathcal{Z}/wL)} = \frac{(1-t)wL}{(1-t)wL + t\mathcal{Z}}.$$

Now $(1-u) = L/L^S$, so the wage-curve (11) can be expressed as

$$\log(w) = \log\left(\frac{(1-t)wL}{(1-t)wL + t\mathcal{Z}}\right) + \log(AB^2\eta) + 2\eta\log(b + (1-b)(L/L^S))$$

$$(13)$$

Substituting for L^S from (12),

$$\log(w) = \log\left(\frac{(1-t)wL}{(1-t)wL + t\mathcal{Z}}\right) + \log(AB^2\eta)$$

$$+ 2\eta\log\left(b + \frac{(1-b)L}{\theta E - (1-\theta)t\mathcal{Z}/[(1-t)w]}\right) \qquad (14)$$

This equation has been left in implicit form for practical reasons and to retain its family resemblance to Equation (11) above. This is now a wage-setting equation (WS) or pseudo labour supply schedule rather than a wage curve, since it combines the household labour supply with the wage curve. When labour supply is fixed, WS and the wage curve coincide.

Considering the properties of this WS, notice that a rise in the marginal tax rate t will now have opposing effects. First, reducing the residual progression index will tend to shift WS down. But second, reducing labour supply L^S will tend to shift WS up. So it seems possible that a more elastic labour supply can reverse the effect of progression on the WS. Whether this happens can be influenced by the generosity or otherwise of the benefit system. If b is high (e.g. 0.8, say), the effects of changes in labour supply are strongly damped (see Equation (13)), so in this case the possibility that labour supply effects will reverse the effect of progression is also strongly damped. Conversely, with low unemployment benefits, labour supply effects could give us the result that an increase in progression raises wages and reduces employment, thus restoring what one expects in fully market clearing models.

There are, however, also demand side effects of progression to be considered. Training costs negatively affect the demand for labour, and the rate of progression affects the quit rate and hence training costs. An increase in progression, *ceteris paribus*, will increase the quit rate and training costs, reducing demand for labour; this effect is again damped for high b. For high b, therefore, an increase in progression will shift both supply and demand down, reducing wages but with an uncertain effect on employment. For low b, the negative demand shift will be greater, making it more likely that employment will fall. The next sections illustrate these possibilities.

2.3 *Labour market equilibrium*

With fixed labour supply, the wage curve plays the role of labour supply curve. To complete the model of the labour market we solve equation (3) for $\dot{\lambda}_t = 0$, the steady-state condition. From (7) $\lambda = Ah$. We also set $h = q = B[1 - u(1 - b)]^\eta$ for $w^* = w_A^*$ (see Equation (5)). The result is

$$-\frac{\partial f(L)}{\partial L} + w + \frac{AB^2}{2}(1 - u(1 - b))^{2\eta} + \rho AB[1 - u(1 - b)]^\eta = 0.$$

To solve in terms of w and L, express u as $1 - L/L^s$, and choose a parametric form for the production function: let

$$f(L) = CL^\alpha, \quad \text{for } 0 < \alpha < 1.$$

Hence the demand curve is (simplifying by taking the static case, or $\rho = 0$)

$$w = \alpha C(L)^{\alpha - 1} - \frac{AB^2}{2}(1 - u(1 - b))^{2\eta}, \tag{15}$$

$$w = \alpha C(L)^{\alpha - 1} - \frac{AB^2}{2}\left[b + \frac{L(1 - b)}{\theta E - (1 - \theta)t Z/[(1 - t)w]}\right]^{2\eta}. \tag{16}$$

The wage equals the marginal product less the marginal cost of training at the equilibrium hiring rate. Labour supply effects enter the demand curve via training costs, since any change in labour supply affects unemployment and so quits and so training costs. A rise in t therefore will tend to raise training costs and reduce the demand for labour.

2.4   Numerical examples

To illustrate numerically, we choose parameters to yield a wage curve elasticity of about -0.1 (see comments above on this), and measures of progression and labour supply elasticity comparable with calibrated AGE models. Let $A = B = 1$, $C = 3$, $\alpha = 0.75$, $\eta = 2.5$, $b = 0.8$, $m = 0.4$ and 0.3, $\rho = 0.0$, $\theta = 0.5$, $Z = 1$, and $E = 4$.

Fixed labour supply case

Figures 15.1 and 15.2 plot Equations (16) and (13) with L^s fixed, showing the wage rate w against relative employment L/L^S. The figures differ in the level of benefits. Changes in progression can easily be seen to have the following consequences: an increase in marginal rate of tax, for given allowances, will shift down the wage-curve, reducing the wage rate and the unemployment rate; changes in the average rate will have the opposite effects. In the figure, the upper wage curve corresponds to $t = 0.3$, the lower to $t = 0.4$. Since labour supply is fixed, progression changes have no effect on labour demand. The effect of a low (zero in this case) level of benefits is to steepen the curves and to reduce the employment gain of increased progression: the effect is still positive.

Variable labour supply case

The next examples introduce variable labour supply as set out above, with a linear-progressive tax and Cobb–Douglas utility function. We again compare high and low benefit regimes.

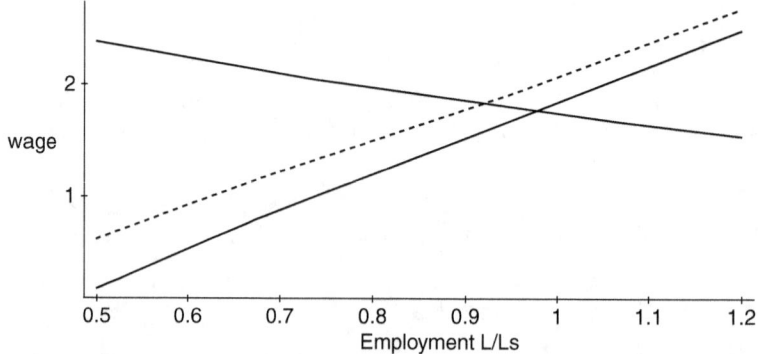

Figure 15.1 Fixed labour supply, $b = 0.8$, dotted line less progressive. Demand and wage-setting curves shown.

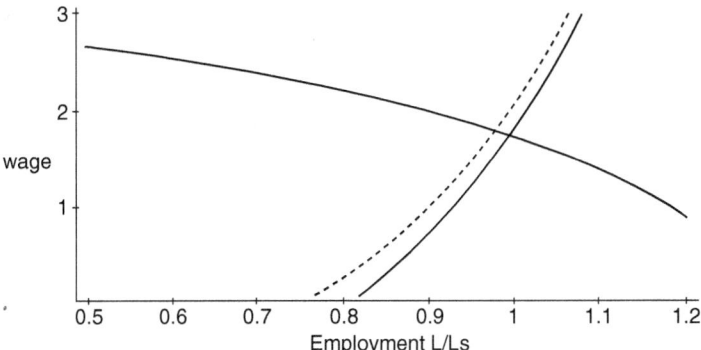

Figure 15.2 Fixed labour supply, $b=0$, dotted line less progressive. Demand and wage-setting curves shown.

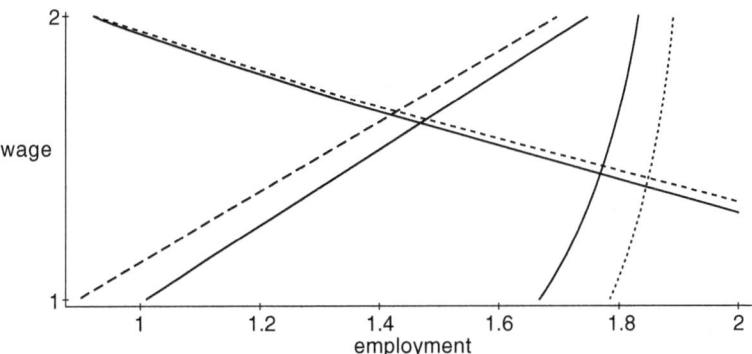

Figure 15.3 Variable labour supply, $b=0.8$, dotted lines less progressive. Demand, supply and wage-setting curves shown.

In Figure 15.3, we can see the effects of including variable labour supply into the analysis. Again, the dotted lines show the less progressive case with marginal rate $t=0.3$, and the more progressive case has $t=0.4$. The maximum labour supply is 2 (since $T=4$ and $\theta=0.5$). The figure shows both the supply schedules and the wage-setting schedules: the latter are shifted to the left, and the gap between them is involuntary unemployment. The effect of increased progression is to move the supply schedule and the wage-setting schedule closer together, reducing unemployment. The more progressive case has higher employment, but the demand schedule also shifts down, damping the employment effect and further reducing wages. This shift in the demand curve is a feature of the variable labour supply model: the variable labour supply changes the relation between employment, unemployment and hence employers' training costs. In this example, however, the demand shift does not reverse the positive employment effect of an increase in progression.

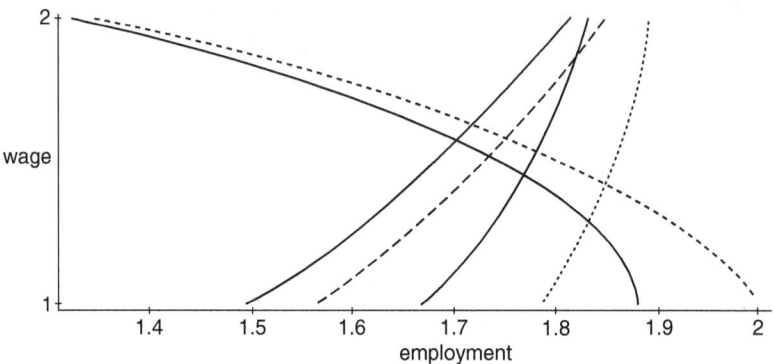

Figure 15.4 Variable labour supply, $b=0$, dotted lines less progressive. Demand, supply and wage-setting curves shown.

In the example discussed above, the residual progression index $(1-t)/(1-t^A)$ is 0.78 and the elasticity of labour supply is 0.12 at the equilibrium with the progressive tax. These figures correspond quite closely to measures reported in the literature (see e.g. Sorensen 1997) and to those in our calibrated models of Germany, France, Italy and the UK discussed below.

We now illustrate the effect of reducing the benefit level. Figure 15.4 shows the effect of setting $b=0$. This time, with higher progression the supply schedule is shifted further to the left, so that the wage-setting schedule is also shifted to the left; since the gap between them is reduced, unemployment falls as well as employment. Two quite distinct effects on employment can be seen. First, reducing benefits increases the level of employment. Comparing Figures 15.3 and 15.4, it can be seen that with $t=0.4$ (for example) the level of employment has risen from about 1.5 to 1.7. Second, however, the more progressive tax has in the zero benefit case both lower demand and lower wage-setting curve, clearly reducing employment. The effect on wages is also slightly negative in this case. So when benefits are zero, the effect of increased progression on employment is reversed. On the other hand, it is still true that increased progression reduces unemployment.

Thus, if the policy-maker starts from a position of high benefit levels, he/she can increase employment by increasing progression, reducing benefits, or both. Since each of these options has quite different distributional consequences, equity considerations might determine the choice. By contrast, if benefits are initially low, there will be less scope for increasing employment by fiscal manipulation, and reducing benefits and/or reducing progression will be the choice: in this case all choices will tend to increase inequality. It may be, therefore, that there is some limit to the degree to which employment can be stimulated in this way before equity considerations become dominant.

These examples show that the effects of progression on employment in this variety of efficiency wage model depend crucially on the benefit level, and work through both demand and supply in the labour market. In a general equilibrium setting, the product market and public sector would provide further feedback. To yield any policy recommendations therefore, it is desirable to incorporate these wider effects, and to calibrate the resulting general equilibrium for the country under consideration. It is already clear that calibration can affect the direction as well as the extent of the consequences of tax reform.

3 Extensions to the theoretical model and Applied General Equilibrium (AGE) model description

The model set out in the previous section is inadequate in several ways that we can remedy by making use of an AGE model. In a multi-country, multi-sector model, with a variety of types of labour, various direct and indirect taxes, and terms of trade effects, the intuition from simple examples must be confirmed. And using a model calibrated to national data, we can obtain quantified estimates of the effects of changes in tax design, and thus judge whether the effects seem trivial or potentially important.

The model described here corresponds in most of its features to that used in Hutton and Ruocco (1999), so we will focus mainly on the innovations of this paper. It is a multi-country AGE model, representing 6 groups of European Union countries. Some of these represent single states while others represent groups as follows: 1. Belgium & Luxembourg–Denmark–Netherlands, 2. Germany, 3. Spain–Greece–Ireland–Portugal, 4. France, 5. Italy, 6. United Kingdom. The Rest of the World (ROW) completes this setting. Aggregating some of the countries will not undermine our simulation results as we concentrate our attention on Germany, France, Italy and the UK.

3.1 The household sector

Formally, the preferences of households are represented by a nested utility function, a formulation implying Hicksian separability, and multi-stage budgeting. Given that the countries differ only in the parameterisation of the functional forms, we will not index the variables by country in what follows. For each country we have modelled a representative household composed of two groups of individuals identifiable by gender, each with distinct time endowments, acting as if maximising a single utility function subject to a household budget constraint. The arguments of the utility function are leisure and aggregate present consumption. On the one hand, the household decides consumption, by choosing different consumption goods, then distinguishing between imported and domestic commodities and finally, between imported consumption goods from different source countries. Collective goods are provided free of charge and enter the utility function in an additively separable manner (and consequently can be omitted). On the other hand, leisure decisions are distinguished by family member, yielding distinct men's and women's labour supplies, as in Ashenfelter and Heckman (1974). In addition, we allow each family member to choose her/his optimal combination of full- and part-time labour supply, distinguishing between the preferences of men and women. The figure in Appendix I provides an overview of the household sector hierarchy. A much more ambitious household model, disaggregated into 40 household types and several categories of labour is developed within the MIMIC model, in for example, Graafland and de Mooij (1999). The model presented here has some similar features, including the choice of full- vs part-time work. We will assume that the part-time market is 'legitimate' but clears competitively, while in MIMIC there is a competitive 'black' labour market.

The difference between the level of the total time endowment and the leisure demand for each group yields the total labour supply for men (L_m^S) and for women (L_w^S).[6] Conditional on the total labour supply for each gender, women and men must still decide whether to work full- or part-time, so the household will offer a combination of full- and part-time work. This choice is taken by each group maximising a homothetic CET preference function subject to a net income constraint. The model differs from our previous work in that we allow the household to take into account, when making its decision, the risk of being unemployed.

Formally, each gender i solves the problem:

Maximise

$$CET \; (L_{f,i}^S/L_i^S, L_{p,i}^S/L_i^S) = -[\beta_{f,i}^{1/\delta_2}(L_{f,i}^S/L_i^S)^{\pi_2} + \beta_{p,i}^1/\delta_2(L_{p,i}^S/L_i^S)^{\pi_2}]^{\pi_2} \qquad (17)$$

subject to

$$L_{f,i}^S/L_i^S + L_{p,i}^S/L_i^S = 1, \qquad (18)$$

$$(1-u)(L_{f,i}^S/L_i^S)w_f(1-t_f) + ub(L_{f,i}^S/L_i^S)w_f(1-t_f)$$
$$+ (L_{p,i}^S/L_i^S)w_p(1-t_p) = w_i, \qquad (19)$$

that is,

$$(L_{f,i}^S/L_i^S)w_f(1-t_f)(1-u(1-b)) + (L_{p,i}^S/L_i^S)w_p(1-t_p) = w_i, \qquad (20)$$

or

$$(L_{f,i}^S/L_i^S)\tilde{w}_f(1-t_f) + (L_{p,i}^S/L_i^S)w_p(1-t_p) = w_i, \qquad (21)$$

where the notation is as follows:

i index for gender (m, w)

j index for full- and part-time labour (f, p)

w_i composite net of tax wage rates for gender i; $i = m, w$

w_j gross wage rates full- and part-time labour; $j = f, p$

$\tilde{w}_f$ 'risk-adjusted' full-time wage $w_f(1 - u(1 - b))$

t_j marginal tax rates for full- and part-time labour

$L^S_{j,i}$ Total full- and part-time labour supply for gender

$\beta_{j,i}$ share parameters for f and p labour supply for gender i

δ_2 elasticity of substitution $(\delta_2 < 0)$

π_2 $(\delta_2 - 1)/\delta_2$.

The share parameters $(\beta_{j,i})$ together with the elasticity of substitution (δ_2) determine the shape of the CET function (see Hutton and Ruocco 1999 for details). The budget constraint Equation (19) has three components: full-time wages from employment, unemployment benefit in the full-time market, and part-time wages. Therefore any variation in unemployment will induce changes in the full-time/part-time choice: increased unemployment reduces the relative attraction of the full-time market, and moves some workers into the part-time market.

For arbitrary values of w_i, w_f and w_p, the full-time and part-time shares would not sum to unity: the general equilibrium set of wages and prices must therefore satisfy Equation (18).

The solution to this problem, therefore, determines the optimal choice of the household, given net wages, the benefit level, unemployment and preferences over full- or part-time work. Each gender's labour supply is

$$L^S_i = L^S_{f,i} + L^S_{p,i} \quad \text{for } i = m, w. \tag{22}$$

Our modelling of household choice between full- and part-time labour is also consistent with a distribution of preferences over mode of work. In this case the threshold value of relative wages is a random variable: that is,

$$0 \leq L^S_{f,i}/L^S_i = F\left(\frac{\tilde{w}_f(1 - t_f)}{w_p(1 - t_p)}\right) \leq 1.$$

Each member of the labour force has a threshold value of $\tilde{w}_f(1 - t_f)/w_p(1 - t_p)$, above which he/she decides to switch from part-time to fulltime work, according to individual preferences. To be consistent with the CET function in (17), these threshold values are distributed according to the log-logistic distribution function, which yields the proportion of the population whose threshold lies below the value $\tilde{w}_f(1 - t_f)/w_p(1 - t_p)$.

3.2   The production sector

The other features of the model are fairly standard in the tradition of Shoven and Whalley (*op. cit.*): the reader can refer to Fehr, Rosenberg, and Wiegard (1995), and to Ruocco (1996) for a more detailed description. In this section we will, therefore, report the main differences between our model and the original model of Fehr, Rosenberg, and Wiegard (1995). Three primary factors of production (capital, full-time and part-time labour) and 11 commodities are identified for each country. Firms do not distinguish between full-time labour offered by men or by women. The different observed market wage rates of women and men depend solely on the fraction of full- or part-time work provided by women and men respectively. This assumption does not necessarily rule out some degree of discrimination.[7]

Full-time (L_f) and part-time (L_p) labour form a Cobb–Douglas nest within a CES value-added production function with aggregate labour and capital as arguments. The gross production function is the usual Leontief-type, depending on value-added and composite intermediate inputs. The introduction of training costs for full-time employees is the major difference between this model and that in Hutton and Ruocco (1999). Appendix I displays the production tree schematically.

3.3   The public sector

We now consider the expenditure side of the government budget. There are two expenditure categories: lump-sum payments to the representative consumer and government outlays for the provision of public goods. Because firms pay for the use of the public good as an intermediate input, only net public expenditures (provided free of charge to the consumer) have to be financed by taxes. Transfers are a linear function of the level of unemployment

$$T = \gamma_0 + \gamma_1 u \sum_i L^S_{f,i}. \tag{23}$$

The parameter γ_1 is the cost in benefits of an additional unemployed person, that is, $\gamma_1 = b w_f (1 - t_f^A)$. The intercept of the transfers function γ_0 corresponds to those transfer payments which the government makes independent of the level of unemployment (e.g. pensions). γ_1 is calibrated to the value of unemployment compensation in the respective countries under consideration.

On the revenue side of the budget, the government collects various taxes: full-time labour income tax, part-time labour income tax (in principle but not in practice), capital income tax, value added taxes, tariffs and production taxes. Taxes on capital and labour income are modelled as linear progressive taxes: we assume single marginal tax rates applicable to income above a threshold. As noted below, capital income tax is levied according to ownership of capital, not the location where the capital is employed, and since this is a static model with the return on capital determined internationally, capital income is in effect exogenous and so capital income tax is like a lump-sum tax.

3.4 *Labour market equilibrium in the AGE model*

The form of the wage curve in this study is a departure from our previous work and has been derived above as Equation (11). Adapting the notation, this now appears as:

$$\log\left(\frac{w_f}{Q}\right) = \log\left(\frac{1-t_f}{1-t_f^A}\right) + \log(AB^2\eta) + 2\eta \log(1-u(1-b)), \qquad (24)$$

where we use the following notation:

t_f^A average full-time labour income tax rate
Q producer price index.

The demand for full-time labour is derived along the lines of Equation (16) above. L_f is solved from

$$\frac{\partial VA}{\partial L}\frac{\partial L}{\partial L_f} = \frac{w_f}{Q} + \frac{AB^2}{2}(1-u(1-b))^{2\eta} + \rho AB[1-u(1-b)]^{\eta}, \qquad (25)$$

where VA is the value added function.

The second and third terms on the RHS of (25) are the full marginal cost of training, acting like a wage tax. Comparing (25) and (24), the marginal cost of training can be solved out as

$$MCT = \frac{w_f}{Q}\left[2\eta\left(\frac{1-t_f}{1-t_f^A}\right)\right]^{-1} + \rho(2A)^{0.5}\left[\frac{w_f}{Q}\left[2\eta\left(\frac{1-t_f}{1-t_f^A}\right)\right]^{-1}\right]^{0.5}.$$

The second part of this expression is very small, so MCT can be approximately measured by the first term. For calibration purposes, we start from the estimated wage curve elasticity of $\partial \log(w_f/Q)/\partial \log(u) = -0.1$. Thus, for an unemployment rate of $u=0.1$ and a benefit level of $b=0.8$, say, we can derive a value of η by solving

$$\partial[2\eta\log(1-u(1-b))]/\partial\log(u) = -\frac{2u(1-b)\eta}{1-u(1-b)} = -0.1.$$

This yields $\eta=2.5$. For a residual progression index value of $(1-t_f)/(1-t_f^A) = 0.8$, training (and other turnover-related) costs can be solved out as $MCT = 0.25(w_f/Q)$. This example illustrates the orders of magnitude implied in the modelling.

In the full-time labour market, we have unemployment equalling the difference between the level of leisure that the consumer (of each sex) would choose at the equilibrium wage rate (ℓ_m or ℓ_w) and the level of leisure that the consumer is forced to choose (ℓ_i^*), thus:

$$\ell_i^* = \ell_i + u L_{f,i}^S.$$

Unemployment therefore corresponds to excess leisure consumption. The market equilibrium condition for the full-time labour market is:

$$\sum_n L_{f,n} = (L_{f,m}^S + L_{f,\omega}^S)(1 - u),$$

where $\sum_n L_{f,n}$ is the demand for full-time labour (summed over production sectors). In the part-time market the conventional clearing condition holds:

$$\sum_n L_{p,n} = L_{p,m}^S + L_{p,\omega}^S.$$

3.5   Policy evaluation

To evaluate policy changes, we need appropriate indicators of their welfare effects. A welfare function which represents the economy as a whole in a world with a single consumer and without rationing is straightforward: the welfare function coincides with the utility function of the representative consumer (U). When some individuals are unemployed, however, this approach is not so satisfactory, since unemployed individuals are forced off their optimal leisure/goods choice. We wish to choose an index which represents the costs of unemployment in a reasonable manner.

We therefore calculate equivalent variations in two ways. The first translates directly from the analysis of the single representative household in unconstrained full employment, comparing utility as a function of consumption and leisure. The second recognises that excess leisure consumption in the form of unemployment for some households will contribute less utility at the margin than freely chosen leisure. The two measures are $EV_{C,\ell+u}$ and $EV_{C,\ell}$, based on utility evaluated using, respectively, total leisure consumed and total leisure demanded. Thus, in the second, we assign zero utility to excess leisure in the form of unemployment. For details see Hutton and Ruocco (1999).

4   The simulations

4.1   Simulation design

To investigate the size of the effects of changes in income tax progression, we conducted some simple experiments on the multi-country model. We measure the effects of increases in the marginal income tax rate, maintaining constant the average income tax rate by varying the level of personal allowances. Since these changes in marginal rates will affect wages and thus the rest of the economy, the government budget constraint will be disturbed. To offset this, we allow the capital income tax rate to vary endogenously. The advantage of using this device is that the capital income tax in this model is in effect a lump-sum tax, since it is levied on domestic income from capital ownership and the domestic supply of capital is fixed (although the domestic capital stock can vary through capital flows). Each experiment is repeated for different levels of unemployment benefit, with and without variable labour supply.

We first, however, construct a full-employment version of the model, by eliminating training costs and hence the wage curve from the full-time market. The tax experiments on this model are necessary to confirm that the progression effects in which we are interested really do depend on the presence of unemployment, and are not the result of some basic misspecification. The results conform to traditional theory: in brief, an increase in marginal rate, with average rate held constant, raises wages and reduces employment and welfare, while an increase in the average rate, with marginal rate constant (achieved by varying either allowances or capital taxation), has similar effects. The question of changing benefit levels does not arise in an interesting way in the absence of unemployment: more generous transfers to households tends to reduce labour supply, with the final effect depending on how the transfer increase is financed. These simulation results are not reported but are available on request.

We now turn to the model with involuntary unemployment. In the presence of unemployment, we conduct the two experiments above (changing marginal and average rates), and investigate the effect of benefit level and labour supply elasticity as sensitivity exercises. Raising the average rate has similar effects with or without unemployment, as expected, and we do not report these results here. We now, however, expect the marginal rate increase (as described above) to reduce wage rates in the full-time market and so tend to encourage full-time employment. Whether employment actually does increase depends also on demand side effects, since as we saw above with the small model, when benefits are low and labour supply variable, the employment effect may be reversed. But since increased progression reduces the wage curve, we can expect unemployment to be reduced in all cases.

Because men are more likely to work full-time, they should be more affected than women. The effect on the part-time market is more difficult to predict. The reduced unemployment rate will encourage workers to switch from the part-time to the full-time market, reducing part-time employment; but on the other hand, the lower full-time wage will have the opposite effect. If the latter effect is stronger, we expect part-time wages to be driven down and part-time employment to increase. Since women have a higher share of part-time work, the effects on women may therefore be smaller than on men. Repeating the experiment, but with a zero benefit level, will steepen the wage curve and generally increase the effects of progression changes on wage rates and so on workers' and employers' decisions. Labour supply effects will be more important: if full-time employment is reduced by higher progression, employers will tend to substitute part-timers, so women's employment should benefit. Finally, as a check for nonlinearity, we repeat the experiments using 3 instead of 1 percentage changes in tax rates.

4.2 Simulation results

Table 15.1 shows the main direct tax rates in our benchmark data set for 1992. The residual progression indices show that France has the least progressive, UK the most progressive income tax systems, excluding social security contributions. The values shown for the marginal tax rates refer to a two-earner couple with two children. We actually use the tax rates of the principal earner as tax rates on full- and part-time labour, where the percentage of the APW (average production worker) income principal/secondary earner is 100/33.

The German case in more detail

Table 15.2 shows the effects of increasing the marginal rate by 1 percentage point for Germany, as a typical example of the results. Details of all simulations are shown in the Appendix tables, with 1 and 3 percentage changes in marginal rates, and also for France, Italy and UK.

Table 15.1 Direct tax rates modelled in 1992 benchmark

	Germany	France	Italy	UK
Marginal tax rate	42.0	28.1	32.7	34.0
Average tax rate	30.5	21.8	20.4	19.2
Social security paid by employers	18.2	35.3	45.9	10.4
π (resid.prog.)	0.83	0.92	0.85	0.82
Benefit ratio b	0.78	0.80	0.50	0.77

Sources: OECD (1995), p.147, 151, 155, 179.

Table 15.2 Effects of increased progression on employment and unemployment: Germany (1992 benchmark)

	Benefit level			
	0.78		0.00	
Labour supply	Fixed	Variable	Fixed	Variable
Marginal rate increased by 1%, average rate constant via variations in allowances				
%Δ employment level	0.57	0.24	0.23	−0.14
%Δ male employment	0.65	0.33	0.26	−0.10
%Δ female employment	0.46	0.11	0.18	−0.19
%Δ full-time employment	0.67	0.33	0.26	−0.10
%Δ part-time employment	0.00	−0.29	0.00	−0.41
%Δ Unemployment rate	−0.62	−0.95	−0.24	−0.32
Welfare measures (% equivalent variation)				
$EV_{C,\ell+u}$	0.48	0.16	0.18	−0.07
$EV_{C,\ell}$	0.48	0.40	0.18	0.03

The first column of figures shows that for fixed labour supply, with full benefit level of 0.78, the largest employment effects are obtained, together with a 0.62 reduction in the percentage unemployment rate (confined by assumption to full-time workers). Part-timers do not benefit, however, since the impact of increased progression is to reduce the full-time wage, encouraging employers to substitute full-time for part-time workers; and because women are more likely to work part-time, women benefit less than men.

The second column shows some interesting contrasts with column one. When labour supply is variable, the tax rise will reduce supply, and all employment effects are less positive. Part-time employment is now reduced by 0.29 per cent. Because full-time employment has risen while labour supply has fallen,

Table 15.3 Increase in tax progression, by increasing the marginal tax rate keeping the average constant and letting allowances vary. Germany

	Benchmark benefit level			
	0.78		0.00	
Labour supply	*Fixed*	*Variable*	*Fixed*	*Variable*
(a) *Increase of 1 percentage point of the marginal tax rate*				
%Δ employment level	0.57	0.24	0.23	− 0.14
%Δ male employment	0.65	0.33	0.26	− 0.10
%Δ female employment	0.46	0.11	0.18	− 0.19
%Δ full-time employment	0.67	0.33	0.26	− 0.10
%Δ part-time employment	—	− 0.29	—	− 0.41
%Δ unemployment rate	− 0.62	− 0.95	− 0.24	− 0.32
Welfare measures				
$EV_{C,\ell+u}$	0.48	0.16	0.18	− 0.07
$EV_{C,\ell}$	0.48	0.40	0.18	0.03
Terms of trade	1.03	1.03	1.03	1.03
Residual income elasticity	0.82	0.82	0.82	0.82
(b) *Increase of 3 percentage points of the marginal tax rate*				
%Δ employment level	1.75	0.69	0.69	− 0.44
%Δ male employment	1.99	0.98	0.79	− 0.32
%Δ female employment	1.42	0.29	0.56	− 0.60
%Δ full-time employment	2.04	0.96	0.81	− 0.30
%Δ part-time employment	—	− 0.92	—	− 1.25
%Δ unemployment rate	− 1.88	− 2.92	− 0.74	− 0.97
Welfare measures				
$EV_{C,\ell+u}$	1.45	0.48	0.55	− 0.22
$EV_{C,\ell}$	1.45	1.19	0.55	0.07
Terms of trade	1.03	1.03	1.03	1.03
Residual income elasticity	0.79	0.79	0.79	0.79

Notes: The EV measures for the variable labour supply cases indicate percentage equivalent variations in disposable money income. For fixed cases, leisure does not enter computed utility, so figures indicate percentage change in utility: these figures will tend to understate EV, but signs will not change.

Table 15.4 Increase in tax progression, by increasing the marginal tax rate keeping the average constant and letting allowances vary. France

	Benchmark benefit level			
	0.80		0.00	
Labour supply	Fixed	Variable	Fixed	Variable
(a) *Increase of 1 percentage point of the marginal tax rate*				
%Δ employment level	0.49	0.24	0.19	− 0.10
%Δ male employment	0.54	0.30	0.21	− 0.07
%Δ female employment	0.42	0.16	0.16	− 0.13
%Δ full-time employment	0.56	0.31	0.22	− 0.06
%Δ part-time employment	—	− 0.22	—	− 0.33
%Δ unemployment rate	− 0.50	− 0.78	− 0.19	− 0.25
Welfare measures				
$EV_{C,\ell+u}$	0.46	0.18	0.17	− 0.06
$EV_{C,\ell}$	0.46	0.41	0.17	0.04
Terms of trade	1.01	1.01	1.01	1.01
Residual income elasticity	0.91	0.91	0.91	0.91
(b) *Increase of 3 percentage points of the marginal tax rate*				
%Δ employment level	1.49	0.72	0.58	− 0.33
%Δ male employment	1.65	0.90	0.64	− 0.22
%Δ female employment	1.29	0.47	0.50	− 0.39
%Δ full-time employment	1.71	0.92	0.66	− 0.19
%Δ part-time employment	—	− 0.68	—	− 1.02
%Δ unemployment rate	− 1.53	− 2.38	− 0.59	− 0.77
Welfare measures				
$EV_{C,\ell+u}$	1.39	0.52	0.52	− 0.19
$EV_{C,\ell}$	1.39	1.24	0.52	0.11
Terms of trade	1.01	1.01	1.01	1.01
Residual income elasticity	0.88	0.88	0.88	0.88

however, the reduction in the unemployment rate is much larger than in the previous case of fixed labour supply: a reduction of 0.95 percentage points is obtained. A further influence on part-time employment is the fall in the unemployment rate making full-time employment more attractive, for given wage rates, so the share of part-time labour in the total labour supply also falls.

Columns three and four repeat the exercise, but with zero benefits for unemployed workers. It is necessary to be clear about this experiment: we have set zero benefits into the benchmark, together with the same benchmark level of unemployment as in the other cases. Thus, although we can predict that reducing benefit levels would also raise employment, as in Section 2 above, employment effects from changing progression are still comparable. If we had shown progression effects relative to employment levels already increased by zero benefits, lower gains would be observed as in Figures 15.3 and 15.4. Column 3 still shows employment gains for the fixed supply case, though the gains are much

Table 15.5 Increase in tax progression, by increasing the marginal tax rate keeping the average constant and letting allowances vary. Italy

| | Benchmark benefit level | | | |
| | 0.50 | | 0.00 | |
Labour supply	Fixed	Variable	Fixed	Variable
(a) *Increase of 1 percentage point of the marginal tax rate*				
%Δ employment level	0.42	0.12	0.26	− 0.03
%Δ male employment	0.43	0.14	0.27	− 0.02
%Δ female employment	0.39	0.09	0.25	− 0.05
%Δ full-time employment	0.45	0.15	0.28	− 0.01
%Δ part-time employment	—	− 0.35	—	− 0.39
%Δ unemployment rate	− 0.41	− 0.58	− 0.25	− 0.33
Welfare measures				
$EV_{C,\ell+u}$	0.34	0.09	0.19	− 0.03
$EV_{C,\ell}$	0.34	0.25	0.19	0.07
Terms of trade	1.04	1.04	1.04	1.04
Residual income elasticity	0.83	0.83	0.83	0.83
(b) *Increase of 3 percentage points of the marginal tax rate*				
%Δ employment level	1.28	0.36	0.80	− 0.11
%Δ male employment	1.32	0.41	0.83	− 0.08
%Δ female employment	1.21	0.26	0.75	− 0.17
%Δ full-time employment	1.36	0.45	0.85	− 0.04
%Δ part-time employment	—	− 1.08	—	− 1.19
%Δ unemployment rate	− 1.24	− 1.77	− 0.77	− 1.02
Welfare measures				
$EV_{C,\ell+u}$	1.04	0.27	0.57	− 0.09
$EV_{C,\ell}$	1.04	0.74	0.57	0.20
Terms of trade	1.05	1.05	1.05	1.05
Residual income elasticity	0.81	0.81	0.81	0.81

less because the flatter wage curve induces smaller wage reductions. When labour supply is variable, the zero benefit case yields employment losses for all categories of worker, especially part-timers. The unemployment rate is still reduced, however, as the labour supply has reduced by more than labour demand. Thus, the predictions from the simple partial model of Section 2 are reproduced here.

The effects on part-time work are worth a further comment. Where income taxation is levied on individual incomes, it is sometimes argued (in e.g. OECD 1995) that more progression would encourage part-time work. We do not replicate this effect since we assume that all workers pay the same marginal rate of tax, so there is no incentive to minimise family tax liability by sharing the work more equally. Our results mainly derive from our modelling the part-time market as competitive, so that the normal disincentive effects on labour supply are obtained.

Table 15.6 Increase in tax progression, by increasing the marginal tax rate keeping the average constant and letting allowances vary. UK

	Benchmark benefit level			
	0.77		*0.00*	
Labour supply	*Fixed*	*Variable*	*Fixed*	*Variable*
(a) *Increase of 1 percentage point of the marginal tax rate*				
%Δ employment level	0.47	0.18	0.19	−0.13
%Δ male employment	0.58	0.30	0.23	−0.08
%Δ female employment	0.34	0.03	0.14	−0.19
%Δ full-time employment	0.62	0.31	0.25	−0.06
%Δ part-time employment	—	−0.26	—	−0.36
%Δ unemployment rate	−0.56	−0.81	−0.22	−0.28
Welfare measures				
$EV_{C,\ell+u}$	0.46	0.15	0.17	−0.07
$EV_{C,\ell}$	0.46	0.39	0.17	0.04
Terms of trade	1.05	1.05	1.05	1.05
Residual income elasticity	0.80	0.80	0.80	0.80
(b) *Increase of 3 percentage points of the marginal tax rate*				
%Δ employment level	1.44	0.52	0.57	−0.39
%Δ male employment	1.76	0.88	0.70	−0.24
%Δ female employment	1.04	0.06	0.41	−0.59
%Δ full-time employment	1.88	0.92	0.75	−0.18
%Δ part-time employment	—	−0.81	—	−1.10
%Δ unemployment rate	−1.69	−2.49	−0.67	−0.84
Welfare measures				
$EV_{C,\ell+u}$	1.38	0.44	0.52	−0.21
$EV_{C,\ell}$	1.38	1.17	0.52	0.10
Terms of trade	1.05	1.05	1.05	1.05
Residual income elasticity	0.78	0.78	0.78	0.78

The welfare measures each tell a different story. The first, 'naïve', measure $EV_{C,\ell+u}$, in which all leisure is treated in the same way shows positive effects particularly for the fixed labour supply cases, but is negative for the fourth column in which employment falls together with unemployment. The second measure, $EV_{C,\ell}$, which removes any welfare benefits from excess leisure consumption through unemployment, is identical for the fixed supply cases since leisure is not a variable, but is more positive for the variable supply cases than $EV_{C,\ell+u}$. This second measure is still positive for the fourth column. Thus, the arguably more realistic measure shows consistently greater benefits from greater progression, remaining positive even when this means lower employment. The reason for the significant discrepancy in the fourth column is that in this case there is a sizeable shift within total leisure $(\ell+u)$ from forced consumption (u)

to chosen consumption (ℓ). Interpretation of these measures is complicated, however, since leisure is not treated as a good when computing utility in the fixed supply case, with the effect that the EV figures will be smaller in absolute value for the fixed case.[8]

With some variations in the details, the same qualitative results are obtained for all other cases considered: see Tables 15.3–15.6. Changing the marginal income tax rate by three instead of one point simply increases all the effects by approximately a multiple of three, indicating the local linearity of the model. The case of Italy is notable in that the 1992 benefit benchmark is only 0.5, reducing the contrast from dropping to zero benefit. The same pattern is observed, however, with zero benefits reversing the employment gains from extra progression. But in Italy, the lower benefit level means that the impact of progression on employment is less. In the central case, with benefit parameter $b = 0.5$, and variable labour supply, a 1 percentage point change in t reduces the percentage unemployment rate by 0.58 compared to 0.95 in Germany, and employment increases by 0.12 per cent compared to 0.24 per cent in Germany. The figures for France and the UK are quite similar to those for Germany.

5 Conclusions

5.1 Employment effect of progression

The numerical results we have obtained are quite consistent with the qualitative predictions of the small theoretical model initially set out. Increased progression above current levels does reduce unemployment; and when unemployment benefit levels are at observed levels, increased progression also increases employment and welfare. Lower levels of benefit would, however, reverse the employment effects, with more progression reducing employment. It also seems that the size of the effects obtained are not trivial, and that there are positive employment and welfare effects from increasing progression in all the cases considered: France, Germany, Italy and the UK. These conclusions are, of course, subject to some reservations. It should be clear that assuming higher levels of supply responsiveness will tend to reverse the results for employment (but not for unemployment), as would increasing progression from much higher levels than currently observed. Diminishing returns must set in at some point, though our simulations do not pick up any strong signs of nonlinearity when comparing 1 and 3 per cent changes. The results for part-time workers are different, because in our model the market for part-time workers is fully competitive and is cleared by the part-time wage. The normal negative effect of progression on employment is therefore to be expected, but other mechanisms work in the same direction: more progression tends to reduce full-time wages and encourage substitution from part-time working; and reduced unemployment makes full-time work more attractive to workers. Women are more likely to work part-time, so they benefit less than men.

5.2   *Distributional effects*

Another aspect of these results which calls for some comment is their distributional implications. We have assumed away distributional issues with the
representative household, but we can speculate on the implications of allowing
a range of households of different types/skills and different wages. We have
assumed a linear-progressive tax schedule, whose index of residual progression
will increase with income (NB this means, perversely, that progression as usually
understood reduces with income). A given percentage change in the marginal rate
will have a bigger effect on residual progression at low incomes, and therefore a
bigger effect on the pre-tax wage at low levels. So a rise in the marginal rate will
tend to reduce low pre-tax wages proportionately more than high pre-tax wages,
and thus increase pre-tax inequality indices such as the Gini. Post-tax inequality
will depend on the average rate structure: average rates must rise at the top end,
and fall at the bottom, if the overall average rate is unchanged. Thus the average
rate structure will tend to reduce post-tax inequality. The net effect is not clear,
but a simple example is suggestive.

Assume there are two classes of labour in equal and fixed supply, sharing the
same wage-curve, but with different levels of demand yielding different wage
rates. The model in Section 2 above yields the result that

$$\log(w) = \log\left(\frac{1-t}{1-t^A}\right) + const. + f(u). \tag{27}$$

To evaluate the proportionate effect of a given change in m, conditional on u, use
the definition

$$\frac{d\log(w)}{dt} = \frac{\partial\log(w(1-t^A))}{\partial t} - \frac{\partial\log(1-t^A)}{\partial t}. \tag{28}$$

And from (27)

$$\frac{d\log(w)}{dt} = \frac{\partial\log(1-t^A)}{\partial t} - \frac{\partial\log(1-t^A)}{\partial t} = -\frac{1}{1-t} + \frac{1-Z/w}{1-t^A}. \tag{29}$$

This is the effect on the gross wage. And combining (28) and (29),

$$\frac{\partial\log(w(1-t^A))}{\partial t} = -\frac{1}{1-t} \tag{30}$$

is the effect on the net wage.

The average rate t^A is higher and Z/w lower for high w, so the second term in
(29) is larger for high w than low w. The whole expression is therefore less negative
for high w, and so more progression is disequalising, provided we assume equal
elasticity of demand for each class of labour. The effect on the post-tax distribution is equi-proportional, however, since the marginal effect on $\log(w(1-t^A))$
is $-1/(1-t)$ in (30), which is independent of w. Thus, in this case, progression
has no effect on the post-tax distribution, while the pre-tax distribution is made
less equal by increased progression.

5.3 Other models

Efficiency wage models can be motivated in a number of different ways. Our training model is one possibility, while 'shirking' models associated with Shapiro and Stiglitz (1984) suggest a different mechanism but with similar predictions. The essential message of these latter models has been expressed by Sorensen (1997):

> ...a higher marginal tax rate implies that a rise in the relative wage will generate a smaller net gain for the individual workers. A higher pre-tax wage will thus become less effective as a means of raising labour productivity. From the viewpoint of each employer, the optimal level of firm's relative wage rate will therefore go down, and in the new general equilibrium, employment will be higher as a result of lower wages. By contrast, if the average tax rate on labour is raised and tax progressivity as well as after-tax unemployment benefits are unchanged, the discipline and productivity-enhancing effects of unemployment will be weakened because the unemployment option becomes relatively more attractive. In order to (partially) restore productivity, employers therefore bid up the level of wages, resulting in higher equilibrium unemployment.

Sorensen's (1999) efficiency wage model assumes fixed hours but variable effort: more progression reduces effort levels, and employment increases with progression; in a search model, similar results flow from the same fixed-wage assumption. In a bargaining model, however, Sorensen shows that the effect on wage rates of increased progression can be offset by reduced hours, but in his model this tends to increase employment (numbers of workers). The net effect is that he finds that progression always increases employment. We have assumed fixed hours for each mode of work, with households adjusting the mix of full- and part-time work, and obtain rather different results.

The different versions have similar properties, but the version we have adopted has its own characteristic features, such as the role of training costs on the demand for labour. This will yield different quantitative properties from alternative efficiency wage, or bargaining models, motivating the wage curve. The mechanisms we have highlighted, however, will exist in any version: the more elastic supply of labour must offset the employment generating feature of progression in any model with a wage curve, and the benefit system must have broadly the same impact as we have demonstrated.

5.4 Summary

The main messages of our paper can be summarised as follows:

1 Simulations suggest that increased progression in the European economies studied would increase employment and welfare, especially for full-time

workers that is, mostly men. Reducing unemployment by this means could even reduce part-time employment.

2   In the efficiency wage model adopted here, the level of unemployment is a function of training (and other turnover-related) costs.

3   The more generous the benefit system, the more unemployment will exist and the more effective is progression in raising employment. When unemployment benefit is sufficiently low, more progression would reduce employment and welfare, but from a higher level. Therefore the distributional consequences of employment policies must be addressed by policy-makers.

4   The model suggests that increased progression may have little or no effect on the post-tax distribution of income, while the pre-tax distribution might become more unequal.

5   The general equilibrium model, calibrated for France, Germany, Italy and the UK showed that the partial equilibrium results hold even in the context of a highly distorted general equilibrium, with international trade, tariffs and various other taxes and subsidies. The numerical effects are similar across countries, and sufficiently large to be relevant for policy.

Appendix I: Utility and production structures

Utility tree

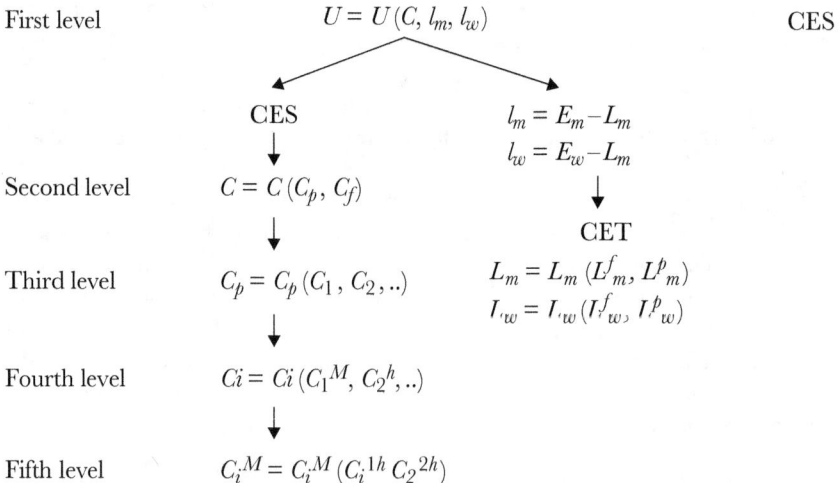

First level	$U = U(C, l_m, l_w)$	CES

At the *first level*, our representative household chooses between an aggregate consumption commodity C and leisure demand l_m for male and l_w for female family members. The utility function $U(\cdot)$ is of the constant elasticity of substitution (CES) type. In the utility tree we now distinguish between the determination of commodity demands in the left-hand part and labour supply in the right-hand part of the diagram. Let us start with the latter branch of the utility tree. Each family member is endowed with a given time endowment E_m and E_w, respectively. The differences between time endowments and leisure demands yield labour supplies L_m and L_w of the different genders. Following Hutton and Ruocco (1999) we introduce at the *second level* an additional labour/leisure choice allowing each family member to choose his or her optimal combination of full- and part-time labour supply $L_{f,m}$ and $L_{p,m}$ for men and $L_{f,w}$ and $L_{p,w}$ for women.

The left-hand side of the utility tree illustrates the partition of consumer choices. On the second level of the utility tree the consumer decides on the demand for different aggregate consumption categories C_i such as, for example, cars or food. The *third level* divides each aggregate consumption commodity into domestic consumption component C_i^h and a composite import component C_i^M. Hence, at this stage the household decides, whether to purchase an imported or a domestically produced commodity. Finally, at the *fourth* and last stage, the decision is about where to buy consumption imports. For example, a German household decides whether to buy an imported car from Italy or from France. Here, C_i^{Fh} and C_i^{Ih} denote the imports from France (F) and Italy (I) of commodity i to country $h \neq F, I$.

As functional forms we have chosen CES functions for the consumption branch of the utility tree.

Production tree

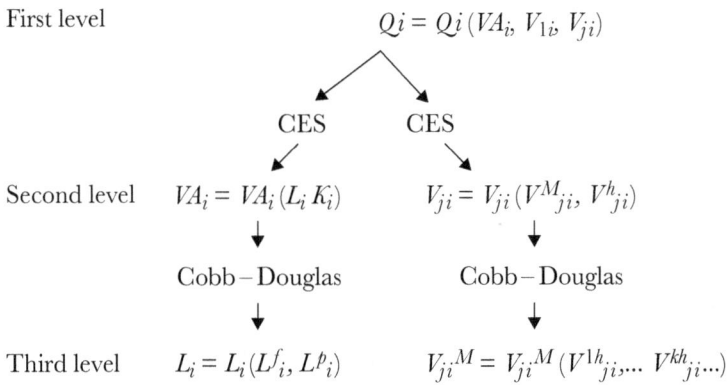

First level	$Qi = Qi\,(VA_i,\ V_{1i},\ V_{ji})$
Second level	$VA_i = VA_i\,(L_i;\,K_i)$ $\qquad$ $V_{ji} = V_{ji}\,(V^M_{ji},\ V^h_{ji})$
	Cobb–Douglas $\qquad$ Cobb–Douglas
Third level	$L_i = L_i\,(L^f_i,\ L^p_i)$ $\qquad$ $V_{ji}{}^M = V_{ji}{}^M\,(V^{1h}_{ji},\dots,\ V^{kh}_{ji}\dots)$

The production function at the first level of the firm's cost minimisation problem is a Leontief-technology. Total output of commodity i, Q_i, depends on value added, VA_i, and on the intermediate use of composite commodities, $j = 1, \dots, 11$ in the production of commodity i, V_{ji}. The left-hand side of the production tree decomposes value added, whereas the right-hand side illustrates the composition of intermediate products. Starting with the value added branch, sector i decides at the second level how much capital, K_i, and aggregate labour, L_i, it needs in production. At the third level aggregate labour demand is decomposed into full-time labour, $L_{f,i}$, and part-time labour $L_{p,i}$. Turning to the left-hand branch of the production tree, the *second level* disaggregates composite intermediate products V_{ji} into domestically produced inputs, V_{ji}^h, and an aggregate of imported intermediate inputs, V_{ji}^M. At the *third level* of the hierarchical cost minimisation problem, the representative firm in sector i decides in which country to purchase its imported intermediates. Here V_{ji}^{kh} denotes the intermediate use of commodity j, originating from country k, in the production of commodity i in country h. At the second level of the production tree we employ CES functions in the value added and the intermediate product branches, while Cobb–Douglas functions are used at the third level.

Notes

1 As a further example, Duncan, Hutton, Laroui, and Ruocco (1998) show in a simulation study that indirect tax harmonisation can be welfare-reducing in the presence of unemployment.
2 Defined as proportion of labour supply.
3 The Jacobsson–Kakwani Theorem shows that a decrease in this index for all incomes will result in a distribution which Lorenz-dominates the pre-change distribution.
4 This argument is further elaborated below in the AGE model in discussing the full-time/part-time choice.
5 In the full general equilibrium model later, we use a nested CES utility structure, but the simpler Cobb–Douglas form is quite suitable at this stage.
6 In Hutton and Ruocco (1999) the notation was slightly different: L^S corresponds to L^T.
7 Discrimination may still take the form of, for example, non-employment or non-promotion, rather than paying a lower wage for identical work.
8 Because when leisure is a good, full income exceeds money income; and the EV equals the percentage change in utility times the ratio of full income to money income.

References

Ashenfelter, O. and Heckman, J. (1974) 'The estimation of income and substitution effects in a model of family labour supply', *Econometrica*, 42: 73–85.
Blanchflower, D. G. and Oswald, A. (1994) *The Wage Curve*. London: M.I.T. Press.
Blum, W. J. and Kalven, H. (1978) *The Uneasy Case for Progressive Taxation*. Chicago and London: University of Chicago Press.
Campbell, C. and Orszag, J. M. (1998) 'A model of the wage curve', *Economics Letters*, 59: 119–25.
Duncan, A. S., Hutton, J. P., Laroui, F. and Ruocco, A. (1998) 'Labour market effects of VAT harmonisation in a multicountry AGE model', in: Fossati, A. and Hutton, J. (eds) *Policy Simulations in the European Union*. London: Routledge, Chap. 4: 59–78.
Fehr, H., Rosenberg C. and Wiegard, W. (1995) *Welfare Effects of Value-Added Tax Harmonization in Europe*. Berlin: SpringerVerlag.
Fuest C. and Huber B. (1999) 'Tax coordination and unemployment', *International Tax and Public Finance*, 6: 7–26.
Goerke, L. (1999) 'Efficiency wages and taxes', *Australian Economic Papers*, 38 (2).
Graafland, J. J. and de Mooij, R. A. (1999) 'Fiscal policy and the labour market: an AGE analysis', *Economic Modelling*, 16: 189–219.
Hoel, M. (1990) 'Efficiency wages and income taxes', *Journal of Economics/Zeitschrift für Nationaloeconomie*, 51: 89–99.

Hutton, J. P. and Ruocco, A. (1999) 'Tax reform and employment in Europe', *International Tax and Public Finance*, 6 (3): 263–88.

Lambert, P. (1993) *The Distribution and Redistribution of Income: A Mathematical Analysis*, 2nd edn. Manchester UK: Manchester University Press.

Lockwood, B. and Manning, A. (1993) 'Wage setting and the tax system: theory and evidence for the United Kingdom', *Journal of Public Economics*, 52: 1–29.

Myles, G. D. (1995) *Public Economics*. Cambridge: Cambridge University Press.

OECD (1995) *The OECD Jobs Study: Taxation, Employment and Unemployment*. Paris: OECD.

Phelps, E. H. (1994) *Structural Slumps: The Modern Equilibrium Theory of Unemployment, Interest and Assets*. Cambridge MA: Harvard University Press.

Ruocco, A. (1996) *A multi-country general equilibrium model for the European Union: the basic features and the coding structure*, Discussion Paper 83. Wirtschaftswissenschaftliche Fakultaet, University of Tubingen.

Shapiro, C. and Stiglitz, J. (1984) 'Equilibrium unemployment as a worker discipline device', *American Economic Review*, 74: 433–44.

Sorensen, P. B. (1999) 'Optimal tax progressivity in imperfect labour markets', *Labour Economics*, 6 (3): 435–52.

Sorensen, P. B. (1997) 'Public finance solutions to European unemployment problems', *Economic Policy*, 24: 222–64.

16 Introducing idiosyncratic uncertainty in a life-cycle CGE-model*

Toke Ward Petersen

1 Introduction

What would happen if uncertainty were introduced in a CGE-model? Would this influence policy conclusions based on these models? And if so, how? The purpose of this paper is to investigate the effects of introducing uncertainty, and understand exactly how the presence of uncertainty makes a difference. This is done by comparing the results of identical policy experiments using three different models: models with and without uncertainty.

A move from progressive to proportional taxation of labour income is often considered welfare-improving, since it is believed to lower distortions. The idea is that lower marginal taxes (under a proportional tax regime) will increase the incentive for high-income groups to work and to accumulate assets. This relationship has been examined in several applied general equilibrium analyses, for instance by Auerbach and Kotlikoff (1987). The question posed in this paper is whether these policy conclusions are altered if idiosyncratic earnings uncertainty is added to the model.

Why would we expect a different outcome under idiosyncratic uncertainty? First of all uninsurable idiosyncratic uncertainty makes the economy work in a different way – among others because agents make precautionary savings to protect themselves against too much variability in income. As pointed out by Engen and Gale (1996), savings of the precautionary type are less sensitive to changes in the rate of return than pure life-cycle savings. Therefore the savings elasticity is likely to be lower in a situation with precautionary savings.[1] A second interesting idea is that with uncertain earnings the 'costs' of progressive taxation may be smaller since progressivity has a risk mitigating effect that may counteract any distortionary effects. Therefore progression may be less 'painful' for the risk-adverse agents since it evens out after-tax income. This chapter analyses this question in a dynamic computable general equilibrium model. Overlapping generations of consumers face an idiosyncratic labour income in each period of their lives. The uncertainty is only present at the individual level, which

*I would like to thank Larry Kotlikoff, Lars Haagen Pedersen, Carlo Perroni as well as my discussant Shantayanan Devarajan for useful comments and suggestions on an earlier version.

means that aggregate variables are not (directly) influenced. Since borrowing is permitted, agents have to self-insure against variability in income. The government sector levies taxes on income and uses the revenue for public expenditures. The production side is standard: firms produce using capital and labour according to a constant return to scale technology.

This study tries to bridge the gap between the traditional deterministic analyses and models with idiosyncratic earnings uncertainty, and attempts to analyse why the two types of models give different results.[2] Interpreting and explaining the difference in simulation results between the deterministic model used by Auerbach and Kotlikoff (from now on referred to as the A–K model) and an almost identical model with idiosyncratic earnings uncertainty turns out to be a bit more complicated than one would expect at a first glance. At least two effects should be taken into account: the effect of having agents with different earning capabilities at any given point in time (which is necessary if the earnings capabilities should be able to vary) and the consequences of having earnings capabilities that fluctuate in a stochastic manner over the life cycle. A simple comparison between the A–K model and the model with idiosyncratic earnings uncertainty would end up mixing these effects together, which is unfortunate because we are only interested in the latter effect.

This chapter is organized as follows: Section 2 contains a description of the model used – this includes a description of the consumers, producers and the government sector. Section 3 describes how the model is calibrated and how the model is solved in stationary state. Section 4 contains the results of the analysis, and finally Section 5 summarizes the findings, and suggests directions for future research.

2 A general equilibrium model

The model described here is a relatively standard stochastic general equilibrium model. To simplify matters, we will only look at the stationary state of the model, which means that all time indices are removed in the formulae below.

2.1 *The consumers*

The consumers in the model are almost similar to Auerbach and Kotlikoff (1987): they live for *j* periods, and seek to maximize their lifetime utility function subject to their budget constraint. Their utility function is additive separable, and they incur utility from consumption and leisure. They face a borrowing constraint in every period, as well as (the usual) lifetime budget constraint. Labour income arises from sale of labour services – the income from this is uncertain, due to a stochastic productivity term (described below). Since income in each period is uncertain, solving the consumers' problem is easier formulated as a dynamic programming problem, which is presented below.

A recursive approach

The recursive maximization problem for a representative consumer with the start-of-period assets a_{j-1} and the productivity category d_{j-1} is given by:

$$V_j(a_{j-1}, d_{j-1}) = \max_{\{c_j, l_j, a_j\}} \left[\frac{1}{1 - (1/\gamma)} u(c_j, l_j)^{(1-(1/\gamma))} + \beta \sum_b \pi_b(d_{j-1})\; V_{j+1}(a_j, b) \right]$$

(1)

with the budget constraint:

$$a_j = (1 + r)\; a_{j-1} + w\; (1 - l_j)\; e_j(d_{j-1}) - p c_j - \mathrm{TAX}$$

(2)

where the agent is subject to liquidity, consumption and leisure constraints:

$$a_j \geq 0 \quad (\forall j)$$

(3)

$$c_j \geq 0 \quad (\forall j)$$

(4)

$$1 \geq l_j \geq 0 \quad (\forall j)$$

(5)

and $V_j(a_{j-1}, d_{j-1})$ is the value function, a_j is the end-of-period assets, $e_j(d_{j-1})$ is the productivity in period j for labour with the start of period[3] productivity d_{j-1}, c_j is the consumption in period j, l_j is the leisure enjoyed by generation j, γ is the household's intertemporal elasticity of substitution, β is the one-period discount factor, $\pi_b(d)$ is the transition probability that next period's labour productivity will be b given it is d in this period, r is the one-period interest rate, w is the wage and p is the consumer price level. TAX is taxes paid, and is the sum of a consumption tax, an interest income tax and a labour income tax:

$$\mathrm{TAX} = \mathrm{TAX}_C(p c_j) + \mathrm{TAX}_A(r a_{j-1}) + \mathrm{TAX}_L((1 - l_j)\, e_j(d_{j-1})\, w)$$

(6)

where TAX_C is the consumption tax, TAX_A is the taxation of interest income and TAX_L is the taxation of labour income.[4]

Earnings

The labour productivity falls in one of D categories, and is age-dependent through the function $e_j(d)$. To simplify matters we assume that productivity can be separated in an age- and a category effect, such that $e_j(d)$ can be written as the product, $e_j(d) = \hat{e}_j \bar{e}_d$. The transition between categories of labour productivity is a first-order Markov process, with age-independent transition probabilities. Uncertainty in earnings is caused by variability in the labour productivity. As formulated above the earnings uncertainty is a first-order Markov process, where the earnings level tomorrow only depends on earnings level today (the Markov formulation makes it possible to introduce 'persistence' in earnings – see below).

Taxes

The tax-functions (TAX$_C$, TAX$_A$ and TAX$_L$) allow for progressive taxation schemes. We use the same progression system as Auerbach and Kotlikoff (1987, ch. 8), and assume that the marginal tax rates take the form:

$$\tau = \underline{\tau} + \kappa B \tag{7}$$

where $\underline{\tau}$ is the marginal tax applicable at zero income (the 'intercept'), B is the taxable amount (the 'base'), and κ is the progressivity parameter (the 'slope'). If $\kappa = 0$ we have a proportional tax system. The average rate of a system given by equation (7) is

$$\bar{\tau} = \underline{\tau} + \kappa \frac{B}{2} \tag{8}$$

This formula is similarly applied to taxation of interest income, labour income taxation and consumption, and the associated progressivity and level parameters are $\{\kappa_a, \underline{\tau}_a\}$, $\{\kappa_l, \underline{\tau}_l\}$ and $\{\kappa_c, \underline{\tau}_c\}$.

Utility

The annual utility function is the CES-function

$$u(c, l) = \left[c^{(1-(1/\rho))} + \alpha l^{(1-(1/\rho))} \right]^{1/(1-(1/\rho))} \tag{9}$$

where α is a taste parameter reflecting the joy of leisure, and ρ is an elasticity of substitution between leisure and consumption.

Solving the consumer's problem

The optimization problem facing an individual is one of finite state, finite horizon dynamic programming.[5] The decision rules can be found by backward recursion from the last period of life. We start by reducing the number of control variables by substituting the budget constraint into the value function.[6] First we isolate c_j in the budget constraint:

$$c_j = \frac{(1+r)a_{j-1} + w(1 - l_j)e_j(d_{j-1}) - \text{TAX} - a_j}{p} \tag{10}$$

which is substituted into the CES-utility function (9), which afterwards is substituted into the value-function (1). This gives an expression for the value-function $V_j(a_{j-1}, d_{j-1})$ where the two control variables in the maximization problem are l_j and a_j (since c_j is defined implicitly).

Last period

Since death is certain beyond period N, and there is no bequest motive in the model, the choice in period N is to consume everything that is left, plus whatever income is generated in that period. With $a_N = 0$ as the optimal solution, we can simplify the last-period problem, and the associated utility is

$$V_N(a_{N-1}, d_{N-1}) = \max_{\{c_N, l_N\}} \left[\frac{1}{1 - (1/\gamma)} \right.$$
$$\left. \times \left[c_N^{(1-(1/\rho))} + \alpha l_N^{(1-(1/\rho))} \right]^{(1/(1-(1/\rho)))^{(1-(1/\gamma))}} \right] \tag{11}$$

We obtain the argmax for l_N (which we will later call l_N^*) by solving equation (11) numerically.

Second-last period (and forwards . . .)

In all periods before the last period, we calculate the optimal plan for the consumer by numerically maximizing the value function $V_j(a_{j-1}, d_{j-1})$, computing the optimal values for the control variables l_j and a_j (and implicitly c_j). This is done in the manner described in Section 3.4.

Individual optimal policy rules

Denote the optimal consumption for a consumer with the decision problem $V_j(a_{j-1}, d_{j-1})$ by $c_j^*(a_{j-1}, d_{j-1})$, the optimal leisure by $l_j^*(a_{j-1}, d_{j-1})$ and the optimal end-of-period asset holdings by $a_j^*(a_{j-1}, d_{j-1})$.[7] We will refer to these as the individual policy rules, and for short refer to them as c_j^*, l_j^* and a_j^*.[8]

2.3 Aggregation

Finally some aggregation and equilibrium conditions for the consumer:

Population transition

The size of each of the overlapping generations has a total measure of unity. Since there is no mortality in the set-up used here, this means that the total (normalized) number of agents at any point in time is fifty-five. At any point in time these agents have characteristics in the $(a, d) \in (A, D)$ space (the two state variables). Let $\Psi_j(a, d)$ denote the number of individuals with assets a, productivity level d and age j. This is a stock variable, and measured at the end of the period; in other words $\Psi_{j-1}(a, d)$ are alive and active in period j of their lives. Calculating how many individuals are in which group – and the transition between groups – is done in the following manner:

   Initial   Individuals entering the economy have no assets, but their distribution on productivity categories is exogenously determined. The probability that an agent starts in category d is η_d. Thus we have that the individuals active in the first period are:

$$\Psi_0(0, d) = \eta_d \tag{12}$$

Transition In the second period individuals can have positive assets in addition to a productivity category. A complicating matter is that the transition in the system is endogenously determined by the consumer's choice of control variable. Thus, for $j = 1, 2, \ldots, N-1$ we have:

$$\psi_0(\hat{a}, d) = \underbrace{\sum_{d \in D} \pi_b(b)}_{\substack{\text{Transition} \\ \text{probability}}} \underbrace{\sum_{a \in A} \Psi_{j-1}(a, d) \chi[a_j^*(a, d) = \hat{a}]}_{\substack{\text{Number of individuals who} \\ \text{choose to transit to this state}}} \qquad (13)$$

where the first term is the (exogenous) transition probability from any productivity category to category b, and the second term is the number of individuals in the previous period who choose their next period assets to equal a_j where $\chi[\bullet]$ is an indicator function (that assumes 1 if true and 0 if false, the condition being whether individuals choose the end-of-period assets we are considering: $\hat{a}$). Thus we sum over all individuals that (choose) to transit to the state $\Psi_j(a, d)$.

Terminal At the final period, the equation above reduces to:

$$\Psi_N(a, d) = 0 \qquad (14)$$

Aggregate factor supply

The next aggregation issue is to figure out the aggregate labour supply by calculating the sum over all individuals. The total labour supply in efficiency units, and the capital stock is given by:

$$L = \sum_{j=1}^{N} \sum_{a \in A} \sum_{d \in D} \Psi_{j-1}(a, d)(1 - l_j^*(a, d))e_j(d) \qquad (15)$$

$$K_{-1} = \sum_{j=1}^{N} \sum_{a \in A} \sum_{d \in D} \Psi_{j-1}(a, d)a_j^*(a, d) \qquad (16)$$

Notice that physical capital does not depreciate.

2.4 The producers and the government

The production side is identical to Auerbach and Kotlikoff (1987). There is a single good that is produced using capital and labour subject to a constant-returns-to-scale technology. Labour across ages and productivity categories differ in efficiency, and we calculate the total labour supply by individuals using equation (15) and the size of the aggregate capital stock using equation (16).

Production takes place using the CES production function:

$$Y(K, L) = \Lambda[\varepsilon K^{(1-1/\sigma)} + (1 - \varepsilon)K^{(1-1/\sigma)}]^{1/(1-1/\sigma)} \qquad (17)$$

where K and L are capital and labour in the period, Y is output, Λ is a scaling constant, ε is a capital-intensity parameter and σ is the elasticity of substitution between K and L. This gives the standard results that the gross wages must equal the marginal revenue product of labour (measured in efficiency units):

$$w = (1 - \varepsilon)\Lambda[\varepsilon K^{(1-1/\sigma)} + (1 - \varepsilon)K^{(1-1/\sigma)}]^{1/(1-1/\sigma)}L^{(-1/\sigma)} \tag{18}$$

and the interest rate equals the marginal revenue product of capital:

$$r = \varepsilon\Lambda[\varepsilon K^{(1-1/\sigma)} + (1 - \varepsilon)K^{(1-1/\sigma)}]^{1/(1-1/\sigma)}K^{(-1/\sigma)} \tag{19}$$

Notice that the output price is numeraire ($p = 1$) and there is no depreciation.

The final part of the model is the government sector that is also kept very simple. Government revenue is raised by taxation of labour income, interest income and a consumption tax. The revenue from taxation is not transferred back to the consumers, but is consumed.

2.5   Equilibrium

Finally we need to define what we understand by an equilibrium in the model:

Definition: A stationary equilibrium for a given set of policy arrangements $\{\kappa_a, \mathcal{T}_a, \kappa_l, \mathcal{T}_l, \kappa_c, \mathcal{T}_c\}$ (progressivity and tax level for the three taxes) is a collection of value functions $V_j(a, d)$, individual policy rules l_j^* and a_j^*, age-dependent measures of agent types $\Psi_j(a, b)$, relative prices of labour and capital $\{w, r\}$ such that:

1   the relative prices $\{w, r\}$ solve the firm's maximization problem (satisfy equation (18) and (19)
2   given the relative prices $\{w, r\}$ and government policies $\{\kappa_a, \mathcal{T}_a, \kappa_l, \mathcal{T}_l, \kappa_c, \mathcal{T}_c\}$ the individual policy rules l_j^*, c_j^* and a_j^* solve the consumer's problem.
3   individual and aggregate behaviour are consistent, that is, that L and K satisfy equations (15) and (16)
4   the population follows the law of motion given by equations (12), (13) and (14)
5   commodity markets clear, that is, that production (given by equation (17)) equals consumption:

$$Y(K, L) = \sum_{j=1}^{N}\sum_{a \in A}\sum_{d \in D} \Psi_{j-1}(a, d)c_j^*(a, d) \tag{21}$$

3   Calibration

This section describes how the model is calibrated, and how the steady state is calculated.

3.1   The consumer side productivity

As mentioned previously $e_j(d_{j-1})$ is separated in $\hat{e}_j$ and $\bar{e}_d \cdot \hat{e}_j$ is the age-dependent part and here we use the same equations for productivity over the life cycle as

Auerbach and Kotlikoff (1987) which in turn originate from a cross-sectional regression study by Welch (1979). This hump-shaped profile gives an earnings profile that peaks at age 30, (corresponding to an actual age of 50) at wages that are 45 per cent higher than at age 1 (corresponding to 21 years).

To keep the model very simple $\bar{e}_d$ (the productivity term that is not age-dependent) can assume one of two productivity values $\{1 - \Phi, 1 + \Phi\}$ where $\Phi \geq 0$. Below we will perform simulations for $\Phi = 0$ and $\Phi = 0.25$ (and in the sensitivity analysis look at what happens when $\Phi = 0.125$ and $\Phi = 0.5$). Notice that when $\Phi = 0$ there is no difference in productivity between the groups – which of course is the same as removing uncertainty and turning to a deterministic model with one productivity level – which is the model used in Auerbach and Kotlikoff (1987).

For the household's intertemporal elasticity of substitution, γ we use the estimate used in Auerbach and Kotlikoff (1987) and set $\gamma = 0.25$.

For the one-period discount factor, β, we again use Auerbach and Kotlikoff (1987). They use a rate of time preference of 0.015, which is equivalent to $\beta = 1/1.015 \approx 0.98522$. For the Markov transition probabilities $\pi_b(d)$ we can use a variety of formulations. π is defined as:

$$\pi_\Omega = \begin{bmatrix} \frac{1}{2} + \Omega & \frac{1}{2} - \Omega \\ \frac{1}{2} - \Omega & \frac{1}{2} + \Omega \end{bmatrix}$$

where Ω is a persistence parameter. Notice that the transition matrix above is balanced (the sum of each column is unity), such that the inflow to any state equals the outflow (which means that the number of individuals in each category is in every period the same as the initial distribution). In the simulations below we will look at different values for Ω. If $\Omega = 0$ (π_0) then previous productivity has no influence on productivity next period. If $\Omega = 0.1$ then transition probabilities are state-dependent, and productivity is persistent. With $\Omega = 0.5$ then the productivity differences at 'birth' are permanent – which is another way of making the model deterministic. If in this case $\Phi > 0$ there are persistent productivity differences, which means that the model turns into a deterministic 2-agent model – this special case is the type of model used by Altig *et al.* (1997).

For the taste parameter reflecting the joy of leisure, α, we use Auerbach and Kotlikoff's value of $\alpha = 1.5$. The elasticity of substitution between leisure and consumption, ρ, is set to 0.8 (again we use the same values as in Auerbach and Kotlikoff 1987).

The population's initial distribution on productivity categories is set to $\Psi_i = 0.5$ for $i \in \{1, 2\}$. Unlike Auerbach and Kotlikoff there is no population growth in the present model.

3.2 The producers

Since the production side is identical to Auerbach and Kotlikoff (except for the absence of installation costs), we use (almost) the same parameters as them: The elasticity of substitution: $\sigma = 1.1$ – Auerbach and Kotlikoff use a Cobb–Douglas production function (i.e. $\sigma = 1$). The capital intensity parameter: $\varepsilon = 0.25$ (as in the A–K model). The production function constant: $\Lambda = 0.89267$ (as in the A–K model).

3.3   The public sector

The tax on labour income is initially the only tax. In all simulations we set the revenue requirement to the level that a 30 per cent labour income tax would yield under proportional taxation (this particular normalization is discussed below).[9] Clearly the size of the government sector is important, and is subject to sensitivity analysis.

3.4   Solving the model in steady state

The model is solved in a manner similar to Auerbach and Kotlikoff (1987) or İmrohoroğlu *et al.* (1993). This means performing the following procedure until convergence:

1   Guess aggregate L and K (and tax rates if they are endogenous)
2   Use the factor-demand equations ((18) and (19)) to calculate guesses for w and r.
3   Solve the dynamic program and obtain the decision rules a_j^* and l_j^*, and hereby c_j^*.
4   Compute the new aggregate capital stock (using equation (16)) and the new labour supply (using equation (15)) (and the tax revenue if it is endogenous).
5   Check if K and L are converging – if not go to step 1, and use a convex combination of the old and the new estimates for K and L as initial guesses (with endogenous tax rates, adjust the tax rates up (down) if the revenue is too low (high)).

Solving the dynamic program

The dynamic program is solved by discritization and enumeration[10] – a method known as value function iteration. In the experiments reported in this paper, assets are discritized in 601 equidistant mesh-points. Mesh-point number 601 is chosen sufficiently high, such that it is never chosen by any agent. The control variable leisure is discritized in 201 mesh-points, which means that the agent can only change his labour supply in units of 0.005. There is a trade-off between computing time and level of detail in these kinds of calculations: we have experimented with several other combinations of mesh-sizes, and it turns out that more mesh-points only slightly alter the results – however the computing time required grows in a non-polynomial fashion.

Solving the dynamic program for an individual of a certain generation means that for each set of state variables (start-of-period assets and productivity) we must search in the space of control variables (next-period assets, labour supply and consumption). With two productivity categories, 601 asset mesh-points and 201 leisure grid-points, this is quite a task.[11]

4   Simulations

As mentioned in the introduction, the purpose of this paper is not to analyse an actual policy issue for a particular country. Rather the purpose is methodological to examine to what extent the presence of an idiosyncratic income risk modifies the analysis, when quantifying the gains of switching from progressive taxation to proportional taxation of labour income (under an equal yield requirement).

The main difference here – compared to Auerbach and Kotlikoff (1987) – is that labour income taxation is the only distortion in the economy. However, for the simulations performed here, this difference has only a minor effect.

4.1   Summary of the findings in the A–K model

Before looking at what happens when introducing idiosyncratic earnings uncertainty, the main findings in Chapter 8 in Auerbach and Kotlikoff (1987) can be reviewed. The principal effect of progressive taxation is that it induces intertemporal speculation in labour supply. With progressive taxation the marginal taxes are higher in the highly productive years in the life cycle, and to avoid these high marginal taxes, agents choose to work less in middle age, and more when old. They find that removing progressivity causes a welfare increase in the new steady state of 0.69 per cent, an increase in labour supply of 3.9 per cent, an increase in the capital stock of 5.1 per cent, and an increase in production of 4.5 per cent.

4.2   What are we comparing?

Before we start comparing the results from the deterministic model to a model with idiosyncratic uncertainty, it is important to realize that the benchmark equilibria we are comparing are different. Most importantly the presence of precautionary savings in the model with uncertainty means that the benchmark capital stock is larger in the models with uncertainty, which of course affects all important variables through the factor prices. Since the size of the national income is different in the models, the benchmark revenue requirement is not a fixed nominal value (relative to the numeraire) but is measured as a ratio to the national income. More precisely we have normalized the labour income tax to 30 per cent, which implies that the size of the government sector is between 22 per cent and 23 per cent of national income in the various models (remember that there is no capital income taxation).

4.3   Aggregate effects in the deterministic case

This section summarizes the findings in the deterministic version of the model with one productivity level ($\Phi = 0$ and $\Omega = 0$). Table 16.1 below summarizes the

Table 16.1 Summary in the deterministic model with one productivity level

	Progressive	*Proportional*	*% change*
Production	26.873	27.830	3.56
K	105.961	111.594	5.32
L	19.451	20.019	2.92
L (hours)	17.265	17.710	2.58
K/Y	3.943	4.010	1.69
w/r	15.076	15.415	2.25
G/Y	22.820	22.035	−3.44
Average labour income tax	31.060	30.000	−3.41
Average utility			3.307

main macroeconomic variables for a move from progressive to proportional taxation of labour income: As expected – based on our expectations from the Auerbach and Kotlikoff study – we see an increase in national income of 3.6 per cent, an increase in the capital stock of 5.3 per cent and an increase in the lifetime utility of a new born of 3.3 per cent. Moving from progressive to pro-portional labour income taxation increases the labour supply in hours, but there is a slightly larger increase in efficiency units (labelled L in the table). Again this effect was expected: agents choose to work more when middle-aged (and highly productive) and less when old (and less productive); therefore productivity per hour worked increases on average.

Comparing these deterministic results with a model with idiosyncratic uncer-tainty would not be straightforward. First of all there is the effect of introduc-ing stochastic fluctuations in income – this is the uncertainty effect that we want to capture. But we also introduce a second effect: agents with different levels of productivity (high and low). To make it easier to understand what is happening when uncertainty is introduced, it turns out to be beneficial to be able to have a deterministic model with two levels of productivity as another point of reference.

4.4   *Introducing two productivity levels*

The second model has two levels of productivity – with permanent differences in productivity over the life cycle (Table 16.2). This is easily accommodated in the set-up presented previously. First we introduce different productivity levels ($\Phi = 0.25$) and secondly we let these productivity differences persist over the life cycle by setting the persistence parameter $\Omega = 0.5$.

Again we see a similar effect but of a different magnitude: an increase in national income of 3.7 per cent, an increase in the capital stock of 5.5 per cent and an increase in the expected lifetime utility of a newborn of 2.1 per cent. Again we notice a slightly larger increase in the labour supply in efficiency units than in hours: the average productivity per hour worked goes up. Notice that these

Table 16.2 Summary in the deterministic model with two productivity levels

	Progressive	*Proportional*	*% change*
Production	26.752	27.744	3.71
K	105.825	111.590	5.45
L	19.340	19.937	3.09
L (hours)	17.355	17.820	2.68
K/Y	3.956	4.022	1.68
w/r	15.139	15.451	2.06
G/Y	22.848	22.031	-3.57
Average labour income tax	31.106	30.000	-3.55
Utility (low productivity)			0.363
Utility (high productivity)			5.444
Average utility			2.089

Table 16.3 Decomposition of the labour supply effect on two productivity levels

	Progressive	*Proportional*	*% change*
Hours worked			
Low productivity	9.048	9.283	2.60
High productivity	8.308	8.537	2.76
Total	17.355	17.820	2.68
Efficiency units			
Low productivity	7.774	7.861	1.12
High productivity	11.566	12.076	4.41
Total	19.340	17.937	3.09

numbers are different from the deterministic model with only one level of productivity. The biggest difference lies in the average utility of a newborn: in the model with one productivity level it increased 3.3 per cent, but here the average increase in utility is 2.1 per cent.

We can also calculate the average utility of a newborn in each of the two productivity categories. The biggest gains from moving to proportional taxation go to individuals that are born with high productivity: their utility increases by 5.4 per cent. For individuals that are born low productive the effect is significantly smaller: they experience an increase in their utility of 0.4 per cent.

The labour supply is decomposed in Table 16.3. It is interesting to notice that individuals with low productivity work more hours than the highly productive (around 9 per cent more), but despite this the highly productive deliver more efficiency units (around 50 per cent) than the low productive. Moving to proportional taxation increases the number of hours worked for both groups. But looking at the number of efficiency units we see that the average productivity per hour worked (this number is not shown in the table but is calculated as efficiency units divided by hours) for the low productive goes down, and increases for the highly productive.

4.5 Aggregate effects with idiosyncratic uncertainty

Finally consider the situation with idiosyncratic earnings uncertainty (for these simulations we use $\Phi = 0.25$ and $\Omega = 0$). This implies differences in productivity of $\{0.75, 1.25\}$ – a magnitude similar to model 2 above. Table 16.4 summarizes the main variables in this situation.

Again we see an increase in national income and the capital stock – however with uncertainty the increase in production is about 0.2 percentage points higher (compared to model 2) and the capital stock increases an additional 1.2–1.3 per cent points compared to model 2 and 1 respectively.

It is interesting to notice that the labour supply measured in efficiency units increases almost as much as in model 1 (the deterministic model with one productivity level) – about 2.9 per cent (which is a little less than in model 2). However the number of hours worked increases by 1.6 per cent compared with 2.6 per cent in the model without uncertainty – thus the average productivity per hour worked increases significantly. This effect turns out to be important.

Comparing Tables 16.1, 16.2 and 16.4 we see that the efficiency per hour worked increases 0.3 per cent in the deterministic model with one productivity level (model 1), 0.4 per cent in the deterministic model with two productivity levels (model 2), whereas it increases 1.3 per cent in the situation with uncertainty (model 3). Table 16.5 decomposes the labour supply effect further.

Table 16.5 reveals what drives these labour supply results: the individuals with high productivity increase their labour supply 5.15 per cent in hours and 5.63 per cent in efficiency units, whereas individuals with lower productivity decrease the number of hours worked by 3.55 per cent, which corresponds to a decrease in efficiency units of 3.50 per cent. This is why the overall effect is a much larger increase in the number of efficiency units of labour than in hours (remember that individuals with low productivity account for around 40 per cent of the hours worked and only account for 30 per cent of the labour supply in efficiency units, whereas individuals with high productivity work

Table 16.4 Summary with idiosyncratic uncertainty

	Progressive	Proportional	% change
Production	27.166	28.221	3.88
K	108.190	115.370	6.64
L	19.592	20.161	2.90
L (hours)	16.726	16.988	1.57
K/Y	3.983	4.088	2.65
w/r	15.268	15.799	3.48
G/Y	22.878	22.023	−3.74
Average labour income tax	31.159	30.000	−3.72
Utility (Low productivity)			3.347
Utility (High productivity)			3.635
Average utility			3.488

Table 16.5 Decomposition of the labour supply effect with uncertainty

	Progressive	*Proportional*	*% change*
Hours worked			
Low productivity	6.883	6.638	−3.55
High productivity	9.843	10.350	5.15
Total	16.726	16.988	1.57
Efficiency units			
Low productivity	5.848	5.643	−3.50
High productivity	13.744	14.518	5.63
Total	19.592	20.161	2.90

around 60 per cent of the number of hours, but account for 70 per cent of the efficiency units).

This division of labour effect (which is only present in the model with idiosyncratic uncertainty) means that the more productive spend their time working, and the less productive spend their time enjoying leisure, and a move from progressive taxation magnifies the scale of this division of labour.

The fact that the highly productive work more hours than the low productive stands in contrast with model 2, where we found that the low productive worked more hours than the high productive. In a sense the income and substitution effect switches around (the notion of income and substitution effect are not used in the traditional manner here). With uncertainty the income effect dominates and productive individuals work more, and the less productive work less. In the deterministic model the substitution effect dominated: highly productive individuals worked less, and the less productive worked more. The overall effect is illustrated by comparing the average productivity per hour worked in the two models: under proportional taxation one hour worked was on average equal to 1.12 productivity units in the deterministic model, whereas it was worth 1.19 efficiency units in the presence of uncertainty.

A final interesting point is the average utility of a newborn. In the A–K model, utility increased 3.3 per cent, in the deterministic model with two categories it goes up 2.1 per cent – but in the situation with idiosyncratic income uncertainty the increase in utility is 3.5 per cent. So the benefit of switching tax system is slightly larger in the situation with uncertainty when compared to the standard A–K model, and significantly larger when compared to the deterministic model with two levels of productivity.

A preliminary conclusion is therefore that the conjecture that progressive taxation is 'less painful' in a situation with uncertainty does not hold – or at least it is dominated by a large efficiency gain. The main factor driving the differing welfare results is the fact that there is an extra effect present in the situation with idiosyncratic uncertainty: the division of labour effect. Since the division of labour becomes more pronounced under proportional taxation, relatively more hours are spent on leisure – which influences welfare.

4.6   *Life cycle behaviour*

Looking at the life cycle behaviour gives some interesting information in addition to the aggregate information presented in the tables. The plots show what happens to assets, leisure and consumption over the life cycle in the three models analysed: the A–K model with no uncertainty and one productivity category, a deterministic model with two productivity categories and finally in the model with idiosyncratic earnings uncertainty.

Figure 16.1 shows what happens to assets, and contains five smaller figures. The first (Figure 16.1a) shows the profile for wealth over the life cycle in the A–K model with one productivity category. This figure shows both the wealth in the case with proportional taxation (the dotted line), and in the case with progressive taxation of labour income (the unbroken line). From Table 16.1 we know that aggregate wealth is higher under proportional taxation; correspondingly the area under the wealth curve must be larger than under proportional taxation.

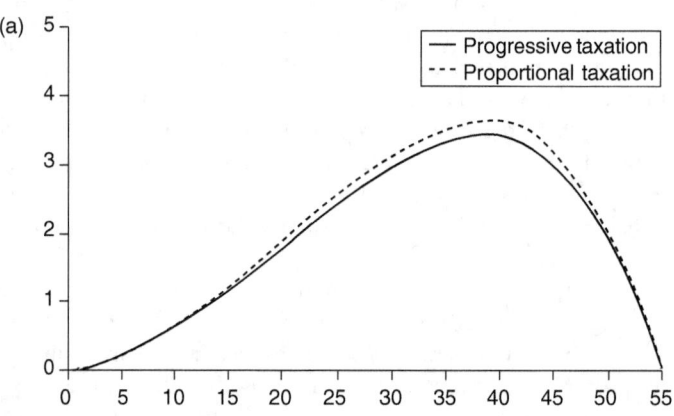

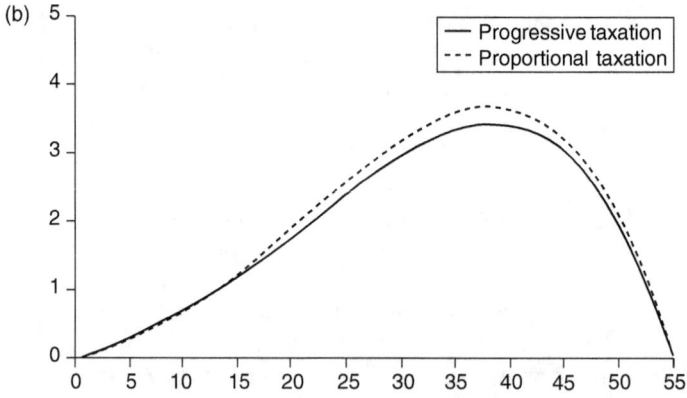

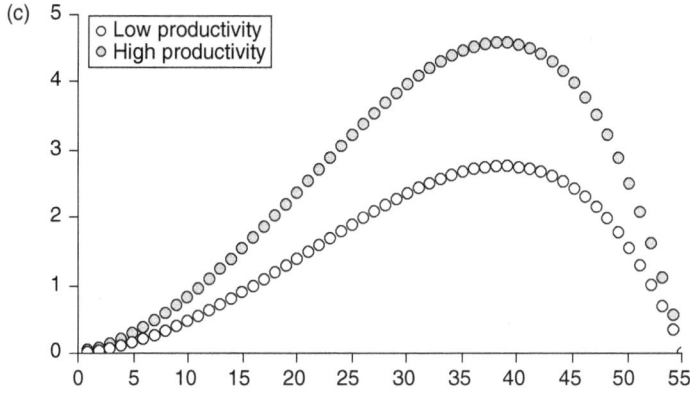

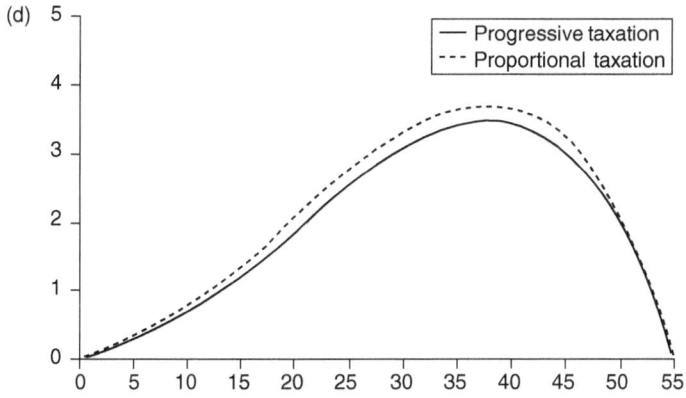

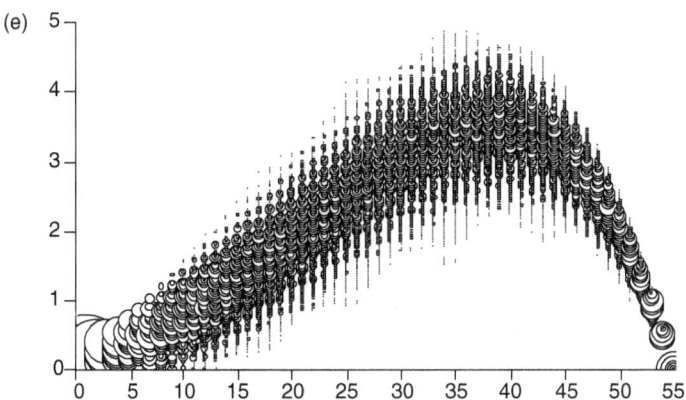

Figure 16.1 Assets. (a) The A–K model (no uncertainty with one productivity category): assets per age group; Deterministic model with two productivity categories: (b) Average assets per age group, (c) Distribution of assets (under proportional taxation); Model with idiosyncratic uncertainty and two productivity levels: (d) Average assets per age group, (e) Distribution of assets (under proportional taxation).

Figure 16.1b shows the average wealth per age group in the deterministic model with two productivity categories and no uncertainty. Figure 16.1c shows (for the same model) the distribution of wealth over the life cycle for individuals with low and high productivity. Since productivity differences are permanent over the life cycle in this case, 50 per cent of the members of each age group will be in each of the two productivity categories.

Notice the significant difference in wealth over the life cycle between the two groups: the wealth for individuals with high productivity peaks after thirty-eight (corresponding to real age fifty-nine) at a 66 per cent higher level than for individuals born with low productivity. Figure 16.1d shows the average wealth (per age group) in the model with idiosyncratic uncertainty. This figure shows the same pattern as in the deterministic case (Figure 16.1a and 16.1b. Figure 16.1e shows the distribution of the wealth in the situation with idiosyncratic earnings uncertainty and progressive taxation. This figure gives some idea of the size of the variation around the average. Additions to this figure are the discs. The size of these discs represents how many agents have the wealth concerned – this is a quick way of depicting 3-dimensional data (the figure does not – like Figure 16.1c – distinguish between individuals with low and high productivity, as there is no significant difference in wealth holdings between the two groups).

Recall that earnings is a process with two states: high and low. In the first period of life, half of the agents are assumed to begin ($\eta_i = 1/2$) in each group – therefore there are two large discs at generation 1 (remember that assets are measured using the end-of-period notation). In the second period there are now $2^2 = 4$ different agents (since all previous period productivity categories can transit to any productivity category next period) – the four groups are all equally large. In period three agents can potentially be divided in 2^3 different states – with a smaller amount of agents in each group. Theoretically agents can – after fifty-five periods of life – end up with $2^{55} = 3.6E16$ different asset holdings, but in reality some agents end up choosing the same end-of-period asset holdings during their life cycle, irrespective of the fact that their productivity life stories have not been identical.[12]

Figure 16.2 shows what happens to the choice of leisure (and implicitly to the labour supply). In the deterministic case (Figure 16.2a), we get the same effect as Auerbach and Kotlikoff (1987): intertemporal speculation in labour makes agents choose to work more in middle age when they are highly productive, and less when old – and they choose to retire earlier under proportional taxation (Figure 16.2b).

In the situation with uncertainty (Figure 16.2d) we get a similar qualitative effect, but of a smaller magnitude: the difference between the unbroken and the dotted line is smaller in the deterministic case (Figure 16.2a) than under uncertainty (Figure 16.2d). But this aggregate effect should be expected when comparing number of hours worked from Tables 16.1 and 16.4 – it is interesting to note that this effect is relatively evenly distributed over the life cycle. With uncertainty the retirement age does not jump, as the 'average agent' works an increasingly smaller amount of hours until retirement.

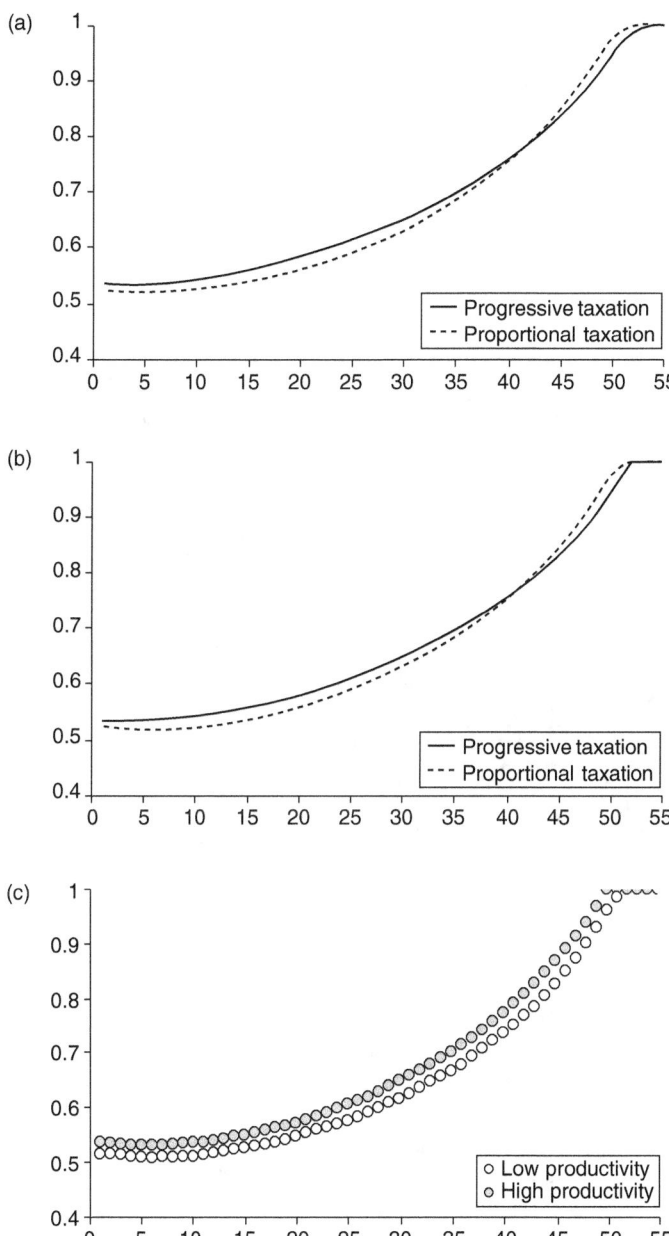

Figure 16.2 Leisure. (a) A–K model (no uncertainty with one productivity category): leisure per age group; Deterministic model with two productivity categories: (b) Leisure per age group, (c) Distribution of leisure (under proportional taxation); Model with idiosyncratic uncertainty and two productivity levels: (d) Average leisure per age group, (e) Distribution of leisure (under proportional taxation).

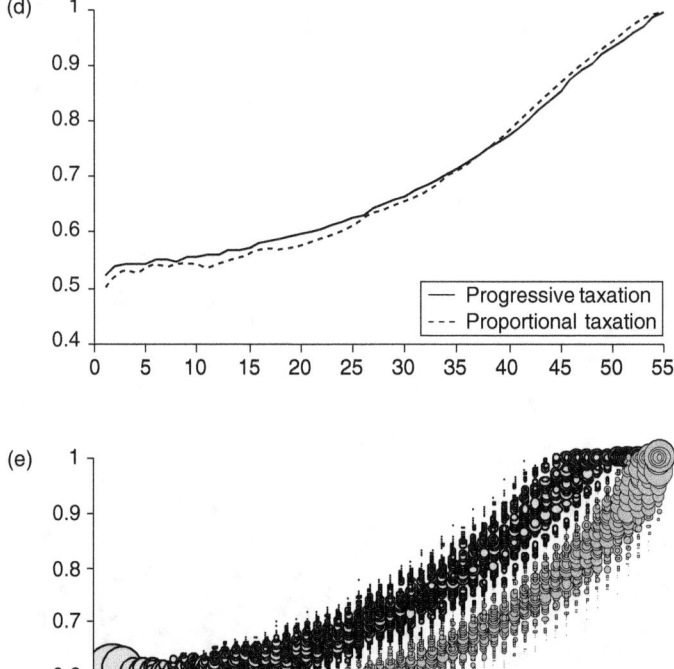

Figure 16.2 (Continued)

When comparing Tables 16.3 and 16.5 we saw an increase in the average productivity when comparing the deterministic model with two levels of productivity (Table 16.3) and the model with idiosyncratic earnings uncertainty (Table 16.5). To understand how this effect arises from the life cycle labour supply compare Figures 16.2c and 16.2e. This comparison is interesting: in the deterministic model agents with low productivity work as previously mentioned more hours and retire later than the agents with high productivity. However in the stochastic model this is the other way around: agents with low productivity choose to work less, and stop working at age fifty (real age: 71) whereas the highly productive work more and retire later. In a sense the uncertainty about future

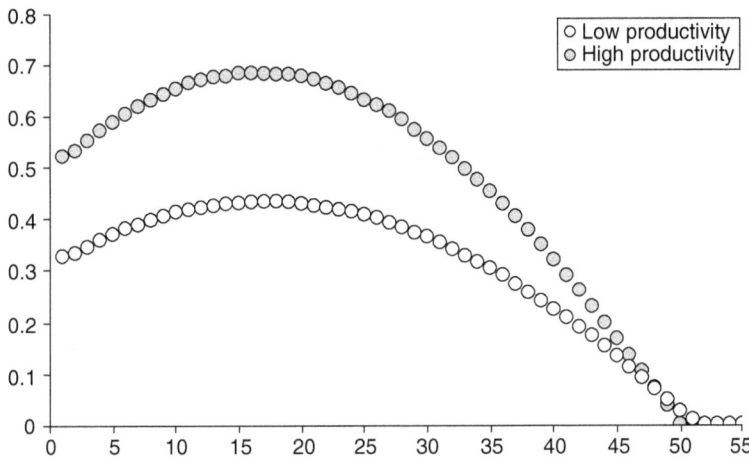

Figure 16.3 Labour earnings in the deterministic model (before tax).

earnings induces an interesting efficiency gain from the division of labour: in periods with high productivity agents work more at every age, whereas they choose to work less in periods with low productivity (and enjoy more leisure). Figures 16.3 and 16.4 show the labour income before taxes in model 2 (with two deterministic productivity levels) and model 3 (with idiosyncratic income uncertainty).[13]

Figure 16.3 shows that despite working fewer hours, individuals with high productivity have a higher income than individuals with low productivity. In the presence of idiosyncratic uncertainty this effect is more pronounced as Figure 16.4 shows.

Finally Figure 16.5 shows what happens to consumption. In the deterministic case (Figure 16.5a and 16.5b) we notice a change in level around the time of retirement. Remember that the Keynes–Ramsey consumption smoothing rule concerns smoothing the value of the annual utility function, which depends on both consumption and leisure (equation (9)). This kink gets less pronounced in the case of idiosyncratic earnings (Figure 16.5d): here the average agent retires gradually, and therefore there is less of a kink. Notice that there is quite a wide variation (Figure 16.5e) behind the smooth average shown in Figure 16.4d. Finally it is interesting to note that the difference in the consumption level between individuals with low and high productivity is larger in the deterministic model with two productivity levels (Figure 16.5c) than in the case with uncertainty. This effect should be expected: using the terminology of Friedman, income in the model with uncertainty can be thought of as being transitory income, and has only a small impact on consumption in the current period. The reason that there is a difference in the consumption level at all (which is not what should be expected from the permanent income hypothesis in its pure form) should be found

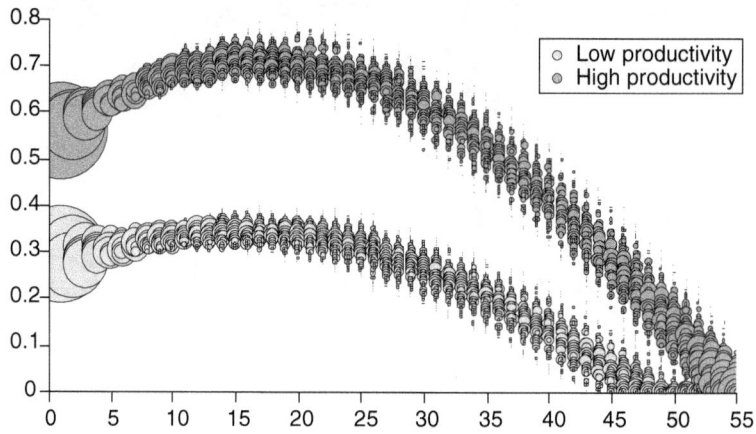

Figure 16.4 Labour earnings with idiosyncratic earnings uncertainty (before tax).

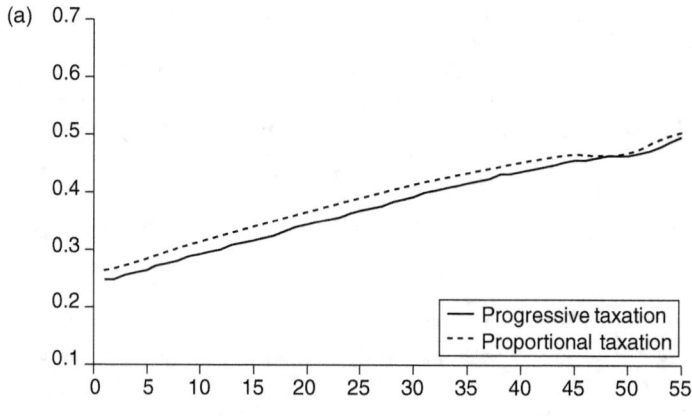

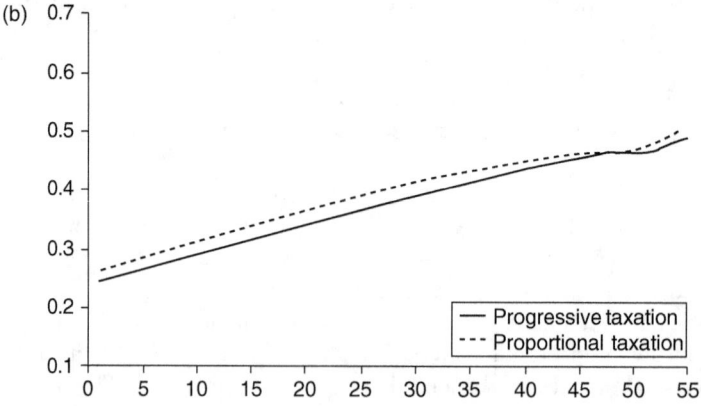

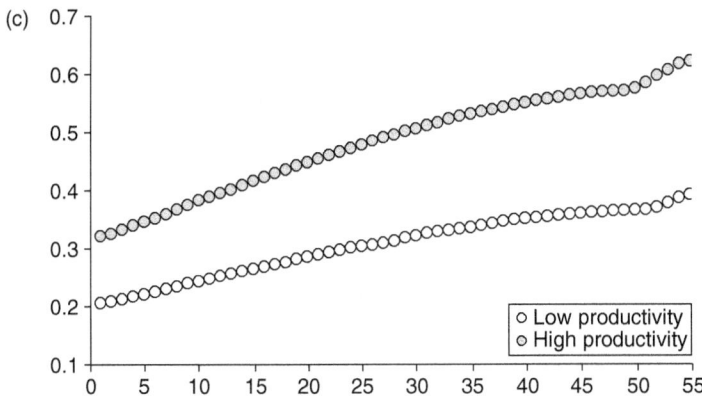

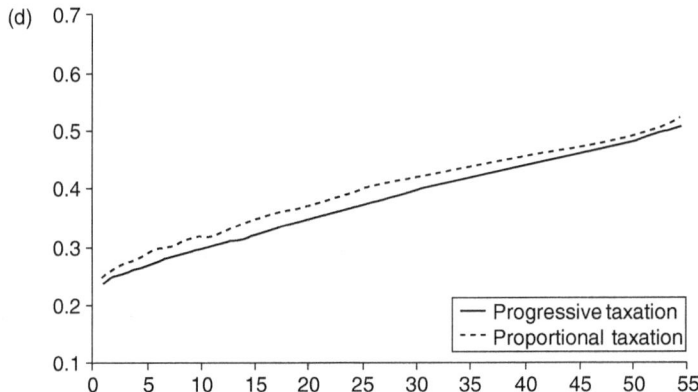

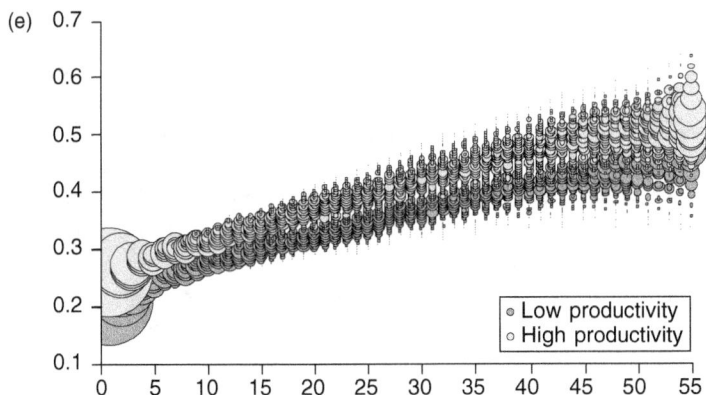

Figure 16.5 Consumption. (a) The A–K model (no uncertainty with one productivity category): Consumption per age group; Deterministic model with two productivity categories: (b) consumption per age group, (c) Distribution of consumption (under proportional taxation); Model with idiosyncratic uncertainty and two productivity levels: (d) Average consumption per age group, (e) Distribution of consumption (under proportional taxation).

in the fact that individuals with high productivity work more, and therefore need a higher level of consumption to compensate their disutility from labour. This stands in contrast with the deterministic model: here the difference in consumption level reflects a difference in permanent income since their lifetime earnings potential differs.

4.7   Sensitivity analysis

The results presented above should of course be subject to sensitivity analysis, and a sensivity analysis of the results is carried out with respect to changes in central parameter values and assumptions. The following parameters were examined (a) the productivity-difference parameter Φ (initially $\Phi = 0.25$), (b) the progressivity parameter κ (initially $\kappa = 0.5$), (c) the government revenue require-ment (initially normalized to a 30 per cent labour income tax) and (d) introducing persistence in Markov-chain that determines productivity (setting $\Omega \neq 0$). Due to exogenous space limitations on the length of this chapter, this part must be downloaded from the book's web site.

5   Summary

The simulations in this chapter have illustrated that when analysing the effects of switching from progressive to proportional taxation, different results are obtained when using an OLG-model with idiosyncratic earnings uncertainty compared to two traditional models without uncertainty (but with different assumptions about productivity).

The analysis showed that the effects we would expect from the A–K model are also present when earnings are uncertain. However the benefits from removing progressive taxation are larger with uncertainty: thus the idea that progressivity is less 'harmful' in the presence of uncertainty does not hold. The main explanation why the results differ in the presence of uncertainty turned out to be a division of labour effect inherent in the specification of uncertainty. The division of labour works better under proportional taxation, since individuals use their comparative advantage: individuals with high productivity work more hours, whereas individuals with low productivity work less hours and enjoy more leisure. The sensitivity analysis showed that the specification of uncertainty is important with respect to which results are obtained: varying the different parameters in the uncertainty specification means that the gains from switching tax system change – but they are in all cases positive.

5.1   Directions for further research

The results from the stochastic earnings model – that people with high productivity work more hours – stand in stark contrast to the results from the deterministic model (with two levels of productivity) where individuals with high productivity work fewer hours. However, the true story is more complex than what can be captured by the simple two-state model used here. The sensitivity analysis showed that the specification of uncertainty is important, and clearly the specification used here is not deployed because of its realism but because of its simplicity. To improve the empirical basis for the modelling of uncertainty, we need to increase the number of productivity categories (to for instance twenty-five or more) and obtain an empirical estimate of the productivity transition frequencies, as well as the associated productivity levels.

Notes

1 This effect is potentially important: Engen and Gale (1996) report that the response in savings to changes in consumption taxation is 80 per cent smaller in a stochastic life cycle model compared to a certainty life cycle model. These smaller elasticities seem to be more in accordance with empirical evidence – see for instance Deaton (1992).

2 Computable models with idiosyncratic income uncertainty have primarily been used to analyse precautionary savings behaviour and social security issues [Hubbard *et al.* (1994), İmrohoroğlu *et al.* (1993, 1998) to mention some prominent examples].

3 Notice that the end-of-period notation is used here.

4 Notice the dating rules used: the end-of-period convention. The first period for the consumer is $j = 1$, which means that the consumer's problem when entering the economy is to solve $V_1(a_0, d_0)$.

5 Using the terminology in Rust (1996) we are dealing with a *Discrete Time Discounted Markov Decision Process*.

6 By substituting consumption (c) away, we reduce the number of control variables to two. We could equally well have substituted the end-of-period assets (a) away – in this case the consumer would explicitly choose labour and consumption (and implicitly the end-of-period assets). However, it is more convenient to substitute consumption away.

7 Consider the optimal choice of assets for an individual that has been active for one period. His optimal end-of-period-one assets are denoted $a_1^*(a_0, d_0)$ – since we know that he entered the economy with zero assets it will in fact be $a_1^*(0, d_0)$.

8 If we think of these as functions we have $a^*: A \times D \to R_+$ and $l^*: A \times D \to R_+$ where A is asset holdings and D is the productivity level.

9 Under the progressive system we need to specify two parameters: the level and the progression, corresponding to τ and κ, in equation (7). One must be determined exogenously, and the other must be determined by the model (using the equal yield constraint). Auerbach and Kotlikoff choose to specify the intercept, and determine the level of progression endogenously. Here the opposite strategy is chosen: we specify the level of progression exogenously and determine the 'intercept' endogenously. This specification gives better opportunity to directly control the level of progression in the sensitivity analysis.

10 The practical aspects of solving dynamic programming models are discussed in Judd (1998). A beginner's guide is Petersen (2000).

11 Several of the techniques discussed in Judd (1998) and İmrohoroğlu *et al.* (1993, 1998) are used to speed up the computations. The practical computations are done in C++ (Microsoft Visual C++ 5.0). The files and program used are available from the book's web site.

12 The discritization of the asset holdings come in handy here, as we force agents to choose one of a finite number of end-of-period asset holdings. This makes the *curse of dimensionality* a little less troublesome. Actually the total number of 'different' agents is 39,444 (different in an age and state-variable sense).

13 Both figures show what happens in the case of a proportional labour income tax of 30 per cent.

References

Altig, D., Auerbach, A. J., Kotlikoff, L., Smetters, K. A and Waliser, J. (1997) *Simulating US Tax Reform*, NBER Working Paper 6248.

Auerbach, A. and Kotlikoff, L. (1987) *Dynamic Fiscal Policy*, Cambridge: Cambridge University Press.

Deaton, A. (1992) *Understanding Consumption*, Oxford: Oxford University Press.

Engen, E. and Gale, W. (1996) 'The effects of fundamental tax reform on savings', in: *Economic Effects of Fundamental Tax Reform*, Washington DC: Brookings Institution Press.

Hubbard, G. R., Skinner, J. and Zeldes, S. P. (1994) 'The importance of precautionary motives in explaining individual behavior and aggregate saving', *Carnegie-Rochester Conference Series on Public Policy*, pp. 59–125.

İmrohoroğlu, A., İmrohoroğlu S. and Joines, D. H. (1993) 'A numerical solution algorithm for solving models with incomplete markets', *International Journal of Supercomputer Applications*, pp. 212–30.

İmrohoroğlu, A., İmrohoroğlu S. and Joines, D. H. (1998) 'Computing models of social security', in: Marimon, R. and Scott, A. (eds), *Computational Methods for the Study of Dynamic Economies*, Oxford: Oxford University Press.

Judd, K. (1998) *Numerical Methods in Economics*, Cambridge, MA: The MIT-Press.

Petersen, T. W. (2000) An introduction to numerical methods and dynamic programming using C++', Statistics Denmark, manuscript available from www.dst.dk/dream

Rust, J. (1996) 'Numerical Dynamic Programming in Economics', in: *Handbook of Computational Economics*, Amsterdam: North-Holland, pp. 619–729.

Welch, F. (1979) 'Effects of Cohort Size on Earnings: The Baby Boom Babies' Financial Bust', *Journal of Political Economy*, 87.

17 International spillover effects of a demographic shock when fiscal policy is politically responsive*

Mehmet Serkan Tosun

1 Introduction

The populations of most developed countries are projected to go through significant ageing during the first half of this century. In the past 25 years the number of people aged 65 and over in OECD countries rose by forty-five million, whereas the working-age population increased by 120 million. However, in the next 25 years, the number of non-working elderly will increase by seventy million while the working population will rise by only five million.[1] Figure 17.1 shows the projected changes in the old-age dependency ratio between 1990 and 2150. This figure indicates that developed countries will experience dramatic population ageing until 2050, after which the dependency ratio levels off.

In the recent literature, the link between population ageing and fiscal policy decisions has not been widely addressed. Instead, the focus has been on predicting the necessary changes in fiscal policy to accommodate the effects of population ageing. Furthermore, in a world connected by an international capital market, population ageing in developed countries may have global repercussions. Hence, in this chapter, I envisage a world economy integrated by an international capital market, where in each country fiscal policy is endogenously determined through a political process. The objective here is to establish the significance of the spillover effects of population ageing in the presence of internationally mobile capital.

The chapter is structured as follows. The next section briefly reviews the recent studies on population ageing. In Section 3, I sketch a two-country overlapping generations model with political economy. I then describe the parameters used in the simulation study and present simulation results together with a sensitivity analysis in Section 4. My concluding remarks follow in Section 5.

*I am indebted to Douglas J. Holtz-Eakin and Mary E. Lovely for helpful comments and encouragement. The research support from the Center for Policy Research at Syracuse University is gratefully acknowledged. I benefited from discussions with John Hutton and other participants of the conference on 'Policy Evaluation with Computable General Equilibrium Models', University of Genova, Italy, 29–30 October 1999. All remaining errors are my responsibility.

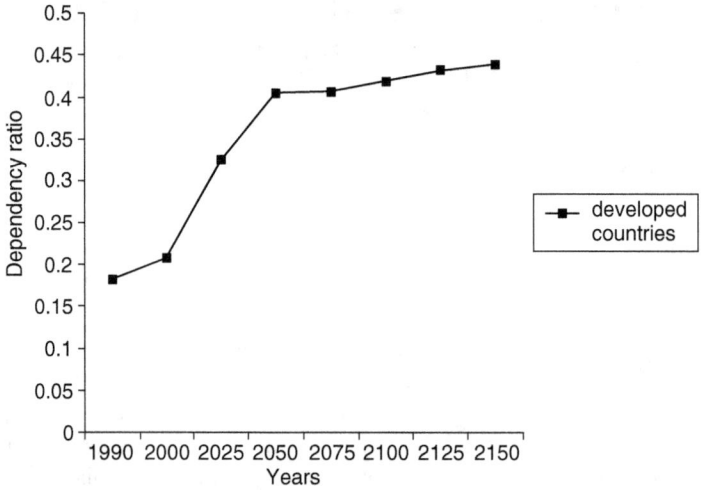

Figure 17.1 Projected old-age dependency ratio in developed countries.

Source: World Population Projections (World Bank 1994) and author's calculations.

Note: Old-age dependency ratio is the proportion of population aged 65 and older to population aged 15–64.

2   Previous studies

Studies that address the effects of population ageing analytically generally lack the consideration of effects that emerge from international capital mobility. However, by allowing for endogenous fiscal policy, some of these studies emphasize the importance of the simultaneity of government policies and the demographic structure of voters. Holtz-Eakin (1993), Meijdam and Verbon (1996) and Holtz-Eakin *et al.* (2000) are closely related to this chapter in terms of the fiscal policy aspect of the model structure. Holtz-Eakin (1993), using a modified version of the standard overlapping generations model, allows for endogenous fiscal policy. The author conducts a series of steady state simulations and shows that demographic change has significant impact on the growth of the economy as well as on the government expenditure and taxation. This paper, however, lacks a transition analysis of the impact of the demographic shock. Holtz-Eakin *et al.* (2000) address in a closed economy setting how government spending for public education is affected by population ageing. This study shows that even though demographic shift favours voters with a lower preference for education spending, reduced taxes may raise capital per worker enough to raise education spending. Meijdam and Verbon (1996), using a similar approach to above studies examine, in a closed economy framework, the effect of ageing on the economy in general and on the evolution of public pension schemes. However, this study does not model political process of fiscal policy determination explicitly.

On the other hand, some simulation studies consider international capital mobility. Cutler *et al.* (1990) and Börsch-Supan (1996) are recent examples that employ the Cass–Ramsey–Solow growth model. Cutler *et al.* (1990) show for the United States that capital flows can significantly change the magnitude of the effects of ageing on consumption. Börsch-Supan predicts considerable capital flows to slowly ageing Southern European Periphery, particularly to Turkey, within the OECD area. Similarly, Kenc and Sayan (1998) show in an over-lapping generations computable general equilibrium model that population ageing in Europe will affect the economy of Turkey substantially in the next several decades through both trade and capital flows. None of these studies, however, model fiscal policy as endogenously determined through a political process in response to ageing.

In the light of this review, I intend to analyse the effects of ageing by focusing on the capital flows between regions. I will also treat fiscal policy as endogenously determined through a political process that is triggered by the changing demographic structure of voters.

3 The model

3.1 Modelling strategy

In this section, I describe the modelling strategy by providing detailed arguments on the three distinct features of my model. First, this chapter employs an extended version of the conventional two-period overlapping generations model with perfect foresight. By explicitly tracing the life-cycle savers, overlapping generations models allow for a generational welfare analysis. This implies that demographic trends can be important determinants of national saving and current account.

Secondly, I explicitly model a political process of fiscal policy making. One issue in the recent discussion of ageing is that the need to share society's resources between non-working elderly and the younger working population may induce generational conflict. For example, Poterba (1997) provides evidence from the US that older citizens prefer lower levels of public spending for education, an expenditure that primarily benefits the young. Similarly, Kahn (2000) shows that population demographics are an important determinant of the support for environmental regulation. His results indicate that senior citizens are more likely to find government spending for the environment too high. In order to simulate this distributional conflict, a political process must be posited. To make the political process of fiscal policy determination rich and interesting, I use a median voter framework[2] with voter heterogeneity. Voter heterogeneity is introduced by assuming a distribution of genetic ability levels for the working generation. The ability level of the individual will, in turn, determine the value she receives from the publicly provided good.

The third and the final aspect of my modelling strategy is a focus on transitions between two common steady states.[3] I introduce demographic shock in one country as a drop in the population growth rate in only the first time period. Although the ageing country becomes smaller in aggregate terms, per worker levels of economic variables are identical in the pre- and post-shock steady states in both countries. Therefore, my analysis is of transitions between two common steady states.

The model extends the conventional Diamond (1965) overlapping generations model in two ways. First, it is a two-country world economy model similar to Buiter (1981) in which countries are perfectly symmetric in the initial steady state equilibrium. Second, it models political decision making in order to examine political economy related effects of ageing. With an increase in the dependency ratio,[4] fiscal policy shifts towards the preferences of the older generation. This combines with the effect of international capital mobility when demographic asymmetries (different population growth rates) between countries or regions are present. Internationally mobile capital is the intermediary in spreading the effects of ageing globally. Using the assumption of initial symmetry between countries, I first present the model for one country only. Then I describe the two-country world equilibrium.

3.2   Household behaviour

Individuals live for two periods and seek to maximize an identical lifetime utility function,

$$U = \ln C_{jt} + \left(\frac{1}{1+\delta}\right) \ln C_{jt+1} \tag{1}$$

where j indexes individuals. C_{jt} is consumption when young and C_{jt+1} is consumption when old. The period specific budget constraints in the first and the second periods are, respectively:

$$\begin{aligned} C_{jt}(a_j) + S_{jt}(a_j) &= \theta_t w_t h_t(a_j) \\ C_{jt+1}(a_j) &= (1 + \theta_{t+1} r_{t+1}) S_{jt}(a_j) \end{aligned} \tag{2}$$

where $\theta_t = (1 - \tau_t)$, $S_{jt}(a_j)$ is first period saving, w_t is the wage rate individual j faces, $h_t(a_j)$ is human capital, where a_j is the ability level of individual j, r_{t+1} is the rate of return to capital, and τ_t is the rate of income taxation.

Tax policy is a flat tax on the labour income of the young and the capital income of the old. Capital income taxation follows a territorial system.[5] I also assume there is a continuous distribution of abilities that is replicated in each new generation. The ability level of individual j is denoted by a_j. This ranges from 0 to 1 and the density function of abilities is denoted by $f(a)$ where by definition:

$$\int_0^1 f(a)\, da = 1 \tag{3}$$

Human capital is accumulated from the interaction of ability level (a_j) of the individual and government spending per worker (g_t):

$$h(a_j)_t = \Phi[a_j g_t + 1]^\psi \tag{4}$$

here, Φ denotes an index on human capital efficiency and ψ is a parameter indicating the return to human capital from the inputs (a_j and g_t).[6] The form of the human capital function is chosen so that individuals with the lowest ability ($a_j = 0$) will contribute to the economy in terms of human capital. From the maximization of (1) subject to (2) and (4); we get the familiar first order condition:

$$C_{jt}(a_j) = \frac{1 + \delta}{(1 + r_{t+1}\theta_{t+1})} C_{jt+1}(a_j) \tag{5}$$

Using (5) and (2), we derive the optimal saving of an individual j:

$$S_{jt}(a_j) = \frac{1}{2 + \delta} \theta_t w_t h_t(a_j) \tag{6}$$

Saving of an individual depends on the net labour earnings, but it is independent of the interest rate. This is due to the Cobb–Douglas form of the utility function. Given (5) and (6), it is easy to derive consumption functions in each period:

$$C_{jt}(a_j) = \frac{1 + \delta}{2 + \delta} \theta_t w_t h_t(a_j)$$
$$C_{jt+1}(a_j) = \frac{(1 + r_{t+1}\theta_{t+1})(\theta_t w_t h_t(a_j))}{2 + \delta} \tag{7}$$

3.3 Political process

The consumption and saving decisions, as seen above, depend on human capital, which is in turn determined by government spending (see equation (4)). By plugging these into (1), we get the indirect utility function, which each voter maximizes subject to the government budget constraint ($\tau_t y_t = g_t$). The preferred tax rate of individual j when young is:

$$\tau_{jt}(a_j) = \frac{a_j \psi y_t - 1}{(1 + \psi)a_j y_t} \tag{8}$$

(8) is the tax rate each individual prefers based on her ability level. This preferred tax rate is increasing in both ability level a_j and in income per young y_t. Because the old do not derive any benefit from publicly provided education and there are no bequests in the model, they incur a cost without enjoying any benefits. Therefore, their preferred tax rate will always be zero, regardless of their ability.

At each period of the model, a cohort of size N_t is born. Then total population in each period is $N_{t-1} + N_t$ where $N_t = (1 + \eta_t)N_{t-1}$ and η_t is the population growth rate at period t. Given this, median voter is defined by

$$N_{t-1} + N_t \int_0^m f(a)\, da = \frac{N_{t-1} + N_t}{2} \qquad (9)$$

where m is the ability level of the median voter.

With population ageing, the median voter becomes a lower ability person (see Appendix) and her preferred tax rate decreases. The intuition behind this is as follows: as the population ages (dependency ratio rises), older people will need fewer young voters to form a majority. These young voters are the ones at the lower end of the ability distribution. They prefer lower taxes than higher ability people because their return from public education is lower.

3.4 Producers' behaviour

Each country produces a single good using a Cobb–Douglas production technology.

$$Y_t = \Lambda H_t^\beta K_t^{1-\beta} \qquad (10)$$

here Λ is the productivity index, K is capital stock and H is aggregate supply of human capital. The aggregate supply of human capital is:

$$H_t = N_t \int_0^1 h(a) f(a)\, da \qquad (11)$$

Competitive factor markets require that real wage and interest rates are equal to the marginal products of labour and capital respectively. Therefore, factor demand equations are:

$$w_t = \beta \Lambda \left(\frac{k_t}{h_t}\right)^{1-\beta} \qquad (12)$$

$$r_t = (1-\beta)\Lambda \left(\frac{k_t}{h_t}\right)^{-\beta} \qquad (13)$$

Here, $k_t = K_t/N_t$ and $h_t = H_t/N_t$ are capital stock per worker and human capital per worker, respectively. Human capital per worker, using (4) and (11), is

$$h_t = \Phi \int_0^1 (ag_t + 1)^\psi f(a)\, da \qquad (14)$$

Using (6) and (14), we can express saving per worker as

$$s_t = \left(\frac{1}{2+\delta}\right) \theta_t w_t \Phi \int_0^1 (ag_t + 1)^\psi f(a)\, da \qquad (15)$$

3.5 World equilibrium

To close the dynamic model, I must specify an international goods market condition and an international capital flow constraint. I assume there is perfect international financial capital mobility. In each country, claims to domestic and foreign capital are perfect substitutes. International goods market equilibrium requires that world saving is equal to world investment:

$$N_{t+1}^A k_{t+1}^A + N_{t+1}^B k_{t+1}^B = N_t^A s_t^A + N_t^B s_t^B \tag{16}$$

where, superscripts A and B denote countries. The implication of (16) is that domestic capital stock may be higher or lower than domestic saving, implying international capital flows. In this model, capital income is taxed where income is earned. Thus, I employ a territorial system of capital income taxation for both countries. This implies that net-of-tax interest rates are equalized between the two countries. Therefore, the international capital flow constraint is:

$$r_{t+1}^A (1 - \tau_{t+1}^A) = r_{t+1}^B (1 - \tau_{t+1}^B) \tag{17}$$

Capital will move between countries until both (16) and (17) hold. I complete the two-country model by introducing balance of payments identities. Balance of payments accounts are especially important in tracing the saving-investment imbalances between countries. Since this is a two-country model, balance of payments of the two countries must sum to zero. Therefore, we have $CA_t^A = -CA_t^B$, $BOT_t^A = -BOT_t^B$, and $FI_t^A = -FI_t^B$; where CA, BOT and FI stand for current account, balance of trade, and net foreign income, respectively. The current account is defined as the difference between national product and domestic absorption. National product consists of domestic product and net foreign income. Domestic absorption equals the sum of consumption and domestic capital accumulation less taxes. I assume that the consumption good can move costlessly between countries. Given this definition, the current account equation can be written as:[7]

$$CA_t = y_t(1 - \tau_t) + r_t(1 - \tau_t) \left[\frac{s_{t-1}}{1 + \eta_t} - k_t \right] - c_{1t} - \frac{c_{2t}}{1 + \eta_t}$$
$$- [(1 + \eta_{t+1})k_{t+1} - k_t] \tag{18}$$

The current account is the sum of balance of trade and net foreign income $(CA_t = BOT_t + FI_t)$. Balance of trade is the difference between domestic product and domestic absorption and can be written as:

$$BOT_t = y_t(1 - \tau_t) - c_{1t} - \frac{c_{2t}}{1 + \eta_t} - [(1 + \eta_{t+1})k_{t+1} - k_t] \tag{19}$$

The net foreign income is earnings from net claims on foreign capital:

$$FI_t = r_t(1 - \tau_t) \left[\frac{s_{t-1}}{1 + \eta_t} - k_t \right] \tag{20}$$

Because this is a one-sector model, 'international trade and international lending and borrowing are part and parcel of the same transaction' (Buiter 1981). The only way for a country to consume and invest more than it produces (have a trade deficit) is to hold a net ownership of claims on foreign capital (receive positive net foreign income).

3.6   Model behaviour

As shown in the appendix, when the population growth rate falls (increased dependency ratio), the ability level of the median voter goes down as well. All else equal, the political transition would reduce provision of the public good. However, if the tax rate decreases, national saving, and thus, physical capital accumulation will be enhanced. This creates a positive effect on income per worker, government spending per worker and human capital per worker. When the feedback effect from human capital dominates the negative effect of a lower preferred tax rate, demographic shock may induce higher income per worker, higher capital stock per worker, and higher human capital and government spending per worker. However, in an international setting, changes in the interest rate in the ageing country due to changes in income per worker and capital per worker may create interest rate differentials between countries, leading to international capital flows. Then, the aforementioned effects will spill over to other countries even though they do not experience any demographic shocks. In the following section, I examine the behaviour of my model in a simulation exercise.

4   The simulation study

The simulation study consists of a transition analysis of the effects of population ageing on the growth of economies. I assume that the countries are identical except for the population growth rates in the first period. The simulations are constructed so that the economies converge back to the same steady state obtained before the demographic shock. This is done by decreasing the population growth rate in the ageing country (A) only in the first time period. The population growth rate in country B remains unchanged throughout the transition. Given this and the fact that initial and final steady states are identical in per worker values, the first two periods of the transition are the focus of my analysis.[8] The parameter values used in the numerical simulation are shown in Table 17.1. The elasticity of output with respect to capital input is set equal to one-third ($\alpha = 0.33$).[9] The annual rate of time preference is chosen to be 4 per cent.[10] Notice that two parameters, the rate of time preference in the utility specification and the population growth rate, are adjusted to the length of the model period (30 years). The values for the scale parameters in the production function (Λ) and in the human capital supply function (Φ) are chosen arbitrarily and not shown in Table 17.1. These parameters determine only the units of measurement and they are not crucial for the simulations. In these simulations, I assume that the ability level, a, is distributed uniformly on the interval [0,1]. These parameter values and the timing

Table 17.1 Benchmark values of the parameters used in the two-country OLG model

	Rates translated into one-period (30 years)	Annual rate
Rate of time preference (δ)	2.24	0.04
Population growth rate (η)	0.55	0.02
Elasticity of human capital/ inputs of ability and government spending (ψ)	0.50	
Elasticity of output/capital (α)	0.33	

Source: Computed by author.

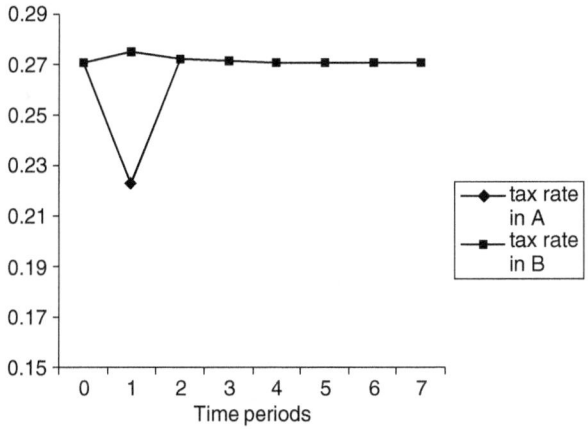

Figure 17.2 Tax rate transitions in A and B.

of population ageing mentioned above describe the benchmark simulation. A series of sensible values for the efficiency of education in raising human capital (ψ) are chosen to conduct a sensitivity analysis as explained in a later section.

4.1   Simulation results

As exposited, with an increase in the dependency ratio, the ability of the median voter is lower than before in country A, but unchanged in country B. Figure 17.2 shows the implications of this on the preferred tax rate. In country A, the lower ability level of the median voter reduces support for the public good. Thus, the median voter prefers a lower tax rate in the first period. However, in country B, there is no change in the median ability and the preferred tax rate, as mentioned before, exhibits positive income elasticity. Therefore, an increase in income per worker in country B leads to a first period increase in the preferred tax rate in that country. In country B, income growth increases the willingness to be taxed at a higher rate. Thus, a politically induced change in fiscal policy in country A spills over to the fiscal policy in country B. In my model, the lower tax rate in the ageing country (A), *ceteris paribus*, causes lower government spending and this causes deterioration in human capital accumulation. In Figure 17.3, human capital per worker decreases in country A and increases in country B in period 1. The increase in the preferred tax rate in country B (see Figure 17.2) explains the first period increase in its human capital per worker. Hence, country B experiences human capital growth due to its increased willingness to have higher government provision of the productivity-enhancing public good.

Figure 17.4 shows that the capital stock per worker increases in both countries in the first period. In country A, a decrease in the tax rate boosts savings through increased net labour earnings. This creates abundance of savings, which depresses the domestic interest rate in country A. At a lower interest rate, demand for capital increases in country B, causing capital to flow to country B. This will continue until net of tax interest rates are equalized between the two countries and the world capital market regains equilibrium. In Figure 17.5, we see an initial drop in the equilibrium net interest rate. For a better understanding of the capital movements, I examine the changes in the balance of payments of the ageing country. Due to the perfect foresight assumption, the decrease in country A's population growth rate in period 1 leads to a drop in period 0 domestic investment. In Figure 17.6, a zero net foreign income means a current account surplus for country A in period 0. Thus, capital moves from country A to country B from period 0 to period 1. This explains the increase in the capital stock per worker in country B in period 1 as we have seen in Figure 17.4. This also leads to a positive net foreign income for country A in period 1. However, due to a large trade deficit, country A incurs a current account deficit in period 1. This means that capital flows from country B back to country A from period 1 to period 2. This

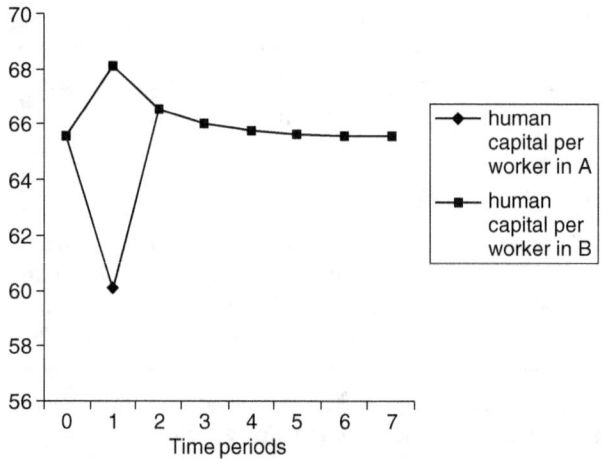

Figure 17.3 Human capital transitions in A and B.

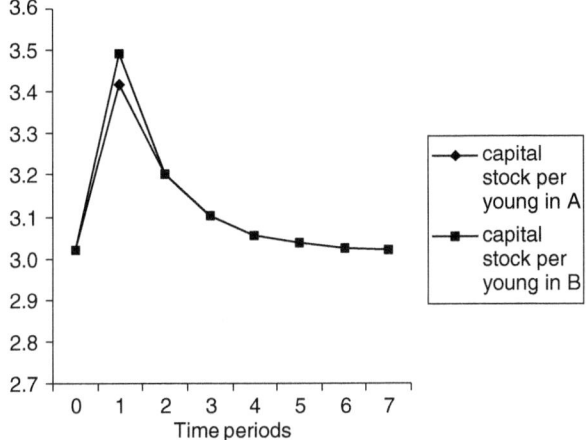

Figure 17.4 Capital stock transitions in A and B.

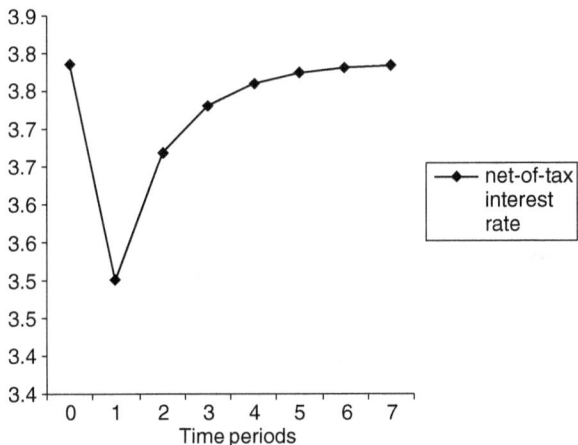

Figure 17.5 World net interest rate transition.

explains the greater decrease in the capital stock per worker in country B in period 2. Also, in period 2, country A has a negative net foreign income and a trade surplus. Because trade surplus outweighs negative net foreign income, country A has a current account surplus and capital flows from country A to country B again. However, since economic variables converge rapidly to their steady state values after period 2, current accounts and trade accounts of both countries are balanced thereafter. Since this is a two-country model of world economy, the balance of payments accounts in country B are just the opposite of what we see in the ageing country.

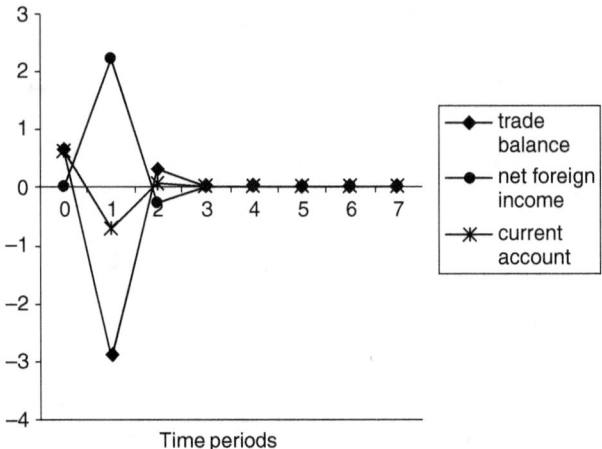

Figure 17.6 Balance of payments transitions for the ageing country (A).

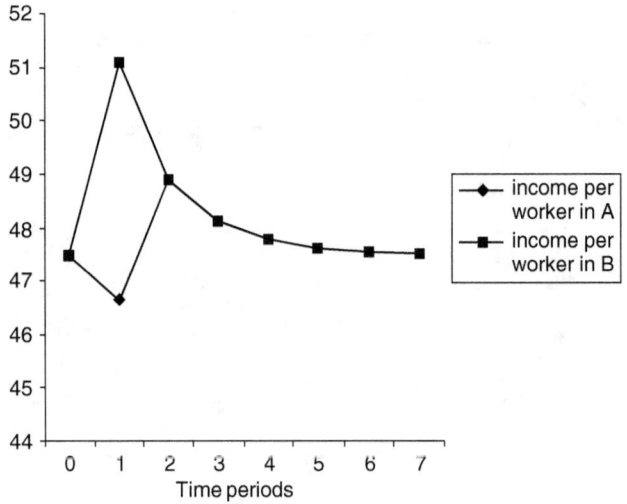

Figure 17.7 Income transitions in A and B.

The results presented above for capital per worker and human capital per worker tell us how income will respond to the demographic shock. Due to capital inflow, both capital and human capital per worker increase in country B leading to an increase in income per worker in the first period. On the other hand, even though the capital per worker increases in A, human capital per worker decreases in period 1. The income transitions in Figure 17.7 show that the decrease in

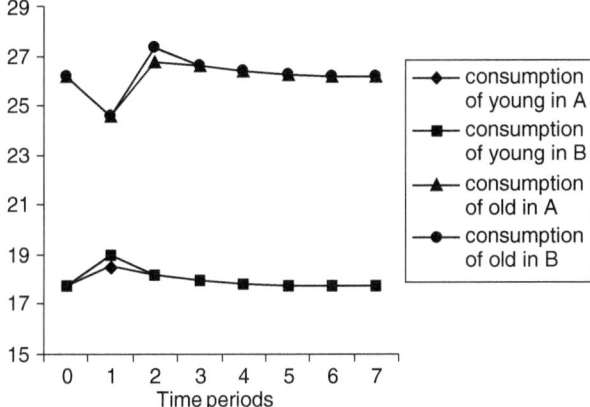

Figure 17.8 Consumption transitions of old and young generations in A and B.

human capital dominates, leading to a decrease in the income per worker in the first period. In the second period however, due to the capital inflow to country A, income per worker increases in country A while it decreases in country B. Welfare effects of ageing can be examined by defining welfare in period t as the lifetime welfare of a person of generation t.[11] Welfare of this person is composed of her consumption when young (in period t) and consumption when old (in period $t+1$), in other words her lifetime consumption. In order to examine the welfare effects, I derive an indirect utility function by substituting consumption solutions in (7) into (1), and I integrate this over the ability distribution. To understand welfare changes, I will first examine consumption transitions. In Figure 17.8, consumption of an old person of generation 0 decreases while that of a young person of generation 1 increases in both countries in period 1. The decrease in the consumption of old in period 1 comes from the perfect foresight assumption. In period 0, consumers internalize the decrease in the net of tax interest rate in the first period (see Figure 17.5). Therefore, a young person who saves in period 0 will get less from her saving in terms of her old age consumption in period 1. This result explains welfare changes in period 0. Figure 17.9 shows that welfare levels of generation 0 drop in both countries. On the other hand, increases in the consumption levels of generation 1 in Figure 17.8 explain the increases in the welfare levels of generation 1. However, both consumption and welfare of generation 1 increase more in country B than in country A. The explanation again lies in the international capital mobility. As shown in this section, capital flows to country B during period 1 lead to an increase in capital stock, human capital, and income per worker, and through these factors lead also to increases in the consumption and welfare of a person of generation 1 in country B. However, in the ageing country (A), human capital and income per worker decrease in period 1 while capital per worker increases, leading to a relatively smaller increase in both

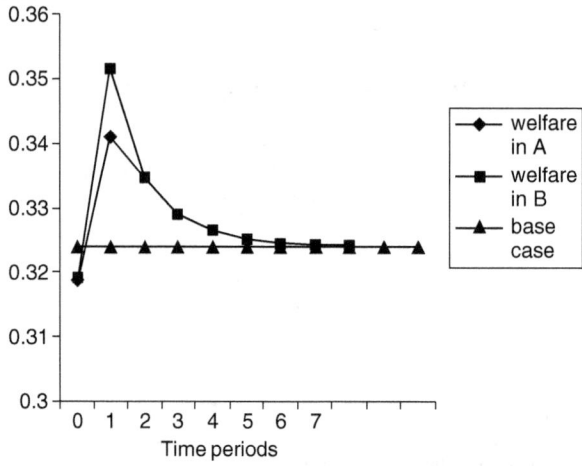

Figure 17.9 Welfare transitions in A and B.

consumption and welfare of a person of generation 1. This is an interesting result from the perspective of country B since it does not experience the same demographic shock as country A. In the following section, in order to establish the significance of capital mobility, I compare the results presented above with the results from an alternative closed economy model.

4.2   Comparison with a closed economy version

International capital flows change the results from a closed economy model significantly. Table 17.2 presents the results from both closed economy and open economy models. One striking result is the change in income per worker. While ageing increases income per worker in closed economy version, it decreases first period income per worker and increases second period income per worker in country A in the open economy model. The explanation lies in the relatively smaller increase in the first period capital stock (due to capital outflows) and greater decrease in first period human capital and government spending per worker in country A. Even though demographic shock enhances short run capital accumulation, and thus economic growth in country A, this positive growth effect on A is undermined due to open capital markets. Country B, on the other hand, benefits in the short run from capital inflows through their effects on the productivity of its economy. When I allow for capital flows, consumption and welfare transitions are smoother for the ageing country (A). Welfare of generation 0 decreases less in country A due to a smaller decrease in the first period interest rate. The interest rate decrease in period 1 causes an initial welfare decrease for country B as well. This is because old in period 1 receive less from their period 0 savings, and as a result they consume less. However, country B has a substantial

Table 17.2 Closed versus open economy results

	Time periods	Closed economy	Open economy	
			Country A	Country B
Capital stock per worker	1	34.3891	13.2621	15.7204
	2	−15.4743	−6.4019	−8.3902
	3	−6.6264	−3.0942	−3.0942
Human capital per worker	1	−3.0868	−8.4217	3.8675
	2	6.6613	10.8679	−2.2496
	3	−1.7649	−0.8143	−0.8143
Income per worker	1	7.9536	−1.7689	7.6383
	2	−1.2195	4.8427	−4.3203
	3	−3.3964	−1.5725	−1.5725
Government spending per worker	1	−7.2475	−19.2216	9.4080
	2	16.6269	28.3516	−5.2351
	3	−4.1241	−1.9239	−1.9239
Consumption of young	1	13.5935	4.7069	6.9817
	2	−6.6265	−1.8870	−3.9732
	3	−3.1209	−1.4409	−1.4409
Consumption of old	1	−12.2408	−5.9744	−5.9744
	2	22.6532	8.6344	10.9946
	3	−3.8943	−0.5717	−2.6859
Welfare	0	−3.9185	−1.8821	−1.8821
	1	20.9056	7.2642	10.5660
	2	−7.6760	−1.8763	−4.8066
	3	−3.6824	−1.7030	−1.7030

Source: Computed by author.

Note: All numbers are percentage changes from the previous period. Period 0 welfare numbers indicate percentage changes in welfare within period 0.

welfare increase in period 1, which is due to an increase in the lifetime consumption of generation 1.

4.3 Sensitivity analysis

The simulations described in Sections 4.1 and 4.2 are based on the set of parameters presented in Table 17.1. Among those, the parameter of the human capital function (ψ), which is the return, in terms of human capital, from government spending, is an important aspect of the model and the welfare results. Accordingly, in Table 17.3, I present the results of a sensitivity analysis for ψ. Higher values of ψ are associated with higher values of the elasticity of human capital with respect to government spending per worker and lower values of the elasticity of the preferred tax rate with respect to median voter's ability. Thus, for a high value of ψ, there will be a relatively smaller decline (or bigger increase) in the tax rate and government spending from a decrease in median voter's ability, while there will be a relatively greater human capital feedback from government spending for a given ability level. For $\psi = 0.7$ country A overall has more favourable transitions than for lower values of ψ, indicated by capital, income and welfare growth throughout the transition periods. However, for $\psi = 0.4$, the decrease in government spending and human capital due to a decrease in median voter's ability in A produces a substantial decrease in the first period income of country A. I also see that for higher values of ψ, the transitions of economic variables in country A and country B become more similar. However, country B goes through similar changes in its economy for all values of ψ in Table 17.3.

Table 17.3 Sensitivity of simulation results to various values of ψ for countries A and B

	Time periods	PSI = 0.4		PSI = 0.5		PSI = 0.7	
		A	B	A	B	A	B
Capital stock	1	11.4134	17.0934	13.2621	15.7204	14.0645	15.1227
per worker	2	−6.2205	−10.7734	−6.4019	−8.3902	−4.8132	−5.6882
	3	−2.5544	−2.5544	−3.0942	−3.0942	−3.1431	−3.1431
Human capital	1	−16.7870	3.2254	−8.4217	3.8675	3.3749	6.3492
per worker	2	21.2460	−2.2633	10.8679	−2.2496	0.2773	−2.5272
	3	−0.5210	−0.5210	−0.8143	−0.8143	−1.3860	−1.3860
Income per	1	−8.3737	7.6105	−1.7689	7.6383	6.7870	9.1681
worker	2	11.3917	−5.1580	4.8427	−4.3203	−1.4322	−3.5821
	3	−1.1967	−1.1967	−1.5725	−1.5725	−1.9691	−1.9691
Government	1	−51.1508	11.5842	−19.2216	9.4080	4.9745	9.4170
spending	2	111.1457	−7.5709	28.3516	−5.2351	0.4056	−3.6710
per worker	3	−1.8029	−1.8029	−1.9239	−1.9239	−2.0198	−2.0198
Interest rate	1	−17.7574	−8.0998	−13.2701	−6.9848	−6.3808	−5.1733
	2	18.7764	6.2945	12.0124	4.4435	3.5532	2.2346
	3	1.3948	1.3948	1.5702	1.5702	1.2112	1.2112
Consumption	1	1.5129	6.6924	4.7069	6.9817	7.9998	9.0015
of young	2	0.2984	−4.5743	−1.8870	−3.9732	−2.6275	−3.5223
	3	−1.0556	−1.0556	−1.4409	−1.4409	−1.9352	−1.9352
Consumption	1	−7.0286	−7.0286	−5.9744	−5.9744	−4.2064	−4.2064
of old	2	6.9785	12.4412	8.6344	10.9946	9.9395	10.9594
	3	1.5125	−3.4192	−0.5717	−2.6859	−1.6737	−2.5775
Welfare	0	−2.2596	−2.2596	−1.8821	−1.8821	−1.3173	−1.3173
	1	3.3092	10.6981	7.2642	10.5660	11.2145	12.5776
	2	1.1409	−5.6102	−1.8763	−4.8066	−3.1316	−4.3044
	3	−1.2581	−1.2581	−1.7030	−1.7030	−2.3472	−2.3472

Source: Computed by author.

Note: All numbers are percentage changes from the previous period. Period 0 welfare numbers indicate percentage changes in welfare within period 0.

5 Concluding remarks

In a world with internationally mobile capital, a demographic shock in the form of falling population growth rate in one part of the world can create substantial adjustments in world economies. In this paper, I addressed this issue from a political economy perspective in a two-country model with overlapping generations. By changing the political balance in favour of the preferences of older generations, population ageing has a direct impact on government spending policy. This triggers changes in the economy of the ageing country and also on other countries through the medium of internationally mobile capital. The simulation exercise shows that these changes can be quite substantial. While international capital flows produce smoother consumption and welfare transitions for the ageing country, they generate substantial short run productivity growth in the country that does not experience any demographic shock. This translates into short run consumption and welfare increases in country B. These results suggest, for instance, that developed country ageing can have significant growth and welfare effects not only on developed countries but also on developing countries. Hence, international spillover effects of population ageing can be too large to ignore.

Appendix: the effect of increasing dependency ratio on the ability level of the median voter

Recall that median voter is defined by

$$N_{t-1} + N_t \int_0^m f(a)\,\mathrm{d}a = \frac{N_{t-1} + N_t}{2}.$$

Rewriting this:

$$N_{t-1} + N_t F(m) - N_t F(0) = \frac{N_{t-1} + N}{2}.$$

Dividing both sides by N_{t-1}:

$$1 + (1 + \eta_t)\{F(m) - F(0)\} = \frac{2 + \eta_t}{2},$$

which can be rearranged as

$$F(m) - F(0) = \frac{\eta_t}{2(1 + \eta_t)}.$$

Differentiating both sides we get,

$$F'(m)\,\mathrm{d}m = \frac{2(1 + \eta_t)\,\mathrm{d}\eta_t - 2\eta_t\,\mathrm{d}\eta_t}{4(1 + \eta_t)^2}.$$

Finally this can be rearranged as

$$\frac{dm}{d\eta_t} = \frac{2}{F'(m)4(1+\eta_t)^2},$$

which is positive. Therefore, with a decrease in the population growth rate the ability level of the median voter will be lower.

Notes

1 OECD Policy Brief No. 5-1998.
2 Political process can be modelled using median voter framework because the conditions for median voter theorem are satisfied. The choice of voters is over a single dimension and the preferences are single peaked.
3 In a world with divergent population growth, the region with the higher growth rate continuously gets bigger than the other region. In that case, the post-demographic shock steady state is not defined.
4 The dependency ratio is defined as the ratio of elderly to non-elderly persons, $(N_{t-1}/N_t) = (1/1+\eta)$ where η_t is the population growth rate. An increase in the dependency ratio is simulated by an exogenous decrease in the population growth rate η_t.
5 Under a territorial system, capital income is taxed where income is earned.
6 ψ should be less than unity to prevent increasing returns from government spending.
7 Since the balance of payments accounts are identical in absolute magnitudes, I can take out the country superscripts and present equations for one country.
8 A relevant allusion to my experiment is throwing a stone into a pool of water. Initial impact creates a big splash, but the circular waves created by the impact dissipate over time, leading the water to its initial calm state. In this chapter, I am particularly interested in that big splash which is observed mainly in the first two periods of my analysis.
9 This elasticity estimate is consistent with the data from the United States. See Laitner (2000) for an argument.
10 Caldwell *et al.* (1999) argue that a premium of riskiness should be added to the widely used 2 per cent rate. They use 3.5 per cent as the discount rate which is the real safe return on indexed Treasury bonds. See Coronado *et al.* (2000) for a recent argument on the variety of discount rates used in studies of social security. They assert that the selection of discount rates ranges between 2 per cent and 5 per cent.
11 Generation *t* refers to persons who are young in period *t* and old in period *t*+1.

References

Borsch-Supan, A. (1996) 'The impact of population aging on savings, investment and growth in the OECD area', in: OECD (ed.) *Future Global Capital Shortages: Real Threat or Pure Fiction?*, Paris, 103–41.

Bos, E., Vu, M. T., Massiah E. and Bulatao, R. A. (1994) *World Population Projections*, World Bank, Baltimore: The Johns Hopkins University.

Buiter, W. H. (1981) 'Time preference and international lending and borrowing in an overlapping generations model', *Journal of Political Economy*, 89(4), 769–97.

Caldwell, S., Favreault, M., Gantman, A., Gokhale, J., Johnson, T. and Kotlikoff, L. J. (1999) 'Social security's treatment of postwar Americans,' in: Summers, L. H. (ed.) *Tax Policy and the Economy*, 13, Cambridge, MA: MIT Press.

Coronado, J. L., Fullerton, D. and Gloss, T. (2000) 'The Progressivity of Social Security', *NBER Working Paper No. 7250*. Cambridge, MA: National Bureau of Economic Research.

Cutler, D., Poterba, J., Sheiner L. and Summers, L. (1990) 'An aging society: opportunity or challenge', *Brookings Papers on Economic Activity*, 1, 1–73.

Diamond, P. (1965) 'National debt in a neoclassical growth model', *American Economic Review*, 55, 1126–50.

Holtz-Eakin, D., Lovely, M. E. and Tosun, M. S. (2000) 'Generational conflict, human capital accumulation, and economic growth', *NBER Working Paper No. 7762*.

Holtz-Eakin, D. (1993) 'Demographics, political power and economic growth', *Public Finance*, 48 (Supplement), 349–65.

Kahn, M. E. (2000) 'Demographic change and the demand for environmental regulation', working paper, Department of Economics, New York: Columbia University.

Kenc, T. and Sayan, S. (forthcoming) 'Demographic shade transmission from large to small countries: An overlapping generations CGE analysis', *Journal of Policy Modeling*.

Laitner, J. (2000) 'Simulating the effect on inequality and wealth accumulation of eliminating the federal gift and estate tax,' *Mimeo*, Ann Arbor, MI: University of Michigan.

Meijdam, L. and Verbon, H. A. A. (1996) 'Aging and political decision making on public pensions', *Journal of Population Economics*, 9, 141–58

Organisation for Economic Co-operation and Development (1998) 'Maintaining Prosperity in an Aging Society', *Policy Brief No. 5*, OECD.

Poterba, J. M. (1997) 'Demographic structure and the political economy of public education', *Journal of Public Policy and Management*, 16, 48–66.

18 An intertemporal evaluation of accession to the European Union*

Daniel Piazolo

1 The issue

The objective of this contribution is to derive an evaluation of the potential consequences of Poland's accession to the European Union (EU). The integration of Poland with advanced industrial countries in the Single European Market can be considered as the formative process for the Polish economy in the next two decades. The analysis is based on a dynamic Computable General Equilibrium (CGE) model of a small open-economy Ramsey-type with intra-industry trade. The intertemporal feature of the Ramsey model allows an examination of the development of the economy. Moreover, it shows clearly that consumption has to be foregone today in order to enable investment which will lead to higher output in the future and higher overall welfare. The effects of Polish accession to the EU run two ways: EU economies will be affected too; however, since the present EU is already a large single market, the effects for the EU will be much smaller in relation to GDP than for Poland. Therefore, the following analysis will not attempt to assess the effects of an enlargement on the present member states, but will look at the effects for the joining country.

To allow a more detailed focus on one country, the quantitative analysis will concentrate on Poland as the largest transition country. However, the results will be qualitatively transferable to the other joining transition countries. Table 18.1 displays the regional trade structure of Poland for the years 1996 and 1997 and shows that 65 per cent of Poland's foreign trade is with the present EU and a further 5 per cent with the countries that belong to the so-called Luxembourg group of EU candidates (i.e. Cyprus, Czech Republic, Estonia, Hungary, Slovenia). Consequently, Poland will find itself in a single market with twenty

*For helpful advice I thank Claudia Buch, Roberto De Santis, Rolf J. Langhammer, Matthias Lücke, Katrin Springer, David Tarr, Rainer Thiele, Erinc Yeldan and the participants at the conference 'Policy Evaluation with Computable General Equilibrium Models' in Genoa, especially Shantayanan Devarajan, Glenn Harrison, Brian Parmenter and Carlo Perroni. I am also grateful to Shantayanan Devarajan and Delfin Go from the World Bank for considerable help and the provision of the GAMS code that was extended for the present purpose. Financial support from the Volkswagen Foundation is gratefully acknowledged.

countries that account for 70 per cent of its foreign trade, which will deeply affect its export and import opportunities. Since EU membership also implies free trade in industrial goods with the other members of the European Economic Space (i.e. Iceland, Liechtenstein, Norway and with a special status Switzerland) and the second so-called Helsinki group of EU Accession countries, about three quarters of all Polish trade will be fully liberalized after accession (cf. Table 18.1).

The chapter is structured in the following way: Section 2 presents very briefly the concept of the dynamic effects of regional integration and the idea behind the dynamic modelling of these effects. Section 3 of the paper presents the main ideas of the dynamic model for the analysis of the integration of Poland into the EU. Section 4 summarizes the potential channels of EU membership effects and Section 5 offers five simulations of such effects. Section 6 concludes and describes some further avenues for research.

2   Dynamic effects of regional integration and dynamic CGE models

Membership in the Single European Market implies not only preferential trade liberalization but also the freedom of movement for goods, capital, labour and firms. The resulting effects can be classified into allocation and accumulation or, alternatively, static and dynamic effects. The static effects relate to the realloca-tion of resources and expenditures in response to changing relative prices. The dynamic effects relate to changes in the amount of resources available, that is, through increases (or decreases) in the capital stock due to changes in the prof-itability of investments.[1]

This paper attempts to model the dynamic effects of Poland's integration into the EU and uses a CGE model for this purpose. The CGE approach for the analysis of regional integration has attracted the Rodrik (1997) critique, stating that the gains from trade liberalization will be overestimated unless the model accounts for the foregone consumption necessary to build up the capital stock. Rodrik's critique is directed at the widespread use of comparative statistics ana-lyses before and after trade liberalization. Dynamic models have also attracted this critique. Baldwin (1999) emphasizes that by focussing on income effects, CGE models based on a Solow-type growth model (i.e. one good economy, neoclassical production function and constant savings rate) might substantially overestimate the actual welfare effects when consumers optimize over time. Also, Harrison *et al.* (1996) note that their calculations based on steady state comparisons ignore the foregone consumption necessary to obtain an increase in the capital stock. Fur-thermore, Rutherford and Tarr (1999) propose that a CGE model analysing dynamic effects of trade liberalization should account for endogenous growth. However, the link between endogenous growth theory and CGE modelling is still a young and fragile one.

The present Ramsey-type model accounts for the foregone consumption necessary to build up the capital stock as well as consumer optimization and includes a welfare measure depending on the present value of all future

Table 18.1 Poland's trade with partner countries in 1996 and 1997

Imports	1996		1997	
	Value in 1000 US$	Percentage of total imports	Value in 1000 US$	Percentage of total imports
World	37,107,424	100.00	42,277,231	100.00
EU	23,383,040	63.01	26,632,449	62.99
Austria	786,791	2.12	831,777	1.97
Belgium-Luxembourg	921,381	2.48	1,137,709	2.69
Denmark	784,050	2.11	797,593	1.89
Finland	597,690	1.61	715,258	1.69
France	1,988,172	5.36	2,461,040	5.82
Germany	9,123,907	24.59	10,143,391	23.99
Greece	71,835	0.19	78,270	0.19
Ireland	183,159	0.49	210,536	0.50
Italy	3,650,713	9.84	4,145,513	9.81
Netherlands	1,374,503	3.70	1,493,213	3.53
Portugal	41,747	0.11	64,351	0.15
Spain	736,195	1.98	1,020,625	2.41
Sweden	970,159	2.61	1,247,812	2.95
United Kingdom	2,152,738	5.80	2,285,361	5.41
Luxembourg group of EU candidates	1,699,422	4.58	2,037,603	4.82
Czech Republic	1,119,859	3.02	1,288,754	3.05
Estonia	20,952	0.06	24,061	0.06
Hungary	411,874	1.11	556,631	1.32
Slovenia	145,123	0.39	166,999	0.40
Cyprus	1,614	0.00	1,158	0.00
Helsinki group of EU candidates	633,377	1.71	725,726	1.72
Bulgaria	28,050	0.08	32,283	0.08
Latvia	14,717	0.04	17,928	0.04
Lithuania	104,747	0.28	106,737	0.25
Romania	67,247	0.18	63,378	0.15
Slovakia	418,616	1.13	505,400	1.20
European economic space (Apart from EU members)	902,808	2.43	1,004,798	2.38
Iceland	7,088	0.02	8,245	0.02
Norway	363,860	0.98	403,745	0.95
Switzerland	531,860	1.43	592,808	1.40
Others	6,015,990	16.21	6,937,754	16.41
Belarus	250,868	0.68	214,666	0.51
Ukraine	409,647	1.10	407,709	0.96
Russian Federation	2,513,529	6.77	2,673,868	6.32
Japan	586,712	1.58	715,939	1.69
Korea	651,596	1.76	1,059,909	2.51
United States	1,603,638	4.32	1,865,663	4.41
Rest of the world	4,472,787	12.05	4,938,901	11.68

Table 18.1 (Continued)

Exports	1996		1997	
	Value in 1000 US$	*Percentage of total exports*	*Value in 1000 US$*	*Percentage of total exports*
World	24,425,663	100	25,747,222	100
EU	*16,004,801*	*65.52*	*16,322,642*	*63.40*
Austria	468,694	1.92	465,567	1.81
Belgium-Luxembourg	593,119	2.43	547,016	2.12
Denmark	727,401	2.98	740,289	2.88
Finland	307,520	1.26	323,516	1.26
France	1,058,704	4.33	1,115,076	4.33
Germany	8,381,125	34.31	8,444,682	32.80
Greece	177,608	0.73	94,117	0.37
Ireland	62,080	0.25	67,798	0.26
Italy	1,288,497	5.28	1,494,801	5.81
Netherlands	1,150,723	4.71	1,182,496	4.59
Portugal	36,142	0.15	25,152	0.10
Spain	243,460	1.00	280,311	1.09
Sweden	565,465	2.32	592,579	2.30
United Kingdom	944,263	3.87	949,242	3.69
Luxembourg group of EU candidates	*1,265,222*	*5.18*	*1,367,336*	*5.31*
Czech Republic	817,730	3.35	882,696	3.43
Estonia	50,363	0.21	47,700	0.19
Hungary	295,838	1.21	367,897	1.43
Slovenia	38,893	0.16	44,747	0.17
Cyprus	62,398	0.26	24,296	0.09
Helsinki group of EU candidates	*647,505*	*2.65*	*834,597*	*3.24*
Bulgaria	42,637	0.17	58,083	0.23
Latvia	69,263	0.28	99,526	0.39
Lithuania	205,977	0.84	308,860	1.20
Romania	68,483	0.28	72,756	0.28
Slovakia	261,145	1.07	295,372	1.15
European economic space (Apart from EU members)	*498,697*	*2.04*	*359,158*	*1.39*
Iceland	9,527	0.04	3,807	0.01
Norway	291,284	1.19	207,952	0.81
Switzerland	197,886	0.81	147,399	0.57
Others	*3,523,002*	*14.42*	*4,380,422*	*17.01*
Belarus	246,695	1.01	294,681	1.14
Ukraine	942,807	3.86	1,170,120	4.54
Russian Federation	1,616,729	6.62	2,118,369	8.23
Japan	50,049	0.20	56,095	0.22
Korea	119,463	0.49	92,779	0.36
United States	547,259	2.24	648,378	2.52
Rest of the world	*2,486,436*	*10.18*	*2,483,067*	*9.64*

Source: OECD (2000), International Trade by Commodities Statistics (ITCS) CD-ROM; own calculations.

consumption. Furthermore, the dynamic model is able to show the time path of most important economic variables. Several static CGE models try to assess the consequences of the accession of the transition countries to the EU. However, only a few CGE models examine the consequences of EU membership for a specific transition country. This paper is to my knowledge the first fully dynamic CGE study for Poland analysing the effects of EU accession.[2]

3   The dynamic computable general equilibrium model for Poland

A dynamic single-country CGE model reflecting the economic conditions of Poland for 1996 is employed to assess the key effects of Poland's membership in the EU. The Poland's Regional Integration Computable Equilibrium (PRINCE) model is of a small open-economy Ramsey-type with intertemporal consumer as well as producer optimization and with intra-industry trade. The PRINCE model is a perfect foresight dynamic model: the decisions of the economic agents are intra- as well as intertemporally consistent. The theoretical framework for the Ramsey model is set out in greater detail in Barro and Sala-i-Martin (1995).[3] The PRINCE model is an extension of the work by Devarajan and Go (1998) for the Philippines which is, in turn, a dynamic and expanded version of Devarajan *et al.* (1997) and Go (1994). The exact structure of the PRINCE model is available as separate appendix from the author and is set out in detail in Piazolo (2000).

In the base structure of the model the economy is divided into two produced goods (exports and domestic goods) and two consumed goods (imports and domestic goods). Consequently, there is only one endogenous price per period (i.e. the price of the domestic good) to be solved for. There are three types of imports, each with a separate import duty: capital imports, which are a fixed share requirement in investment, intermediate imports, and final imports, which compete with the domestic good. Imperfect substitution characterizes the competition between foreign and domestic goods as reflected by the so-called Armington substitution elasticity between the domestic goods and final imports and by a constant elasticity of transformation (CET) between sales to the domestic market and sales to the export markets. The Armington specification assumes that the domestic products in consumer preferences differ from foreign goods. This allows the prices of domestic products to vary at given world market prices, exchange rates and import duties (cf. Blonigen and Wilson 1999). Consequently, it is possible to model two-way flows of goods, that is, intra-industry trade.

3.1   Equilibrium conditions

Intratemporal and intertemporal equilibrium conditions have to be fulfilled for the model to be solved. The intratemporal general equilibrium conditions are: demand equals supply for all goods and for labour, the current account balance is matched by the capital account balance, government savings plus government current expenditure (consisting of public consumption, transfers and subsidies) equals government revenue (derived from tariffs, domestic indirect taxes, income taxes and external borrowing). Concerning the intertemporal equilibrium, it is important to note that the decisions about investment and domestic savings are made independently and that foreign savings fill the gap. Changes in future debt repayments due to the consequent increase in debt are fully anticipated in the household's decision between consumption and savings. A further intertemporal aspect of the model is that future prices and future quantities are fully incorporated into the decisions concerning savings and investment. Consequently, in the steady state, prices and exchange rates are stable and convergence after a shock to the new steady state is unique. During the adjustment after a shock, savings and investment decisions may diverge due to the existence of two discount rates and different adjustment mechanisms for the consumer and the producer.

3.2 Database for the Poland's regional integration computable equilibrium (PRINCE) model

The PRINCE model is implemented to approximate the Polish economy. The database reflects mainly the situation in 1996, with data supplied partly by the Gdansk Institute for Market Economics in Poland. Table 18.2 describes the aggregated social accounting matrix (SAM) for Poland for the year 1996 and shows the financial flows between the various economic agents in the economy. Thus, the SAM provides a 'snap-shot' for a certain year on the development path of the Polish economy. Furthermore, data about the exchange rate, debt and the import structure are needed. As mentioned before, imports are divided up according to the broad categories of consumer, intermediate, and capital imports, each with its own tariff level. On the basis of the tax information, the components of the gross national product (GNP) at factor prices and the various tax ratios and price indices in the model are derived.

3.3 Calibration of the dynamic general equilibrium model for Poland

The economic relationships within a CGE model are calibrated on the benchmark dataset. In the calibration process, exogenous variables (like tax rates) and exogenous parameters (like substitution elasticities) are combined with endogenous variables (like output) to determine the endogenous parameters (like the share parameters of the Armington elasticities). This calibration process computes parameters in such a way that the equilibrium solution of the model reproduces the observed data.

For simplicity, the paper assumes that the balanced growth rate equals zero. This allows a better interpretation of the results of the policy simulations in comparison to the reference run, since one escapes the otherwise necessary detrending of the exogenous growth rate. Consequently, the reference run steady state is in this case actually a stationary state. However, this model and the dynamic calibration procedure could incorporate an exogeneously determined

Table 18.2 SAM for Poland 1996 in million Zloties

Income	Expenditures								Total
	Production		Factors	Institutions			Capital account	Abroad	
	Sectors	Goods		Firms	Households	Government			
	1	2	3	4	5	6	7	8	9
Sectors		685,986.0						90,091.7	776,077.7
Goods	424,619.6				236,326.4	63,428.0	73,191.7		797,565.7
Factors	305,464.5								305,464.5
Firms			139,441.5						139,441.5
Households			166,023.0	139441.5					305,464.5
Government	45,993.6	11,356.1							57,349.7
Capital account					69,138.1	−6,275.1		10,328.7	73,191.7
Abroad		100,223.6				196.8			100,420.4
Total	776,077.7	797,565.7	305,464.5	139441.5	305,464.5	57,349.7	73,191.7	10,0420.4	2,554,975.7

Source: Gdansk Institute for Market Economies (1999), GUS (1998), WIIW (2000), own calculations.

Note: For SAM structure cf. Thiele (1996: 101).

balanced growth rate which is larger than zero. For further simplification, all relevant data are scaled to per capita terms (i.e. divided by the population). In the present form, a stationary population (i.e. no population growth) is assumed. Again, this restriction could be relaxed in an extension of this model.

For dynamic models, it is not feasible to calibrate the model exactly to the database of a particular year (as one would do in the case of a static model). This approach may violate the intertemporal consistency requirements, because the database may be inconsistent with the assumptions of the stationary or steady state. Therefore the dynamic model is calibrated to a base-year, but adjusted to reproduce a reference run with a base-year according to what a hypothetical stationary state for this year would have looked like. (cf. Knudsen *et al.* 1997: 83). The parameters are calibrated for such a reference run, which ensures that the model will generate an equilibrium solution with values that approximate the benchmark data of the economy in question. A change in policy or the advent of an external shock will lead to an alternative path which will reflect the deviation from the steady state reference run.

In the dynamic calibration for the PRINCE model, the depreciation rate is determined endogenously to achieve consistency between the observed investment and the capital stock and consequently the required replenishment of the capital stock due to depreciation. In the steady state of an economy the investment ratio has to equal the depreciation rate if one abstracts from technological progress and population growth.

4   Channels of EU membership effects

4.1   Tariff reduction and adoption of the common external tariffs of the EU

The Europe Agreements between the present EU members and ten Central and Eastern European countries have already led to a substantial reduction in bilateral tariffs and have in fact already created a kind of regional trading area. By 2001, only few industrial goods from the EU to Europe Agreements partner countries or vice versa face any tariff. However, Poland charges an average tariff of 12 per cent on industrial imports from third countries on a most favoured nation (MFN) basis, whereas the EU has an MFN average tariff of only 2 per cent. Poland will adopt the common external tariff of the EU via full EU membership. Furthermore, Poland will have to align its fiscal and agricultural polices with EU regulations, especially the Common Agricultural Policies (CAP). However, this alignment of agricultural policies involves a complex set of policy issues including various subsidy flows and price support schemes. For the present analysis, the detailed mechanisms of the CAP are neglected. The relevant issue is that full EU membership will lead to further overall tariff reduction in Poland, especially *vis-à-vis* third countries. In the following simulations, tariff reductions between Poland and the EU as well as between Poland and non-EU countries are included.

4.2   Reduction in trade costs resulting from borders

Before the implementation of the Single Market, the border cost for trade between the member states of the European Community was estimated to sum up to 1.7 per cent of the value of trade (Cawley and Davenport 1988). This border cost before 1992 was due to customs and fiscal controls between the member states. With the Single Market in force, no customs clearance is required at the borders and the remaining necessary forms documenting the flows of trade (e.g. for statistical purposes) can be completed in the European headquarters. The 1.7 per cent border cost of the total amount traded has recently been used to derive the gains for the present EU member states from the Single Market with CGE analysis (Hoffmann 2000) and can be employed to assess the benefits for acceding countries.

4.3   Reduction of technical barriers to trade

Exporters have to modify their products in order to achieve compliance with the technical standards and regulations of the importing country. In certain cases, the product has to be examined again by certifying institutions to obtain the permit to be sold abroad. These procedures incur substantial costs for the exporting company. The European Single Market attempts to reduce and eventually to abolish these technical barriers to trade between member countries, in most cases by the European harmonization of standards and in fewer cases by enforcing the mutual recognition principle. The extra costs due to the technical barriers of trade arise at production for the export market.

This approach has been used for CGE modelling of the completion of the Single Market and its effect on the present members. Harrison *et al.* (1996) estimate that the reduction in the real trade costs from decreases in border costs and standardization costs sum up to 2.5 per cent of the value traded. Based on this estimate Hoffmann (2000) uses a value of 0.8 per cent of the value of trade as the additional trading costs due to technical barriers before the implementation of the European Single Market (i.e. the difference between the 2.5 per cent estimated by Harrison *et al.* and the 1.7 per cent used for the border costs – see Section 4.2).

4.4   Transfers from Brussels

EU members contribute to the common EU budget according to an algorithm based on each country's VAT revenues. More important, however, for the joining countries are the transfers from the common EU budget. Most of these transfers are either connected to the structural funds or to the CAP. Due to the uncertainties related to the development of the EU CAP and its compliance with the forthcoming millennium WTO round, the focus here is on the structural funds. A share of 5 per cent of GNP probably represents an upper bound for the amount of structural funds flows to a present EU member country (cf. Baldwin *et al.* 1997). However, Baldwin *et al.* argue that due to the political economy of the

EU and the reduced bargaining power of the new entrants, the gross flows from Brussels will be about 4 per cent of GNP in the case of Poland and that the net flows will amount to about 1.5 per cent GNP. The net transfer from the common EU budget to Poland is modelled in the following simulations.

4.5 Other effects

EU membership might affect Poland also through its effects on the migration pattern (Hille 2001) or through the reduction in the risk premia (cf. Piazolo 1999). However, it is quite difficult to find plausible magnitudes of the necessary parameter changes for the CGE analysis. Therefore, the gains derived in the simulation analysis are likely to represent the lower bound of the EU accession effects for Poland.

5 Simulations with the PRINCE model

5.1 Integration scenarios

Five simulations of EU membership effects are carried out examining four different channels of membership effects and the overall consequences if all changes are implemented simultaneously.

Scenario 1

Tariff reduction for products from the EU, EU-associated countries and European Economic Space countries Poland's trade with these countries amounts to 75 per cent already. However, many product categories in bilateral trade with these countries already benefit from duty free treatment due to the European Agreements. The implementation of the common external tariff of the EU will also lead to a tariff reduction for trade with other countries except that the CAP will establish high barriers for agricultural goods toward non-EU members. For total trade, a reduction of tariffs by 50 per cent is simulated.

Scenario 2

Reduction in border costs As mentioned before, the border costs before the implementation of the Single Market were assessed to amount to 1.7 per cent of the total trade. Since more than 75 per cent of trade will be affected, the reduction in trade costs for exports and imports is modelled through a decrease of three-quarters of 1.7 per cent, that is, about 1.3 per cent. In the single-country PRINCE model, a reduction in trade costs is represented through a decrease in import prices and an increase in export prices.

Scenario 3

Reduction of technical barriers to trade It is assumed that technical barriers to trade incur additional trading costs of 1 per cent of the amount traded. Again, since more than three-quarters of trade will benefit from this reduction of trade costs, export and import trade costs are reduced by three-quarters of 1 per cent, that is, by about 0.8 per cent of the amount traded.

Scenario 4

Based on the arguments and calculations of Baldwin *et al.* (1997) a net transfer of 1.5 per cent of the Polish GNP from the EU-budget is assumed. This is modelled as a permanent flow of resources similar to the remittances of Polish workers living abroad.

Scenario 5

All four simulations are implemented simultaneously.

5.2   *Results*

Table 18.3 shows the effects of these five simulations on welfare and on the most important macroeconomic variables (consumption, investment, exports, imports, domestic good production, borrowing, debt and capital stock) relative to the reference run (i.e. without any changes). For the variables, values for the periods 1, 10, 20, 30 and 40 are presented allowing an examination of the intertemporal aspect of the simulated changes for all five scenarios. Additionally, one column (column five) is included representing the multiplicative aggregate (i.e. the pro-duct) of the four sub-scenarios for comparison with the overall effects stemming from the simultaneous simulation of these four scenarios. This comparison shows that the membership effects according to the multiplicative aggregate (column five) are far greater than in the case of the simultaneous implementation of the same four scenarios (column six). This is partly due to the adjustment costs for capital formation preventing a more rapid rise for investment. Furthermore, Figures 18.1 and 18.2 plot the development of the macroeconomic variables for all time periods from 1 to 40 for the overall effects (i.e. the four scenarios simultaneously).

In all simulations, investment goes up in period 1, whereas consumption drops. The increased capital stock is then employed to produce more goods for domestic use and for exports in later periods with consumption rising above the reference-run level approximately from period 5 onwards.

It might be considered counter-intuitive how much consumption renounce-ment the utility maximizing household is willing to undertake, especially since borrowing from abroad is always possible at a fixed interest rate in the world market. However, consumption and investment decisions are fully decentralized and separate. Given a trade policy shock and the resulting relative price changes, the representative firm will react and optimize its investment decision as deter-mined by the investment function and the intertemporal supply problem. The relevant interest rate for the producer depends on the real exchange rate given

Table 18.3 Simulations of full EU membership effects for Poland – relative to the reference run

	Tariff reduction	Border cost reduction	Reduction of tech. barriers to trade	Net-EU-transfers to Poland	Overall effects	
					Aggregated of the 4 simulations	New simulation with 4 effects simultaneously
Consumption						
Period 1	0.958	0.954	0.972	0.938	0.833	0.925
10	1.015	1.033	1.021	1.055	1.129	1.083
20	1.037	1.063	1.039	1.101	1.261	1.146
30	1.044	1.073	1.045	1.116	1.306	1.168
40	1.047	1.076	1.047	1.121	1.322	1.175
Investment						
Period 1	1.204	1.279	1.170	1.414	2.548	1.555
10	1.160	1.221	1.132	1.335	2.140	1.468
20	1.141	1.195	1.116	1.295	1.971	1.416
30	1.134	1.185	1.111	1.280	1.911	1.395
40	1.129	1.178	1.107	1.269	1.868	1.379
Exports						
Period 1	1.009	0.984	0.990	0.959	0.943	0.934
10	1.061	1.054	1.033	1.062	1.227	1.071
20	1.081	1.081	1.049	1.101	1.350	1.125
30	1.088	1.090	1.055	1.114	1.394	1.142
40	1.089	1.092	1.056	1.117	1.403	1.147
Imports						
Period 1	1.054	1.060	1.036	1.111	1.286	1.135
10	1.068	1.079	1.048	1.141	1.378	1.180
20	1.073	1.086	1.052	1.151	1.411	1.194
30	1.075	1.088	1.053	1.153	1.420	1.198
40	1.074	1.087	1.053	1.152	1.416	1.196
Domestic good prod.						
Period 1	0.997	1.005	1.003	1.012	1.017	1.019
10	1.031	1.051	1.031	1.081	1.208	1.114
20	1.043	1.068	1.042	1.107	1.285	1.150
30	1.047	1.074	1.045	1.115	1.310	1.162
40	1.048	1.075	1.046	1.117	1.316	1.164
Borrowing						
Period 1	1.534	1.729	1.443	2.032	7.784	2.378
10	1.318	1.438	1.262	1.633	3.906	1.881
20	1.177	1.243	1.145	1.353	2.265	1.500
30	1.081	1.112	1.067	1.163	1.492	1.233
40	1.000	1.000	1.000	1.000	1.000	1.000
Debt						
Period 1	1.000	1.000	1.000	1.000	1.000	1.000
10	1.203	1.278	1.167	1.400	2.512	1.549
20	1.216	1.296	1.177	1.428	2.648	1.596
30	1.160	1.220	1.131	1.319	2.113	1.448
40	1.089	1.122	1.073	1.177	1.543	1.250

Table 18.3 (Continued)

	Tariff reduction	Border cost reduction	Reduction of tech. barriers to trade	Net-EU-transfers to Poland	Overall effects	
					Aggregated of the 4 simulations	New simulation with 4 effects simultaneously
Capital stock						
Period 1	1.000	1.000	1.000	1.000	1.000	1.000
10	1.083	1.114	1.069	1.172	1.512	1.236
20	1.116	1.160	1.096	1.242	1.761	1.337
30	1.126	1.174	1.104	1.264	1.846	1.370
40	1.129	1.178	1.107	1.269	1.868	1.379
Overall welfare effects (in %)	*0.1397*	*0.3085*	*0.1957*	*0.5154*	*1.1639*	*0.7676*

Source: Calculations with the PRINCE model.

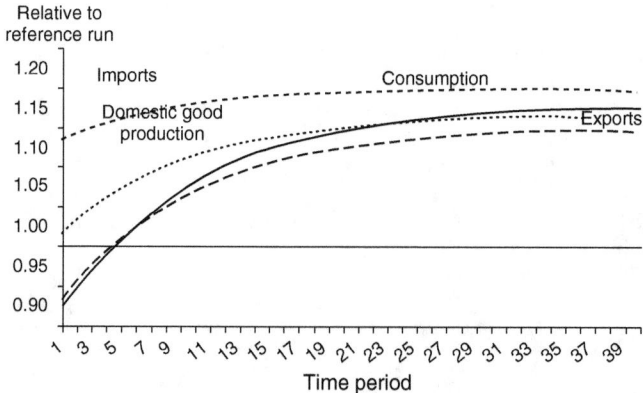

Figure 18.1 Overall effects of EU membership on consumption, exports, imports and domestic good production – relative to the reference run.

Note: The modelled 'Overall Effects of EU Membership' consist of the simultaneous implementation of the four scenarios tariff reduction, border cost reduction, reduction of technical barriers to trade and net-EU transfers.

Source: Calculations with the PRINCE model.

by the price ratio of exports and domestic goods. If this price ratio changes due to a trade policy shock, the firm will adapt its investment to maintain asset equilibrium.

The increase in investment as a result of the trade policy change leads to an increase in the use of inputs for investment goods. The increased demand drives up the costs of inputs and, consequently, the initial price for consumption, which is not under the control of the household. Furthermore, the path of consumption is affected by the discount rate for consumption which includes the forward

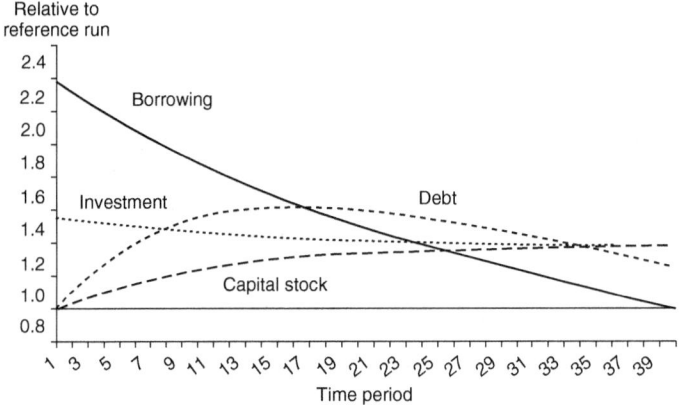

Figure 18.2 Overall effects of EU membership on investment, capital stock, borrowing and debt – relative to the reference run.

Note: The modelled 'Overall Effects of EU membership' consist of the simultaneous implementation of the four scenarios tariff reduction, border cost reduction, reduction of technical barriers to trade and net-EU transfers.

Source: Calculations with the PRINCE model.

percentage change in the relevant exchange rate, the relative price between imports (PM) and domestic goods (PD) (cf. Equations (4) and (5) in the separate Appendix). After the initial appreciation (PM/PD declines), the real exchange rate for consumption depreciates slowly year after year. As Equation (9) in the Appendix determines, a slowly depreciating exchange rate leads to a slowly rising consumption path. To achieve intertemporal consistency, the consumption path has to shift downwards as a result of the trade policy change so that consumption is at the beginning indeed lower than in the reference run. However, consumption is higher than in the reference run for the fifth and all following periods. Borrowing increases considerably relative to the reference run, but a further increase in borrowing (to facilitate higher consumption at the beginning) would not be optimal since the capital inflow changes the exchange rate (away from the optimal level) and since the level of borrowing has to return at the terminal period to the original level (a requirement exogeneously specified).

5.3   The overall effects of Poland's accession to the EU

Welfare (as defined by the utility measure introduced earlier) increases in all five simulations.[4] The simultaneous implementation of all four effects leads to an increase in welfare by 7.7 per million (0.7676 per cent in the last row of the last column in Table 18.3). Maybe, the size of the increase in welfare is judged to be surprisingly low. However, it has to be remembered that, in the reference run, the representative household maximizes utility and is at the optimal level of investment. Consequently, the household is neutral towards having a marginal additional unit of capital since it requires a reduction in consumption. The discounted value of potential future additional income due to a marginal increase in the capital stock equals the value of the forgone consumption today. The changes due to EU membership might have considerable effects in the substitution between investment and consumption, yet the welfare effects are much smaller, since the welfare measure accounts for the foregone consumption.

The values for period forty approximate the new steady state. For example, the scenario of the tariff reduction, consumption and domestic good production in the new steady state is 4.7 per cent higher relative to the base scenario. The increase in consumption can act as a proxy for the income effect of the trade policy changes. The comparison of the different EU membership effects shows that the modelled net transfer from the EU budget to Poland has the most profound effect on the welfare measure (with an increase by 5.1 per million). This is due to the substantial increase in investment that is made possible through the funds of the EU partner countries: the simulation shows that investment increases by more than 40 per cent in the first period whereas consumption has to be reduced by only 6 per cent. This sharp rise in investment points to necessary amendments concerning the modelling of adjustment costs for investments. Some sensitivity analyses for the adjustment cost parameter and also for the intertemporal elasticity of substitution are represented in an appendix that is available on request from the author.

5.4   Issues for further research

EU membership is represented in these CGE models as a sudden and unexpected shock, which is not entirely realistic. Consequently, it is also not reasonable to believe that the year of EU accession will bring a dramatic increase in investment. Due to the anticipation of full EU membership and the gradualism practised in accession, economic agents will adapt (and have already adapted in the cases of the advanced Central and Eastern European countries) their behaviour beforehand. Actually, dynamic CGE modelling also allows the possibility of phasing in trade policy changes over a longer time period. If, however, the rational economic agent expects changes in the future, he or she will change the behaviour accordingly to maximize utility.

Several research opportunities follow from this paper. First, the other three mentioned channels of EU membership effects (reduction in the risk premia, migration and demand side effects) could be modelled. Second, the announcement effects of regional integration could be investigated with this CGE model along the lines of Willenbockel (1998). Third, the model could be extended either to a further disaggregation of sectors or to a multi-country level.

6   Conclusions

The simulations of Poland's membership in the EU with the PRINCE model reveal positive effects stemming from regional integration. EU membership effects were modelled through tariff reduction, border cost reduction, reduction of technical barriers to trade, and net EU-transfers from Brussels to Poland. The simulations show that the higher future consumption stemming from the increased capital stock requires considerable investment today, that is, foregone consumption. This 'disutility' of consumption renouncement is reflected in the welfare measure, which discounts the consumption of all periods.

For the simultaneous implementation of all four effects of EU membership, consumption in the new steady state is 17.5 per cent higher than at the starting point. But at the beginning consumption is actually lower than in the reference run. Consequently, this evaluation of Poland's accession to the EU also reflects the painful adjustment process for transition countries wanting to join a regional integration arrangement. Overall, however, Poland will benefit considerably from the European integration.

Notes

1 This is set out in greater detail in Piazolo (2001). For a general discussion of the dynamic effects of regional integration the reader is referred to the relevant surveys by Walz (1997) and Baldwin and Forslid (1999).
2 Banse (1999) offers a recursive dynamic CGE model for Hungary and Poland. Lensink (1999) examines the effects of interest rate deregulation and changes in reserve requirements for Poland with a CGE model containing a commercial banking sector and a central bank.
3 Implementations of the Ramsey model as CGE models for the General Algebraic Modelling System (GAMS) are offered by Manne (1986), Go (1994), Lau *et al.* (2001) and Devarajan and Go (1998).
4 Given that the utility function represents the rational preferences of a representative household with perfect foresight, the utility function can act as a proxy for a welfare measure (cfr. Ng 1983: 7–12). The utility function embedded within a CGE model is frequently used as an exact and convenient evaluation of welfare changes (Martin 1997: 77). It should be noted that the used welfare measure here is given in 'utils'.

References

Baldwin, R. E., (1999) 'Discussion of Francois, Nordström and Shiells, 1999. 'Transition dynamics and trade policy reform in developing countries'', in: Baldwin, R. E. and Francois, J. F. (eds), *Dynamic Issues in Applied Commercial Policy Analysis*, Cambridge: Cambridge University Press, 41–3.

Baldwin, R. E., Francois, J. F. and Portes, R. (1997) 'The costs and benefits of Eastern enlargement: the impact on the EU and Central Europe', *Economic Policy*, 24, 127–70.

Baldwin, R. E. and Forslid, R. (1999) 'Putting growth effects in computable equilibrium trade model', in Baldwin, R. E. and Francois, J. F. (eds), *Dynamic Issues in Applied Commercial Policy Analysis*, Cambridge: Cambridge University Press, 44–84.

Banse, M. (1999) 'Impact of EU-accession on consumers' welfare in Central European countries', *Paper presented at the 2. GTAP Conference*.

Barro, R. J. and Sala-i-Martin, X. (1995) *Economic Growth*, New York: McGraw-Hill.

Blonigen, B. A. and Wilson, W. W. (1999) 'Explaining Armington: what determines substitutability between home and foreign goods?', *Canadian Journal of Economics*, 32(1), 1–21.

Cawley, R. and Davenport, M. (1988) 'Partial equilibrium calculations of the impact of internal market barriers in the European Community', *Research on the Cost of Non-Europe Basic Findings 2*. European Commission, Brussels.

Devarajan, S., Go, D. S., Lewis, J. D., Robinson, S. and Sinko, P. (1997) 'Simple general equilibrium modeling', in: Francois, J. F. and Reinert, K. A. (eds.), *Applied Methods for Trade Policy Analysis – A Handbook*, Cambridge: Cambridge University Press, 156–85.

Devarajan, S. and Go, D. S. (1998) 'The simplest dynamic general-equilibrium model of an open economy', *Journal of Policy Modeling* 20(6), 677–714.

Gdansk Institute for Market Economies (1999) 'Polish Database 1996', *Mimeo*.

Go, D. S. (1994) 'External shocks, adjustment polices, and investment in a developing economy – illustrations from a forward-looking CGE model of the Philippines', *Journal of Development Economics*, 44, 229–61.

GUS (Glowny Urzad Statystyczny) (1998) *National Accounts 1992–6*, Warsaw.

Harrison, G. W., Rutherford, T. F. and Tarr, D. G. (1996) 'Increased competition and completion of the market in the European Union: static and steady state effects', *Journal of Economic Integration*, 11(3), 332–65.

Hille, H. (2001) *Enlarging the European Union: a computable general equilibrium assessment of different integration scenarios of Central and Eastern Europe*, Frankfurt a.M: Lang.

Hoffmann, A. (2000) 'The gains from partial completion of the single market', *Weltwirtschaftliches Archiv*, 136(4): 601–30.

Knudsen, M. B., Pedersen, L. H., Petersen, T. W., Stephensen, P. and Trier, P. (1997) 'A prototype of a DREAM (Danish Rational Economic Agents Model)', *Mimeo*.

Lau, M. I., Pahlke, A. and Rutherford, T. F. (2001) Modeling economic adjustment – a primer in dynamic equilibrium analysis, *Journal of Economic Dynamics and control*, 25.

Lensink, R. (1999) 'Financial reforms in Poland: an analysis with a computable general equilibrium model', in: Mullineux, A. W. and Green, C. J. (eds), *Economic Performance and Financial Sector Reform in Central and Eastern Europe*, Cheltenham: Edward Elgar, 164–82.

Manne, A. S. (1986) *GAMS/MINOS: Three examples*, Department of Operations Research (Stanford University), May.

OECD (2000) *International trade by commodities statistics* (ITCS) CD-ROM.

Piazolo, D. (1997) 'Trade integration between Eastern and Western Europe: policies follow the market', *Journal of Economic Integration*, 12(3), 259–97.

Piazolo, D. (1999) 'Growth effects of institutional change and European integration', *Economic Systems*, 23(4), 305–30.

Piazolo, D. (2000) 'Poland's membership in the European Union: An analysis with a computable general equilibrium (CGE) model', LICOS Discussion paper no. 89, Leuven.

Piazolo, D. (2001) 'The integration process between Eastern and Western Europe', Kiel Studies 310, Berlin: Springer.

Rodrik, D. (1997) 'Discussion of Baldwin, Francois and Portes "The costs and benefits of Eastern enlargement: the impact on the EU and Central Europe"', *Economic Policy*, 24, 170–3.

Rutherford, T. F. and Tarr, D. G. (1999) 'Blueprints, spillovers, and the dynamic gains from trade liberalization in a small open economy', in: Baldwin, R. E. and Francois, J. F. (eds), *Dynamic Issues in Applied Commercial Policy Analysis*, Cambridge: Cambridge University Press, 269–309.

Thiele, R. (1996) *Wirtschaftspolitische Optionen zum Schutz tropischer Wälder*, Kiel Studies 278.

Uzawa, H. (1969) 'Time preference and the Penrose effect in a two-class model of economic growth', *Journal of Political Economy*, 77, 628–52.

Walz, U. (1997) 'Dynamic effects of economic integration: a survey', *Open Economies Review*, 8(3), 309–26.

WIIW (Vienna Institute for International Economic Studies) (2000) *Countries in Transition*, Vienna.

Willenbockel, D. (1998) 'Growth effects of anticipated trade liberalization and the Baldwin multiplier', *Economic Letters*, 59, 231–5.

Index

1987 Household Expenditure Survey 23
1992 World Bank *World Development Report* 163

Aaron, H.J. 250
AGE *see* applied general equilibrium model
Ahmad, E. 40
Ahmed, S. 40
A&K methodology 205, 211; implementation of model 206–11
A–K model 301, 313; *see also* Auerbach and Kotlikoff (AK) model
Altig, D. 307
Amato reform 216, 218–19, 223–5, 228
Anderson, B. 125
Antichi, M. 219
applied general equilibrium (AGE) model 219–20, 281–6
applied intertemporal general equilibrium model 85; calibration and computational strategy 95–8; dynamic structure 86–93; instantaneous equilibrium structure 87–91; results 98–101
Armington approach 161
Armington assumption 144–5
Armington good *146*
Armington specification 164
Ashenfelter, O. 282
Atkinson, A.B. 40
Auerbach, A. 203–4, 233, 237–8, 300–1, 305, 307, 309–10
Auerbach and Kotlikoff (AK) model 217, 232–3, 237, 251
Australia 56, 64; CGE model 56; foreign students 63–5; IMPACT project 56; ORANI model 56–9
Australian Bureau of Agricultural and Resource Economics (ABARE) 67

Australian Bureau of Statistics (ABS) 64
Australian Capital Territory (ACT) 79
Australian Commonwealth Department of Education, Training and Youth Affairs (DETYA) 63–4
Australian Tourism Forecasting Council (TFC) 67

balance of trade 73
Baldwin, R.E. 345, 352, 354
Ballard, C.L. 6–7, 14, 16–18, 40–1
Barro, R.J. 4, 348
Belgian economy 204, 207
Belgium 203, 208, 213
Bergman, L. 125
Blanchflower, D.G. 275
Blum, W.J. 271
Boehringer, C. 161–2
Börsch-Supan, A. 250, 327
Breyer, F. 250
British pharmaceutical industry 99
Broer, D.P. 233, 250–1
Brooke, A. 26
Browning, E.K. 40
Buiter, W.H. 328

Campbell, C. 273
Campbell, J.Y. 146
capital market distortions 51–2
capital mobility 143, 147–51; international 140–1, 157; theoretical implications 140–2
capital stock 76
carbon taxation 160–77
Cass–Ramsey–Solow growth model 327
Central Bank 234
Central Statistical Office (CSO) 253

Centre of Policy Studies (CoPS) 56, 67
CES function 26
CES-utility function 64, 234
CGE *see* computable general equilibrium model
Chaveau, T. 233
Clarke, R. 160
closure rules 42
Cobb–Douglas utility function 112, 234, 276, 278, 284, 308, 329–30
competitive industries 88–9
computable general equilibrium (CGE) model 6, 21, 140, 160–2, 334, 345–8; Australia 56; conjectural variation 105–21; idiosyncratic uncertainty 312–13; overview 42–4; structure 107–9; Turkey 111–17
Conrad, K. 162
constant elasticity of substitution (CES) utility function 22
constant returns to scale (CRTS) 186, 189
Cournot competition 189
Cournot–Nash equilibrium 128–33
Cournot–Nash–Walras GE model 102
Croushore, D. 40
Cutler, D. 327

Danish economy 20–1; quantitative model 20; small open economy model 22–7
Danish model *24*; empirical implementation of the model 23–7; sectors *24*;
DART *see* Dynamic Applied Regional Trade (DART) model
Dasgupta, P.S. 40
De Melo, J. 22
De Mooij, R.A. 282
Denmark 27
Denmarks Statistics 23
Devarajan, S. 105, 348
deviation simulations 67
developing countries 39; Bangladesh 40; Cameroon 40; empirical magnitudes 40; Indonesia 40; marginal cost of funds (MCF) 39–40
Diamond, P. 328
Dini reform 216–19, 222–5, 228
Dirkse, S.P. 27

Dixit–Stiglitz utility function 105
Dixon, P.B. 56, 59
Docquier, F. 204
Dynamic Applied Regional Trade (DART) model 143–8
Dynamic CGE modelling 80–1

economic crisis 63; Asia 63; Australia 63
economic growth 253; ageing effects 253–9
Edwards, T.H. 162
efficiency wage model 272–81; examples 278–81; labour market equilibrium 277–8; variable labour supply 276–7; the wage curve 274–6; *see also* Sorensen's efficiency wage model
Engen, E. 300
Ethier, W.J. 141
EU-aggregated demand 93
EU *see* European Union
Europe 160–1, 166; carbon taxation 160–73; carbon tax simulations 166–71
European electricity directive 132
European Single Market 85, 93; trade experiment 93–4
European trade integration: welfare gains *101*
European Union (EU) 160–2, 344–5, 351
excise tax reductions: welfare effects 27, 32
excise taxes 27; compensating losers 32–4; reform of 27; welfare effects 27–32

Federal tax-policy changes 10
Fehr, H. 163, 234, 242, 250, 284
Fehr, Rosenberg and Wiegard (FRW) model 161–4
Feldstein, M. 250
Ferris, M.C. 27
foreign students *see* Australia
France 288
FRW model 160
Fuest, C. 272
Fullerton, D. 6, 11, 14, 16–17, 40–1

Gale, W. 300
Gasiorek, M. 105
Gauss–Seidel algorithm 17
GEMTAP model 6, 7, 15–16

Germany 162–3, 167–70, 225, 234, 288, 293
Global Trade Analysis Project (GTAP) 149
global warming 58, 183
Go, D.S. 348
Goerke, L. 271
Goulder, L.H. 7, 14, 17–18
Graafland, J.J. 282
Green, R.J. 124
Greenwood, J. 4
GTAP *see* Global Trade Analysis Project (GTAP)

Hammond, P.J. 35
Hansson, I. 41
Harberger, A.C. 40
Harris, R. 94, 105
Harrison, G.W. 17, 22, 26, 37, 105, 345, 352
Harrison, J. 57
Harrison–Rutherford–Tarr (HRT) approach 114–17
Heckman, J. 282
Heckscher–Ohlin–Samuelson (HOS) model 141, 156
Herfindahl–Hirschman index (HHI) 123
Hicksian equivalent variation 153
Hicksian separability 281
Hoel, M. 271
Hoffmann, A. 352
Holtz-Eakin, D. 326
HOS *see* Heckscher–Ohlin–Samuelson (HOS) model
HRT *see* Harrison–Rutherford–Tarr (HRT) approach
Huber, B. 272
Huffman, G.W. 4
Hutton, J.P. 164, 281, 284, 286

IEA *see* International Energy Agency
IMPACT project 56
İmrohoroğlu, A. 308
infinite-horizon simulation model 3–16; analysis 10–13; infinite-horizon consumer model 7–10; production side 6; results 10–13
international capital mobility *see* capital mobility

International Energy Agency (IEA) 149, 182; *Energy Statistics of OECD Countries and Energy Prices and Taxes* 163
international trade: theoretical implications 140–2
Italian numerical model 128; results 128–33
Italy 122–33, 162, 216, 225–8, 293; ageing population 216–17, 224–6; market power 122–5, 128, 129 *see also* liberalized power markets; pension insurance scheme 217–19; pension reform 216–19, 220–7; price formation 128–9

Japan 162, 225
Johansen, L. 57
Jorgenson, D.W. 4
Judd, K.L. 4

Kahn, M.E. 327
Kalven, H. 271
Kehoe, T.J. 17
Kenc 327
Kendrick, D. 26
Keynes–Ramsey consumption smoothing rule 319
Kimbell, L.J. 17
King, A.T. 17
Kotlikoff, L.J. 203–4, 233, 238, 250, 300–10
Kyoto Conference, 1997 160
Kyoto Protocol 139, 152–5, 157; climate policy analysis 151–6

labour market distortions 51–2
Lambert, P. 275
Lane, P. 142
leaky bucket 35–6
Leontief technology 26
Lerner formula 105
Lerner index 124
Lerner's equation 90
liberalized power markets 122–34
Liégeois, P. 204
Lockwood, B. 271, 275
Loufir, R. 233
Lübke, E. 219
Lucas, R. 4

McDonald, D. 59
McDougall, R.A. 56
Mankiew, N.G. 146
Manning, A. 271, 275
marginal cost of funds (MCF) 27, 39, 44–8, 54; Bangladesh 44–5, 48, 54; Cameroon 44, 46, 54; Indonesia 44–7, 54
marginal excess burden (MEB) 40
market power 123
Markov process 302
Markusen, J.R. 141
Meagher, G.A. 56
Meeraus, A. 26
Meijdam, L. 326
Mendoza, E. 4
Mercenier, J. 96–8
Michel, P. 96–8
Miles, D. 233
Milesi-Ferretti, G.M. 142
MIMIC model 282
MIT Global Climate Change programme 160
MONASH 56–67; dynamic policy analysis 59–63; forecasting 59–62; structure of 59–61
Morgan Research Centre (MRC) 63
multi-regional trade model 140
Mundell, R. 141
Myles, G.D. 271

national commodities 78
Negishi, T. 97
Netherlands 250, 272
Newbery, D.M. 125
non-tariff barriers (NTBs) 93
Norman, V.D. 142
Norway 232, 234; fiscal system 234–7
Norwegian economy: simulation model 233–40
numerical model 124–8

OECD countries 182, 225, 228, 249, 325
Okun's leaky bucket *see* leaky bucket
oligopolistic markups 91–3
Orszag, J.M. 273
Oswald, A. 275
overlapping generations (OLG) framework 3–4, 206

Parmenter, B.R. 59
pay-as-you-go (PAYG) basis 216–20; 251–65
PCMI 124
Pearson, K.R. 57
Pechman, J.A. 17
Pench, A. 162
pension funding reforms 232–46
pension reforms: simulation experiments 240–6
Phelps, E.H. 272–3
Philippines 348
Pigou, K. 40
Poland 344, 348–51, 353; general equilibrium model 348–51; SAM 350
Poland's Regional Integration Computable Equilibrium (PRINCE) model 348–51, 353; simulations 353–8
policy reforms 20–3
Polo, C. 17
Poterba, J.M. 327
power exchange markets (PX) 122
Prachowny, M.F.J. 17
Price-Cost Margin Index (PCMI) 123
PRINCE *see* Poland's Regional Integration Computable Equilibrium (PRINCE) model

Raffelhüschen, B. 250
RAINS *see* Regional Acidification Information and Simulation (RAINS) model
Ramsey model 345, 348
real depreciation 73
real wage 76
recycled tax revenues: uses 161
Regional Acidification Information and Simulation (RAINS) model 160, 162, 165–6, 170, 173
regional integration: dynamic effects 345–8
regulated third party access (RTPA) 122
Rennings, K. 183
rental distortions 49–50
Rimmer, M.T. 56
Rodrik, D. 105, 345
Rosenberg, C. 284
Ruocco, A. 161, 164, 281, 284, 286
Rutherford, T.F. 22, 26, 105, 345

Rutström, E.E. 22
Rybczynski effect 141–2

Sahasakul, C. 4
Sala-i-Martin, X. 348
Samuelson, P.A. 40
Sancho, F. 17
Sayan 327
scale elasticities 95
Schmidt, T.F.N. 162
Sempere, J. 35
Shapiro, C. 295
Shoven, J.B. 6, 11, 14–17, 41, 284
small open economy (SOE) model 22–7, 208
Smith, A. 108–9
Snow, A. 41
social accounting matrix (SAM) 349–350
social security reform 259–65
social welfare function (SWF) 31
Solow-type growth model 345
Sorensen, P.B. 271, 273, 275, 295
Sorensen's efficiency wage model 295
Starrett, D.A. 7, 9–10
static equilibrium conditions 90–1
Steigum, E. 233
Stern, N.H. 40
Stiglitz, J.E. 40, 295
Stijns, J.P. 204
Stijns, J.-Ph. 203
Straub, M. 250
Stuart, C. 41
Summers, L.H. 10
Survey of Current Business 1963–6
Svensson, L.E.O. 141

Tarr, D.G. 22, 26, 105, 345
tax export 162

tax progression: effect on labour market 272–81; and employment 271–93; simulations 286–93
temporal aggregation 98–9
Tesar, L. 4
Turkey 107, 327; economy 107; partial trade liberalization 117; structure of CGE model 107–9

UK 163–9, 288, 293
United Nations 249
UN World Investment Report 1998 150
US tax policy 4–6

VA *see* voluntary agreements
Venables, A.J. 108–9, 142
Verbon, H.A.A. 326
voluntary agreements (VA) 182–95; analytical framework 186–90; numerical results 190–4; practice and economic intuition 183–6

wage distortions 49–50
Warren, R. Jr. 41
Westerhout, E.M.W.T. 233, 251
Whalley, J. 11–17, 41, 284
Wiegard, W. 284
Wilcoxen, P.J. 4
Wildasin, D.P. 40
Willenbockel, D. 142, 358
Wong, K.-Y. 141
World Energy Council (1999) 149

Yun, K.-Y. 4